Achieving Organizational Agility, Intelligence, and Resilience Through Information Systems

Hakikur Rahman
Institute of Computer Management and Science, Bangladesh

A volume in the Advances in Business Information Systems and Analytics (ABISA) Book Series

IGI Global
PUBLISHER of TIMELY KNOWLEDGE

Published in the United States of America by
IGI Global
Business Science Reference (an imprint of IGI Global)
701 E. Chocolate Avenue
Hershey PA, USA 17033
Tel: 717-533-8845
Fax: 717-533-8661
E-mail: cust@igi-global.com
Web site: http://www.igi-global.com

Library of Congress Cataloging-in-Publication Data

Names: Rahman, Hakikur, 1957- editor.
Title: Achieving organizational agility, intelligence, and resilience through information systems / Hakikur Rahman, editor.
Description: Hershey, PA : Business Science Reference, [2022] | Includes bibliographical references and index. | Summary: "This book presents the latest scholarly research on the widespread integration of technological innovations around the globe and examines how organizational agility, intelligence and resilience interprets, affects, and improves the entrepreneurship around the globe"-- Provided by publisher.
Identifiers: LCCN 2021028551 (print) | LCCN 2021028552 (ebook) | ISBN 9781799847991 (hardcover) | ISBN 9781799871385 (paperback) | ISBN 9781799848004 (ebook)
Subjects: LCSH: Organizational resilience. | Entrepreneurship. | Technological innovations.
Classification: LCC HD58.9 .A28 2022 (print) | LCC HD58.9 (ebook) | DDC 658.4/013--dc23
LC record available at https://lccn.loc.gov/2021028551
LC ebook record available at https://lccn.loc.gov/2021028552

This book is published in the IGI Global book series Advances in Business Information Systems and Analytics (ABISA) (ISSN: 2327-3275; eISSN: 2327-3283)

British Cataloguing in Publication Data
A Cataloguing in Publication record for this book is available from the British Library.

All work contributed to this book is new, previously-unpublished material.
The views expressed in this book are those of the authors, but not necessarily of the publisher.

For electronic access to this publication, please contact: eresources@igi-global.com.

Advances in Business Information Systems and Analytics (ABISA) Book Series

ISSN:2327-3275
EISSN:2327-3283

Editor-in-Chief: Madjid Tavana La Salle University, USA

MISSION

The successful development and management of information systems and business analytics is crucial to the success of an organization. New technological developments and methods for data analysis have allowed organizations to not only improve their processes and allow for greater productivity, but have also provided businesses with a venue through which to cut costs, plan for the future, and maintain competitive advantage in the information age.

The **Advances in Business Information Systems and Analytics (ABISA) Book Series** aims to present diverse and timely research in the development, deployment, and management of business information systems and business analytics for continued organizational development and improved business value.

COVERAGE

- Business Intelligence
- Data Analytics
- Data Governance
- Data Strategy
- Business Process Management
- Management Information Systems
- Geo-BIS
- Algorithms
- Data Management
- Business Systems Engineering

IGI Global is currently accepting manuscripts for publication within this series. To submit a proposal for a volume in this series, please contact our Acquisition Editors at Acquisitions@igi-global.com or visit: http://www.igi-global.com/publish/.

The Advances in Business Information Systems and Analytics (ABISA) Book Series (ISSN 2327-3275) is published by IGI Global, 701 E. Chocolate Avenue, Hershey, PA 17033-1240, USA, www.igi-global.com. This series is composed of titles available for purchase individually; each title is edited to be contextually exclusive from any other title within the series. For pricing and ordering information please visit http://www.igi-global.com/book-series/advances-business-information-systems-analytics/37155. Postmaster: Send all address changes to above address.

Titles in this Series

For a list of additional titles in this series, please visit:
www.igi-global.com/book-series/advances-business-information-systems-analytics/37155

Handbook of Research on Applied Data Science and Artificial Intelligence in Business and Industry
Valentina Chkoniya (University of Aveiro, Portugal)
Engineering Science Reference • © 2021 • 653pp • H/C (ISBN: 9781799869856) • US $425.00

Using Strategy Analytics to Measure Corporate Performance and Business Value Creation
Sandeep Kautish (Lord Buddha Education Foundation, Nepal)
Business Science Reference • © 2021 • 287pp • H/C (ISBN: 9781799877165) • US $225.00

Adapting and Mitigating Environmental, Social, and Governance Risk in Business
Magdalena Ziolo (University of Szczecin, Poland)
Business Science Reference • © 2021 • 313pp • H/C (ISBN: 9781799867883) • US $195.00

Innovative and Agile Contracting for Digital Transformation and Industry 4.0
Mohammad Ali Shalan (Aqarat Real Estate Development Company, Saudi Arabia) and Mohammed Ayedh Algarni (Information and Documents Center, Institute of Public Administration, Saudi Arabia)
Business Science Reference • © 2021 • 415pp • H/C (ISBN: 9781799845010) • US $225.00

Opportunities and Strategic Use of Agribusiness Information Systems
Ferdinand Ndifor Che (W3-Research, USA & APPC Research, Australia) Kenneth David Strang (W3-Research, USA & APPC Research, Australia) and Narasimha Rao Vajjhala (University of New York Tirana, Albania)
Business Science Reference • © 2021 • 333pp • H/C (ISBN: 9781799848493) • US $195.00

Integration Challenges for Analytics, Business Intelligence, and Data Mining
Ana Azevedo (CEOS:PP, ISCAP, Polytechnic of Porto, Portugal) and Manuel Filipe Santos (Algoritmi Centre, University of Minho, Guimarães, Portugal)
Engineering Science Reference • © 2021 • 250pp • H/C (ISBN: 9781799857815) • US $225.00

For an entire list of titles in this series, please visit:
www.igi-global.com/book-series/advances-business-information-systems-analytics/37155

IGI Global
PUBLISHER of TIMELY KNOWLEDGE

701 East Chocolate Avenue, Hershey, PA 17033, USA
Tel: 717-533-8845 x100 • Fax: 717-533-8661
E-Mail: cust@igi-global.com • www.igi-global.com

Table of Contents

Preface xiii

Acknowledgment xvii

Chapter 1
Digital Organizations: The Social Business Contribution 1
Maria João Ferreira, REMIT, Universidade Portucalense, Portugal & ISTTOS, Centro Algoritmi, Universidad do Minho, Portugal
Fernando Moreira, REMIT, IJP, Universidade Portucalense, Portugal & IEETA, Universidade de Aveiro, Portugal
Isabel Seruca, REMIT, Universidade Portucalense, Portugal & ISTTOS, Centro Algoritmi, Universidad do Minho, Portugal

Chapter 2
Implementing Cloud Information Systems for Organizational Agility and Competitive Advantage: SaaS Migration 39
Kamran Janamian, Independent Researcher, Slovakia

Chapter 3
Organizational Sustainability: Characteristics of Agility 72
Hakikur Rahman, Ansted University Sustainability Research Institute, Malaysia

Chapter 4
Long Tail Leadership: A Covid Case Study Illustrates the Importance of Understanding Soft Power Affecting Organizations 103
Diane Spencer-Scarr, Curtin University, Australia

Chapter 5
Open Innovation Strategies in SMEs: Development of a Business Model 137
Hakikur Rahman, Ansted University Sustainability Research Institute, Malaysia

Chapter 6
Assurance for Change Management With COBIT 2019 and CMMC Maturity Frameworks........163
Jeffrey S. Zanzig, Jacksonville State University, USA
Guillermo A. Francia, III, University of West Florida, USA

Chapter 7
BI and Analytics for Effective Disaster Recovery Management Lessons From the Bayou........197
Gregory Smith, Xavier University, USA
Thilini Ariyachandra, Xavier University, USA

Chapter 8
From Business Intelligence to Data Science: A Decade of Evolution........218
Virginia M. Miori, Saint Joseph's University, USA
John Yi, Saint Joseph's University, USA
Rashmi Malhotra, Saint Joseph's University, USA
Ronald K. Klimberg, Saint Joseph's University, USA

Chapter 9
Towards Making a Sustainable Organization........238
Hakikur Rahman, Ansted University Sustainability Research Institute, Malaysia

Chapter 10
Critical Success Factors for Organizational Agility: Q-Study and the Place of IT........269
Mohamed Amine Marhraoui, ENSIAS Engineering School, Mohammed V University in Rabat, Morocco
Mohammed Abdou Janati Idrissi, ENSIAS Engineering School, Mohammed V University in Rabat, Morocco
Abdellah El Manouar, ENSIAS Engineering School, Mohammed V University in Rabat, Morocco

Compilation of References........299

About the Contributors........342

Index........348

Detailed Table of Contents

Preface...xiii

Acknowledgment...xvii

Chapter 1
Digital Organizations: The Social Business Contribution....................................1
Maria João Ferreira, REMIT, Universidade Portucalense, Portugal & ISTTOS, Centro Algoritmi, Universidad do Minho, Portugal
Fernando Moreira, REMIT, IJP, Universidade Portucalense, Portugal & IEETA, Universidade de Aveiro, Portugal
Isabel Seruca, REMIT, Universidade Portucalense, Portugal & ISTTOS, Centro Algoritmi, Universidad do Minho, Portugal

Digitalization is changing business and organizations. In the organizational context, the potential that can be realized through digitalization is manifest, namely the expenditure reduction and higher innovative power. However, it is not enough to integrate digitalization; a change of culture and behavior is necessary. To this extent, social media relations have the potential to create communication capabilities that can be turned into useful resources, which in turn will result in more significant competitive advantage and performance. Taking advantage of social tools within social business contexts requires an exercise in how to demonstrate usefulness regarding the creation, access, and sharing of content securely. To this end, this chapter will provide a comprehensive view of a new context of labor (i.e., social business supported by mobile IST-m_CSDIT2) to improve the organizational well-being through the collective intelligence and agility dimensions.

Chapter 2
Implementing Cloud Information Systems for Organizational Agility and Competitive Advantage: SaaS Migration..39
Kamran Janamian, Independent Researcher, Slovakia

In today's competitive business environment, information systems are not a luxury; rather they are vital for survival. A new generation of ISs has been established on cloud capabilities. Moving toward software as a service is not the goal in a business, and if not implemented properly, competitive advantage may even suffer. Managers and change agents should undertake deep study over SaaS implementation before migration. In this chapter, the main elements and features in which CEOs and IT managers should consider in evaluating the SaaS migration option will be provided, and enterprises may be acquainted with the concept, goals, and theoretical foundations of SaaS as a main cloud-based service in the business environment. On the other hand, businesses should undertake some necessary changes in the operating circumstances which are utilization of a proper and modified business models established over a knowledge base strategic movement. This will lead enterprises to achieve the main goals of migrating to SaaS and cloud platforms (i.e., agility, competitive advantage, and innovation).

Chapter 3
Organizational Sustainability: Characteristics of Agility 72
Hakikur Rahman, Ansted University Sustainability Research Institute, Malaysia

An organization with its capacity to endure, add up value, and promote value chain could be seen as a sustainable organization. Sustainability could be in the form of short-, medium-, and long-term effect to an entity. Through the utilization of the information and communication technology, organizations now can adopt various business techniques to tackle or minimize risks, reduce costs, and make profit. Among many such techniques, this particular research looks into the aspects of agility within organizations that may lead to sustained business platform. This chapter tries to argue that an organization with this characteristic, in the longer run, can lead to sustainability and elevate the business intelligence. In this discourse, through a vertical literature review, this study has tried to construct a framework of sustainability with the aspect of an organization and thereby proposed a business model for ideation and future implementation.

Chapter 4
Long Tail Leadership: A Covid Case Study Illustrates the Importance of Understanding Soft Power Affecting Organizations..103
Diane Spencer-Scarr, Curtin University, Australia

The increased weighting of digital natives in a fattening long tail has added complexity to organizational leadership, particularly during the global COVID-19 pandemic. Trends affecting the individual come from social, economic, and technological sources and affect leadership behaviors, and this in turn affects society. In order to understand this interconnection, lower-level influences and how they affect the higher-level visible signs are discussed. These lead to influences on behavior. Influences are felt as intensity and embeddedness of engagement, decision-management, feedback ability, and motivators. This chapter begins with a discussion of causes for this phenomenon and concludes with ways to work with the long tail, either from within as a member or externally as a leader. The chapter ends with a brief comment on future research based on findings discussed in this chapter.

Chapter 5
Open Innovation Strategies in SMEs: Development of a Business Model........137
Hakikur Rahman, Ansted University Sustainability Research Institute, Malaysia

Open innovation in enterprises has already obtained its acceptance at all levels of the business industry for adding worth to the business. The value could be in the form of economic expanse or enhancement of knowledge leading to a sustained financial base. Open innovation adopts various strategies to accomplish the task for enhancing the value gain. Varying by size, nature, pattern, or characteristics of the firm, various strategies are being adopted by enterprises. Though largely known to be familiar in corporate business houses, in recent years, open innovation is also becoming increasingly recognizable in small and medium enterprises (SMEs), and the trend is rapidly escalating. However, despite the potency of open innovation strategies, most of the enterprises are yet to find a sustained business model, especially for the SMEs working at the outmost periphery of that value chain. This chapter is trying to formulate a business model incorporating partnership approach from academia, research houses, intermediaries, practitioners, and other stakeholders.

Chapter 6
Assurance for Change Management With COBIT 2019 and CMMC Maturity Frameworks...163
Jeffrey S. Zanzig, Jacksonville State University, USA
Guillermo A. Francia, III, University of West Florida, USA

As technology plays an ever-increasing role in carrying out structured tasks in today's society, people are given more time to focus their attention on higher levels of service and personal development. However, technology is in a constant state of change and assurance services are needed to help ensure that technology changes are accomplished properly. The Institute of Internal Auditors has identified 10 steps that can be used to effectively implement changes in technology. This process and its accompanying internal controls can be assessed through an internal audit function that considers issues of both functionality and security. In addition, continuous improvement of the change management process for technology can be evaluated though capability/maturity models to see if organizations are achieving higher levels of accomplishment over time. Such models include the COBIT 2019-supported capability maturity model integration (CMMI) model and the cybersecurity maturity model certification (CMMC) framework used by defense industrial base organizations.

Chapter 7
BI and Analytics for Effective Disaster Recovery Management Lessons From the Bayou 197
Gregory Smith, Xavier University, USA
Thilini Ariyachandra, Xavier University, USA

Disaster recovery management requires agile decision making and action that can be supported through business intelligence (BI) and analytics. Yet, fundamental data issues such as challenges in data quality have continued to plague disaster recovery efforts leading to delays and high costs in disaster support. This chapter presents an example of these issues from the 2005 Atlantic hurricane season, where Hurricane Katrina wreaked havoc upon the city of New Orleans forcing the Federal Emergency Management Agency (FEMA) to begin an unprecedented cleanup effort. The chapter brings to light the failings in record keeping during this disaster and highlight how a simple BI application can improve the accuracy and quality of data and save costs. It also highlights the ongoing data driven issues in disaster recovery management that FEMA continues to confront and the need for integrated centralized BI and analytics solutions extending to the supply chain that FEMA needs to become more nimble and effective when dealing with disasters.

Chapter 8
From Business Intelligence to Data Science: A Decade of Evolution...............218
Virginia M. Miori, Saint Joseph's University, USA
John Yi, Saint Joseph's University, USA
Rashmi Malhotra, Saint Joseph's University, USA
Ronald K. Klimberg, Saint Joseph's University, USA

The use of information technology and decision support concepts at the operational business level were slow to take hold in the 20th century. In 2010, the authors documented the evolution and current state of the field of business intelligence and analytics (BIA). In the last decade, however, through the resurgence and mainstream use of artificial intelligence, machine learning algorithms, the development of inexpensive cloud-based mass storage, and the internet-of-things, business intelligence has evolved into data science. In this chapter, the authors trace this evolution across the diverse areas of data science and identify extremely useful advancements and best practices in the field.

Chapter 9
Towards Making a Sustainable Organization 238
Hakikur Rahman, Ansted University Sustainability Research Institute, Malaysia

Sustainable development refers to an economic, environmental, and social development aspect that meets the demands of the contemporary context and does not prevent future generations from fulfilling their requirements. In this perspective, businesses play an imperative role. However, studies reveal that the progress towards sustainable development has been slow, indicating the need for more concrete guidance that would allow businesses to act strategically and successfully in a sustainable way. There are three distinct, but complementary, dimensions of strategic management as viewed from the perspective of sustainability in order to encourage the integration of sustainability issues into corporate activities and strategies. This chapter looks through various aspects of sustainability towards making a sustainable organization through a vertical literature review. This theoretical discussion contributes to existing research to find relationships between strategic management and sustainable development and tries to provide a schema for further empirical research.

Chapter 10
Critical Success Factors for Organizational Agility: Q-Study and the Place of IT 269
Mohamed Amine Marhraoui, ENSIAS Engineering School, Mohammed V University in Rabat, Morocco
Mohammed Abdou Janati Idrissi, ENSIAS Engineering School, Mohammed V University in Rabat, Morocco
Abdellah El Manouar, ENSIAS Engineering School, Mohammed V University in Rabat, Morocco

Companies are facing important challenges related to markets' internationalization, regulatory restrictions, and fierce competition especially during the COVID-19 context. Environment is thus characterized by rapid and volatile changes. Organizational agility is the key capability allowing firms to adapt continuously by sensing changes in their environment and responding in an efficient and rapid manner. Previous work has addressed organizational agility enablers, including IT ones, allowing the firm to be more agile. In this chapter, the authors first extend their organizational agility enablers list through an in-depth analysis of consulting firms and governmental agencies reports on agility during the COVID-19 context. The final list contains 28 organizational agility enablers belonging to 10 groups. Then, the authors conduct a Q-study in order to identify what factors are critical for a successful journey towards agility and to analyze the results from an IT perspective.

Compilation of References 299

About the Contributors 342

Index 348

Preface

As the world relentlessly improving towards organizational development through the utilization of information technology and in recent years technology continues to be a ubiquitous force that propels businesses to success, it is imperative that updated studies are continuously undertaken to ensure that the most efficient tools and techniques are being utilized. In the contemporary business environment, organizations that can improve their agility and business intelligence are able to become much more resilient and viable competitors in the global economy.

Achieving Organizational Agility, Intelligence, and Resilience Through Information Systems is a significant reference book that provides the latest empirical studies, conceptual research, and methodologies that facilitate organizations to enhance and improve their agility, competitiveness, and sustainability in order to position them for paramount success in today's economy. Covering topics that include knowledge management, human development, and sustainable development, this book is ideal for managers, executives, entrepreneurs, IT specialists and consultants, academicians, researchers, and students.

ORGANIZATION OF BOOK CHAPTERS

The book is comprised of 10 chapters and includes topics from business intelligence, change management, disaster recovery management, and organizational agility to sustainable organization.

It has been observed that the world digitalization is transforming business and organizations. In the organizational context, the potentials that can be realized through digitalization are many, namely the expenditure reduction and higher innovative power. However, it is not enough to integrate digitalization on their own; a change of culture and behavior is necessary. To this extent Chapter 1 emphasizes that social media relations have the potential to create communication capabilities that can be turned into useful resources, which in turn will result in more significant competitive advantage and performance. Taking advantage of social tools within

Social Business context requires an exercise in how to demonstrate their usefulness regarding the creation, access and sharing of contents securely. This chapter provides a comprehensive view of a new context of labor, i.e. Social Business supported by mobile IST-m_CSDIT2, to improve the organizations well-being through the collective intelligence and agility dimensions.

Chapter 2 discusses on cloud information systems to improve organizational agility. It mentions that in today's competitive business environment, Information Systems are not a luxury necessity; rather they are vital for survival. A new generation of ISs has been established on cloud capabilities. Moving toward Software as a Service is not the goal in a business and if not implemented properly competitive advantage may even suffer. Managers and change agents should undertake deep study over SaaS implementation before migration. In this chapter, the main elements and features in which CEOs and IT managers should consider in evaluating the SaaS migration option is being provided, and theoretical foundations of SaaS as a main Cloud-based service in the business environment has been put forwarded.

An organization with its capacity to endure, add up value and promote value chain could be seen as a sustainable organization. Moreover, sustainability could be in the form of short-medium-and-long term effect to an entity. To an organization, in this global economic crisis and increased competition, long term sustainability means to be able to compete, expand margin, and append knowledge, notwithstanding mere survival. Through the utilization of the information and communication technology, organizations are now can adopt various business techniques to tackle or minimize risks, reduce costs, and make profit. Chapter 3 has tried to argue that an organization with this characteristic, in the longer run, can lead to sustainability and elevate the business intelligence. In this discourse, through a vertical literature review, the study has tried to construct a framework of sustainability with the aspect of an organization and thereby proposed a business model for ideation and future implementation.

Chapter 4 showcases a Covid case study illustrating the importance of understanding soft power affecting various organizations. It mentions that the increased weighting of digital natives in a fattening long tail has added complexity to organizational leadership, particularly during the global Covid-19 pandemic. In order to understand this interconnection, lower-level influences and how they affect the higher-level visible signs are discussed. This chapter begins with a discussion of causes for this phenomenon and concludes with ways to work with the long tail, either from within as a member, or externally as a leader.

During the last decades, open innovation in enterprises has already obtains its acceptance at all levels of the business industry for adding worth to the business. Furthermore, the value could be in the form of economic expand or enhancement of knowledge leading to a sustained financial base. Varying by size, nature, pattern or characteristics of the firm various strategies are being adopted by enterprises.

Though largely known to be familiar in corporate business houses, in recent years open innovation is also becoming increasingly recognizable in small and medium enterprises (SMEs) and the trend is rapidly escalating. Chapter 5 has tried to formulate a business model incorporating partnership approach from academia, research houses, intermediaries, practitioners and other stakeholders.

As contemporary technology plays an ever-increasing role in carrying out structured tasks in today's society, people are given more time to focus their attention on higher levels of service and personal development. However, technology is in a constant state of change and assurance services are needed to help ensure that technology changes are accomplished properly. As another case study, Chapter 6 puts forward a case of effective utilization of information technology towards achieving organizational agility. During the study, it finds out that the Institute of Internal Auditors has identified ten steps that can be used to effectively implement changes in technology. This process and its accompanying internal controls can be assessed through an internal audit function that considers issues of both functionality and security. Such models include the COBIT 2019 supported Capability Maturity Model Integration (CMMI) model and the Cybersecurity Maturity Model Certification (CMMC) Framework used by Defense Industrial Base organizations.

Disaster recovery management requires agile decision making and action that can be supported through business intelligence (BI) and analytics. However, fundamental data issues such as challenges in data quality have continued to plague disaster recovery efforts leading to delays and high costs in disaster support. Chapter 7 presents an example of these issues from the 2005 Atlantic hurricane season, where Hurricane Katrina wreaked havoc upon the city of New Orleans forcing the Federal Emergency Management Agency (FEMA) to begin an unprecedented cleanup effort. The chapter brings to light the failings in record keeping during this disaster and highlight how a simple BI application can improve the accuracy and quality of data and save costs.

It has been observed that the effective utilization of information technology and decision support concepts at the operational business level is slow to take hold in the twentieth century. As a research study, Chapter 8 documented the evolution and current state of the field of Business Intelligence and Analytics (BIA). It states that in the last decade, however, through the resurgence and mainstream use of artificial intelligence, machine learning algorithms, the development of inexpensive cloud-based mass storage, and the internet-of-things, business intelligence has evolved into data science.

Sustainable development refers to an economic, environmental and social development aspect that meets the demands of the contemporary context and does not prevent future generations from fulfilling their requirements. In this perspective, businesses play an imperative role. However, researches reveal that the progress towards sustainable development has been slow, indicating the need for more concrete guidance that would allow businesses to act strategically and successfully in a sustainable way. Chapter 9 looks through various aspects of sustainability towards making a sustainable organization through a vertical literature review.

Chapter 10 puts forward a contemporary context of organizational agility in the prevailing pandemic. It mentions that companies are facing important challenges related to markets' internationalization, regulatory restrictions and fierce competition especially during the COVID19 context. Environment is thus characterized by rapid and volatile changes. Organizational agility is the key capability allowing firms to adapt continuously by sensing changes in their environment and responding in an efficient and rapid manner. The study goes through a list of 28 organizational agility enablers belonging to 10 groups.

CONCLUSION

It has been observed that at an organization level, creating a well-designed knowledge management system that improves knowledge sharing and retention can speed both decision making and response time. Henceforth, further in-depth studies need to be carried out towards achieving organizational agility, intelligence, and resilience through effective utilization of information systems.

This book put forwards those issues in relevance to strengthen the organizational well-being by upholding the essential elements in relation to this emerging arena of organizational agility, intelligence and resilience. The book includes concepts, theories, case studies and practices around the niche global market, especially focusing the contemporary economic barriers. It is expected that the book will become apparent as a potential resource material in the existing market, not only for academic researchers, but also for the practitioners.

Hakikur Rahman
Institute of Computer Management and Science, Bangladesh
July 2021

Acknowledgment

Editor with pleasure recognizes the relentless support and generous assistance from all authors that are involved in the accumulation of manuscripts, revision and finalization of various research outcomes and case studies without which the project could not have been satisfactorily accomplished.

Special thanks go to the enthusiastic and brilliant publishing team at the IGI Global. Particularly to Crystal Moyer, Eric Whalen and Maria Rohde for their supports and co-operations for keeping the project on schedule, and to Jan Travers and Lindsay Wertman for their continuous professional guidance.

Finally, heartfelt thanks go to my family, friends and colleagues for their care and support.

Hakikur Rahman
Institute of Computer Management and Science, Bangladesh
July 2021

Chapter 1
Digital Organizations:
The Social Business Contribution

Maria João Ferreira
https://orcid.org/0000-0003-4274-8845
REMIT, Universidade Portucalense, Portugal & ISTTOS, Centro Algoritmi, Universidad do Minho, Portugal

Fernando Moreira
https://orcid.org/0000-0002-0816-1445
REMIT, IJP, Universidade Portucalense, Portugal & IEETA, Universidade de Aveiro, Portugal

Isabel Seruca
https://orcid.org/0000-0002-9951-6378
REMIT, Universidade Portucalense, Portugal & ISTTOS, Centro Algoritmi, Universidad do Minho, Portugal

ABSTRACT

Digitalization is changing business and organizations. In the organizational context, the potential that can be realized through digitalization is manifest, namely the expenditure reduction and higher innovative power. However, it is not enough to integrate digitalization; a change of culture and behavior is necessary. To this extent, social media relations have the potential to create communication capabilities that can be turned into useful resources, which in turn will result in more significant competitive advantage and performance. Taking advantage of social tools within social business contexts requires an exercise in how to demonstrate usefulness regarding the creation, access, and sharing of content securely. To this end, this chapter will provide a comprehensive view of a new context of labor (i.e., social business supported by mobile IST-m_CSDIT2) to improve the organizational well-being through the collective intelligence and agility dimensions.

DOI: 10.4018/978-1-7998-4799-1.ch001

INTRODUCTION

Organizations in recent years, due to digitalization, have undergone an enormous r(evolution) at the social, economic, and technological levels where the traditional barriers of information transfer and knowledge silos have been progressively eliminated. Finding experts and knowledge within an organization is now easier through Social Business.

Social Business (Yunus, 2007; IBM, 2013; Spieth et al., 2019) can be defined as the ability of an organization to share information, produce knowledge collaboratively, manage knowledge, eliminate communication and sharing barriers, accelerate business processes, approaching the business partners, namely suppliers and customers, and create innovative products, services and business models. It is thus essential that such products, services and models are created and properly documented, managed and shared.

A change of paradigm in what comes to the use of information systems and technologies (IST) in the day-to-day life of every citizen, by itself, does not sustain such a transformation; it is also necessary a change of culture and behavior. On the one hand, the use of IST in an appropriate and integrated way with the organization's processes will depend on an individual and collective effort, which may be called "collective leadership" (Friedrich et al., 2009; Eva et al., 2019). On the other hand, the younger generation, accustomed to sharing, often through mobile devices, personal information on Facebook, Twitter, among others, enters the job market looking for similar tools. These new "social tools" allow the production, sharing and management of information and knowledge within the organization between peers and other stakeholders, allowing the barriers elimination of the communication and sharing.

Therefore, we may infer that Social Business is much more than just collaboration and sharing, since the IST that are currently available allow the organizations' processes to be more dynamic, more "social".

Following these developments, and according to the European Commission report "Towards a sustainable Europe by 2030" EU is harnessing the power of the digital transformation to meet the Sustainable Development Goals (SDGs), and it is fully committed to develop capacity and expertise in key digital technologies such as connectivity, the 'internet of things', cybersecurity, blockchain or high-performance computing, while simultaneously paying attention to the potential negative externalities of digital infrastructures. (Timmermans & Katainen, 2019).

The growth of social media is already happening at a tremendous rhythm. The arrival and development of mobile internet applications has set to double the intensity of social media use. Currently, according to Kemp (2020), internet worldwide users are 4.57 billion with a penetration rate of 59%, mobile internet users as a percentage of total internet users are 91% and the active social media worldwide users are 396 billion with a penetration rate of 51%. This makes mobile internet the fastest penetrating technology in the history of mankind (CISCO, 2020).

In this context, Social Business Intelligence (SBI) – the combination of business intelligence software with collaboration tools - allows organizations to see, discuss and act on changes and insights that are happening in their business data. SBI combines corporate data with user-generated content in social media, contributing to better decision making in the organization. Social networks are analysed from different user perspectives, such as content, relationships, and behaviour, becoming an abundant source of information about opinions, interests, needs and attitudes of users. The challenge of the SBI is, then, an efficient management of information from social networks considered as Big Data, characterized by an immense amount and variety of unstructured data that changes at high speed (Berlanga et al., 2019).

Taking advantage of these technologies for organizations within the context of Social Business, in particular for nomadic workers, requires a comprehension exercise in how to demonstrate their usefulness with regard to the creation, sharing and documentation of information and knowledge in and out of an organization, the education and training of organizational workers and ad-hoc discussion, in a safe way. In this chapter, we propose an approach using mobile devices, called mobile Create, Share, Document, Improve and Training (m_CSDIT^2). The Case Study approach will be used as the research method (Yin, 2009).

We argue that Social Business, supported by different ISTs including mobile devices that comply with the approach of m_CSDIT^2 will contribute in a particular way for the organizational well-being (Dodge et al., 2012) raising indicators of the collective intelligence (Malone et al., 2009; Jandrić, 2020) and agility (Sherehiy et al., 2007; Joiner, 2019) dimensions.

The intelligence dimension, on its different indicators is achieved through "collective leadership" (De Brún & McAuliffe, 2020), since it is more efficient than hierarchic management, for certain types of tasks, allowing the internal relations of cooperation to increase and improving the flow of knowledge. Broad participation is usually more effective and leads to more information that can be processed and used in decision-making.

The agility dimension is achieved, through collaborative work, supported mainly by nomadic workers, allowing a systemic perception, especially taking advantage of the interconnections between the organization's capabilities and market opportunities (Cheng et al., 2020).

As a result, the chapter will provide a comprehensive view of the prevalent issues of a new dimension of labour for traditional organizations i.e. Social Business supported by mobile IST – m_CSDIT^2 – in order to improve the well-being of these organizations through the collective intelligence and agility dimensions.

THE NEW DIMENSION OF LABOUR FOR ORGANISATIONS: SOCIAL BUSINESS

The Social Business Concept

The concept of Social Business was firstly associated with Yunus´ work (Yunus, 2007). According to Yunus, the concept involved both economic and social perspectives: Social Business is supposed to solve a social problem and to achieve financial sustainability rather than to generate profits.

A new perspective was introduced by Kim (2012) in a blog post where the concept was applied to evolutionary marketing and technology strategies. Social Business is a recent but popular trend that is revolutionizing organizational work and generating value for all of its elements, i.e. employees, customers, partners and suppliers. It means that all departments in an organization integrate their social capabilities into traditional business processes (Dorn et al., 2007) to change the way of working in order to create value. A Social Business organization uses social software technology to communicate with its rich ecosystem of customers, business partners and employees.

A Business is created and managed by people. The individual or group who is taking decisions will determine either the success or failure of an organization, i.e. if it will survive or will eventually die in market (Hiriyappa, 2008; Guamushig et al. 2019). In order to achieve that success long term goals are needed to be set, i.e. profitability, productivity, competitive position, employee's development, employee relationships, public responsibility, and technological leadership (Hiriyappa, 2008) that are converted into internal efforts and organizational transformations. However, those organizations often fail due to internal (Kotter, 1995) and external forces (Zakić et al., 2008).

An organization in the 21st century, known as Enterprise 2.0 (McAfee, 2009; Wong, 2020), to achieve success, must be a connected entity that supports internal and external networks of people and knowledge in order to obtain competitive advantage and to face the constant and mutable external environmental forces. The potential of Social Business allows this challenge. Hagel et al. (2010) claim that "*each of us, individually and together, are now, for the first time in history, in a position to collaborate in a complete reimagination of our biggest private and public-sector institutions that will eventually remake society as a whole*". Following this imperative, organizations must be open to be supported by Social Business, which constitutes a shift in how people work, moving from hierarchies to networks. Nowadays, complex work is the most valuable, as well as the type of work that cannot be automated or outsourced. It is work that requires creativity and passion. Doing complex work in networks means that information, knowledge and power no longer flow up and down. They flow in all directions. Brown (2012) claims that to understand complex systems it is necessary to submerge in them. This requires social learning. Complex work is not linear. Social Business is giving up centralized control and harnessing the power of networks.

Organizations must be able to share knowledge quicker than before. This requires a shift towards something like a starfish framework that not only allows for independent action but also distributes knowledge through all parts. Social learning is about how organizational knowledge gets distributed.

The work of Social Business can only be achieved through social learning; Jarche (2011) synthesized this idea into ten statements:

- The increasing complexity of work is a result of global interconnectedness.
- Today, simple work is being automated (e.g. bank tellers).
- Complicated work (e.g. accounting) is getting outsourced.
- Complex and creative work is what gives organizations unique business advantages.
- Complex and creative work is difficult to replicate, is constantly changing and requires greater tacit knowledge.
- Tacit knowledge is best developed through conversations and social relationships.
- Training courses are artefacts of a time when information was scarce and connections were few; that time has passed.
- Social learning networks enable better and faster knowledge feedback loops.
- Hierarchies constrain social interactions so traditional management models must change.
- Learning amongst us is the real work in Social Businesses and management's role is to support social learning.

Undertaking Social Business is not the same of an organization that just uses a Facebook page or/and a Twitter account. Social Business means that all departments of an organization, from human resources to marketing, to product development, to customer service, to sales, use social media in the same way they use any other tool and channel to do their job. It is an organization that uses social networking tools often to communicate inside and outside the organization. It is a strategic approach to shaping a business culture, highly dependent upon executive leadership and corporate strategy, including business process design, risk management, leadership development, financial controls and use of business analytics. Becoming a Social Business can help an organization to deepen the relationship with its customers, generate new ideas faster, identify expertise and enable a more effective workforce (Forbes, 2011).

According to i-SCOOP (n.a.), social business incorporates four dimensions: technological, social (in this case, organizational/economic), managerial and human (see fig.1).

Figure 1. Social business – connected and people business
(Font: i-SCOOP, n.a.)

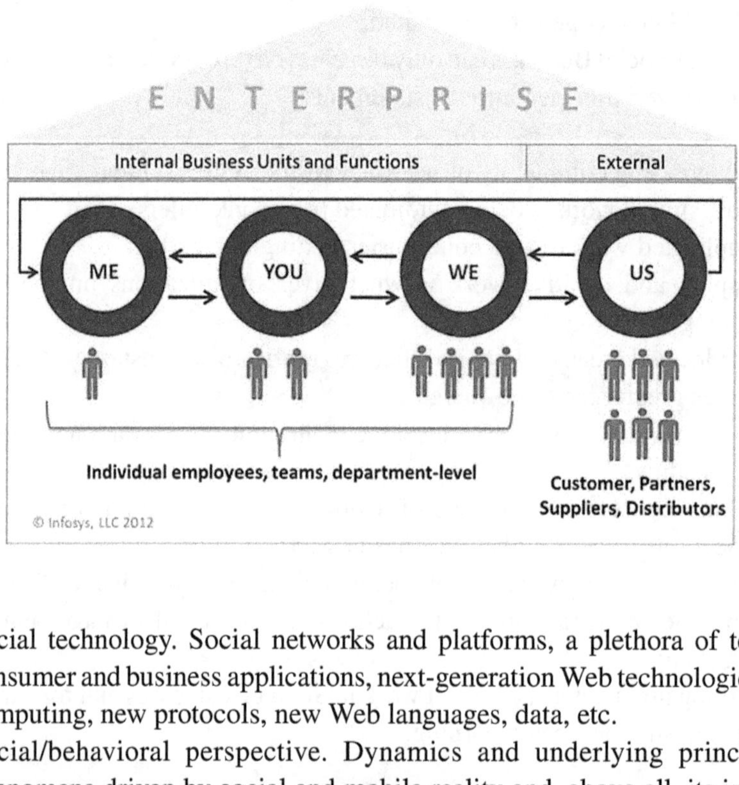

1. Social technology. Social networks and platforms, a plethora of tools and consumer and business applications, next-generation Web technologies, cloud computing, new protocols, new Web languages, data, etc.
2. Social/behavioral perspective. Dynamics and underlying principles of phenomena driven by social and mobile reality and, above all, its impact on how people behave, interact, inform themselves, form communities, co-create, etc. Gamification, the reversal of processes by which the "customer" takes centre stage; the principles of sharing and networking and crowd-sourcing are some of these phenomena.
3. Process and management. This dimension includes management styles and processes, the creation of different approaches to processes within the organization and its ecosystem, new business models, changes in the ways of working, building agile teams and making decisions in addition to traditional and slow management structures. In essence, this amounts to making existing business functions more efficient, fluent, and free from conventional silo models. Information and content play a fundamental role in these processes and in the

mutual exchange of value between people and customers, and customers are also internal customers. Intelligent data and information, proactive content management and even content marketing play a role here (in two directions) with a clear link between, for example, social business and social content strategy.

4. Social and human. It emphasizes more humane principles in the way of doing business. Centralization in people, a greater focus on "human values", social good and even social responsibility. From a more human dimension, it can also add the psychological needs that, on the one hand, are made possible by the two previous dimensions and on the other hand, drive them. The need for recognition, equality, trust, involvement, honesty, authenticity, self-realization, etc.

In a nutshell, Social Business is more than being present in a social network. The organization needs to interact on different channels if it intends to implement a Social Business strategy. The Social Business requires the transformation of the organization so that sociability and interaction are prioritized. This means that the mere existence of social networks is insufficient. The media should be valued and worked in a collaborative way, either as part of the tasks performed, or in an integrated way with business applications. In this context, it is essential to understand that Social Business is not the destination to be reached, but the path that will be outlined. Social Business is a way of doing business and, therefore, requires training, endurance, agility and teamwork. The involvement of stakeholders in the strategy to improve internal communication is a key factor. However, its implementation is only a start since this is a continuous and gradual process. Likewise, it is also essential to indicate to the organization's professionals the importance of the strategy and at the same time present the policies for the use of social tools inside and outside the business (Positivo Tecnologia, 2018).

Integrating Social Business Into an Organization

Besides the well-known potential for organizations in the use of social media, most organizations show a paradoxical behavior in the way they perform business and in the way they manage their institutional social media. This paradoxical behavior results most often in the underuse of conversation potential. These issues are discussed in Van Belleghem (2012) and may be summarized as follows:

- Almost every organization thinks that word-of-mouth advertising is important, but they make little or no effort to manage it. There is a (mistaken) perception that organizations can do little to influence consumer conversations.

- Organizations communicate impersonally, while their customers are demanding a more human approach. The customer wants just one thing: to be treated in a manner that makes him happy. Organizations seem more concerned with processes, structures and budgets.
- One of the global trends in the business world is a growing requirement for good service. Many organizations see customer service as a budget item where savings can and should be done.
- Consumers now have relatively sophisticated technology at their disposal. Many organizations are still working with outdated technology.
- Customers often want to help organizations, to be their friends. On the other hand, organizations often do not think that just a few hundred fans are worth investing in.
- Organizations spend a small fortune on advertising in which they essentially make promises. The modern consumer wants proof, not promises; wants action, not just communication.
- Consumers talk to each other, and often have interesting and relevant things to say. Organizations make little effort to track down these comments and even less effort to take account of them.
- Staff is often proud of their organizations and would like to talk about them, but sometimes is forbidden to do so by their employers.

Perhaps the two last issues in the list provided constitute the biggest paradoxes of all the mentioned issues. Organizations keep referring that satisfied customers and satisfied staff are important, but very often their actions do little or nothing to reflect these words. These are the fundamental causes of unused conversation potential. This problem is exemplified in a further section with the discussion of real cases study.

The future of organizational work is social, collaborative and mobile (Streitz, 2003). The introduction of Social Business into an organization requires important changes in the way its collaborators work in all the organization structure (Cortada et al., 2012). According to Cortada et al. (2012), in order to integrate Social Business in the core of an organization three key issues must be addressed:

1. Organizations need to consider how to incorporate social metrics in themselves and in their processes;
2. Organizations need to understand and manage the risks associated with the integration of social business; and
3. Organizations need to manage change, which is a fundamental requirement to undertake with success social business practices.

Moreover, in SideraWorks (2013) seven dimensions are proposed that must be questioned and defined: (1) vision and goals; (2) cultural readiness; (3) organizational structure; (4) social strategy; (5) communication; (6) social technologies; and (7) training and education.

In this context, the two last dimensions (social technologies and training and education) should allow knowledge to flow in the organization. The primary function of social technologies and training and educating professionals in the networked organization is to connect and communicate based on three core processes:

1. Facilitating collaborative work and learning amongst workers, especially as peers;
2. Sensing patterns and helping to develop emergent work and learning practices; and
3. Working with management to fund and develop appropriate tools and processes for workers.

According to Zhao & Kemp (2012) employees tend to use blogs, wikis and social bookmarks to search and retrieve information about the organization, to connect with coworkers or to build relationships. Another survey, according to these authors, shows that the main goal of using social media tools, such as Facebook in the workplace is to maintain and develop connections with friends not work-related. The adoption of such tools in the workplace has therefore raised several issues and challenges for organizations. One of the most important issues is the virtual disappearance for employees of boundaries between the personal and professional life, as well as personal and professional connections.

Social Business Contributes for a More Competitive Organization

In a few short years, social technologies have given social interactions the speed and scale of the Internet. Whether discussing consumer products or organizing political movements, people around the world constantly use social media tools to seek and share information. And, in this context, business is changing their behavior and social media becomes an important business tool (McKinsey& Company, 2012).

The value of organizations that use social media tools is determined by how they are harnessed to create value for the organization (Majchrzack, Cherbakov & Ives, 2009). Martin & van Bavel, presents a set of a number of potential benefits, i.e., tangible and intangible gains, when the organizations use social media tools, which they classified in terms of a) employ uses of the technologies, b) customer engagement activities, and c) external partner activities (Martin & van Bavel, 2013).

For employees the benefits are: (i) Fast access to organizational knowledge; (ii) Fast access to internal expertise; (iii) Greater collaboration opportunities; (iv) Reduced internal communication costs; (v) Improved training processes and (vi) Improved recruitment of new employees. For customer engagement: (i) More effective branding (Barwise & Meehan, 2010), stronger brand loyalty (Syncapse, 2013), and improved marketing, including stronger customer dialog (Gallaugher & Ransbotham, 2010); (ii) Ability to mine and analyze customer data more effectively; (iii) Ability to personalize marketing activities based on customer interests; (iv) Improved customer service and support; (v) Better product development; (v) Increased customer satisfaction, and (vi) Reduced marketing costs. For external partners the benefits are: (i) Fast access to external knowledge and improved information sharing; (ii) Reduced external communication costs; (iii) Improved collaboration and innovation opportunities, and (iv) Exploiting new marketing opportunities.

Those potential benefits are quantified in some studies, namely McKinsey & Company (2012) and PulsePoint Group and The Economist Intelligence Unit (2012). The McKinsey & Company (2012) study emphasizes that the use of social media in the interaction between employees of an organization could increase the productivity by 20 to 25 percent (see fig. 2) since it improves their communication and collaboration.

Figure 2. Productivity indices with the use of social media tools

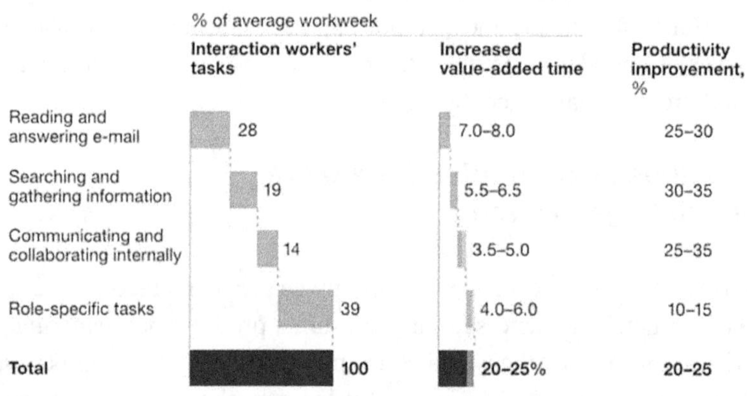

The study driven by the PulsePoint Group in collaboration with The Economist Intelligence Unit (2012) indicates that organizations that wholly embrace social business initiatives are experiencing four times greater business impact than organizations that do not. In the study were identified and analyzed eight facets that improve business, through the adoption of social business, and consequently have a positive economic impact (see fig. 3).

Figure 3. Impact of adopting social business by the organizations

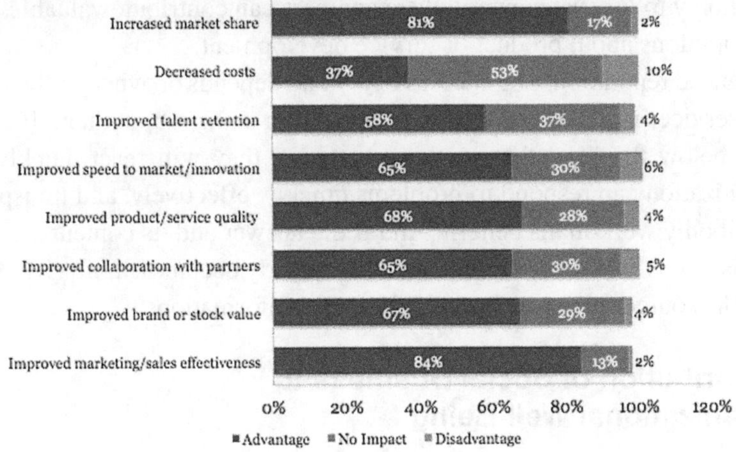

These studies show the importance of social business to organizations, not only inside the organization itself, but also in its relations with the outside, i.e., with the organizational ecosystem.

According to Edwards (2016) the benefits of Social Business in an organization are:

1. Better customer relationship. As a social business, the organization is seen as open, transparent, accessible and responsive. If a customer can communicate with the organization in real-time and through an appropriate platform, he will feel valued and respected. Better yet, if the organization exceeds response expectations, it will not only have satisfied customers, it will have potential brand advocates.
2. Improved insight. Social business can gain more and better insights into the behaviors, feelings and actions of customers. This, in turn, can create more targeted and relevant campaigns and product development.
3. Employee satisfaction. The social business allows employees to participate in the conversation, both internally and externally. The result is more involved, collaborative and motivated teams that can and have the autonomy to make a difference.

4. Higher productivity. By encouraging open collaboration and involvement, a social business allows for a better flow of communication internally and a culture of "doing things" as a team.
5. More innovation. New ideas are more like being shared, built, developed and put into action. Internally, employees from all parts of the organization have the autonomy to innovate; externally, customers can contribute valuable insights and opinions about product or service development.
6. Enhanced reputation. The success of a brand depends on whether the products and services match the claims an organization makes about them. If a service falls below the level that customers expect, they will react quickly. If the organization can respond to problems quickly, effectively, and transparently, it will only work in his benefit. And if the answer and its content are correct, that is, if it is useful, the organization can quickly become a more visible expert and the source from which to obtain useful information.

The Contribution of Social Business to the Organizational Well-Being

As referred in previously social business is the creation of an organization that is using social technology to benefit its entire ecosystem by embedding several aspects including collaboration. In this way the core of social business and the activities that it supports will have an impact in the organization through six dimensions (SideraWorks, 2013), which are presented in Figure 1: adaptability, empowerment, agility, connection, openness and collective intelligence (Malone et al., 2009). We highlight two of these – the agility and collective intelligence dimensions.

Organizational agility is defined, in the Business dictionary, as the capability of an organization to rapidly change or adapt in response to changes in the market. A high degree of organizational agility can help an organization to react successfully to the emergence of new competitors, the development of new industry-changing technologies or sudden shifts in overall market conditions.

Organizational agility helps balancing speed of response, communication and information sharing with thoughtful coordination and long-term scalability. In this context, according to Charbonnier-Voirin (2011), organizational agility is the organization capacity to incorporate new elements such as innovations or improvements in order to enhance its performance.

Levy (1999) argues that collective intelligence is the "*capacity of human communities to co-operate intellectually in creation innovation and invention*". Levy also adds that collective intelligence is a "*fully distributed intelligence that is continuously enhanced and synergized in real time*" which results in effective mobilization of skills with social business. And in this context, collective intelligence leverages the capacity to listen and use established information as well as new sources of information. Evaluating and analyzing data is not just to track activity, but to actively support business decisions in order to improve products, services, and processes of an organization (SideraWorks, 2013).

Organizational well-being is the process of creating well-being across an organization (Dodge et al., 2012). Therefore, if agility and collective intelligence are incremented in an organization, well-being will also be incremented.

The Support of Social Media Tools in Social Business Context

Social media tools are supposed to inflict a sharp transformation in the employees' private and professional lives. Through careful observation of the use of such tools it is widely acknowledged that they are vital in the process of communication in society today (Ham et al., 2019).

Organizations worldwide are adopting social media tools in many critical applications to create, share and documenting. Some industry executives from advertising and marketing consider their use crucial. Despite its growing ubiquity, social media tools are still not well understood from a strategic business perspective, and also regarding its use in education and training in the workplace (Barczk & Duncan, 2012).

Studies on the organizational impacts of the use of social media tools to date have been mentioned only speculatively (Vannoy & Palvia 2010). According to (Boyd, 2008; Lampe, Ellison & Steinfield, 2006) a possible explanation for this is the growing use of social media tools outside the organization or explicitly social contexts, which are used mostly by youth and students.

According to Jarrahi & Sawyer (2013) the increase in the number and variety of information and communication technologies in the workplace, as well as the practices of knowledge sharing which are becoming increasingly digital allow traditional organizations to benefit from the wide variety of social technologies. The social media tools constitute the subset of social technologies that have allowed new possibilities for sharing organizational knowledge. The use of social media tools offer opportunities for collaboration and social exchange, and are well positioned to increase and prolong the interpersonal social connections (Skeels & Grudin, 2009).

Jarrahi & Sawyer (2013) mention that what is known so far on the use of social media tools at work is based on studies focused on the use of a social media technology by itself. These studies provide useful information about some organizational implications of its use, but do not consider how technologies can be used together. However, it is easy to acknowledge that the vast majority of organizations have employees interacting with several technologies.

For a successful organization to have social business, social media must be understood as a means, not an end. Social media is the ideal partner for such an organization. The advantages are obvious: speed, a wide potential reach, a human method of communicating, no hierarchy, full transparency, creation of communities, etc. It is the only channel where feedback from the outside world is transparent and direct. Social media force organizations to be more honest, quicker and clearer in their communication. This trend has allowed organizations to develop in the direction of genuine customer-orientation.

Despite these advantages, the checklist mentality which some organizations use when dealing with social media is not the right way to maximize the company conversation potential. Regarding Facebook pages and Twitter accounts as some kind of magic trick is not the good way of achieving success and will only lead to disappointment. The reality is that, with a few exceptions, any company is likely to have a million fans on the first day. For the vast majority of organizations, it takes time and effort to build up a community of fans and followers. Besides, wide reach on social media is only one of the important criteria. Building up a strong relationship with the customer is just as important. The role of company employees in helping to make the company's culture tangible is another relevant issue to consider. Social media are then the ideal way to spread the company's culture and stories on a wide scale.

Social media tools refer to social networks (Facebook, Google+, Twitter, Instagram, TicTok), in addition to sharing videos platforms (YouTube), blogging platforms and platforms of communication (Zoom, Teams) (Ham et al.,2019).

Social media tools provide their users a profile, a list of friends, a chat room and the ability to send public or private messages, create events, comment, get feedback, etc. From a general perspective we can say that they have in common the ease of use, and free use, for good or for evil, representing the day-to-day lives of young people, mostly.

Some studies about social networks show that about a third of employees from different organizations use social media tools (Demyen, 2020). Thus, a social media tool can be used to create a large community of employees, both new and old, ensuring that within this community, new employees will have the opportunity to interact with more experienced employees, with the objective of exchanging organization's information.

Twitter is a social media tool similar to Facebook. Both sites are considered social networking sites where people can communicate with each other, keep in touch and share information, although Twitter limits the amount of information that you can share at any time within a single tweet (Tagtmeier, 2010).

The Use of Social Business Intelligence (SBI) Within Social Business

As mentioned in the previous sections, the inclusion of social business in an organization implies the use of social media by those same organizations. Organizations that make use of social media have in their power a great source of data in the most diverse formats that grows every day all the time. In this context, the SBI, which is the confluence of two domains - business intelligence (BI) and social media and other Web 2.0 platforms - allows the creation of new added value organizational processes and enhanced business capabilities used by organizations all over the world to effectively harness social media data and analyze them in order to produce added value information such as customer profiles and demographics, search habits, and social behaviors (Gioti et al., 2018).

Social Business Intelligence (SBI) consists of tools, technologies, applications and processes that help organizations through the collection, processing and analysis of data with different structures and formats from different distribution channels, such as social media. It creates the possibility of comprehensive monitoring of the external environment and helps to use user-generated content and unstructured knowledge for the organization. According to Jafari et al. (2017) the factors for the use of social business intelligence in the organization are classified into five categories: organizational, media, process, technical and human factors. Each of these factors includes different items to guide an organization in the use of user-generated content and unstructured knowledge on social media.

Therefore, the purpose of an SBI is to provide solid data analysis, and its results can be strategic or tactical improvements in the organization. The SBI builds a vision of the external forces that affect and guide organizations' daily business (Choi et al., 2020). By using an SBI, organizations can gain key benefits, including improving customer satisfaction, improving service quality, reducing missed opportunities, increasing revenue, brand reputation, continually improving efficiency, optimization, reducing risks and overall costs, ROI improvement, marketing optimization, situational awareness, the capture of unsatisfied ideas and needs, opportunity to take care of the client, sentiment analysis, use of social CRM, audience creation, reputation management and more effective marketing (Jafari et al., 2017).

THE USE AND UNDERUSE OF CONVERSATION POTENTIAL

Social media can enable and significantly increase the collaboration and learning from customers in various ways, for instance by novel social ways of providing and receiving feedback of a brand, an organization's products or services and practices.

Today's consumers want an organization that is open and receptive to their opinions, an organization that puts the customer first, in a central position.

Thanks to social media, organizations can get their information out to the public faster than ever. However, social media can spread bad information about a business just as fast as it can spread good information, due to its powerful amplifying effect. Social media builds brand awareness in ways that no other form of media can and reaches customers who would be otherwise unreachable. The conversation potential and the reach provided by the use of social media can lay the foundations for an organization's future growth or damage of reputation or brand image.

Designing a social strategy for the organization and learning from the interaction with customers so as to re-design strategy or improve organization procedures and practices should allow the right balance for an organization to ensure success in engaging with social media. The two case studies provided in this section describe real stories of how organizations can underuse or use the conversation potential enabled by social media and the consequent impact on the businesses' brand image in both cases.

The 'United Breaks Guitars' Case

"United Breaks Guitars" is a song by Canadian musician David Caroll and his band, Sons of Maxwell. It chronicles a real-life experience of how his guitar was broken during a trip on United Airlines in 2008, and the subsequent reaction from the airline. The song becomes an immediate YouTube and iTunes hit upon its release in July 2009 (Wikipedia, 2013; Van Belleghem, 2012).

Background

Musician Dave Caroll said his guitar was broken while in the airline's custody. He alleged that he and fellow passengers on board a flight plane saw baggage-handling crew throwing guitars on the tarmac in Chicago O'Hare on his flight from Halifax, Nova Scotia to Omaha, Nebraska. He arrived at his destination to discover that his $3,500 Taylor guitar had indeed suffered a broken neck (shown in his video).

The incident happened in March 2008, when singer Dave Caroll was sitting on board of a United Airlines flight. The plane was still on the tarmac, and through the window he could see how the baggage staff was dealing less than gently with his luggage. In his case, this included his expensive guitar, so he warned the United Airlines staff on the plane that he was concerned about its safety. He was not being thorny; all he wanted was the handlers to exercise a little more care. The cabin crew showed little interest and said that they could not 'interfere' with the work of their colleagues on the ground. They simply referred Caroll to the ground crew at his place of final destination. When he arrived, Caroll found that his fears had been justified: his costly Taylor guitar had been badly damaged. As he had been told, he reported to the ground personnel and explained his problem. No one was really prepared to listen, and he was passed from one person to another. Nobody did anything and nobody accepted responsibility. In the end, Caroll gave up in frustration. He tried to claim compensation through the airline's head office, with no results. His fruitless negotiations with the airline for compensation lasted nine months.

The Song and the Response

After nine months of fruitless negotiations with the airline, Caroll decided to put his frustration to creative use. He wrote a song and created a music video about his experience: 'United breaks guitars'. The lyrics include the verse "I should have flown with someone else, or gone by car, 'cause United breaks guitars".

The video, posted on YouTube on July 6, 2009, became a huge internet hit. It amassed 150,000 views within one day and garnered over half a million hits by July 9, 5 million by mid-August 2009 and 10 million by February 2011.

In less than a week, more than a million people had seen the video. Dave was by no means a famous singer, but people could associate with his feelings and share in his story: they had also already felt the same sense of exasperation and powerlessness when dealing with a giant organization. During the first days, more than 100 bloggers picked up the story. United Airlines decided not to react.

Unfortunately for United Airlines, however, the snowball was already rolling – and there was no way of stopping it. By the middle of the second week, the story had reached the ears of the traditional media. CNN ran a piece on the song, the newspapers followed, and all of a sudden Dave was a popular guest on several radio stations. The story seemed to have a life of its own.

Because no reaction from United Airlines was forthcoming, Dave launched a second video, United Breaks Guitars: Song 2, released on YouTube on August 18, 2009. The song takes a humorous look at Carroll's dealings with "the unflappable" United customer service employee Ms. Irlweg and targets the "flawed policies" that she was forced to uphold. A few months later, Caroll was finally invited to meet three of United Airlines' senior managers. They personally apologized him for the inconvenience he had suffered and asked if the carrier could use the video internally for training. United mentioned they hoped to learn from the incident, and to change its customer service policy as a result of the incident. A week later Caroll was invited to the American Senate, to discuss the rights of airlines passengers. Since the incident, he has been in great demand as a speaker on customer service.

Figure 4. The United Breaks Guitars YouTube video

The Paradoxical Behavior of United Airlines and Lessons Learned

Throughout this entire saga, United Airlines had chosen not to react in public forums. This was a missed opportunity. Dave's story caused many other dissatisfied customers to come out in the open. The best reaction would have been to listen to these people and try to help them.

There were probably other less than satisfied customers in the past, and they had probably talked online about the organization's poor service. The major crisis with Dave could have been avoided, if United Airlines had acted earlier to put these matters right. It is also clear that before the incident customer service at United Airlines was a department, not a philosophy. To make matters even worse, it was more than one department, all of whom were keen to pass on the responsibility to each other. The cabin crew on Dave's plane should have taken action immediately: good service means that everyone must be prepared to take their responsibility seriously. Even though airlines are not always directly in charge of their own baggage handling, there still needs to be clear communication and sense of commitment toward the customer.

Even though the United slogan 'We invite you to come and fly the friendly skies' is a good slogan, the behavior of the organization's staff showed that it was no more than that: the reality behind the slogan, as Dave experienced, was very different. Modern consumers will only believe in organization advertising if they can see the proof with their own eyes in organization actions.

The paradoxical behavior of United Airlines was not only confined to its underuse of conversation potential. In fact, they actually provoked a flood of negative conversations. The memory banks of Google mean that crises of this kind can continue to haunt a organization. In August 2011, three years down the line, the link to the 'United breaks guitars' video still occupies the 15th spot when searching for information about 'United Airlines' and 'baggage'.

In this whole regrettable tale, there is however a relevant mitigating factor in the organization's favour which constitutes also a lesson learned from the incident: the video is now used by United Airlines (and many others) as didactic material during customer service training.

The 'Become the Doritos Guru' Case

This case describes a complete change in how the Canadian based chips brand Doritos (Paul, 2009; StuzoGroup, 2013) got through to its teen audience, and the success the organization had with a totally re-imagined, user-generated campaign based on the use of social media. The campaign was based on the proposition: "name the new Doritos flavor, create a 30-second commercial for it and in return we will pay the winner, who will be declared "The Doritos Guru", $25,000 cash and 1% of the flavor's Canadian net sales, forever". Although the effort was centered on the mystery flavor, the impact lifted overall Doritos sales. The case also showed excellent results for brand health and engagement through the use of social media.

Background

In early 2009 Doritos released a new chip flavor and wanted to use this as an opportunity to drive brand awareness and engagement through an innovative promotion that leveraged social media. Working with multiple partners, Doritos decided to pursue a cross-platform promotion focused on a viral video.

The campaign, called "Become the Doritos Guru", was a video upload contest wherein users were tasked to create a catchy TV spot and name for the new chip flavor. Doritos was prepared to offer a prize of $25,000 and 1% of future consumer sales to the winning commercial and name for the new flavor. At the outset of the campaign, Doritos identified the ideal business outcomes for the promotion:

- Reach consumers across multiple social channels to create high brand awareness and engagement;
- Launch brand presence on Facebook and build out a Facebook fan base and Social CRM;
- Drive sales of the brand and the new flavor.

The Solution

The social promotion experts at Stuzo Group (StuzoGroup, 2013) conceived and developed the interactive components of the program. A first of its kind, the Stuzo Group proposed a solution which would launch an interconnected promotion on Facebook, YouTube, and a standalone website using Facebook Connect.

Figure 5. The Become the Doritos Guru campaign

Consumers were able to engage with the promotion in the environment of their choice. Facebook and the Doritos Guru microsite served as the interfaces for video uploads and related promotion interactions, while a branded YouTube Channel was used to host the videos and provide additional exposure. Data such as number of votes, comments, and video views was transferred seamlessly between the three sites.

The platform's administrative controls allowed Doritos to screen and approve video submissions before publishing them simultaneously to all three channels. Using the many tactical component features of the platform, users could vote, comment and share submissions, greatly encouraging viral spread. The winning video was based on votes from other users, showing the power of social media.

Campaign Results

This innovative promotion crushed all expectations set by Doritos and its agency partners. The campaign' participants took the opportunity to name the new flavor and to momentarily embody the Doritos brand. Furthermore, massive consumer engagement was achieved. Viewers came out in full force to express their opinions driving an enormous amount of traffic to all three channels. Overall, 75,000 people participated. 4,000 clever and well-produced ads were submitted, 570% more than the original goal. The Doritos YouTube channel became the #1 Subscribed Channel with 2.1 million video views. Viewers spent an average of 6 minutes on the sites, 2 minutes over the original goal. Viewer participation was exceptional with 560,000 votes and 188,000 comments. In one week after its official launch, Doritos' Facebook page gained 31,000 fans. Throughout the campaign, over 900,000 consumers visited the page. As a result of the integrated marketing program, Doritos sales increased dramatically in just two months. In particular, Doritos sales including the new flavor increased by an unprecedented 23% during the campaign period.

SOCIAL BUSINESS SUPPORTED BY MOBILE IST

Social business in organizations is a reality that needs to be improved and even, in some cases systematized, as already discussed. Acknowledging this context, the m_CSDT framework was formerly proposed in Ferreira et al. (2015) and updated Ferreira et al. (2019); at that stage, the framework was used to introduce and/or systematizes social business in organizations and the use of social business intelligence (SBI) within social business. The main aim is to contribute to the improvement of business processes, relationships with stakeholders (business partners, customers) and continuous training of employees within organizations. The following subsections present the m_CSDIT^2 approach, a usage scenario of it and some ethical issues that should be taken in consideration when social business is adopted by an organization.

Mobile_Create, Share, Document, Improve and Training: m_CSDIT²

The relevance of conducting social business supported by social media tools and SBI is widely acknowledged and recognized by the scientific community and organizations, as discussed throughout the previous sections. However, there is a lack of approaches that allow the systematization and that guide its implementation within an organization. To address this end, we propose an approach consisting in a three-layer framework (m_CSDIT²) which covers the:

1. Creation, sharing documentation of information and knowledge in and out of an organization, improvement of organizational processes and relationships with stakeholders, based on information and knowledge;
2. Training of organizational workers – ToOW model (Ferreira et al., 2017); and
3. Promotion of ad-hoc discussion.

Figure 6. The m_CSDIT² approach

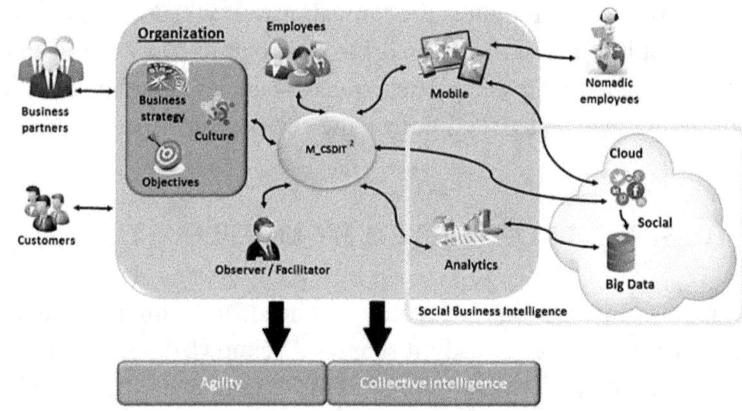

As shown in Figure 6, it is possible to develop a generic approach for implementing a social business through the use of social media tools and the support of social business intelligence (SBI), in order to achieve the well-being of the organization considering the agility and collective intelligence dimensions. In this approach, emphasis is given in the production of value for the organizational ecosystem.

Creating value often occurs in different social contexts. This approach includes individual and organizational contextual factors. It identifies the crucial role that an organization plays in promoting a culture of lifelong learning, collaboration and innovation in order to achieve the organization's strategic objectives. The model identifies and presents the relationships and interaction between employees, the social media tools, the social business intelligent, the business strategy and the organization.

The approach focuses the collaboration issue and its relationship with the accomplishment of the organizational goals. The employees are at the center of the collaboration and are mostly members of social networks. The approach illustrates the nature of collaboration in the workplace, with mobile devices, where social business is largely organized and conducted by the organization, and is based on the social context.

The approach may be briefly described as the collaboration in the workplace based in social media tools. This means that the organization learn through the participation and involvement of its employees through a network, connecting, interacting, and collaborating to obtain or share information and / or knowledge through social media tools. That information and / or knowledge is also obtained from the social business intelligence.

We propose that the collaboration in the workplace is achieved through the integration of suitable social media tools to the needs of organizational development and learning. To that end, we suggest a mixed form of peer tutoring with an instructor who acts as observer / facilitator. To realize the potential benefits of collaboration in the workplace based on social media tools, we recommend that organizations support rather than restrict the adequate use of social media tools in the workplace. Thus, organizations have to define the best long-term strategies and implement action plans to take advantage of collaboration based social media tools.

A Scenario for Using Social Media Tools for Employees' Training

In this section, we outline a scenario for a possible training action that will incorporate social media tools – 2nd framework's layer. The scenario describes how Facebook, Twitter and YouTube, can be included in the training program.

At the beginning of the training program some accounts on Facebook and Twitter are created. Subsequently, a group is created on Facebook, where employees are invited to join. At this stage it is expected that some inexperienced employees present some concerns with the safety issues related with the addition to the group of their profiles, as well as the information that they are writing on Twitter. In response to these concerns it is possible to change the Facebook settings to allow access only to "friends" of the group's creator, who is the action's instructor. Regarding Twitter, only the instructor and other employees allowed to follow. Furthermore, only one group member can send invitations to others to join the group. Thus, it is not possible for any other user of Facebook to access the group without an invitation. In these training actions, there will likely be employees who have never used this kind of tools, so it may be necessary a first action training to learn how to use Facebook and Twitter effectively.

During the course of the training the instructor can put YouTube videos on the mural of the Facebook group created and learners are invited to comment the videos with their opinions. Simultaneously, students may ask any questions about the videos on the Facebook wall, as well as through Twitter by writing small messages. At this stage, there is no difference between employees who are in the organization and those who are on the move, as there is no difference in treatment and "equal" opportunities are given. If precise indications on how to make comments are not given, it is quite possible that in early stages there are few answers and that "Like" button is just used. One way to encourage the production of reviews is, for example, to assign a grade to improve the final classification of the action training. During the training action, Facebook and Twitter can be used for the instructor to send messages to learners, tasks to be performed, evaluation dates, to use the calendar, among other issues related to the action. What is expected is to have great interaction in the communication between the instructor and the trainees and between the trainees themselves, achieving, for example, shorter response times to several problems.

It is expected that instructors will increase the number of questions on Facebook and Twitter, on the next subjects taught, the kind of assessments to be performed, deadlines for submission of tasks, among other tasks. This type of interaction will allow, for example, a collaborator who knows the answer to some question to "post" it even before the instructor realizes it, which can improve communication and a spirit of sharing and collaboration. It is also expected that as the action progresses more training videos are available in Youtube and their respective reviews increase in quantity and quality. It is believed that, at the end of the training action, the pedagogical use of Facebook, YouTube and Twitter have a positive impact on organizational learning through the use of mobile devices and with the contribution of the community of group training creating, sharing and documenting.

At the end of the training action a formal evaluation of the action will be carried out, through the use of a questionnaire and the results obtained will be compared with the results of training activities that do not use social media tools.

Ethical Issues

Many ethical issues arise when social media tools are used in an organizational context, one of which is the existence of a conflict of interest. First, social media tools users, particularly social networks users, cannot be sure that the published contents remain private. In case social networks are effectively integrated into the organizational environment, users should become aware that there can be no expectation of privacy. Secondly, there may be consequences when personal information provided to be private, is mixed with the information used in the organizational environment. The information provided should reflect / represent the user only under a professional setting.

Another issue related to the use of social media tools consists in age and previous experience. One cannot assume that, for example, all students enrolled in a particular course are experienced in the use of social media tools. According to Foulger et al. (2009), students aged over 40 years have little or no familiarity with the functions of social media tools in comparison with younger students. These results suggest that it is necessary to have special attention for competencies of employees who participate in any activity that uses social media tools.

Before adopting the tools of social media in organization, it is necessary to consider the definition of institutional and / or personal guidelines to maximize the potential of this kind of tools, minimizing legal responsibilities (Barczk & Duncan, 2012). Therefore, it is possible to list the following measures: (i) separating the personal from professional issues, thus creating different accounts, (ii) making full use of privacy settings and review them frequently, (iii) deactivating the mural through privacy settings to prevent the placement of undesirable messages, (iv) being aware of the possibility of having a maliciously audience, and (v) being aware that the information posted in these tools is out of control.

Following certain guidelines and using common sense, the employees of the organizations where social media tools are used can tailor organizational activities with the lowest possible risk to them and / or for the organization, provided that they have in mind the issues mentioned above.

FUTURE RESEARCH DIRECTIONS

Despite the successes and progress made to date, many important topics remain open for investigation with respect to providing appropriate approaches to undertake social business in organizations supported by the use of social media tools.

Many of the results achieved so far in social business supported by social media tools have come from joint work between researchers and organizations. Awareness, education and systematization remain three of the biggest issues to develop for those working in social business.

Researchers need to have practical experience as well as a sound theoretical foundation. Practitioners need to be equipped with a variety of approaches to use where appropriate depending on what is best suited to a given situation. Customers need to understand the importance of the process, believe in it, and support the efforts involved in doing it right. So, it is in this context that it is proposed the m_CSDIT^2 approach.

The m_CSDIT^2 approach proposed – a three-layer framework – needs to be conceptualized, implemented and validated in an organizational context.

The conceptualization of the model, in particular the first layer, will go through a preliminary study on identifying indicators of measurement. The indicators will be used to determine an activity pattern to select and use social media tools either producing organization's information "out" and in their input, i.e. what type and how the information should be made available to one or more stakeholders, and also how the feedback given by this/these stakeholder(s) should be analyzed in order to make the organization more competitive.

As far as out information is concerned, the indicators should guide the selection of tools to use against the objectives, the "drawing" of the content and the form of dissemination. Meanwhile indicators for analysis of information indicate how to handle this same information in order to draw conclusions on the basis of the proposed objectives e.g. likes and dislikes analysis and their comments within one or more social networks. In defining the indicators, qualitative and quantitative methods will be used.

In what comes to the conceptualization of the second layer of the framework, it is under development, i.e. studies (Gracia & Ferreira, 2012) have been performed and a model has been outlined as one can ascertain from the section entitled The scenario for social using average tools for employees ' training, in which the referred model is presented in an instantiated form.

Finally, the third layer will not be the object of study in its conceptualization, because as it can be concluded from the name itself, it is intended that the promotion of ad- hoc discussion is unrestricted and not planned. However, the analysis of the results will be held through the in indicators set for the first layer.

CONCLUSION

This chapter aimed to give an overview of the state-of-the art of the issues underlying the undertaking by organizations of social business supported by social media tools. Then it introduces an approach consisting in a three-layer framework (m_CSDIT^2) that covers the systematization of the creation, sharing and documentation of information and knowledge in and out of an organization, the education and training of organizational workers and ad-hoc discussion.

Even though the m_CSIDT^2 approach seems to be a valuable contribution to offer a new context to the traditional way of performing business - the social business context, in order to achieve organizational well-being in the agility and collective intelligence dimensions, the approach needs a greater degree of formalization.

The main difference between a traditional organization with and without social business is the involvement of the customers, business partners and employees in the life of an organization. Both visions present benefits and drawbacks. In particular, it is envisaged that the m_CSDIT[2] approach will allow the implementation of social business in an organization. The approach focus on the production of value for the customer reducing whatever does not add value from his point of view as well as to the organization itself. Therefore, the involvement of the organization ecosystem is of paramount importance to achieve this goal. On the contrary, traditional approaches allow the conduction of business within an organization in a closed way.

REFERENCES

Barczyk, C. C., & Duncan, D. G. (2012). Social Networking Media: An Approach for the Teaching of International Business. *Journal of Teaching in International Business, 23*(2), 98–122. doi:10.1080/08975930.2012.718703

Barwise, P., & Meehan, S. (2010). The One Thing You Must Get Right When Building a Brand. *Harvard Business Review*, 80–84.

Berlanga, R., Lanza-Cruz, I., & Aramburu, M. J. (2019). Quality Indicators for Social Business Intelligence. *Sixth International Conference on Social Networks Analysis, Management and Security (SNAMS)*, 229-236. 10.1109/SNAMS.2019.8931862

Boyd, D. (2008). *Taken out of context: American teen sociality in networked publics*. School of Information, University of California-Berkeley.

Boyd, D. M., & Ellison, N. B. (2008). Social network sites: Definition, history, and scholarship. *Journal of Computer-Mediated Communication, 13*(1), 210–230. doi:10.1111/j.1083-6101.2007.00393.x

Brown, J. S. (2012). *Learning in and for the 21st Century. Singapure*. National Institute of Education.

Charbonnier-Voirin, A. (2011). The development and partial testing of the psychometric properties of a measurement scale of organizational agility. *M@n@gement, 14*(2), 119-156.

Charlton, T., Devlin, M., & Drummond, S. (2009). Using Facebook to improve communication in undergraduate software development teams. *Computer Science Education, 19*(4), 273–292. doi:10.1080/08993400903384935

Cheng, C., Zhong, H., & Cao, L. (2020). Facilitating speed of internationalization: The roles of business intelligence and organizational agility. *Journal of Business Research, 110*, 95–103. doi:10.1016/j.jbusres.2020.01.003

CISCO. (2020). *Cisco Annual Internet Report (2018–2023) White Paper*. Retrieved July, 2020, from https://www.cisco.com/c/en/us/solutions/collateral/executive-perspectives/annual-internet-report/white-paper-c11-741490.html

Consulting, I. (2011a). *"Social media around the world" study*. Retrieved July 05, 2013, from www.slideshare.net/InSitesConsulting/social-media-around-the-world-2011-9537752

Cortada, J. (2012). *The Business of Social Business: What works and how its done*. IBM Institute for Business Value. Retrieved August 02, 2013, from https://www.ibm.com/midmarket/common/att/pdf/IBV_2012_The_business_of_social_business.pdf

De Brún, A., & McAuliffe, E. (2020). Identifying the context, mechanisms and outcomes underlying collective leadership in teams: Building a realist programme theory. *BMC Health Services Research, 20*(1), 1–13. doi:10.118612913-020-05129-1 PMID:32228574

Dede, C. (2005). Planning for Neomillenial learning styles: Implications for investments in technology and faculty, In D. G. Oblinger & J. L. Oblinger (Eds.), *Educating the Net Generation*, (pp. 228–249). Retrieved August 02, 2013, from https://www.educause.edu/educatingthenetgen

Demyen, S. (2020). Employees' Perspective on the Usefulness of Social Media for an Organisation. Analele Universitatii "Eftimie Murgu" Resita. Fascicola II. *Studii Economice, 27*, 17–31.

Dodge, R., Daly, A., Huyton, J., & Sanders, L. (2012). The challenge of defining wellbeing. *International Journal of Wellbeing, 2*(3), 222–235. doi:10.5502/ijw.v2i3.4

Dorn, J., Grün, C., Werthner, H., & Zapletal, M. (2007). A Survey of B2B Methodologies and Technologies: From Business Models towards Deployment Artifacts. *Proceedings of 40th Hawaii International Conference on Systems Science (HICSS-40-2007).*

Downes, S. (2008). *Places to go: YouTube*. Innovate. Retrieved July 02, 2013, from https://innovateonline.info/

Dunlap, J. C., & Lowenthal, P. R. (2011). Learning, unlearning, and relearning: Using Web 2.0 technologies to support the development of lifelong learning skills. In G. D. Magoulas (Ed.), *E-infrastructures and technologies for lifelong learning: Next generation environments* (pp. 292–315). University of London. doi:10.4018/978-1-61520-983-5.ch012

Edwards, J. (2016). *6 benefits of being a social business*. Retrieved July, 2020, from https://www.theidm.com/blog/6-benefits-of-being-a-social-business

Eva, N., Cox, J. W., Tse, H. M., & Lowe, K. B. (2019). From competency to conversation: A multi-perspective approach to collective leadership development. *The Leadership Quarterly*, *101346*. Advance online publication. doi:10.1016/j.leaqua.2019.101346

Ferreira, M. J., Moreira, F., & Seruca, I. (2014). *A traditional organization towards a new dimension of labour – social business. In Information systems and Technology for Organizational Agility, Intelligence, and Resilience*. Information Science Reference. doi:10.4018/978-1-4666-5970-4.ch009

Ferreira, M. J., Moreira, F., & Seruca, I. (2017). Organizational training within Digital Transformation: The ToOW model. *Proceedings of the 19th International Conference on Enterprise Information Systems (ICEIS 2017)*, *2*, 526-532. 10.5220/0006366105260532

Ferreira, M. J., Moreira, F., & Seruca, I. (2019). Digital Transformation Towards a New Context of Labour: Enterprise 4.0. In Technological Developments in Industry 4.0 for Business Applications (vol. 1, pp 26-49). Information Science Reference (IGI). DOI: doi:10.4018/978-1-5225-4936-9.ch002

Ferriter, W. H. (2010). Digitally speaking. *Educational Leadership*, *68*, 87–88.

Forbes. (2011). *How to Build a Social Business*. Retrieved July 02, 2013, from https://www.forbes.com/sites/danschawbel/2011/10/13/how-to-build-a-social-business/

Foulger, T., Ewbank, A., Kay, A., Popp, S., & Cater, H. (2009). Moral spaces in MySpace: Preservice teachers' perspectives about ethical issues in social networking. *Journal of Research on Technology in Education*, *42*(1), 1–28. doi:10.1080/15391523.2009.10782539

Friedrich, T. L., Vessey, W. B., Schuelke, M. J., Ruark, G. A., & Mumford, M. D. (2009). A framework for understanding collective leadership: The selective utilization of leader and team expertise within networks. *The Leadership Quarterly*, *20*(6), 933–958. doi:10.1016/j.leaqua.2009.09.008

Gallaugher, J., & Ransbotham, S. (2010). Social Media and Customer Dialog Management at Starbucks. *MIS Quarterly Executive*, *9*(4), 197–212.

Garcia, L., & Ferreira, M. J. (2012). *Facebook as a supporting tool for collaborative/ cooperative teaching. Global Journal of Educational Research.*

Gioti, H., Ponis, S. T., & Panayiotou, N. (2018). Social business intelligence: Review and research directions. *Journal of Intelligence Studies in Business*, *8*(2), 23–42. doi:10.37380/jisib.v8i2.320

Gray, K., Annabell, L., & Kennedy, G. (2010). Medical students' use of Facebook to support learning: Insights from four case studies. *Medical Teacher*, *32*(12), 971–976. doi:10.3109/0142159X.2010.497826 PMID:21090950

Green, T., & Bailey, B. (2010). Academic uses of Facebook: Endless possibilities or endless peril? *TechTrends*, *54*(3), 20–22. doi:10.100711528-010-0398-z

Greenhow, C. (2011). Online social networking and learning: What are the interesting research questions? *International Journal of Cyber Behavior, Psychology and Learning*, *1*(1), 36–50. doi:10.4018/ijcbpl.2011010104

Greenhow, C., Robelia, B., & Hughes, J. E. (2009). Web 2.0 and classroom research: What path should we take now? *Educational Researcher*, *38*, 246–259. doi:10.3102/0013189X09336671

Guamushig, T.-M., Lopez, C.-P., Santorum, M., & Aguilar, J. (2019). Characterization of a Fourth Generation Virtual Organization Based on Industry 4.0. *2019 International Conference on Information Systems and Software Technologies (ICI2ST), Information Systems and Software Technologies (ICI2ST), 2019 International Conference On*, 182–186. 10.1109/ICI2ST.2019.00033

Hagel, J., Brown, J. S., & Davison, L. (2010). *The Power of Pull: How Small Moves, Smartly Made, Can Set Big Things in Motion*. Basic Books.

Ham, C.-D., Lee, J., Hayes, J. L., & Bae, Y. H. (2019). Exploring sharing behaviors across social media platforms. *International Journal of Market Research*, *61*(2), 157–177. doi:10.1177/1470785318782790

Harris, A. L., & Rea, A. (2009). Web 2.0 and virtual world technologies: A growing impact on IS education. *Journal of Information Systems Education*, *20*(2), 137–144.

Hew, K. F. (2011). Students' and teachers' use of Facebook. *Computers in Human Behavior*, *27*(2), 662–676. doi:10.1016/j.chb.2010.11.020

Hibbard, C. (2010). How Twitter helped Discovery Channel during a hostage crisis. *Social Media Examiner*. Retrieved July 04, 2013, from www.socialmediaexaminer.com/discovery-channel-case-study/

Hinchcliffe, D. (2020). *Revisiting How to Cultivate Connected Organizations in an Age of Coronavirus*. Retrieved August, 2020, from https://dionhinchcliffe.com/category/social-business/social-collaboration/

Hiriyappa, B. (2008). *Strategic Management for Chartered Accountants*. New Age International Pvt Ltd Publishers.

i-SCOOP. (n.d.). *Social business guide: Context and business dimensions*. https://www.i-scoop.eu/social-business/

IBM. (2012). *The business of social business: What works and how it's done*. Retrieved July 04, 2013, from https://www.ibm.com/midmarket/common/att/pdf/IBV_2012_The_business_of_social_business.pdf

IBM. (2013). *Social Business: Patterns in achieving social business success by leading and pioneering organizations*. IBM Institute for Business Value. Retrieved July 05, 2013, from IBM website: http://social.bz/download/IBM-social-patterns.pdf

Jafari, S. M., & Asgarnajafi, F. (2017). Social Business Intelligence Utilization in Organization: The Importance of Unstructured Knowledge. *Proceedings of the International Conference on Intellectual Capital, Knowledge Management & Organizational Learning*, 109–115.

Jandrić, P. (2020). Creativity and Collective Intelligence. In M. Peters & R. Heraud (Eds.), *Encyclopedia of Educational Innovation*. Springer. doi:10.1007/978-981-13-2262-4_65-1

Jarche, H. (2011). *Social learning for business*. Retrieved July 9, 2013, from http://www.jarche.com/2011/01/social-learning-for-business/

Jarrahi, M. H., & Sawyer, S. (2013). Social Technologies, Informal Knowledge Practices, and the Enterprise. *Journal of Organizational Computing and Electronic Commerce*, *23*(1-2), 110–137. doi:10.1080/10919392.2013.748613

Joiner, B. (2019). Leadership Agility for Organizational Agility. *Journal of Creating Value*, *5*(2), 139–149. doi:10.1177/2394964319868321

Junco, R., & Cole-Avent, G. A. (2008). An introduction to technologies commonly used by college students. *New Directions for Student Services*, *124*(124), 3–17. doi:10.1002s.292

Kaplan, A. M., & Haenlein, M. (2010). Users of the world, unite! The challenges and opportunities of social media. *Business Horizons*, *53*(1), 59–68. doi:10.1016/j.bushor.2009.09.003

Kemp, S. (2020). *Digital 2020 Global Overview Report, DataReportal*. https://datareportal.com/reports/digital-2020-global-digital-overview

Kim, P. (2012). *The definition of social business*. Retrieved from http://dachisgroup.com/2012/06/the-definition-of-social-business/

Kotter, J. P. (1995). Leading Change: Why Transformation Efforts Fail. *Harvard Business Review OnPoint*, 60-67.

Lampe, C., Ellison, N., & Steinfield, C. (2006). A Face (book) in the crowd: Social searching vs. social browsing. CSCW '06, Banff, Alberta.

Lehman, C. M., DuFrene, D. D., & Lehman, M. W. (2010). YouTube video project: A "Cool" way to learn communication ethics. *Business Communication Quarterly*, *73*(4), 444–449. doi:10.1177/1080569910385382

Levy, P. (1999). *Collective Intelligence: Mankind's Emerging World in Cyberspace*. Perseus Books.

Liu, Y. (2010). Social media tools as a learning resource. *Journal of Educational Technology Development and Exchange*, *3*(1), 101–114. doi:10.18785/jetde.0301.08

Mackay, F. (2010). Business schools respond to demand for use of social media. *The New York Times*. Retrieved July 10, 2013, from http://www.nytimes.com/2010/03/31/education/31iht-riedmba.html?p

Majchrzack, A., Cherbakov, L., & Ives, B. (2009). Harnessing the Power of the Crowds with Corporate Social Networking "How IBM does it". *MIS Quarterly Executive*, *8*(2), 103–198.

Malone, T. W., Laubacher, R., & Dellarocas, C. N. (2009). *Harnessing Crowds: Mapping the Genome of Collective Intelligence*. MIT Sloan Research Paper No. 4732-09. Retrieved July 12, 2013, from http://ssrn.com/abstract=1381502 doi:10.2139/ssrn.1381502

Martin, A., & van Bavel, R. (2013). *Assessing the Benefits of Social Networks for Organizations*. Retrieved November 18, from http://ftp.jrc.es/EURdoc/JRC78641.pdf

McAfee, A. (2009). *Enterprise 2.0: New Collaborative Tools for Your Organization's Toughest Challenges*. Harvard Business Review Press.

McKinsey & Company. (2012). *The social economy: Unlocking value and productivity through social technologies*. Retrieved November 19 from https://www.mckinsey.com/insights/high_tech_telecoms_internet/the_social_economy

Moran, M., Seaman, J., & Tinti-Kane, H. (2011). *Teaching, learning, and sharing: How today's higher education faculty use social media*. Pearson Learning Solutions and Babson Survey Research Group. Retrieved July 15, 2013, from http://www.pearsonlearningsolutions.com/educators/pearson-social-media-survey-2011-bw.pdf

Mullen, R., & Wedwick, L. (2008). Avoiding the digital abyss: Getting started in the classroom with YouTube, digital stories, and blogs. *The Clearing House: A Journal of Educational Strategies, Issues and Ideas*, *82*(2), 66–69. doi:10.3200/TCHS.82.2.66-69

Myers, A. (2013). *McKensey Global Survey Finds Social Tools Tacking Hold in the Networked Enterprise*. Retrieved August 02, 2013, from https://www.cmswire.com/cms/social-business/mackinse

Orr, E., Mita, S., Ross, C., Simmering, M., Arseneault, J., & Orr, R. (2009). The influence of shyness on the use of Facebook in an undergraduate sample. *Cyberpsychology & Behavior*, *12*(3), 337–340. doi:10.1089/cpb.2008.0214 PMID:19250019

Paul, J. (2009). *The Doritos Guru chips in*. Retrieved November 29, 2013, from https://strategyonline.ca/2009/04/01/decondoritos-20090401/

Pinto, B. (2009). *Using Twitter to teach*. ABC News. Retrieved July 15, 2013, from https://abcnews.go.com/GMA/Weekend/story?id=7140272&page=1

Prensky, M. (2001). Digital natives, digital immigrants. *On the Horizon, 9*(5), 1–6. Retrieves July, 2020, from https://www.meupositivo.com.br/panoramapositivo/social-business-entenda-o-que-e-e-quais-sao-as-melhores-praticas/

PulsePoint Group and The Economist Intelligence Unit. (2012). *The Economics of the Socially Engaged Enterprise*. Retrieved November 18, from http://www.pulsepointgroup.com/sites/default/files/AP-Presentation-4_27_12.pdf

Sherehiy, B., Karwowski, W., & Layer, J. K. (2007). A review of enterprise agility: Concepts, frameworks, and attributes. *International Journal of Industrial Ergonomics*, *37*(5), 445–460. doi:10.1016/j.ergon.2007.01.007

Sideraworks. (2013). *What Is Social Business?* Retrieved July 17, 2013, from https://www.sideraworks.com/wp-content/uploads/2012/03/WhatIsSocialBusiness_SideraWorks.pdf

Silius, K., Kailanto, M. & Tervakari, A-M. (2011). Evaluating the Quality of Social Media in an Educational Context. *iJET, 6*(3), 21-26.

Spieth, P., Schneider, S., Clauß, T., & Eichenberg, D. (2019). Value drivers of social businesses: A business model perspective. *Long Range Planning Journal, 52*(3), 427–444. doi:10.1016/j.lrp.2018.04.004

Streitz, N., Prante, T., Röcker, C., Alphen, D. V., Magerkurth, C., Stenzel, R. & Plewe, D. A. (2003). Ambient Displays and Mobile Devices for the Creation of Social Architectural Spaces. *The Kluwer International series on Computer Supported Cooperative Work, 2*, 387-409.

StuzoGroup. (2013). *Doritos-Become The Doritos Guru.* Retrieved November 29, 2013, from http://www.stuzo.com/case-studies/Stuzo_CaseStudy_Doritos_BecometheDoritosGuru.pdf

Syncapse. (2013). *The Value of a Facebook Fan 2013: Revisiting Consumer Brand Currency In Social Media.* Retrieved November 25, 2013, from www2.syncapse.com/e/15032/Value-of-a-Fan-Report-2013-pdf/4mqfc/328355212

Tagtmeier, C. (2010). Facebook vs. Twitter: Battle of the social network stars. *Computers in Libraries, 30*, 6–10.

Positivo Tecnologia. (2018). *Social business: entenda o que é e quais são as melhores práticas.* Author.

Timmermans, F., & Katainen, J. (2019). *Towards a sustainable Europe by 2030.* European Commission. Retrieved August, 2020, https://ec.europa.eu/commission/sites/beta-political/files/rp_sustainable_europe_30-01_en_web.pdf

Van Belleghem, S. (2012). *The Conversation Company, Boost your Business Through Culture. People & Social Media.* Kogan Page.

Vannoy, S. A., & Palvia, P. (2010). The Social Influence Model of Technology Adoption. *Communications of the ACM, 53*(8), 149–153. doi:10.1145/1743546.1743585

Wankel, L., & Wankel, C. (2011). Connecting on campus with new media: Introduction to higher education administration with social media. *Cutting Edge Technologies in Higher Education, 2*, xi–xviii.

Wikipedia. (2013). *United Breaks Guitars.* Retrieved March 03, 2013, from https://en.wikipedia.org/wiki/United_Breaks_Guitars

Wong, D. M. L. (2020). *Individual use of Enterprise 2.0 and its impact on social capital within large organisations* [PhD Thesis]. Computing and Information Systems - Theses [380]. Retrieved September, 2030, from https://minerva-access.unimelb.edu.au/handle/11343/241865

Yin, R. (2009). *Case Study Research: Design and Methods*. SAGE Publication, Inc.

Young, J. (2010). How social networking helps teaching (and worries some professors). *The Chronicle of Higher Education*. Retrieved July 18, 2013, from http://chronicle.com/article/How-Social-Networking-Helps/123654/

Yunus, M. (2007). *Creating a World Without Poverty: Social Business and the Future of Capitalism*. Public Affairs.

Zakić, N., Jovanović, A., & Stamatović, M. (2008). External and Internal Factors Affecting the Product and Business Process Innovation. *Facta Universitatis Series: Economics and Organization*, *5*(1), 17–29.

Zhao, F., & Kemp, L. (2012). Integrating Web 2.0-based informal learning with workplace training. *Educational Media International*, *49*(3), 231–245. doi:10.1080/09523987.2012.738015

ADDITIONAL READING

Alloway, T. P., Horton, J., Alloway, R. G., & Dawson, C. (2013). Social networking sites and cognitive abilities: Do they make you smarter? *Computers & Education*, *63*, 10–16. doi:10.1016/j.compedu.2012.10.030

Baran, B. (2010). Facebook as a formal instructional environment. *British Journal of Educational Technology*, *41*(6), 146–149. doi:10.1111/j.1467-8535.2010.01115.x

Belle, L., Meghan, C., & Nicole, D. (2010). Using Social Mediate Engage Youth:Education, Social Justice & Humanitarianism. *Prevention Researcher*, *17*(5), 13–16.

Billiot, T. (2011). In one online class, Twitter brings students together. The Chronicle of Higher Education. Retrieved July 02, 2013, from http://chronicle.com/article/In-One-Online-Class-Twitter/129120/

Boateng, R., Victor, M., & Thomas, C. (2010). When Web 2.0 becomes an organizational learning tool: Evaluating Web 2.0 tools. *Development and Learning in Organizations*, *24*(3), 17–20. doi:10.1108/14777281011037254

Bonabeau, E. (2009). Decisions 2.0: The Power of Collective Intelligence. *MITSloan Management Review, 50*(2), 45-52 Retrieved July 02, 2013, from the MIT Sloan website: https://sloanreview.mit.edu/article/decisions-20-the-power-of-collective-intelligence/

Educause (2007). 7 things you should know about Twitter. Retrieved August 02, 2013, from https://www.educause.edu/ELI/7ThingsYouShouldKnowAboutTwitt/161801

Hargittai, E. (2007). Whose space? Differences among users and non-users of social network sites. *Journal of Computer-Mediated Communication, 13*(1), 276–297. doi:10.1111/j.1083-6101.2007.00396.x

Hinchcliffe, D., & Kim, P. (2012). *Social Business By Design: Transformative Social Media Strategies for the Connected Company*. Jossey-Bass.

Koutsabasis, P., Stavrakis, M., Spyrou, T., & Darzentas, J. (2011). Perceived impact of asynchronous e-Learning after long-term use: Implications for design and development. *International Journal of Human-Computer Interaction, 27*(2), 191–213. doi:10.1080/10447318.2011.537206

Liu, Y. (2010). Social media tools as a learning resource. *Journal of Educational Technology Development and Exchange, 3*(1), 101–114. doi:10.18785/jetde.0301.08

Mazman, S. G., & Yasemin, K. U. (2010). Modeling educational usage of Facebook. *Computers & Education, 55*(2), 444–453. doi:10.1016/j.compedu.2010.02.008

Moreira, F., & Ferreira, M. J. (2012). Exploring Integration Issues in A Blended Mobile Learning Model context oriented applied to a Requirement Engineering course – Mobility, Context And Cloud. *The Proceedings of the Information Systems Education Conference, 29*(2088), New Orleans, LA.

Moreira, F., Ferreira, M. J., & Sobral, S. R. (2010). Proposta de um modelo Blended Mobile Learning orientado ao contexto, *IEEE-RITA. Edición Especial, 5*(4), 132–137.

Murphy, G., & Salomone, S. (2013). Using social media to facilitate knowledge transfer in complex engineering environments: A primer for educators. *European Journal of Engineering Education, 38*(1), 70–84. doi:10.1080/03043797.2012.742871

Parker, G. L. (2010). Strategic Planning with Critical Success Factors and Future Scenarios: An Integrated Strategic Planning Framework (CMU/SEI-2010-TR-037). Retrieved August 02, 2013, from the Software Engineering Institute, Carnegie Mellon University website: https://www.sei.cmu.edu/library/abstracts/reports/10tr037.cfm

Roblyer, M. D., Michelle, M., Marsena, W., James, H., & Witty, J. (2010). Findings on Facebook in higher education: A comparison of college faculty and student uses and perceptions of social networking sites. *The Internet and Higher Education*, *13*(3), 134–140. doi:10.1016/j.iheduc.2010.03.002

Stana, A., Meka, E., Sevrani, K., & Baholli, I. (2013). From Traditional Business toward Social Business: A Single Window E-Platform for the Albanian Port Community System. *Academic Journal of Interdisciplinary Studies*, *2*(2). Advance online publication. doi:10.5901/ajis.2013.v2n2p191

Tallon, P. P., & Pinsonneault, A. (2011). Competing Perspectives on the link between strategic information technology alignment and organizational agility: Insights from a mediation model. *Management Information Systems Quarterly*, *35*(2), 463–486. doi:10.2307/23044052

Tian, S. W., Yu, A. Y., Vogel, D., & Ron Chi-Wai Kwok, R. C. (2011). The impact of online social networking on learning: A social integration perspective. *International Journal of Networking and Virtual Organisations*, *8*(3/4), 264–280. doi:10.1504/IJNVO.2011.039999

Wankel, C. (2010). Cutting-Edge Social Media Approaches to Business education: Teaching with LinkedIn, Facebook, Twitter, Second Life, and Blogs. Series: Research in Management Education and Development. Charlotte, NC: Information Age Publishing.

Wise, S. (2012). Collective Intelligence in the Public Sector: Crowd sourcing through Multi-stakeholder Networks. *Entrepreneurial Practice Review*, 2(2), Retrieved August 03, 2013, from http://www.entryerson.com/epr/index.php/jep/article/viewFile/109/82

Zaman, A. (2012). Developing a Social Business Model for Zero Waste Management Systems: A Case Study Analysis. *Journal of Environmental Protection*, *3*(11), 1458–1469. doi:10.4236/jep.2012.311163

KEY TERMS AND DEFINITIONS

Agility: The capability of an organization to rapidly change or adapt in response to changes in the market.

Collective Intelligence: Shared knowledge jointly constructed by a group of people through their collaborations and instructions.

Mobile Learning: Any sort of learning that happens when the learner is not at a fixed, predetermined location, or learning that happens when the learner takes advantage of the learning opportunities offered by mobile technologies.

Nomadic Workers: Someone who works in different places while away from their office, often using a mobile phone and the internet:

Social Business: A company that embeds social tools and practices both internally (employee-oriented) and external (oriented to other stakeholders such as customers or other business partners) with and integrated approach.

Social Software: Software inspired by the functionalities of Web 2.0 tools such as blogs, wikis, microblogging, social networks, and others.

Training and Education Professionals: Training and education in the networked organizations is to connect and communicate based on facilitating collaborative work and learning amongst workers, especially as peers.

Well-Being: Is when individuals have the psychological, social, and physical resources they need to meet a particular psychological, social, and/or physical challenge.

Chapter 2
Implementing Cloud Information Systems for Organizational Agility and Competitive Advantage:
SaaS Migration

Kamran Janamian
Independent Researcher, Slovakia

ABSTRACT

In today's competitive business environment, information systems are not a luxury; rather they are vital for survival. A new generation of ISs has been established on cloud capabilities. Moving toward software as a service is not the goal in a business, and if not implemented properly, competitive advantage may even suffer. Managers and change agents should undertake deep study over SaaS implementation before migration. In this chapter, the main elements and features in which CEOs and IT managers should consider in evaluating the SaaS migration option will be provided, and enterprises may be acquainted with the concept, goals, and theoretical foundations of SaaS as a main cloud-based service in the business environment. On the other hand, businesses should undertake some necessary changes in the operating circumstances which are utilization of a proper and modified business models established over a knowledge base strategic movement. This will lead enterprises to achieve the main goals of migrating to SaaS and cloud platforms (i.e., agility, competitive advantage, and innovation).

DOI: 10.4018/978-1-7998-4799-1.ch002

INTRODUCTION

Information Systems as Carr (2004) states appear to be like electricity. Publicity and essentiality of electricity forced managers not to depend on electricity for their strategic decisions, and so is true for ISs. Carr argues, "When a resource becomes essential to competition but inconsequential to strategy, the risks it creates become more important than the advantages it provides" (2004, P.11). Traditional desktop ISs are more or less known for more than three decades, and managers are following new routes to the quality, timeliness, and effectiveness of information flow for gaining competitive advantage. The main disadvantages of traditional desktop ISs are high costs, implementation difficulties, and information blockage. The arrival of the Internet has extended the way ISs can perform, however network-enabled Information Systems have been in use for more than two decades. Now there is no need to pay heavy costs for Information System implementation and license purchases. "Cloud Computing" emerged a new generation of ISs, i.e., "Cloud Information Systems (CISs)". With this new phenomenon as Martin (cited by Geelan, 2009) explains, there is no need for new IT structures, user training, or licensing procedures; on the other hand and at the same time the company will benefit from increased IT capabilities and capacities.

NIST's[1] definition of Cloud Computing (2011) implies that every application that uses the internet as a tool for enabling "ubiquitous, convenient, on-demand network access" (Mell & Grance, 2011) to shared computing resources, data, information or services, can be grouped in the Cloud Computing Model. To name a few Cloud Computing services offered since far, we can point to Software as a Service (SaaS), Platform as a Service (PaaS), and Infrastructure as a Service (IaaS). These so-called Cloud-models have moved business IT to a new era, which is based on hybrid and virtual worlds. This chapter attempted to guide managers and change agents through choosing and using the SaaS model in the new Cloud-era. Feasibility and suitability of SaaS and CIS will be studied in different business environments, and SaaS business maturity models will be explained. Change as a vital element of implementing the SaaS model will be described and few delivery methods to SaaS implementation challenges will be offered as well. Thus, this chapter can be a guideline toward SaaS-migration.

Importance of SaaS

SaaS has been modified, explained and defined by almost any expert in the field. However, the most known definition of SaaS explains that any application running on the cloud platform enabling consumers to run the program on a thin-client (Internet browser) or a program interface can be known as SaaS (D. C. Chou &

Chou, 2008; Mell & Grance, 2011; SIIA, 2001). Others defined SaaS as a software in which the application is based on the Internet and is available via network and can be accessed remotely (Churakova & Mikhramova, 2010). In SaaS, the operation is executed on the host's server and databases are saved on the virtual space owned by the SaaS provider. Application operation, safety, security and storage may not controlled by the consumer.

Rapid growth of IT technologies bring advantages for companies, although at the same time it creates certain risks and challenges. Reacting to these changes is paramount for the companies to take advantage and to counteract threads of this new digital-cloud-era (SIIA, 2001). SaaS mainly provides cost savings, resource utilization, application access scalability, and global outsourcing possibilities for the organization (D. C. Chou & Chou, 2008) along with many other advantages such as opening the global information flow to the company's management layers, using up-to-date IT expertise, and bringing core competency to the enterprise. Lynn Elwood, the vice president of OpenText (a known cloud solution enterprise) claims cloud based services and software as a service solutions will bring businesses better agility, flexibility and insight (2016) however on the other hand she suggests those who want to consider cloud options first should ensure if the cloud and SaaS will bring benefits or not and this is the time, some questions will rise: how would a manager understand the suitability of the SaaS model for the business, and why should a change agent offer SaaS as a strategic movement?

SAAS MIGRATION

Generally speaking, businesses cannot target their initial enterprise without proper outsourcing. Outsourcing IT is essential as outsourcing raw materials and resources. Software as a Service is in fact a motivation for enterprises to eliminate their hopeless effort on IT and target those essential goals in today's competitive environment. But the main question remains why? when? what? and how? to implement this IT infrastructure. Is SaaS implementation procedure the same as those processes essential for traditional IT implementation? These questions will be discussed in following section.

Why Migrate to SaaS?

Although the SaaS model may provide many advantages for businesses, but feasibility of migrating to SaaS should be studied in every specific transition situation. The main dilemma remaining for managers and change agents here is "What is the essentiality for migrating to the SaaS model?"

- Argued in almost every literature, one of the major drivers of SaaS migration is cost (Carr, 2003; Carraro & Chong, 2006; D. C. Chou & Chou, 2008; Herbert, Ross, & Rose, 2010; Hogan, 2008). Carr (2004) states, "studies of corporate IT spending consistently shows that greater expenditures rarely translate into superior financial results." (P.12) Indeed he says, the opposite is often true. Desktop ISs need to be installed, maintained periodically, debugged in the first implementation months, and managed by an IT expert inside the corporation; and these all impose expenses on the company's limited financial resources. Why not spend money on core competencies and leave the IT to experts outside of the company? This way not only will expenses be guided through main features of the organization, but also it will lead shifting risks. A Berkeley report shows that using CIS or SaaS may convert capital expenses (CapEx) to operating expenses (OpEx) and this will allow the capital to be spent on the core business investments (Armbrust et al., 2009; Herbert et al., 2010). The total cost of ownership is another factor explained by Nema (2010). Using the SaaS model, businesses are able to avoid hidden and apparent costs of legacy system implementation and maintenance, while with SaaS; the company pays just monthly or annual fees. Purchased software is worth nothing for the company and the whole price will be an expense, while in a monthly or annually based model, financial liquidity flows out of the company continually. As a result, the risk of IT failure, costs, maintenance, security and scalability will be imposed to the third party.
- Fast and easy implementation is the second important factor (Herbert et al., 2010). When purchasing SaaS, there is no need for physical download, installation and maintenance procedures. Customers of SaaS also can access the most recent versions of the software at the fastest time. Software configuration, infrastructure capitalization and installation process is also minimized (Elwood, 2016). This is about SaaS deployment, but managers should be aware of business-model changes their respective company should experience. This will be discussed further in the second part of this chapter.
- Innovation and agility according to Herbert et al. (2010) and Hogan (2008) are other factors dramatically affecting business processes. SaaS brings innovative and on-demand applications for customers. When a company wants to start a fast on-demand project, SaaS may be a good choice. It can respond quickly and properly to the innovative changes and modifications managers, employees, and customers of the company may need on the software.
- Using IT expertise in comparison with software licensing states to be another factor (Carraro & Chong, 2006; Herbert et al., 2010; Hogan, 2008). "With SaaS, the job of application deployment and keeping it running… testing and

installing patches, managing upgrades, monitoring performance, ensuring high availability, and so forth is handled by the provider" (Carraro & Chong, 2006). Transferring time and money are the other core business affairs of the organization. In the SaaS model, it has been claimed (Herbert et al., 2010) that vendors act more responsive and proactive, because the future road map of SaaS vendors depends highly on every single customer. In case of SME[2]s, many believe that security confidence maintained by SaaS vendors are way out of business's abilities when using in-house package software. IT expertise in the SaaS model is hired rather than purchased and this will convert the responsibilities of software vendors. A SaaS vendor should understand that software is not offered as a single package anymore, rather it is their services that bear the most significance.

- Opening new opportunities and abilities to the business is another driver of SaaS migration. With ever-growing business environments, managers are not aware of future changes. For instance, outsourcing main business processes can be implemented using high quality services offered by overseas SaaS vendors. Business performance highly depends on the strategic decision making process. Whatever strategy may be used in the company, "SaaS serves as an ongoing, democratizing force, putting more computer power into the hands of all kinds of end users, and delivering more expertise and services to them." (Babcock, 2010) Claimed by Buyya, Yeo and Venugopal (2008) enterprises now use Cloud services such as SaaS to enhance scalability of their services and products considering their financial deficit; this way, managers may bring value to the business. Value creation of SaaS in businesses highly depends on the degree in which a company shows agility and fluctuation to the new opportunities and gates of new digital-era business environments.
- Last but not least is the competitive advantage. Argued by Govindaraju et al. (2018) IT capabilities establish organizational agility and competitive advantage by developing "trust and strong collaborations" between IT and business elements and this will lead to better decision making by the managers since they can always be updated by the most recent facts inside business environment. IT capabilities also trigger proactive business environment. Major IT innovations will lead to huge changes in business processes and business innovation. Figure 1 shows the process in which competitive advantage will be achieved through IT capabilities in the business environment.

Figure 1. Path towards Competitive Advantage through IT Capability
adapted from "IT Infrastructure Transformation and its Impact on IT Capabilities in the Cloud Computing Context" by Govindaraju, Akbar and Suryadi, "International Journal on Electrical Engineering and Informatics- Vol. 10, No. 2, June 2018"

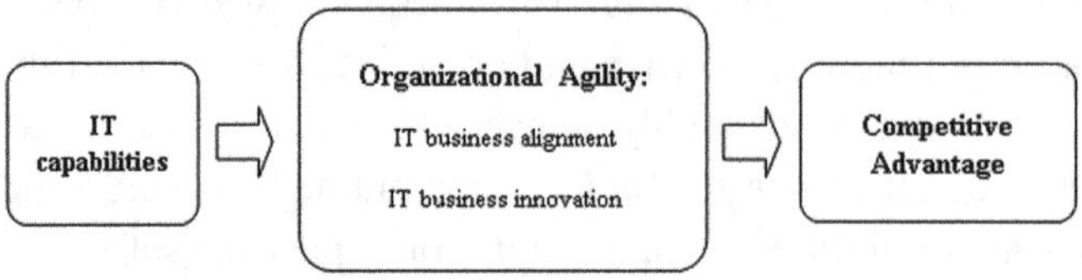

When to Start SaaS Migration?

Since manager concern is always about creating value for the business, the best IT strategic movement shall be compared to the value creation characteristics of the new model. Information Systems are major elements for business process improvement. ISs as claimed by Whitten and Bentley (2007) (cited by Chou & Chou, 2011) are developed to 1) improve business knowledge; 2) improve business processes; and 3) improve business communication. Whenever important goals cannot be attained by means of existing IS in the organization, the signs of migrating to the new Information System era arise.

SaaS and CIS services are very flexible in content. In many cases, managers and change agents do not want to risk the whole business's information and data to be placed on the Internet with a third party's control. SaaS comes in two forms (Murthy, 2010): 1) on-demand, which is service completely transferred over the internet with application, data, and control over provider's servers; and 2) on-premise, which is the same services over organizational internal servers and physical hardware locations. A healthy mix of applications running on the vendor's servers and software running on in-house servers can be a good choice for starters. On the other hand, while the manager's major concern with SaaS is security, implementing CIS as an on-premise service will solve much of the problem. Integrating existing ISs with SaaS is another factor playing a paramount role in SaaS migration decision. When a huge amount of data is locked in, the existing IS of the organization, SaaS or any other Information System model cannot be of much help. Routes to the legacy system integration may lead to SaaS implementation easiness.

Evaluation checklist of SaaS vendors can help managers on choosing the right time to start SaaS migration. Change agents of the organization considering different factors vital for the business competitive advantage should prepare such checklists; take price, security, innovation, integration, availability, performance, adaptability, and reliability (Churakova & Mikhramova, 2010) as examples. In fact, these issues are manager's concerns, which should be properly covered at the time of migration decision making.

Microelements have been claimed to affect SaaS time-to-migration (Churakova & Mikhramova, 2010). In a stable, uncompetitive, monopolistic sector of economy, managers do not feel the need for modifying IT. Take steel companies as an example. Such fundamental industries are often owned by the government or controlled in a semi-public economic sector. Except for internal (B2B) information exchange, there is no need for using SaaS or CIS. These companies can implement huge ERP software with unlimited amount of money, time, and governmental protection. Rather than economic factors, political, social and technological micro-factors may help enterprises to move from older information systems to the new Cloud-era. On the other hand, because of the uncontrollable environment the Cloud will provide, legal and political factors may act as an obstacle (Churakova & Mikhramova, 2010).

Overall, managers should have proper insights of the status quo in the organization. When legacy systems cannot handle business processes, at the time when there is no package software with an affordable price, implementation time is a major concern, and business shift to the Web is unavoidable, SaaS can be a better alternative for non-core and non-critical Information System areas. Considering that the outright conversion to the SaaS business model may pose risks to the business, managers should know that migrating to SaaS is not a single step, rather it is a long process with intense changes in business models of the organization. Some literature bring checklists that can help managers in choosing in-house information systems or SaaS (cloud-based information systems) (Bemrose, 2014):

- IT Expertise: if a company cannot afford in-house IT expertise and infrastructure the best choice is then using services rather than investing in capital.
- Flow of Data and Vendor Compliance: security is one of the most important factors banning businesses to use SaaS, since flow of data in SaaS business model is often out of hands of the company.
- Customization Level: effort to customize in the shelf software is a very rigorous and expensive process. Software as a Services often establish solutions rather than a raw application or service.
- Total Cost of Ownership: while in SaaS business model, companies will not invest in IT infrastructure and installation but higher annual fees and solution charges might lead to higher total cost of ownership.
- Benefits, Opportunities, Costs and Risks: Driving factors of migrating to SaaS should exceed those risks posed to the business environment, otherwise implementing desktop or Web Information Systems (WIS) may be enough for the status quo.

- Balanced Score Card: "another method to help ensure a SaaS solution meets an organization's strategy is to evaluate a SaaS based on its effect on an organization's: learning and growth, internal business processes, customer performance, and financial performance." (P.46) when using score cards it is important to note effect of each factor on the other factors.

What to Migrate to SaaS?

Nowadays the Cloud platform and CIS have been offered mostly in Customer Relationship Management (CRM), Human Resource Management (HRM), Archival, Business Intelligence (BI), portfolio and risk management, trade valuation, online backup, supply chain management, and enterprise content management fields (Murthy, 2010; Nema, 2010). These are the most proper segments of the business, which can be modified over the SaaS business model. In other words, these sections are the best to start with. However, it is the manager's concern and analysis, which shows the place to start. Core business information systems should not be the start point in SaaS migration, while these ISs must be integrated with SaaS during implementation procedures, otherwise islands of information may create in the business environment, and competitive advantage is the first thing to suffer. Web-enabled customized applications as Salesforce.com[3] argues (2008) can be a good solution. This way organization may use SaaS, as an on-demand IS alternative.

According to Cadambi and Easwaran (2016) the primary segments in which SaaS providers offer IT services include: 1) Pure SaaS solution: distinctive application is offered to broad number of customers in multiple segments; 2) On-premise software: specific software is offered in the shelf while further support and solution is provided as a service; and 3) Integrated technology and products: software, hardware and licensing is provided as well as intellectual property leasing and on-demand services.

Security is the first obstacle for many SMEs to migrate to the cloud platform. These companies should not start from vital IS sectors. For some others availability of information system is the most important factor. Software Level Agreements (SLA) may help organizations in reaching their desired level of expected service. On the other hand, using legacy systems for some kind of emerging business opportunities seems to be, let us say, impossible. Take monitoring user Internet consumption for an Internet Service Provider (ISP) as an example. It is almost impossible to monitor Internet usage by legacy systems. Other examples are time tracking and procurement services provided by Workday for human capital management. Although legacy systems are available for the task, consider an organization with global spread of employees and you will be convicted that using SaaS is the best solution. With ever-growing acceptance of the Internet as a proper tool for Business to Cosumer (B2C) market, SaaS providers like SalesForce or Constant-Contact are targeting this market helping both the consumer for choosing the right product and the business to choose the right consumer. Legacy systems are useless in this field.

Many Small or Medium sized businesses do not have enough resources for IT infrastructure capitalization and as a result they cannot afford to pay for on premise software. Using SaaS as a result can be the best choice since they do not need any capitalization on IT infrastructure, nor they need any investments on the software itself. Fees payable during the use of service is mostly affordable by the company and full services will be offered to them at the utmost quality available. A study implemented by Bemrose (2014) argues that selecting where to migrate to SaaS can be seen in two different perspectives: "selecting solutions based on current internal needs, and selecting solutions based on the benefits a solution can provide" (P.44)

How to Migrate to SaaS, Implementing SaaS

After the managers and change agents have analyzed feasibility, possibility, and adaptability of SaaS deeply, and chosen to start SaaS migration on a specific part of IS, then comes the implementation plan. Chou & Chou argue (2011) that business owners should "define their business, express their requirements, find and engage cloud services that match their needs, compose services if needed, and monitor their business operation over outsourced services" (P.1095). Define, analyze, plan, engage, feedback, and modify. This is a simple and comprehensive action plan for implementing almost all kinds of ISs. This modified model offered in figure 2 is a kind of checklist plan provided by the author for gaining a cost effective, speedy, and proactive implementation process.

Murthy (2010), Carraro & Chong (2006), and Buyya et al. (2008) models have been modified and altered for this model.

1. Define: the problem definition has been introduced in section 1.3. The manager will understand bottlenecks and problems in the existing Information System and decide to make required changes. After defining the problem for managers and change agents, it is now important to persuade executive managers and business owners to prepare the environment for the big change. Finding a leader as Salesforce.com (2008) claims, is vital for the rest of the implementation procedures.
2. Analyze: the first thing to consider in this step is to build an IT strategic plan. The company's IT plan may be for a small temporary project, or for an important long-term policy. Then according to Murthy (2010), the organizational IT plan may be short-term, medium term, or long term. In short-term IT plans, it is better to consider implementing SaaS in non-core business ISs, and integrating them with existing legacy systems. If the company is preparing for a medium-

Figure 2. SaaS Implementation plan

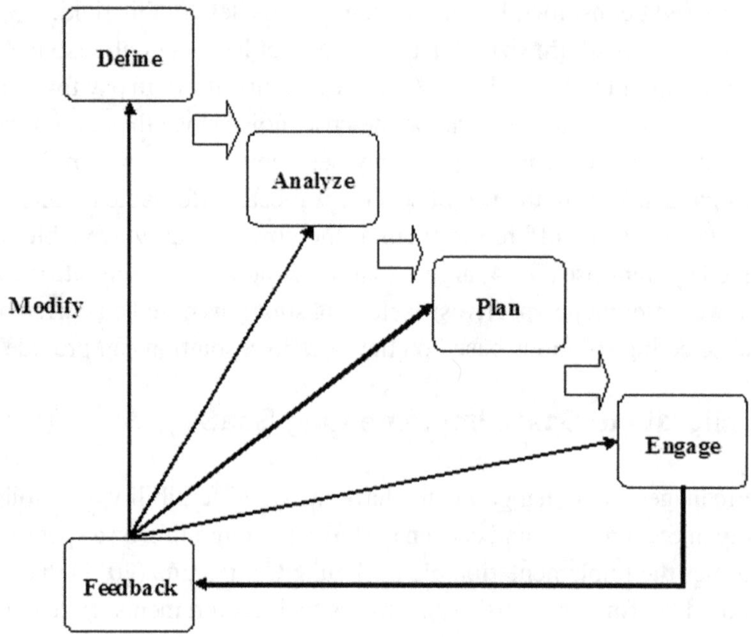

term plan, it is better to enhance legacy system abilities on the Web, and see if legacy software vendors provide SaaS services or not. On long-term strategies, businesses should experience huge changes on their IT infrastructure and sometimes on their business models as well. Provided by Carraro & Chong (2006) there is three aspects of embracing SaaS in business, i.e. licensing model, location of application, and software management model. In this perspective, there are two ends in a line. The right end would be pure SaaS implementation and on the left end,lays the traditional in-house IT implementation model. Managers should analyze the desired circumstances and place their business properly on this continuum. Figure 3 shows three SaaS embracing continuum as explained by Carraro & Chong (2006).

3. Plan: planning SaaS implementation highly depends on vendor selection. After defining the problems and bottlenecks of legacy systems and analyzing procedures for an effective migration, managers know the exact amount of resources (time, money, and human resources) they have in hand. On the other hand, they know exactly what they want from the SaaS model. Here, they should search on different vendor's technical capabilities and financial viability (Nema, 2010). Choosing the right SaaS provider is astep-by-step checklist procedure (Nema, 2010): SaaS vendor and the business managers

should come to a common agreement about the level of services, expectations, prices, and so on. Strong SLAs should be offered in this step. Feasibility of integrating SaaS with existing systems should be studied. Vendors' experiences with other companies should be studied deeply, because many problems are unveiled this way. Choosing a vendor with strong security maintenance, backup system, support mechanism, integration options, Website, and customization offerings should be put into consideration.

4. Engage: engaging in the action is always the most critical step. Business executives should understand that migrating to SaaS is not a single step; rather it is a continuous procedure. Referring to previous sections, the best way to start SaaS implementation is to start from those non-core business IS sectors, and it is also better to start implementing SaaS on a specific business unit, integrating the segment with existing IS and observing the results. In case of success, other parts of the company will follow the migration process automatically. In case of failure, while managers and change agents investigate on bottlenecks, the whole business will probably not suffer from the failure.
5. Feedback: Feedback is an unavoidable part of the IS implementation plan, whether it is a traditional IS or SaaS implementation. In this step, negative or positive outcomes of previous steps will be known. Availability, security issues, vendor's support policy, compliance, and interoperability offered by Won Kim (2009) should be studied along with other factors such as cost reduction, implementation easiness, and task fulfillment. These elements are critical success factors of SaaS implementation, and if provided by the new IT strategy, it can be claimed that SaaS has been successful in the company. This case rarely becomes true, because problems and bottlenecks exist in almost every IT implementation situation. The ability of vendor in modifying and customizing SaaS applications and level of services plays an important role on feedback maintenance.
6. Modify: now it is time to implement modifications of findings on the previous step (feedback). In almost every case, Information and Communication Technology needs to be aligned with business strategy as claimed by Galliers (2006); the vice versa situation can sometimes help the company; thus personalizing, modifying, and customizing SaaS is the best attractive way of satisfying users in the executive layers of management. Salesforce.com executives (2008) believe that this would be the cheapest way of attraction.

Figure 3. SaaS Embracing Continuum
(adapted from Carraro & Chong, 2006)

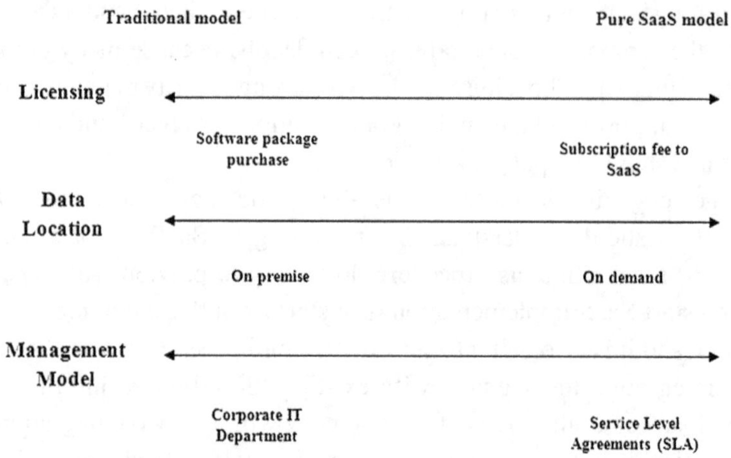

SAAS BUSINESS MODEL

Here the manager chose to migrate to SaaS. S/he knows the path, how, when, and what to do accordingly, but what would be the changes and consequences? Changing a simple routine in a company will affect the whole production process, more or less. For sure implementing such a vast IT infrastructure will bring about changing issues for the enterprise. As a result a business model should be then provided by the change agents and managers.

A study on 226 companies showed that aligning information systems and business strategies improve business performance (Osterwalder & Pigneur, 2005). Although in many cases after SaaS implementation, business strategy will move to the next performance stage, and then it comes to mind that both business and IT strategy are compliments to each other.

Before studying on business strategy, a manager should understand the business model in which the company is operating. One of the best-known business models has been introduced by Osterwalder. This model explains five pillars and nine business model building blocks shown in table 1. Companies that want to move their IT strategy from a traditional one to a new Cloud platform need to define their respective business characteristics in each business building block of this model. After this research, executive managers and change agents may come to this conclusion that their business model does not welcome the new IT infrastructure. In the real world, there are many of such cases. In fact, not all businesses, and not all business models can tolerate changes incurred by the SaaS business model.

Table 1. Nine business models

Pillar	Business Building Block	Description
Product	Value Proposition	Mixture of products and services which satisfy specific segments of customers
Customer Interface	Target Customer	Groups of people the organization plans to target on services or products
	Distribution Channel	Channels in which a company can communicate with targeted customers for reaching value proposition
	Relationship	Different types of relationship established for communicating with specific customer segments
Infrastructure Management	Value Configuration	Arrangement of assets, activities, resources, and requirements to make the business model work
	Core Competency	The most important factors to make the business model work
	Partner Network	The network of partners, suppliers, and customers that make the business model work
Financial Aspects	Cost Structure	All costs incurred to make the business model work
	Revenue Model	Revenues captured by each customer segment and with the help of business model

(adapted from Osterwalder et al., 2005; Stuckenberg et al., 2011)

In this part of the chapter, an analysis and modification of Osterwalder's business model on SaaS implementation is provided. In conclusion, to this model a maturity model for SaaS business model will be proposed. Figure 4 shows relationships between SaaS business model components the way Osterwalder argues and adapted by Churakova and Mikharamova (2010).

- **Value proposition:** is the mixture of products or services provided by the company to the customers. With SaaS, companies can communicate with customers in an effective way. This will lead to better customer satisfaction. The strategic path toward customer satisfaction requires thorough understanding of market changes and product modifications. On the other hand, stated by Timmers (1998) a business should propose what would be needed to accomplish nine value chain elements introduced by Porter[4]. Many companies operate as a branch of a multinational corporation. They do not need to communicate with the corporate customers, thus their value proposition is not toward the final consumer. SaaS migration for such companies may not be wise, considering risks incurred for the business. Churakova & Mikharamova (2010) state that the Total Cost of Ownership (TCO), IT expenses, and IT risks will reduce with the use of SaaS. They also

Figure 4. SaaS business model
(adapted from Osterwalder et al, 2005; Churakova and Mikharamova, 2010)

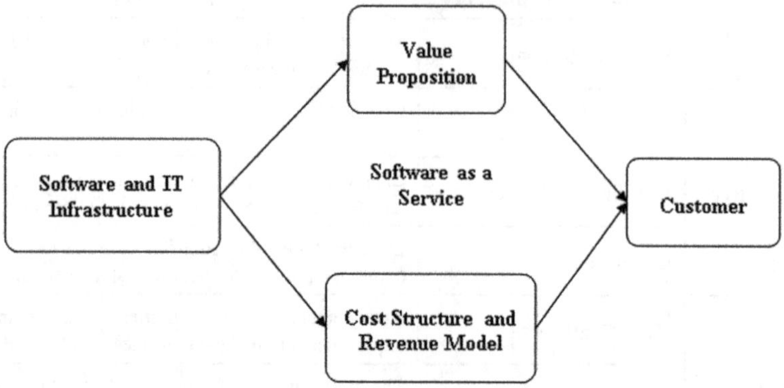

argue that for small or medium projects, the time to reach benefits and short-term goals will be rebated, and opportunities for outsourcing IT will rise (2010). This opportunity results in using the cheapest and best IT expertise from around the world.

- **Target Customer:** after defining values of the organization in serving customers, here they should target their proper market and pick valuable customers. A flatter business model puts enough power in the hands of executive managers to choose the best market and customers. Today it is not sufficient to prepare a general marketing rule for the whole company. Each segment may target the market as a different strategic choice. Migrating to SaaS may produce opportunities for companies to better target customers with potentialities of the internet. Legacy IS may not be able to communicate well to these opportunities, as they are offline or in the best situation integrated on the Web, which is far from abilities of a Web-based cloud platform.
- **Distribution Channel and Customer Relationships:** is the route to the market in which a company may satisfy customers and establish communication with them. The information era forces companies to provide utmost available data to customers. Whoever has on time, enough, and proper information feels the power in their hands. On-time information offering is not available through legacy systems. Stuckenberg et al. state "Communication, distribution and sales channels are making extensive use of the internet" (2011, P.12) forums, blogs, idea platforms, and video streams also integrated with SaaS may help the company provide better products or services (2011). Physical presence is not necessary using SaaS, because the internet will sometimes work better for bringing customer comments inside the organization. (Churakova & Mikhramova, 2010)

- **Value Configuration and Core Competencies:** IT has always been a high resource consumer in companies. When outsourced with lowest risks possible and with best SLA conditions, better opportunities on core business functions can be obtained. A research by Saaksjarvi et al. (2005) shows that business value creation results from a combination of "information, products and services, innovative configuration of transactions, and the reconfiguration and integration of resources, capabilities, roles, and relationships" (P.181). The same research unveiled that the most important characteristic of the SaaS business model is the opportunity of a company to seize core competence opportunities while their IT is outsourced to a SaaS vendor (2005).
- **Partner Network:** information flow between and among customers, suppliers and the company may strengthen the partnership produced in a business block. SaaS is both an opportunity and an obstacle in this regard. Since many SaaS vendors do not offer suitable integration services as seen by Saaksjarviet al. (2005), those companies with strategic information flow to other company databases, may see SaaS migration a risk, while on the other hand many experts believe that with proper the SLA, such services are available in a desired manner, and deemed not an obstacle when considering SaaS migration (Churakova & Mikhramova, 2010; Kang et al., 2010; Stuckenberg, Fielt, & Loser, 2011).
- **Cost Structure and Revenue Model:** since in the cost area, almost every literature insists on cost reduction of SaaS implementation (Carraro & Chong, 2006; Chou & Chou, 2011; Churakova & Mikhramova, 2010; Herbert et al., 2010; Kim, 2009; Rosenberg, 2009; Sääksjärvi, Lassila, & Nordström, 2005; Stuckenberg et al., 2011), in the long-term, there is not yet enough research to propose a proper revenue model for SaaS implementation. In addition, it is yet unknown whether implementing SaaS in a company may result in future revenue streams or not. One reason is that SaaS is no older than 10 years (according to (Churakova & Mikhramova, 2010) and long-run research is not yet available. The other reason is that calculating risks generated for the company in SaaS migration is not feasible, and continuously changing due to different circumstances. Although it is apparent that with managing and adjusting risks and disadvantages of SaaS migration, due to lower TCO, lower CapEx, and totally lower costs, the NPV[5] of SaaS is beneficial in many cases.

Analyzing and defining the role of these business building blocks on SaaS implementation, there is always a runaway situation. Application Service Providers (ASPs) are the previous generation of IT. They have brought applications for businesses in specific segments and they offered special integration services over these applications. However, one of the main differences between ASPs and SaaS vendors is that ASPs do not offer services and they do not offer customized applications (Sääksjärvi et al., 2005). This was a major shortcoming of ASPs. Like packaged software sellers, they sold their product with no services. On the other hand, SaaS vendors are selling their services, and the main element of their service is their application. Thus, for fulfilling their task, SaaS vendors should provide customized applications and in any case, business managers may implement the adapted and customized SaaS business model. However, it should be mentioned that SaaS migration is not always an opportunity. Due to different business building blocks, and considering different situations, it is managers and change agents who are responsible for this huge IT infrastructural change.

Business models smooth the path toward understanding hidden agendas of the business. Although SaaS business models offered since far may help managers to better understand feasibility of SaaS migration for their specific status quo. The SaaS business model should be studied regarding four main domains i.e. business representation, IT infrastructure, IT function, and IT usage:

1. SaaS business model due to business representation: Rappa introduces nine models of business on the Web. Business model as he describes is "the method of doing business by which a company can … generate revenue" (Rappa, 2010). The list of business models offered by Rappa in the Internet era is brokerage, advertising, infomediary, merchant, manufacturer, affiliate, community, subscription, and utility. SaaS should be implemented differently for each model. SaaS described by Kang et al. (2010), may be offered in four different domains namely business, service, system, and data. For instance, an advertising firm may need just data configuration SaaS and there is no need to risk the whole business structure on SaaS migration.
2. SaaS business model due to IT infrastructure: Osterwalder et al. (2005) propose that studying business models of a company improves the choice of IT infrastructure and on the other hand, IT infrastructure choice may facilitate business model selection. In this regard, Osterwalder et al. (2005) carried out a detailed study and introduced nine main elements of an IT infrastructure, which should be considered by managers: 1) application infrastructure; 2) communications management; 3) data management; 4) IT management; 5) security; 6) architecture and standards; 7) channel management; 8) IT research and development; and 9) training and education in IT. Every specific factor should be graded according to these nine business building blocks, and then decision on migrating to a new IT infrastructure should be maintained upon this scoreboard. For instance, if the business's security is almost critical to all nine business building blocks described in table 1, then SaaS migration may

not be logical. However, as mentioned before, critical modifications may be established on SLA, and SaaS implementation would be possible in these cases.

3. SaaS business model due to IT function: SaaS may function as a new technical adventure or as a new business phenomenon in a company as argued by Kang et al. (2010). SaaS usage may have a major impact on implementation decision and the way it should be maintained in an organization. When implemented as a technical function, core business data and processes may be kept in-house, whereas implementing SaaS for business functions, managers should prepare the organizational business layers for a huge change in implementation procedures.
4. SaaS business model due to IT usage: SaaS may be used for six main reasons according to Ried, Rymer and Iqbal (2008), a) Outsourcing: provides delegate operations of existing software; b) Manual ASP business: provides similar applications to multiple clients; c) Industrial ASP: provides configurable applications for many clients; d) Single application SaaS: provides one software through a multi-tenant structure to many clients; e) Business domain SaaS: provides multiple applications through a multi-tenant structure to many clients; and f) Dynamic business application as a service: provides user configurable software and custom business application for multi-tenant users. First levels introduced here provide primary applications on the Web, while in the fifth or sixth level; SaaS vendors provide full integration and migration toward a dynamic business transition.

Introduction of these four main domains leads us to a maturity model mainly captured and adapted from Kang et al. (2009) and Churakova & Mikharamova (2010). There are two axes in this SaaS model. The “maturity level” and “service domain”.

Maturity level as described by Kang et al. (2010) with modification includes:

1. Ad-hoc is the same level offered by traditional ASPs. Applications in this level offers to the business a customized hosted software with no services or modifications.
2. Configurable is the next level in which configuration and modification needs not to be maintained in the code level of application, however options are available separately for each business.
3. Multi-tenant is the third level, which supports the multi-tenant architecture. Different businesses use the same instance implemented by SaaS vendors simultaneously, without interrupting other user activities in a multi-tenant architecture, which is configurable on the user level. In other words, the vendor in this level offers a Software Oriented Architecture (SOA) to the business environment; although it is not yet a fully customized SaaS.

4. Customized virtualization is the utmost service level offered by a SaaS vendor. In this level, different instances are available in one general structure. Every instance can be customized toward business expectations.

On the other hand, service domain axe includes four main levels introduced by Microsoft and Forrester group (cited by Kang et al., 2009): 1) Data, 2) System, 3) Service, and 4) Business. In the data level, physical databases are placed and integrated on the Web. In the second level, physical data along with system integration services are offered. On the service level, SaaS vendors offer on-demand IT technologies on the Web, and in the fourth level, customized SLAs propose the scope of services needed to be delivered on the network. Figure 5 introduces a modified SaaS model for businesses adapted from the Microsoft and Forrester models cited and modified by Kang et al. (2009) along with the Churakova & Mikharamova (2010) model of the SaaS business model. Each manager and change agent should analyze the status quo and expectations of the business from SaaS migration and then decide on the place s/he might accommodate the organization on this model. As mentioned before, it is better to start SaaS migration from low-levels of this model. Improvements in the business layer will grow the business model as well.

Figure 5. SaaS model for business
(Adapted from Kang et al., 2008; Churakova & Mikharamova, 2010)

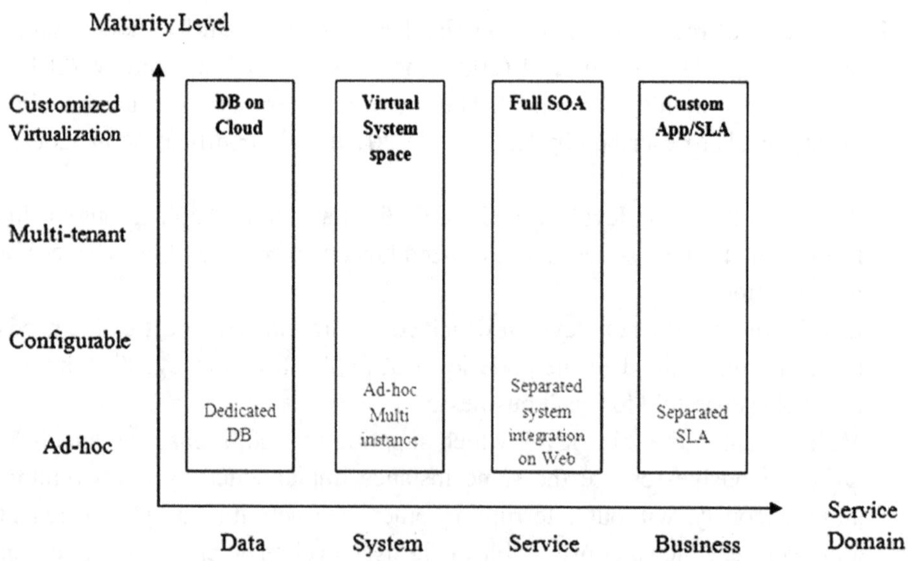

Business models provided here in this study eventually clears the fact that SaaS does not provide a happy ending for any organization with any business environment. SaaS consist of different phases, advantages and disadvantages, through which might help some businesses to gain competitive advantage.

SAAS MIGRATION, A STRATEGIC MOVEMENT

Changing business model not only means important changes in whole business procedures, but also needs strategic movements from old and traditional management routines to innovative, agile, and self-building processes. A quick look at successful examples of SaaS like Salesforce, Basecamp, Quickbook, and Oracle's different applications based on cloud services shows that these enterprises have been built completely with new business models and their strategic structure has less in common with traditional layer-base companies.

Implementing SaaS in a company is not a goal. The goal toward SaaS migration is to provide competitive advantage for the business. This advantage brings forth specific tools and methods. One of the most known techniques is that SaaS enables information flow toward different layers of executive forces inside and outside of the business entity. Babcock (2010) argues Cloud Information Systems is a "revolt against centralized computing" and business model (P.204). In this model, flatter organizational structures will emerge and new business ideas appear, and as Pearce and Robinson describe, this will create a full organizational communication in which it aims to "deliver speedy, customized, service-enhanced products to savvy customers from an integrated boundary-less B-Web (Business Web) organization, pulling together abundant, world class resources digitally" (2009, P.363). A flatter organizational structure is in close connection to the level of agility in the business environment. The more flat the infrastructure is, the better business can respond to changes and opportunities, and the more the level of business agility will be. Agility and change management are identical in nature. Bodker et al. (2004) have segmented changes in business environments to three main domains. Enterprises may face these three changes when deciding to start SaaS migration: anticipated change, which is planned changes; emergent change, which is changes not intended or anticipated, and opportunity based changes, which are changes and fluctuations in the enterprise environment, which open new doors of business improvement for the company. On the other hand, Gonçalves and Sapateiro claim that every organization decides to step toward huge IT infrastructural changes needs to shift its six main elements (2008): 1) Nature and quality of work; 2) Individual's status, job satisfaction, stress position, and identity; 3) Organizational communication; 4) Interpersonal relationships; 5) Interdepartmental relationships; and 6) Organizational values chains. Thus, SaaS migration is not a single step; rather it is a process in which every single business component will be involved. In most circumstances, an approach toward SaaS migration should be based on value recognition of business as argued by Timmers (1998). Re-identifying and reconstructing value chains of business should be maintained before and during SaaS implementation phases because stated by Weill, Subramani, Broadbent and Building (2002) it is critical to understand which IT infrastructure is needed for what kind of value creation chain, so that managers can decide on proper long-term investments in IT strategies. This is the process of aligning IT strategies and business core policies. Galliers (2006) claims in some situations developments in IT not only did not help the business grow in the competitive environment, but also made the enterprise suffer the organizational learning process, a process vital for gaining knowledge and competitive advantage. The main reason he introduces is that software vendors try to copy "best-practice" experiences over different businesses. For instance, when a company decides on IT revolution, a software vendor may offer packages in which same enterprises in the same industry implemented recently and demonstrated success. Galliers (2006) with the aim of many researches and findings shows that this "best-practice" model should be strongly adapted and modified in order to be suitable for the business status quo. In other words, managers and change agents should understand that implementing whatever SaaS vendors offer to suite their business needs and to change business strategies just to be aligned with SaaS capabilities is an illogical IT strategic movement. In contrary it is the business core policies and IT strategies that should dictate whatever it needs to vendors and SaaS providers should be ready to modify and customize their application for each enterprise with proper SLAs. Considering SaaS implementation without understanding customization capabilities of Cloud Information Systems is considered risky and illogical.

Knowledge and innovation in the business are other fundamental tools toward gaining competitive advantage. Innovation and organizational learning suffers in cases, which enterprises do not respond to ever-changing environments. SaaS should be implemented as means of facilitating formal and informal information flow inside and outside of the enterprise; otherwise SaaS is a barrier toward competitive advantage, since stated by Galliers (2006), efficiency and effectiveness comes from innovation and organizational learning process. Koelliker argues (2016) a centralized knowledge based management is an approach to provide a smooth, identical, uniform and resembling service to the customers. At this point of business history "more than ever, agility is a key asset and differentiator. Through the benefits of cloud-based knowledge management, your enterprise can achieve the agility it requires to provide high quality experiences to customers and service delivery that offers the accuracy, speed and consistency they demand" (Koelliker, 2016, P.17).

A study on IT transformation shows that implementing new information systems in a business not only needs strategic movement but also enforces change management requirements (Govindaraju et al. 2018). Nowadays short life-cycle of IT-capabilities ties agility, change management and strategic movement together. Without a balanced relationship between and among enterprise structure, there will not be a happy ending for the business as the amount of change, SaaS will create on the business is enormous and huge.

SWOT ANALYSIS ON SAAS IMPLEMENTATION

As any other strategic movement, SaaS implementation brings about strengths, weaknesses, opportunities and threats (SWOT). SWOT analysis in any business environment is different and there is no unique role of thumb. However Rostami, Akbari and Javan (2014, P.83-84) mentioned some important notes on aspects which are more common on most of business environments:

- Strengths: a) access information from anywhere, b) zero IT infrastructure investment, c) lowest possible software maintenance costs.
- Weaknesses: a) immaturity in many SaaS models and services that companies offer, b) ambiguous and complex prices of services, c) high risks of data due to dependence on the SaaS provider, d) high risk of usage due to Internet availability.
- Opportunities: a) cost savings and higher profit for the company, b) strategic innovation and flexibility, d) focusing on the core activities, e) accessing the latest IT-tech and applications on the lowest possible cost.
- Threat: a) lack of data control risk, b) unacceptable SaaS performance risk, c) Internet resilience and bandwidth risk, d) integrating SaaS application/ data with the in-house application/data, and e) high risks of data theft (SaaS providers due to SLA agreements often are responsible for possible data loss, hacking and spoliation, but in some cases important data leakage will cost the company it's competitive advantage and even ends up to the complete business destruction which is not insurable).

SOLUTIONS TO SAAS IMPLEMENTATION CHALLENGES

There has been a large amount of research over SaaS and Cloud Information Systems in their context; however few contemplate SaaS implementation action plans. In real world cases, sometimes-theoretical phenomenon may not be available in certain circumstances. This is also true about SaaS implementation plans. On the other hand, fast paced IS improvements forced many companies to enter the information-era environment, in which information systems are not considered strategic movement anymore (Carr, 2003). In such circumstances, organizations may need their IT infrastructure to be changed due to specific status quo. Then how about the companies who want to migrate to SaaS, while the SaaS model might seem to be too risky and fragile for them? As mentioned before Change management processes and policies should be defined and recognized by the strategists of the business before any serious SaaS implementation decision or else the failure probability will be high.

Innovation is a must for businesses deciding to migrate into SaaS model. In cases which business model is so solid, SaaS will overcome as an IT promotion in the best case scenario, which is considered failure because it is like investing on an expensive and luxury Maserati for working in Uber! There is no logic behind investing time, money and effort on SaaS just to be in cloud. Enterprises deciding to migrate to the SaaS model should have proper system's thinking in mind. SaaS is an innovation model itself and will bring about innovation for the business, as a cycle competitive advantage is then engendered via enterprise innovation (Govindaraju et al. 2018). SaaS in itself not only cannot create competitive advantage, but also if not implemented thoroughly it will cause huge failure because of high costs and efforts placed in it.

In this section, the main literature-claimed disadvantages of SaaS have been introduced and solutions have been provided. However, the author believes that these are not actually disadvantages; rather these are "misunderstandings" that can be overcome.

Business and IT Agility in SaaS Environments

Woodly and Hobbs claim that an enterprise may survive over this IT competition just by enhancing abilities for change and responding to the environment in order to adapt circumstances (2008). Today's highly global competitive environments have made traditional IT methodologies inoperative, thus traditional methods such as the waterfall life cycle may not be feasible in SaaS engineering and implementation. According to a research by Vision Consulting Group in 2006, "over 45% of features and functions built into the average software product are never used" (Morton, Lindsay, & Ching, 2006). Then why to waste heavy investment on applications which we need half of capabilities? While on the other hand, these applications may not have proper features to satisfy our needs. Vision consulting group has introduced quality of software as "fitness to use" (Morton et al., 2006). Just with agile methods and policies, businesses may be ready to produce and use proper IS for their specific range of applications. The main pace toward IT agility is to prepare the business environment to be sensible for the changes and to monitor IT usage and value creation in order to modify and create feedback (Woolley & Hobbs, 2008). In this agile business model incremental, cooperative, straightforward, and adaptive software development may create value argued by Abrahamsson, Salo, Ronkainen and Warsta (2002), such environments create "complex adaptive systems" and business models in which "decentralized, independent individuals interact to create innovative, emergent results" (Highsmith & Cockburn, 2001). Operational implementation of SaaS using traditional methods is infeasible and sometimes illogical; agility on the other hand will create SaaS implementation success, while SaaS implementation enforces IT agility. Briefly, IT agility is both the cause and consequence of SaaS implementation, while feedback and monitoring information on SaaS implementation is vital for the IT infrastructure to be flexible enough to respond changes as quickly and properly as possible.

A study over several companies conducted by Lu and Ramamurthy (2011) showed IT capabilities and innovations such as the ones like SaaS or cloud-based systems will bring about agility in two main segments; external and internal. The external agility is achieved via market capitalization and external communications of the business with customers and other related parties, while internal agility is engendered due to operational adjustment. But the other side of the coin is that in some circumstances the more we spend on the IT (in terms of dollars, human resources or other business sources) does not lead to better agility, while "spending it in such a way as to enhance and foster IT capabilities does" (P.949).

User Involvement in SaaS Implementation Phases

A research conducted by Aydin, Harmsen, Van Slooten and STEGWEE in the IT department of a financial institution in Europe (2004) shows that one of the most critical aspects of implementing agile methods in an organizational IT structure is active user involvement. Information systems claimed by Kovács and Ueno are means of maturing data from raw stage to usable, analyzable, and stable information, this process however is impossible without the inevitable role of human participation (2004). Fitness of purpose in agile software development method is attained just by realizing purposes and the changing environment. Managers and change agents along with users, employees, and executive agents should analyze the purpose and status quo. Implementing IS packages mainly developed by software professionals inside rooms with closed doors, aims to act as a separated island in the enterprise surrounding.

Solutions to SaaS Disadvantages

Many scholars address SaaS disadvantages and business misbehavior due to SaaS migration, while there are always solutions. Here a list of literally claimed SaaS disadvantages and Cons with respective solutions have been provided for managers and change agents to consider before deciding to commence SaaS migration:

- Security: is the most repeated disadvantage of SaaS migration. According to Murthy (2010), SaaS implementation can be established both on-premise and on-demand. Using on-premise option of SaaS implementation may help solve many security issues. This will also promise the future expansion of higher volume data storage without extra costs or new SLAs (Xin & Levina, 2008). In this model, all application data and infrastructure are placed in the owner's physical location. Security breaches and leakages will be hard, if not impossible. Strong SLAs also have been claimed to be a solution to security issues by Salseforce.com (2008). When considering the importance of customer satisfaction in Software-as-a-Service SLA, then vendors should prove their abilities for keeping customer applications and data secure. Hogan also describes a solution to SaaS security issues (2008). He explains SaaS database as the main and sole target of security issues. Then protecting database is the same as protecting the whole Cloud platform. Encrypting data in these databases can protect them from being hacked or stolen according to Armbrust et al., 2009. In cases of leakage, information may not be clearly understood, and in cases of using strong cryptography techniques, stolen data is useless for hackers. Ghorbel et al. argue privacy techniques that will strengthen the security of SaaS include (2017): 1) encryption, 2) processing encrypted data, 3) obfuscation or masking data, 4) sticking data to policies rather than relations, 5) using trusted platform module, 6) data segmentation so that a segment loss of data will not lead to all-data loss and 7) using trusted third party mediator models. Each technique has its own strength and weakness furthermore there is always a reasonable risk of security even though we execute the most updated security protocols and as a result using a hybrid cloud-in-house software services might be the ultimate answer for those businesses who want to use cloud advantages and at the same time escaping cloud security issues as Carson, Botter and Krujelskis argued (2013).
- SaaS Integration: In many cases, managers prefer to start SaaS migration with specific parts of their IT structure. Here they want SaaS to be integrated with legacy systems and interact with them appropriately. Introduced by Gartner[6] (2009) there are two main methods of SaaS integration: 1) Batch

synchronization, in which after modification on the user's side data can be synchronized in schedules basis; and 2) Real-time integration, in which database, application, and services are always online for users, clients, and servers. The third method can be a modified mixture of those two methods, in which technologies such as Microsoft's AJAX or Sun Microsystems's JavaScript enable the application to be offline, while on the other hand the software is capable of sending packages of data in the time of data modification.

- Performance unpredictability: in many places of the world, internet bandwidth and capabilities are not the same provided in developed countries according to Peng, Cui & Li, and Internet downtimes may cause the business critical data to be locked-in for hours (2009). Thus, managers in developing countries with limited Internet connection capabilities should be aware of obstacles in the path of SaaS migration. However with the use of specific methods such as the one mentioned by Gartner (2009) as "batch synchronization" SaaS implementation method, application and databases can be always in the hand of critical organizational segments, while the others (including less-important distant-users and customers) may be updated in a scheduled basis. Another solution according to Armbrust et al is to use scheduled backups and Virtual Machine Supports (2009).
- Is SaaS the ultimate IT capability for business? This is one of the most asked questions of managers according to Gartner (2009) when deciding to implement SaaS. The answer cannot be provided with full confidence. In most cases, modifying and using existing legacy systems can be operationally and financially feasible in the financial crisis environment of the recent years. However migrating to cloud platform for gaining competitive advantage over rivals in the globally grown markets is inevitable. There are also many limitations so forth with this young technology according to Gartner (2009), but the level of business agility, system configurability, and customization capabilities filled the gap created with these limitations.
- Implementation issues: SaaS is still an unknown domain for many managers. Change agents also do not know where to start. Considering that Saas vendors are offering services rather than software, implementation is guaranteed by the SaaS provider (Salesforce.com, 2008). However, in accordance with the business model desired to be used in the migration phases, employees and organization main users of the SaaS should cooperate in every specific implementation step.
- SaaS, is it a real cost saving IT option? Gartner claimed in 2009 that the Total Cost of ownership for SaaS is lower in the first two years and after that because of capital assets used in IT infrastructure gets depreciated, in an accounting

perspective, TCO will be higher in comparison with desktop ISs! On the other hand, Motahari-Nezhad, Stephenson and Singhal argued that loss of direct control over resources, IT infrastructure and software might create indirect future costs (2009). So, is SaaS really a cost saving IT option? The answer is, not always, and not in all circumstances. As mentioned before in this chapter, SaaS can be feasible as a certain IT solution in specific circumstances just when analyzed deeply in accordance with the business model and enterprise status quo. For instance, when considering an impermanent project needing to be aligned with existing legacy ISs, SaaS stands in the top of IT choices. However, when considering an ERP implementation project for the coming ten years in a low-bandwidth internet area with limited capabilities of existing SaaS vendors, it might not be financially feasible to hire professionals and establish Virtual Private Networks to construct a modified private SaaS for the organization. Nevertheless, it might be the last resort for the enterprise to enter the global market; hence the incurred costs should be accepted.

FUTURE RESEARCH

After SaaS has proven to be a new phenomenon for the businesses, nowadays I think there are a lot to search because SaaS and Cloud platform is moderately new and there are lots of gaps and unknown areas facing multi-national organizations. The main aspect I think needs immediate research is the amount of change SaaS will enforce on the business ground. In fact change will bring about innovation and innovation will bring up agility, but the other side of the coin is that change hurts! The main question is then if benefits overcome the pain and if business tolerance over the change pain is enough. Relationships between change management, strategic management, and quality of performance should be studied thoroughly.

CONCLUSION

In this chapter, we outlined the concepts and features of SaaS as a Cloud Information System and Service. A manager in the first place should know the necessity of migrating to the new IT environment in the Cloud platform. Understanding why, when, and how to migrate to SaaS is vital for the strategic foundations of an enterprise. The necessity originates from the business model in which the company strategized over. A modified business model and maturity model of SaaS has been introduced using main existing business models in the literature. Knowledge-based model which is enforced by the strategic movement and change management will fit the business environment the best. This way, managers may be ready to adapt their organizational layers toward a continuous change, which comes with SaaS implementation phases. After understanding the scope and size of change incurred over businesses, managers and change agents should decide on the maturity model the SaaS should be based upon in the enterprise. This may be a simple ad-hoc service over the database, or it can be a customized virtualization of every single business element. It is recommended that businesses start using SaaS model from the lowest level possible. Improvements in business models will occur sooner or later, and then the time for moving to the next SaaS maturity model will come. SaaS migration is not a single step, like installing and purchasing packaged software, rather it is a strategic movement in which every organizational element will be involved and may needs to be change. This change does not only consist of the simple changes, but it may require fundamental changes which itself will bring about agility and innovation. As a cycle in a system, this agility will strengthen the business model of the enterprise. At the end of this chapter, SWOT analysis on the SaaS implementation has been discussed but the main factor which should be considered by the managers is that there is no role of thumb as any business needs its specific SWOT analysis and in some cases (as in case of government-based companies with serious data and information in hand) SaaS implementation weaknesses and threats may overcome strengths and opportunities. Cloud platform and SaaS as one of its segments is an evolving phenomenon in the business environment. Definition, use cases, issues, risks, Pros, Cons, and benefits are not fully discovered yet. Wide public and private use of SaaS may illuminate the proper business models in which SaaS may be beneficial in the utmost level. However, pioneer enterprises who uncover opportunities of SaaS before pervasive Cloud usage will win the business competitive advantage race.

REFERENCES

Abrahamsson, P., Salo, O., Ronkainen, J., & Warsta, J. (2002). *Agile software development methods.* VTT Publishing.

Armbrust, M., Fox, A., Griffith, R., Joseph, A. D., Katz, R. H., Konwinski, A., . . . Zaharia, M. (2009). *Above the clouds: a Berkeley view of cloud computing* (Report No. UCB/EECS-2009-28). University of Berkeley, UC Berkeley reliable adaptive distributed systems laboratory.

Aydin, M. N., Harmsen, F., & Van Slooten, K., & Stegwee, R. (2009). An agile information systems development method in use. *Turkish Journal of Electrical Engineering and Computer Sciences, 12*(2), 127–138.

Babcock, C. (2010). *Management Strategies for the Cloud Revolution*. McGraw Hill Professional.

Bemrose Bob. (2014). *Implementing and Integrating SaaS Solutions at Small Businesses*. Presented to the Interdisciplinary Studies Program of University of Oregon Applied Information Management. Approved by Dr. Kara McFall. Small Business SAAS Integration.

Buyya, R., Yeo, C. S., & Venugopal, S. (2008). *Market-oriented cloud computing: Vision, hype, and reality for delivering it services as computing utilities*. Academic Press.

Cadambi P., Easwaran S. (2016). *Transforming Your SaaS Business a strategic guide for optimizing business performance*. KPMG LLP International Whitepaper.

Carr, N. G. (2003). IT doesn't matter. *EDUCAUSE Review, 38*, 24–38. PMID:12747161

Carraro, G., & Chong, F. (2006). *Software as a service (SaaS): An enterprise perspective, A Microsoft Whitepaper*. Retrieved March 24th, 2012 from http://msdn.microsoft.com/en-us/library/aa905332.aspx

Carson P., Botter L., Krujelskis S. (2013, July). Going to The Cloud vs Doing It In-House. *Information Today,* 4-10.

Chou, A., & Chou, D. (2011). *Cloud Computing from the perspective of system analysis*. Paper presented at the 2011 Southwest Decision Science Institute Conference.

Chou, D. C., & Chou, A. Y. (2008). *Software as a Service (SaaS) as an outsourcing model: an economic analysis*. Paper presented at the 2011 Southwest Decision Science Institute Conference.

Churakova, I., & Mikhramova, R. (2009-2010). *Software as a service: Study and analysis of saas business model and innovation ecosystems* [Unpublished Master's thesis]. Universiteit Gent.

Galliers, R. D. (2006). Strategizing for agility: confronting information systems inflexibility in dynamic environments. *The Transfer and Diffusion of Information Technology for Organizational Resilience*, 361-362.

Gartner. (2009). *Gartner fact checks the five most-common SaaS assumption*. Gartner Report.

Ghorbel, A., Ghorbel, M., & Jmaiel, M. (2017). Privacy in Cloud Computing Environment: A Survey and Research Challenges. *Journal of Supercomputing*. . doi:10.1007/s11227-016-1953-y

Gonçalves, N. P., & Sapateiro, C. M. (2008). Aspects for Information Systems Implementation: Challenges and impacts. A higher education institution experience. *Tékhne-Revista de Estudos Politécnicos*, (9), 225–241.

Govindaraju, R., Akbar, R., & Suryadi, K. (2018). IT Infrastructure Transformation and Its impact on IT Capabilities in the Cloud Computing Context. International Journal on Electrical Engineering and Informatics, 10(2).

Herbert, L., Ross, C. F., & Rose, E. (2010). *Real-world insights into SaaS implementation success*. Report to Forrester Group.

Highsmith, J., & Cockburn, A. (2001). Agile software development: the business of innovation. *International Journal of Computer, 34*(9), 120-122.

Hogan, M. (2008). *Cloud computing & databases, how databases can meet the demands of cloud computing*. Whitepaper report to ScaleDB.

Kang, S., Myung, J., Yeon, J., Ha, S.-w., Cho, T., Chung, J.-m., & Lee, S.-g. (2009). *A Standardized Maturity Model for Designing SaaS Service Guideline*. Academic Press.

Kang, S., Myung, J., Yeon, J., Ha, S.-w., Cho, T., Chung, J.-m., & Lee, S.-g. (2010). *A Standardized Maturity Model for Designing SaaS Service Guideline*. Academic Press.

Kim, W. (2009). Cloud Computing: Today and Tomorrow. *Journal of Object Technology*, *8*(1), 65–72. doi:10.5381/jot.2009.8.1.c4

Koelliker. (2016). Maximize Business Agility with Cloud-Based Knowledge Management. *KMWorld, S17*.

Kovács, A. I., & Ueno, H. (2004). Towards complex adaptive information systems. *Proceedings of the 2nd International Conference on Information Technology and Application*.

Lu, Y., & Ramamurthy, K. (2011). Understanding The Link Between Information Technology Capability and Organizational Aglity: An Empirical Examination. MIS Quarterly, 35(4), 931-954.

Lynn. (2016). Agility, Flexibility & Insight. Is That Your Cloud? *KMWorld, S21*.

Mell, P., & Grance, T. (2011). *The NIST Definition of Cloud Computing-Recommendations of the National Institute of Standards and Technology.* NIST Special Publication, 800-145.

Morton, R., Lindsay, C., & Ching, C. (2006). *Why your business needs agile software development*. Report to Vision Consulting Group.

Motahari-Nezhad, H. R., Stephenson, B., & Singhal, S. (2009). Outsourcing business to cloud computing services: Opportunities and challenges. *IEEE Internet Computing*, 10.

Murthy, A. (2010). Tapping into SaaS and pre-packaged products to drive optimization. *Infosys, FINsights Issue on IT Optimization*.

Nema, P. (2010). *Best practices for adopting SaaS: a holistic evaluation approach: A Silicon Valley*. Bank report and white paper.

Osterwalder, A., Pigneur, Y., & Tucci, C. L. (2005). Clarifying business models: Origins, present, and future of the concept. *Communications of the Association for Information Systems*, *16*, 16. doi:10.17705/1CAIS.01601

Peng, B., Cui, B., & Li, X. (2009). Implementation Issues of A Cloud Computing Platform. *Bulletin of the IEEE Computer Society Technical Committee on Data Engineering*.

Rappa, M. (2010). *Business models on the Web*. Retrieved Feb 11th, 2012 from http://digitalenterprise.org/models/models.html

Ried, S., Rymer, J. R., & Iqbal, R. (2008). *SaaS Maturity Model by Forrester*. Report to Forrester Group. Retrieved Feb 23rd, 2012 from https://www.forrester.com/Forresters+SaaS+Maturity+Model/fulltext/-/E-RES46817?docid=46817

Rosenberg, D. (2009). *How to evaluate SaaS for your business*. Retrieved March 20th, 2012 from http://news.cnet.com/8301-13846_3-10172508-62.html

Rostami, T., Akbari, M. K., & Javan, M. S. (2014). Benefits, Weaknesses, Opportunities and Risks of SaaS Adoption from Iranian Organizaitons Perspective. Advances in Computer Science: an International Journal, 3(1).

Sääksjärvi, M., Lassila, A., & Nordström, H. (2005). *Evaluating the software as a service business model: From CPU time-sharing to online innovation sharing*. Paper presented at the IADIS International Conference e-Society.

Salesforce.com. (2008). *The 7 secrets of SaaS startup success*. Whitepaper report of Salesforce.com over SaaS implementation issues.

SIIA. (2001). *Software as a Service strategic background, Software and Information Industry Association report on SaaS*. SIIA.

Stuckenberg, S., Fielt, E., & Loser, T. (2011). The impact of software-as-a-service on business models of leading software vendors: experiences from three exploratory case studies. *Proceedings of the 15th Pacific Asia Conference on Information Systems (PACIS 2011)*.

Timmers, P. (1998). Business models for electronic markets. *Electronic Markets*, *8*(2), 3–8. doi:10.1080/10196789800000016

Weill, P., Subramani, M., Broadbent, M., & Building, I. (2002). Infrastructure for Strategic Agility. *Sloan Management Review*, *44*(1), 57–65.

Woolley, B., & Hobbs, G. (2008). Agility in Information System. *ACIS 2008 Proceedings*.

Xin, M., & Levina, N. (2008). Software-as-a-service model: Elaborating client-side adoption factors. *Proceedings of the 29th International Conference on Information Systems*.

ADDITIONAL READING

Barna, P., Frasincar, F., Houben, G.-J., & Vdovjak, R. (2002). *Methodologies for Web Information System Design*. Technische Universiteit Eindoven.

Bodker, K., Pors, J. K., & Simonsen, J. (2004). Implementation of Web-based Information Systems in Distributed Organizations. *Scandinavian Journal of Information Systems*, 16.

Carstensen, P. H., & Vogelsang, L. (2001). *Design of Web-Based Information Systems-New Challenges for Systems Development?* Paper presented at the ECIS.

Gonçalves, N. P., & Sapateiro, C. M. (2008). Aspects for Information Systems Implementation: challenges and impacts. A higher education institution experience. *Tékhne-Revista de Estudos Politécnicos,* (6).

Mowshowitz, A. (2002). *Virtual Organization, Toward a Theory of Societal Transformation stimulated by Information Technology*. Quorum Books.

Paiano, R., Guido, A. L., & Pandurino, A. (2009). *Designing Complex Web Information Systems*. IGI Global Publications. doi:10.4018/978-1-60566-300-5

Pardellas, J. (2004). *Knowledge Map for Distributed Information System Reengineering*. Presented at the university of Geneva, Switzerland.

Pearce, I. I. J., & Robinson, R. J. B. (2009). *Strategic Management, Formulation, Implementation, and Control*. McGraw Hill Publication.

Pearce, J., & Robinson, R. B. (2006). *Strategic Management, Formulation, Implementation, and Control*. McGrwa Hill Publication.

Porter, M. E. (2001). Strategy and the Internet. *Harvard Business Review*. PMID:11246925

Vidgen, R. T. (2002). *What's so different about developing web-based information systems?* Paper presented at the ECIS.

KEY TERMS AND DEFINITIONS

ASP, Application Service Provider: Any company or contractor who offers software as a service like Amazon's AWS or Google's cloud.

Business Agility: Is the level of business tolerance toward changes and circumstance. The more agile a business is, the better it can be matched to ever-changing business circumstances of this tech-era.

CIS, Cloud Information System: Briefly is a kind of Information System which is placed on the Web rather than on a physical server in client's site. Many Pros and Cons have been illustrated for the CIS since far.

SaaS, Software as a Service: Is both a phenomenon and a new model to offer application to the customer far different from the old application packaging era. In this model software is not sold as a good, rather it is offered as a service with a long service agreement, backup, and maintenance.

SLA, Service-Level Agreement: Is a kind of agreement between the customer and SaaS provider in which the level of cooperation, terms of services, and many other SaaS agreement conditions has been established in. SLA is vital for both client and provider to illuminate the coming horizons of their business views.

ENDNOTES

1. National Institute of Standards and Technology (NIST) is an agency of the U.S. Department of Commerce responsible for developing standards and guidelines.
2. Small to Medium Enterprise
3. Salesforce.com is one of the successful SaaS pioneers and has implemented many researches over SaaS implementation and SaaS success.

4 Nine value chain elements introduced by Porter are: 1) inbound logistics, 2) operations, 3) outbound logistics, 4) marketing and sales, 5) services, 6) technology development, 7) procurement, 8) human resource management, and 9) corporate infrastructure (Timmers, 1998).

5 Net Present Value, Which is a financial indicator showing present value of a project due to discounted revenues minus discounted costs. If the result is positive, the project will be beneficial; otherwise, the project may be harmful for the company.

6 Gartner is the world's leading information technology research and advisory company.

Chapter 3
Organizational Sustainability:
Characteristics of Agility

Hakikur Rahman
Ansted University Sustainability Research Institute, Malaysia

ABSTRACT

An organization with its capacity to endure, add up value, and promote value chain could be seen as a sustainable organization. Sustainability could be in the form of short-, medium-, and long-term effect to an entity. Through the utilization of the information and communication technology, organizations now can adopt various business techniques to tackle or minimize risks, reduce costs, and make profit. Among many such techniques, this particular research looks into the aspects of agility within organizations that may lead to sustained business platform. This chapter tries to argue that an organization with this characteristic, in the longer run, can lead to sustainability and elevate the business intelligence. In this discourse, through a vertical literature review, this study has tried to construct a framework of sustainability with the aspect of an organization and thereby proposed a business model for ideation and future implementation.

INTRODUCTION

Organizations in a disparate range of markets are facing the challenges of new product innovations, decreasing product lifecycles, product proliferation and customers who are becoming ever more demanding. This has resulted in markets that can be characterized as increasingly unstable and unpredictable, and has caused many organizations to seek to improve their performance through various activities, alignments and sustainable responses (Brown and Eisenhardt, 1998; White, Daniel

DOI: 10.4018/978-1-7998-4799-1.ch003

and Mohdzain, 2005). These activities, alignments and sustainable responses may not only be considered as means for the business development, but also considered for increased business (and or market) intelligence (Roberts and Grover, 2012).

Fowler (2000) calls this type of sustainable response to issues of poverty a "virtuous spiral" that involves three dimensions, such as external impact, human and financial resources, and continuous regeneration that keeps an organization healthy, relevant and feasible in a turbulent environment over a long period of time. A related concept that involves similar issues is social venture. It combines both social and economic activity to achieve three key objectives, such as economic capability, sustainability and social change (Lucas & Vardanyan, 2005).

In this aspect, many nonprofit organizations engage in social enterprise strategies to expand their organizational capacity and to ensure their financial sustainability. These type of organizations are not only interested in generating individual profits, but also in promoting social change in underdeveloped areas and promoting sustainability and job growth (Fowler, 2003; Lucas and

Vardanyan, 2005; Ersing, Loeffler, Tracy and Onu, 2007; Brower, 2011). As a result of rapid depletion of natural resources and concerns over wealth disparity and corporate social responsibility, sustainability has increasingly become imperative to business research and practice over the past decades. Within this domain, the so-called triple bottom line seeks to evaluate business performance on its impacts on the environment and interested stakeholders besides profitability concerns.

Until now, management information systems (MIS) research on sustainability has been somewhat constrained in the realm of green information technology (IT), which focuses mostly on the reduction of energy consumption of corporate IT systems. However, the expeditious changing and dynamic global business environment requires firms to be more flexible to quickly adapt and respond to market variations. Among the forces that drive changes, requirements for corporate responsibility and sustainability are getting more urgent. During such difficult time as this economic recession, companies are faced with hard choices to survive. Research has acknowledged that addressing sustainability issues is critical to the long-term survival and flourishing of companies (Porter and Kramer, 2006).

Thus, it is imperative to increase the business intelligence of an organization by addressing the sustainability issue through agile and intelligent ways (Lichtenthaler, 2007). At the same time, sustainability has increasingly become an important issue for both management scholars and practitioners. This recent push can be attributed to the facts that while the last two decades have brought much economic growth, there is much concern surrounding both wealth discrepancy and natural resource diminution. This concern has displayed itself in legislation expanding the responsibility of firms, increasing attention on training managers in sustainable management, and the development of theory to support sustainable managerial decision making in intelligent manner (Mintzberg, Simons and Basu, 2002; Hart and Milstein, 2003).

Sustainability has commonly been regarded as a crucial objective for organizations. Dilemmas which have arisen from environmental degradation, social and economic inequality, and changes in public opinions about the roles organizations play in maintaining sustainability has stimulated scholars and researchers to study the relationships of organizational practices and sustainability. (Florea, Cheung and Herndon, 2013). Sustainability has taken a prominent role in the popular media, corporate boardrooms, political arenas, and academia. Conversations and deliberations about what it is, why it is important, what should be done about it, and how quickly one should act are all-encompassing. It is an important, but often unspoken, and urgency accompanies these conversations. However, life as it is known– the elevated standard of living that many people have become accustomed to– is directly threatened by the very patterns of organizational activity that created the comfortable lives in the first place. For these reasons, the society is confronted with how deeply held this pattern of activities prevail in an organization (Mohrman and Worley, 2010).

Meanwhile a growing number of companies are integrating sustainability concerns into their strategic and operational decision-making processes alongside other traditional business imperatives as such profit maximization, cost reduction, revenue growth, and quality enhancement. In fact, the extent to which executives and managers embrace or resist this trend can determine the success or failure of a firm's efforts to operate in a more sustainable approach. Along this process, on-the-job training that introduces managers to sustainability principles and practices is one increasingly popular approach to securing cooperation and support for sustainability initiatives (Haugh and Talwar, 2010; Thomas and Lamm, 2012).

In this context, it is often professed that globalization serves as both a catalyst of accelerated development as well as an agent of chaotic disruption resulting in the contemporary socio-economic and political dislocations. In light of this, a key idea may be that heterogeneity could be understood as a mind-set and an exercise where complexity and diversity are leveraged strategically in a manner that promotes organizational sustainability. Carayannis and Provance (2008) have argued that innovation emerges from posture, the organizations position within a business ecosystem, propensity, as a manifestation of processes, routines and capabilities including the organizational culture and performance (3P), which are not only financial, but also products, patents and environmental impacts. Hence, organizational design for innovation is the effective alignments of the organization to the firm's business model in order to generate an optimal environment for the 3P's (Carayannis and Provance, 2008; Carayannis, Sindakis and Walter, 2015).

However, if it can be mentioned that organizations are already adopting a sustainable approach to their activities, then arises several questions, as what are the reasons for this? Is it just another exercise in public relations? Is it for purely business reasons (i.e., profit), or are social/ethical issues increasingly significant? Along these contexts, Eccles, Ioannou and Serafeim (2011) argue that research evidence suggests that organizations are not adopting sustainability policies purely for public relations reasons, but rather that they reflect "substantive changes in business processes" (Wales, 2013).

Towards this contribution, organizational sustainability is being considered as a normative underpinning that considers an organization or a community sustainable when it contributes to a more sustainable world as can be understood with the current knowledge and understanding of what sustainability might entail in the society. In other words, a sustainable organization does not refer to an organization that succeeds in keeping itself going by maintaining, for instance, profitability, but rather to one that, given what is known today, successfully balances people, prosperity and planet by searching for a dynamic equilibrium between these 3P's. Eventually such a balancing act may necessitate a shift altogether from the maximization of profit to something completely different such as the maximization of connotation.

In recent years, a perspective has emerged that defines sustainability to include three omponents, such as the natural environment (the planet), society (the people), and economic performance (the profit) (Elkington, 1994; 1998; 2004). This perspective is generally referred to as the triple bottom line (TBL). TBL approach recommends that besides economic performance, organizations need to engage in activities that positively affect the environment and the society. Furthermore, it is argued that a firm's long-term profitability and existence are best served by balancing them with social and environmental aims (Hart and Milstein, 2003; Porter and Kramer, 2006; Dao, Langella and Carbo, 2011; Weerawardena, McDonald and Mort, 2010).

The TBL perspective of sustainability, as illustrated in Figure 1, has been adopted which considers organizational sustainability to include three components (planet, people and profit). By considering people and planet in addition to profit, effects on the environment and stakeholders will be incorporated when contemplating alternatives, leading to a more sustainable outcome in intelligent and appropriate forms (Elkington, 1994; Aguilera, Rupp, Williams and Ganapathi, 2007; Hart and Milstein, 2003; Porter and Kramer, 2006; Dao, Langella and Carbo, 2011).

Limiting our focus on organizational sustainability and its implications due to the agility of an organization, we further progress to discuss about a few features of agility. In today's extremely competitive environment, it has been observed that firms that are agile tend to be more successful. However, despite the widely accepted importance of agility in organizations, there is limited research on this construct (Roberts and Grover, 2012).

Agility can be seen as a dynamic organization design capability that can sense the need for change from both internal and external sources, carry out those changes proactively and routinely, thus sustaining the above-average performance. The final characteristics, sustained above-average performance, is the outcome of agility. Many firms are able to push their performance to above average in the short run; however, the real issue is dynamically aligning structures, processes, and systems to sustain the entire organization (Worley and Lawler III, 2010).

Figure 1. Bonding of the three parameters of sustainability (triple bottom line) (adapted from Dao, Langella and Carbo, 2011)

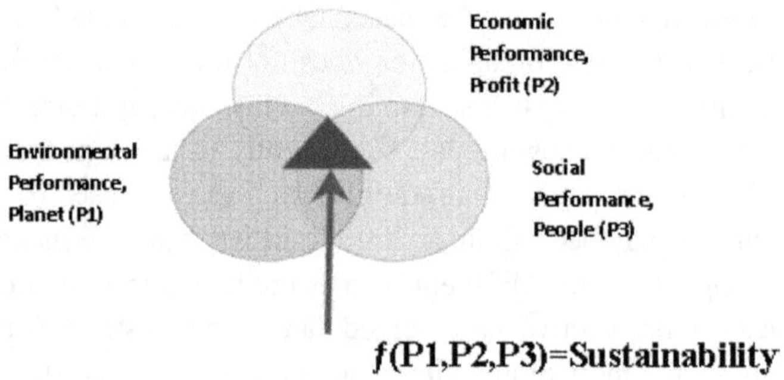

Agility is widely accepted, especially in the manufacturing industry as a new competitive concept. Agility as a term reflects a comprehensive response to the business challenges of profiting from rapidly changing, continually fragmenting markets for high performance, elevated quality, enhanced customer configured goods or, services. However, it has been observed that, how to develop a manufacturing strategy based around agility is not fully understood yet. Uncertainty has been found as a major topic for management research long before the term agility was introduced. In spite of the differences in defining "agility", one may emphasize on the speed and flexibility as the primary attributes of an agile organization. Another important attribute of agility is the effective response to sudden changes and uncertainties. Some other schools of thoughts mention that responding to change in proper ways and exploiting the advantages of changes are the most important factors of agility. Another important attribute that has been found is the ability to produce high quality and highly customized products (Gunasekaran, 1999; Sharifi and Zhang, 1999; 2001; Tsourveloudis and Valavanis, 2002; Sherehiy, Karwowski and Layer, 2007).

As the brief overview of the agility definitions shows, this concept of agility is comprised of characteristics like adaptability and flexibility. It seems that these two terms represent the advancement of the idea of the organization that is able to adjust. The agile organization may represent the latest stage of development of this idea, which could combine all important perceptions from the adaptable and flexible organization concepts. Although, studies on agility utilize some ideas and practices related to the adaptable and flexible organization, it has been observed that many important developments on this topic from the organizational and management field were overlooked (Sherehiy, Karwowski and Layer, 2007).

Thus, in order to clarify the agility concept and to classify the large diversity of strategies, techniques, and practices that are mentioned in the literature as components of agile enterprise need to have their origins explored. Further, in order to synthesize the agile enterprise concept, important knowledge related to managing the unpredictable and changing environment needs to be evaluated (Sherehiy, Karwowski and Layer, 2007).

This chapter attempts to make an overview of the existing frameworks of agile organizations and its various attributes. For this overview, a longitudinal literature review has been conducted. This review includes various frameworks that encompass elements and structures of an organization, in terms of agility. It was out of scope of this research to make a comprehensive literature review of research and concepts in relation to other parameters of a sustainable organization, such as organizational intelligence or organizational resilience. However, where applicable, emphasis has been given to the context that organizational sustainability through agility not only makes the business process more sustained, but also assists to make intelligent business decisions. Furthermore, efforts have been given in the context to make implications about the impact of this be applicable for academics and researchers in the field of making intelligent business decisions through organizational sustainability and agility. The main aim of this study is to identify the origins and theoretical background of some ideas that are available about an agile enterprise and described in the literature as a part of organizational sustainability incorporating agility.

2. LITERATURE REVIEW

An organization can be seen as a social entity that has a collective goal and is linked to an external environment. There are a variety of legal types of organizations, including corporations, government organizations (GOs), non-governmental organizations (NGOs), international organizations, armed forces, charities, not-for-profit corporations, partnerships, cooperatives, universities, and research. A hybrid organization is a body that operates in both the public sector and the private sector simultaneously, thus fulfilling public duties and simultaneously developing commercial market activities (Google and Wiki definitions).

In the field of social sciences, organizations are the object of analysis for various disciplines, like sociology, economics, political science, psychology, management, and organizational communication. The broader analysis of organizations is usually referred to as organizational structure, organizational studies, organizational behavior, or organization analysis. In this aspect, a number of perspectives exist, such as:

- From a process-related perspective, an organization is viewed as an entity is being reorganized, and the focus is on the organization as a set of tasks or actions;
- From a functional perspective, the focus is on how entities like businesses or state authorities are used; and
- From an institutional perspective, an organization is viewed as a purposeful structure within a social context (Douma and Schreuder, 2012; Google and Wiki definitions).

Sustainability is being seen as the capacity to tolerate. In ecology the word describes how biological systems remain diverse and productive over the time. Long lived and healthy wetlands and forests are examples of sustainable biological systems. For humans, sustainability is the potential for long-term maintenance of well being, which has ecological, economic, political and cultural dimensions. Healthy ecosystems and environments are necessary to the survival and flourishing of humans and other organisms. For organizations, sustainability is to survive under the adverse conditions (internal and external) through the ability to endure, add value and promote supply chain (Google and Wiki definitions) thus applying various methods such as being agile, intelligent and resilient. In the context of agility, it is a concept that is widely adapted to the area of contemporary business. The existing literature presents agility as a broad concept, which can be easily adopted in the field of business processes, such as manufacturing.

Sustainability can be treated as a recent and comprehensive issue for the economy, the companies, and the population, being considered a systemic concept related to the stability of economic, social (including cultural), and environmental issues. The United Nations' Brundtland Report defined sustainable development as"[...] the one that meets present needs without compromising the ability of future generations to meet their own needs" (Brundtland Report, 1987: pp.16). Hence, sustainability is a manner of driving civilization in order to the society and its members (companies included) safeguard biodiversity and natural ecosystems, planning and acting to achieve the indefinite maintenance that can fill their needs and express their greatest potential in the present (Lee and Saen, 2012; Buys et al., 2014; Longoni et al., 2014; Ribeiro et al., 2015; Lopes, et. al., 2017).

Naturally, the organizational configuration of any business is vital for its success in acting as a driver for the company to accomplish its vision. At its most basic level, an organization is either an individual or a group of people who work collectively to achieve a shared aim or set of aims. The impact of changing demographics, the global market, social inequity and climate change on organizations has been considered in contemporary times. One common response is for organizations to implement sustainable processes with a view toward having a positive influence on the environment, thereby creating social as well as financial capital. According to the Chartered Institute of Personnel and Development in London, CIPD (2012), the essence of organizational sustainability is the principle of strengthening the environmental, societal and economic systems within business operations. This principle is essential since the perception of sustainability will keep the business running by helping the business prosper without compromising the needs of the future (CIPD, 2012; Wales, 2013); McNamara, 2015); Zawawi and Abd Wahab, 2019).

At the same time there are a few theoretical and empirical studies on inter-organizational agility, which frequently involves just the application of system engineering thinking to describe and optimize factors influencing the transfer of material and information among companies. The US Agility Forum presents agility as the ability to flourish and prosper in a competitive environment of continuous and unanticipated change, to respond fast to rapidly changing markets driven by customer-based valuing of products and services. Some mention, it is the future business system that will replace the mass production businesses of today (Kidd, 2006; Kisperska-Moron and Swierczek, 2009).

In this aspect, Conboy and Fitzgerald (2001) has defined agility as the continual readiness of an entity to rapidly or inherently, proactively or reactively, embrace transformation, through high quality, simplistic, economic components and relationships with its environment. The literature review suggests that the agile capabilities of companies can be analyzed from the perspective of their relations with the major business partners or stakeholders (clients, suppliers, service providers and other competitors) and the role of information technology in initiating and sustaining those relationships (Kisperska-Moron and Swierczek, 2009).

It has been observed that the current ubiquity of networks, and various forms of networking, at the industry, firm, and individual levels is reshaping the global business architecture and thus attracting significant research interest (Lin, Desouza and Roy, 2010). Through the utilization of information and communication technologies (ICTs) and applications of various facets of information technology (IT), entities are no longer isolated as before, and the interaction among each other is more vibrant nowadays. Firms are able to communicate among partners, suppliers, and clients in a more intelligent way than ever before. This sort of technological advancement has lead to technological transformations at the business process level, such as incremental or radical.

The management of technological transformation in companies is of high interest to both theory and practice. Incremental technological transformation introduces relatively minor changes on the existing products, exploits the potential of the established design and often reinforces the dominance of established firms. But, radical technological transformation requires a new set of engineering and scientific principles and can open up new applications and market segments which may challenge the position of established firms. However, many studies have shown that the insufficient reaction of established companies to radical technological change can lead to their demise. In this respect, researchers have identified insufficient information on technological trends and managerial incompetence as main reasons for the limited learning capability of established companies. On the other hand, for established companies, radical technological transformation is not only a challenge, but it also constitutes a major source of failure. It has been observed that by establishing effective technology intelligence processes, companies may react to radical trends in time which is a prerequisite for coping with technological transformation (Lichtenthaler, 2007).

Furthermore, in order to identify technological discontinuities in an early stage and to increase the effectiveness of technological decision-making, many researchers have called for a more systematic observation of technological trends already in the early 1970s. In the literature, many terms are used for this process of systematic acquisition, assessment and communication of information on technological trends in order to detect opportunities and threats in a timely manner. The expressions range from technology monitoring, technology assessment and technology forecasting to technology intelligence. In this study, the term technology intelligence is adopted because it has been increasingly used in recent years by both researchers and practitioners (Lichtenthaler, 2007).

Given the background details, we refer to the organizational sustainability as the capability of an organization in adverse environment with agility that is to be able to react fast and adjust accordingly to sustain the organization. Adopting different practices and tools to improve the competitiveness, might well be by hand of agile methods or principles, which concepts have penetrated the thinking of managers, especially in manufacturing industries for decades (Smart et al., 2003) and which has been much debated in research and practice over the past years. Furthermore, it is clear that more and more organizations are exhibiting flexibility and agility coupled with the ability to create and apply innovative ideas, acting collaboratively. (Green, 1999; Browaeys and Fisser, 2012). This study is now trying to relate how agility in an organization leads to the sustainability of the organization through establishing a theoretical framework.

3. THEORETICAL FRAMEWORK

The concept of agility was initiated by researchers of the Iacocca Institute of Lehigh University in 1991. Initially, it was introduced within the field of manufacturing, especially in the concept of flexible manufacturing systems, and later on it has been applied to other business sectors.

This newly evolved concept has received increasing attention from both academic and commercial fields. (Sarker et al., 2009; Sarker and Sarker, 2009; White et al., 2005; Bottani, 2009; Ngai, Chau and Chan, 2011).

As mentioned, agility has been the subject of increasing research interest, and there are both academic and practical calls for a better understanding of its genesis, development, and consequences. The importance of organizations to engage at the sophisticated levels of fostering the organizational traits of agility (leading to sustainability), complexity management and learning is called for universally. For example, consultants, executives, and management theorists have tried to comprehend the components and consequences of agile strategies, while others have studied the characteristics of reconfigurable and ambidextrous structures. However it has been observed that the number of frameworks that comprehensively explore agile organization designs is much smaller (Worley and Lawler III, 2010; Flumerfelt, Siriban- Manalang and Kahlen, 2012).

One agility framework (see Figure 2), suggests that organizations need to break away from traditional design assumptions, think about how each element or feature must be constructed with flexibility in mind, and then align them dynamically to support both adaptability and sustained high levels of performance. Worley and Lawler III (2010) termed it as the built to-change model, and it has been adapted and integrated with concepts from strategic leadership to create the agility framework. The basic features of this framework are a robust strategy, an adaptable organization design, and shared leadership and identity in value-creating capabilities.

Traditionally, an enterprise keeps a relatively large organizational structure that is usually hierarchical. The structure is to handle various customers' needs, when the service or production provided by the enterprise involves complex activities. If customers' demands are similar and are maintained on a requirement basis, the company may gain enough payoffs to support the equipment and workforce for customers' needs. However, if customers' needs are changing frequently in terms of time, quantity, and design, a relatively large organization structure may not react to customers' needs on a timely basis.

Moreover, when customers' needs change or the market demands decrease, some facilities in the organization may become obsolete or redundant. Thus, the obsolete or redundant facilities incur excessive overhead and endanger the enterprise's viability. The good news is that with the effective support of IT, an enterprise does not need to maintain a large, complex organization, yet it can still work on large projects through collaborating with other relatively small organizations, such as suppliers, vendors, subcontractors, etc. Those small organizations can form and re-form various networked organizations, depending on the customers' demands (Huang, Ceroni and Nof, 2000).

3.1. Agile Organization

An agile organization is said to be adaptive to innovations, flexible and responsive to transformations, and at the same time, robust and resilient to damages. Being agile and utilizing IT, an organization is able to involve more reasoning, intelligence, collaboration and autonomy for adjustment (Huang, Ceroni and Nof, 2000). The organization should be also able to achieve all these in productive and cost-effective ways (Alberts and Hayes, 2003; Lin, Desouza and Roy, 2010).

Figure 2. A framework involving agile parameters
(adopted from Worley and Lawler III, 2010)

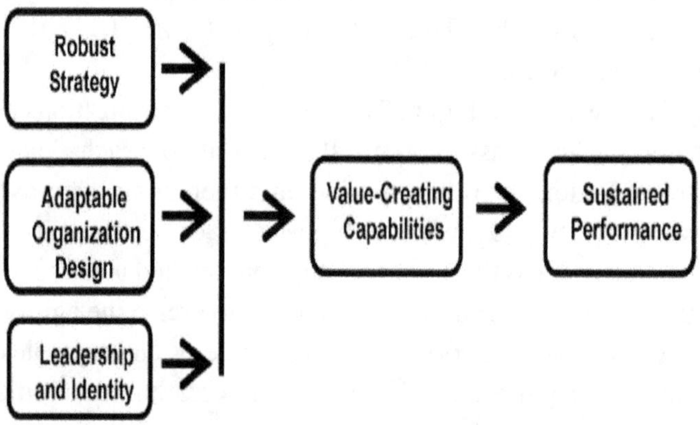

While the agility of networked organizational structures is important for organizational accomplishment, studies on how to appraise it remain scant, probably because the difficulty in measuring network evolution. An agile organization is said to be adaptive to innovations, and at the same time, flexible and responsive to changes by being robust and resilient to damages (internal and external) (Alberts and Hayes, 2003). And the organization should be able to achieve all these in productive and cost-effective ways. Currently there are a few measures that are available to adequately capture the structural agility of organizational networks. However, the main challenge remains is that the ongoing changes in the networks, which has been characterized as network evolution. Lin, Desouza and Roy (2010) argue that, one need to measure and predict network evolution as a continuous process rather than discrete snapshots.

In the perspective of agile organization, agility is the capability of an enterprise to operate profitably in a rapidly changing (abrupt) and continuously fragmenting (dynamic) global market environment by producing high-quality, high-performance, customer-configured products and services (Tsourveloudis and Valavanis, 2002). Literature in areas like, human resources, supply chain management, organizational design, and even information systems have examined organizational agility from a historic and descriptive approach, involving collecting survey data or writing case studies (Giachetti, Martinez, Sáenz and Chen, 2003). These studies though seem helpful, but they do not provide with perceptive tools and techniques to improve organizational agility. Lin, Desouza and Roy (2010) continue to argue that, in this aspect, quantitative measures need to be taken that can evaluate and predict outcomes that are more preferable. However, a question arises at this point, as what are the agile methods or which are the characteristics of an agile method?

As mentioned above, agile methods have received considerable attention during the last 2 decades, since 1991 (Dybå and Dingsøyr, 2008). Furthermore, in comparison to other systems development methods, they seem to be exceptionally well-received by practitioners. One question arises here, as what could be the explanation for this success? In this aspect, Livari and Livari (2011) go on explaining that, one possibility could be the fashion factor, which is the early excitement with the idea. Although this possibility may not be excluded, but one can conceive of more fundamental changes in the systems development arena that favors agile methods. Moreover, when arguing for agile systems development methods (SDMs), its promoters often refer to the increased turbulence and unpredictability of the world, and for that reason organizations and enterprises need to be more agile, more responsive to changes (Sherehiy, Karwowski and Layer, 2007).

Ideally, agile methods sustain this organizational agility. It is not necessarily self-evident what methods are agile, since they are not based on any clear common core idea (such as the systems development life-cycle in the case of the waterfall model, prototype in the case of prototyping, the concept of object in the case of object-oriented methods), apart from on the concept of agility. At the same time, agility seems to provide quite a complicated definitional basis for agile methods (Livari and Livari, 2011).

In recent years, the urgency for business environment change came from a new business paradigm now referred to as the agility. In addition to the mentioning in earlier places, agility, in its original incarnation, emphasized the power of relationships to create value through knowledge and information sharing. Furthermore, as observed earlier, the definition of agility has evolved. Nowadays, agility calls upon social computing to unlock knowledge, experience and expertise distributed among unrelated and previously unidentifiable individuals (Li, Nagel and Sun, 2011). Also, questions are revolving around as how to structure and design organizations that could support agility and adaptability, which are of strategic significance. Evidences support that interactions and the dynamics of complexity are origins of new knowledge, diversity, and innovation are the main exciting advancement for organizations struggling to survive and compete in a dynamic, fast-paced and highly interrelated global environment (Martinez, 2008).

Hence, apart from being adaptable and flexible, more and more the organization is reaching towards social sectors, more and more it is leaning towards fulfillment of social and corporate responsibilities, in addition to empowerment. In this aspect, agility can be seen as the capacity to redefine a business process in order to adjust it to changing external conditions. What is under stake here is the effort and time that is required to adapt an existing business process. In the case of mechanistic business process management (BPM), adaptations may take a long time to accomplish and involve a significant effort.

The central reason is that changes in the BPM system (BPMS) must be carefully managed at the technical level so that the transition to the new system does not generate operational problems. However, in the case of humanistic BPM (empowerment), agility may be easier to accomplish since changes do not involve the technicality. In addition to BPMS, Web services organizations utilize Business Intelligence (BI) and Data Warehousing (DW) to enable them to better understand the competition and take fast decision through enhance knowledge management (de Oliveira, Balloni, de Oliveira and Toda, 2012). Of course one should consider that the adaptation cost is also partially dependent on the required levels of formalization and factor, which gives some advantage to the humanistic approach. For example, there may be no effort associated with adaptation in the case of a system using ad hoc workflows to implement a business (Antunes, Simões, Carriço and Pino, 2013). Therefore, the theoretical framework needs to be attentive towards the social dimension of the agile organization. Thus, a brief discussion on social agility is being given next. Thereafter, we talk about the organizational agility and ecosystem agility to complete the framework.

3.1.1. Social Agility

In these days, agility calls upon social computing to unlock knowledge, experience and expertise distributed among unrelated and previously unidentifiable individuals. Social agility can be seen as the process of enhancing the productivity of individuals and the effectiveness of teams by making it easier for the people to relate to one another on the basis of shared goals. The power of social agility derives from social computing, which evolves from enhanced relationships that amplify tacit interaction.

According to Li, Nagel and Sun (2011) McKinsey and Co. is the first organization to explicitly place a value on tacit interaction. The company has defined tacit interaction as collaborations that involve unscripted information interchange, judgment making, and multifaceted forms of knowledge exchange with coworkers, clients, suppliers and other partners. Figure 3 shows the utilization of social computing to achieve business goals for effective innovation and growth through agility.

Lawler III and Worley (2012) perform an analysis of firm profitability in 14 industries over 30 years and shows that a few firms have been able to sustain above average levels of financial performance. Besides, they find that, consistently high financial performers are not only more likely to score high on agility, but also likely to lead in environmental and social performance. However, they argue that, the correlation between financial sustainability and agility is stronger than the correlation between financial sustainability and social or environmental performance. Furthermore, it has been observed that social agility with effective business goals leads to organizational agility.

3.1.2. Organizational Agility

In many organizations, the potential for significant benefit from collaboration has remained untapped because of adherence to traditional forms of business organization and management.

This could be due to the persistent belief that it is always difficult to bridge internal organizational boundaries, and that it is almost impossible to bridge external organizational boundaries. Hence, operating under such beliefs allows only a small portion of employee knowledge and know-how to be accessible from outside of the organization. This results in missed opportunities for many organizations. Organizational agility appears from the removal of organizational walls and silos to create opportunity-driven structures, and the adoption of evaluation processes to sustain processes and incentives that motivate and reward collaboration. This enables an organizational environment in which knowledge and expertise can be easily reconfigured in response to business challenges and prospects. It also makes large organizations more searchable and analyzable and, in some ways, more navigable than smaller ones, and, therefore, makes it easier to precisely determine what people demand. This creates new possibilities for the implementation of business processes, innovative business models, and market-positioning strategies (Li, Nagel and Sun, 2011).

Figure 3. The use of social computing to achieve business goals
(adopted from Li, Nagel and Sun, 2011)

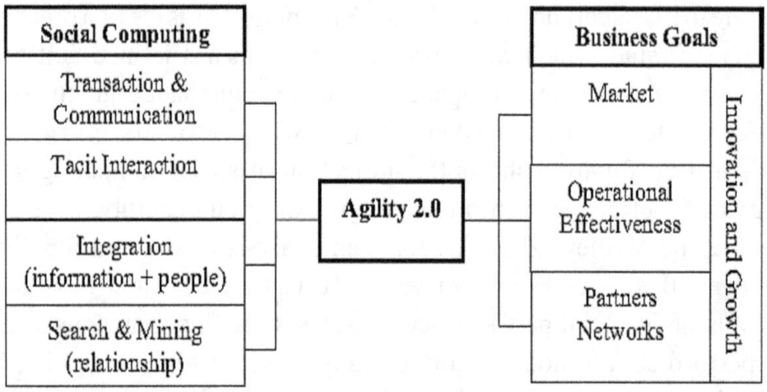

A number of definitions for organizational agility have been recommended. The definitions generally convey the idea of rapidity and the changing market environment. Organizational agility is a response to the disputes posed by a business environment dominated by change and uncertainty. It engages a new way of doing business. It reveals a new mind-set on making, selling, and buying a form of openness to new forms of commercial relationships, and new measures for assessing the performance of organizations and people. Organizational agility necessitates an organization to be quick in assembling its technology, employees, and management with communication infrastructure in response to changing customer demands in a continuous and unanticipated changing market environment. Simply stated, it is an organization's ability to generate the requisite information for management decision-making in a turbulent situation (Kodish, Gibson and Amos, 1995; Zain, Rose, Abdullah and Masrom, 2005).

Figure 4 constructs a framework of organizational agility from various technology adoption influences. Furthermore, organizational agility refers to the framework for technological, managerial and production expertise supporting organizational sustainability. To develop organizational agility, an organization has to possess a number of competencies, such as technological competency, managerial competency, and operational competency (Ngai, Chau and Chan, 2011).

The framework for organizational agility in terms of competency is shown in Figure 5. Table 1 shows the extended framework based on the three competency parameters, and their agility index. Next discussion is on ecosystem agility, which suffices the organizational perspective of an organization on its entirety.

Figure 4. Organizational agility framework from technology adoption influence viewpoints
(adopted from Zain, et. al., 2005)

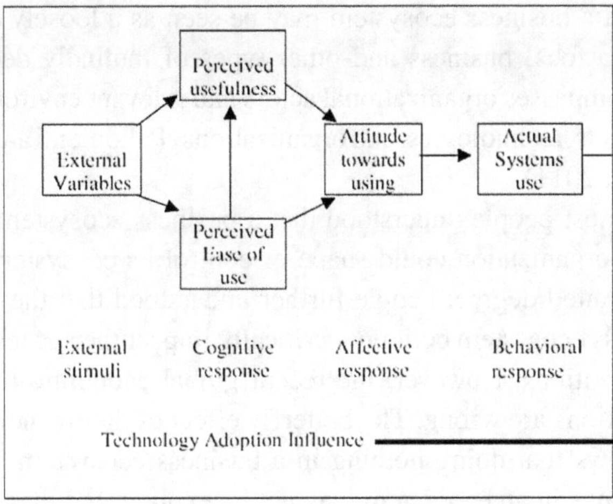

Figure 5. Organizational agility in the aspect of various competencies
(Author)

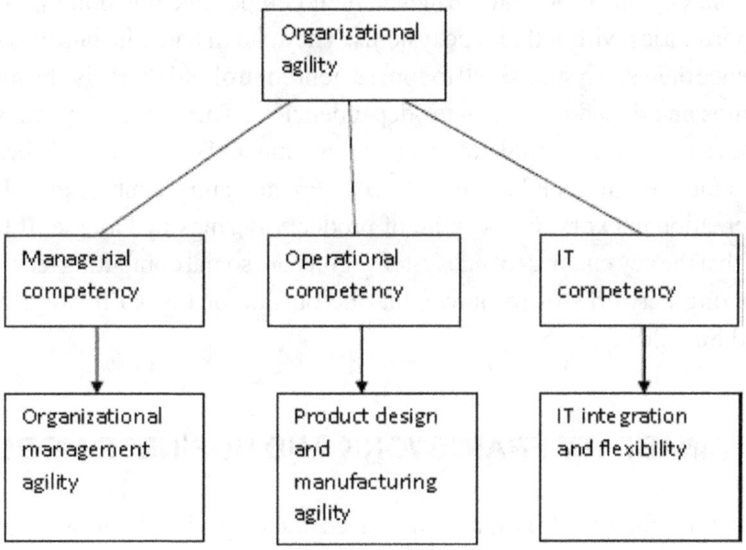

3.1.3. Ecosystem Agility

Frosch and Gallopoulos (1989) originally presented the concept of industrial ecosystem in Scientific American. Later on J.F. Moore (1996) proposed the concept of a business ecosystem in 1996. Moore describes business ecosystem as an economic community supported by a foundation of interacting organizations and individuals. He further describes that a business ecosystem may be seen as a loosely coupled system that consists of a focal business and other types of mutually dependent businesses, and that encompasses organizational actors and relevant environmental components such as markets, technologies, and organizations (Peltoniemi and Vuori, 2004; Li, Nagel and Sun, 2011).

Until very recently, most people understood that a business ecosystem simply exists as is, and that an organization could shape or control its ecosystem for its own benefit only to a limited degree. People further understood that the implicit relationships in a business ecosystem could not critically impact the success of the ecosystem's core organizations. However, the recent global economic recession shows that these assumptions are wrong. The butterfly effect of the financial crisis in the United States shows that doing nothing in a business ecosystem is doing something, though the links in an ecosystem may not be explicit, but they are still real links (Li, Nagel and Sun, 2011).

In these aspects, ecosystem agility refers to how social computing may be utilized by companies to identify, exploit and manage the inter-dependencies, relationships and strategies in their business ecosystems to enhance the chances of achievement. Organizations can influence their competitive position to create new value opportunities within their ecosystems. They can in some instances transform and influence their ecosystems, and to some extent control and share risk by managing relationships and dependencies (inter-dependencies). The iTunes application store can be seen as a simple example of this phenomenon. Other examples of ecosystem business strategies may include the P&G´s (Proctor and Gamble) establishment of value creation network, or the suite of product offerings by Google. It has been observed that the key enablers of ecosystem agility are social computing technologies for organizing networks of resources that lie outside of formal relationships (Li, Nagel and Sun, 2011).

4. SUSTAINABILITY FRAMEWORK AND BUSINESS MODEL

A Business Sustainability Framework may need to satisfy what the present generation wants without decreasing opportunity and at the same time be able to satisfy what the next generation wants. In this aspect, business sustainability management (BSM) integrates management strategy and operational activities corresponding to the interested parties, protecting human resources and natural resources those

Table 1. Organization agility framework based on the agility index

Organizational Management Agility	Inter-Organization Cooperation	Degree of Cooperation With Other Organizations
	Intra-organization cooperation	Time and space needed for production process
	Institutional framework agility	Team building speed and efficiency
Product design and manufacturing agility	Speed of product and manufacturing design	Period of product and manufacturing design
	Product design flexibility	Degree of product structure similarity
	Re-configurability	Integrated modular packaging unit
IT integration and flexibility	Availability of customer demand information	Increased information access
	Information management agility	Organizational information system quality

(adopted from Sherehiy, Karwowski and Layer, 2007; Ngai, Chau and Chan, 2011)

are necessary for future business activity and operation (von Rosing, Hove and von Scheel, 2013).

The sustainability framework requires that organizations and enterprises need to be more agile, and more responsive to changes, in terms of agile systems development methods (SDMs), where its proponents are exposed to the increased turbulence and unpredictability of the world around.

In this aspect, firstly, the group culture is primarily concerned with human relations and flexibility. Here, belonging, trust and participation are its core values. Further, effectiveness of the criteria includes the development of human potential and member commitment. Secondly, the developmental culture is future-oriented, considering what might be. The effectiveness of the criteria, here, emphasizes growth, resource acquisition, creativity and adaptation to the external environment. Thirdly, the rational culture (stability, sustainability and external focus) is achievement-oriented, focusing on productivity, efficiency and goal achievement.

Finally, the hierarchical culture (stability, sustainability and internal focus) is oriented towards security, order, routine, and control. It emphasizes management, sustainability and efficiency through a defined set of regulations (Livari and Livari, 2011). Figure 6 shows the sustainability framework that incorporates four transformational parameters leading to organizational agility.

The sustainability maturity model (SMM) can be depicted as a structured collection of elements describing the aspects of sustainability maturity in an organization. Like

Figure 6. Framework for sustainability
(adopted from Livari and Livari, 2011)

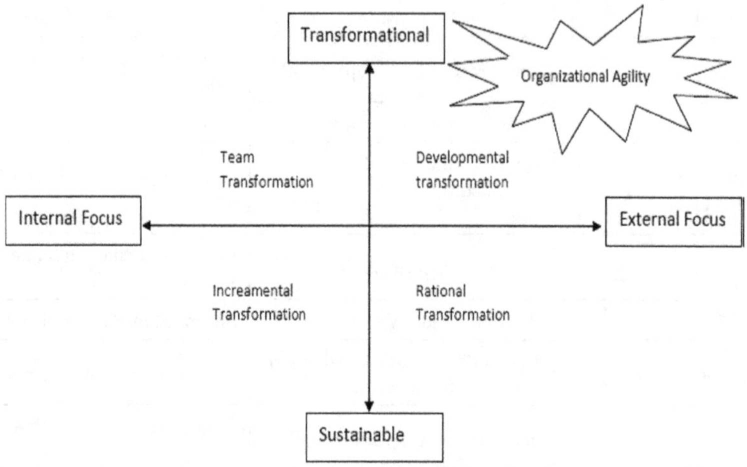

any other model it should be treated as an abstraction of an existing system (von Rosing, Hove and von Scheel, 2013).

The proposed business model is based on the basic business model building block suggested by Noran (2013), which is comprised of three parameters, such as input (IT, Operational and managerial competencies), control (organizational agility) and resource (organizational framework elements) that enable the activity (the business model), which leads to the output (here, the organizational sustainability). Figure 7 illustrates the proposed business model based on the basic building block of a business model as suggested by Noran (2013).

5. FUTURE WORKS AND CONCLUSION

If one looks at the future research on sustainability and related topics in terms of organizations and external funding, one need to pay more attention to capacity building as a possible outcome of short-term programs (Scheirer, 2005). Within the scope of this particular research, one essential factor comes as a question, as whether an organization becomes sustainable depending on its capacity to able to be agile? Or, we may need to pay attention to other issues, such as resilience, intelligence, competencies, collaboration, IS, innovation, and culture (Sherehiy, Karwowski and Layer, 2007). What could be the medium and long term effects of agility (as a lone influencer) on organizational sustainability?

Figure 7. Proposed business model
(Author)

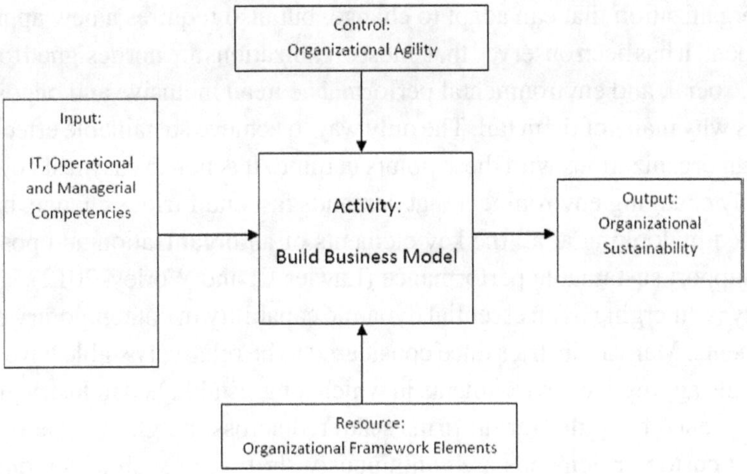

Over the last 50 years, globalization has transformed companies to enterprises, while computing and communication have transformed production and service organizations to innovative organizations (Huang, et. al., 2000). This instigates extended study on the role of agility in organizations to be able to be competent and sustain in the longer run.

It has been observed that there is a lack of research on the organization of the technology intelligence process in situations of radical technological change. Current research has not taken a holistic view on the technology intelligence processes, especially in situations of radical technological change that covers all process steps from information acquisition, business modeling to decision-making. Furthermore, it is not clearly understood as how hierarchical levels and the different forms of coordinating the technology intelligence process interact and how they influence the quality of the product, process and the quality of decision making.

Additionally, industry characteristics seem to influence the quality of the technology intelligence process. Therefore, the objective of this study remains confined to identify different organizational forms of agility processes in situations of radical technological transformations and organizational decision-making (Lichtenthaler, 2007). Future studies may seek for the impact of technology intelligence and resilience on organizational sustainability. Furthermore, so far the sustainability concerns, in aspect of low awareness among the organizations, including the financial constraints and high risk of investment in the period of economic crisis, future researches should take them into account for investigative research.

Creating organizations that perform well in terms of the environment, profit, and people (triple bottom line approach) is a not a simple process. Rather, it requires more than an organization that can adapt to change, but also requires a new approach to management. It has been observed that, most organizations are not designed to address financial, social, and environmental performance in an inclusive and ongoing way, and this is why many of them fail. The only way to achieve sustainable effectiveness is to design organizations with these points in mind. It is not an easy task, especially in a rapidly changing environment that demands fast and furious change, but it can be achieved by looking at all the key elements of an organization and positioning them to support sustainable performance (Lawler III and Worley, 2012).

Agility is emerging as an essential dynamic capability in contemporary business environments. Many industries once considered to be relatively stable have evolved into severely aggressive environments in which long-established industry giants are being threatened by agile startup firms scattered across the globe. One reason for this is that customer demands are continuously shifting in such hypercompetitive environments. In this aspect, to create competitive advantage, organizations must sense and respond rapidly to changes in customer preferences. In other words, a firm's customer agility, its ability to sense and respond quickly to customer based opportunities for innovation and competitive action, is extremely critical for survival and success (Jarratt and Fayed, 2001; Jayachandran, Hewett, and Kaufman, 2004; D'Aveni, Dagnino and Smith, 2010; Roberts and Grover, 2012).

While the agility of networked organizational structures is essential for organizational performance, but studies on how to evaluate it remain scant, probably because of the difficulty in measuring network evolution (Lin, Desouza and Roy, 2010).

This study thus concludes that organizations acting in challenging situations with low awareness about agility, low financial capability, and at the same time with high risk of investment seem to expedite extended research to measure the impact of these potential risk factors to be able to be a sustainable organization in the longer run.

REFERENCES

Aguilera, R., Rupp, D., Williams, C., & Ganapathi, J. (2007). Putting the S back in corporate social responsibility: A multilevel theory of social change in organizations. *Academy of Management Review*, *32*(3), 836–863. doi:10.5465/amr.2007.25275678

Alberts, D. S., & Hayes, R. E. (2003). *Power to the Edge: Command, Control in the Information Age*. US Department of Defense, Command and Control Research Program.

Antunes, P., Simões, D., Carriço, L., & Pino, J. A. (2013). An end-user approach to business process modeling. *Journal of Network and Computer Applications, 36*(6), 1466–1479. doi:.jnca.2013.03.014 doi:10.1016/j

Bottani, E. (2009). On the assessment of enterprise agility: Issues from two case studies. *International Journal of Logistics: Research and Applications*, *12*(3), 213–230. doi:10.1080/13675560802395160

Browaeys, M.-J., & Fisser, S. (2012). Lean and agile: An epistemological Reflection. *The Learning Organization*, *19*(3), 207–218. doi:10.1108/09696471211219903

Brower, H. H. (2011). Sustainable development through service learning: A pedagogical framework and case example in a third world context. *Academy of Management Learning & Education*, *10*(1), 58–76. doi:10.5465/AMLE.2011.59513273

Brown, S. L., & Eisenhardt, K. M. (1998). *Competing on the edge, strategy as structured Chaos*. Harvard Business School Press.

Buys, L., Mengersen, K., Johnson, S., Buuren, N. V., & Chauvin, A. (2014). Creating asustainability scorecard as a predictive tool for measuring the complex social, economic and environmental impacts of industries, a case study: Assessing the viability and sustainability of the dairy company A. *Journal of Environmental Management*, *133*, 184–192. doi:10.1016/j.jenvman.2013.12.013 PMID:24374467

Carayannis, E. G., & Provance, M. (2008). Managing firm innovativeness: Towards a composite index builton firm innovative posture, propensity and performance attributes. *International Journal of Innovationand Regional Development*, *1*(1), 90–107. doi:10.1504/IJIRD.2008.016861

Carayannis, E. G., Sindakis, S., & Walter, C. (2015). Business model innovation as lever of organizational sustainability. *The Journal of Technology Transfer*, *40*(1), 85–104. doi:10.100710961-013-9330-y

CIPD. (2012). *Responsible and Sustainable Business: HR leading the way – A collection of "thought pieces"*. CIPD.

D'Aveni, R. A., Dagnino, G. B., & Smith, K. G. (2010). *The age of temporary advantage*. Academic Press.

D'Aveni, R. A., Dagnino, G. B., & Smith, K. G. (2010, December). The age of temporary advantage. *Strategic Management Journal*, *31*(13), 1371–1547. doi:10.1002mj.897

Dao, V., Langella, I., & Carbo, J. (2011). From green to sustainability: Information Technology and an integrated sustainability framework. *The Journal of Strategic Information Systems*, *20*(1), 63–79. doi:10.1016/j.jsis.2011.01.002

De Oliveira, S. B., Balloni, A. J., de Oliveira, F. N. B., & Toda, F. A. (2012). Information and Service-Oriented Architecture & Web Services: Enabling integration and organizational agility. *Procedia Technology*, *5*, 141–151. doi:.protcy.2012.09.016 doi:10.1016/j

Douma, S., & Schreuder, H. (2012). *Economic Approaches to Organizations*. Pearson Education.

Dybå, T., & Dingsøyr, T. (2008). Empirical studies of agile software development: A systematic review. *Information and Software Technology*, *50*(9-10), 833–859. doi:10.1016/j.infsof.2008.01.006

Eccles, R., Ioannou, I., & Serafeim, G. (2011). *The Impact of a Corporate Culture of Sustainability on Corporate Behaviour and Performance*. Harvard Business School Working Paper 12-035.

Eersing, R. L., Loeffler, D. N., Tracy, M. B., & Onu, L. (2007). Pentru Voi Fundatia. *Journal of Community Practice*, *15*(1), 193–215. doi:10.1300/J125v15n01_09

Elkington, J. (1994). Towards the sustainable corporation. *California Management Review*, *36*(2), 90–100. doi:10.2307/41165746

Elkington, J. (1998). *Cannibals with forks: The triple bottom line of the 21st Century*. New Society Publishers.

Elkington, J. (2004). Enter the triple bottom line. In A. Henriques & J. Richardson (Eds.), *The Triple Bottom Line: Does It All Add up?* (pp. 1–16). Earthscan.

Florea, L., Cheung, Y. H., & Herndon, N. C. (2013). For all good reasons: Role of values in organizational sustainability. *Journal of Business Ethics*, *114*(3), 393–408. doi:10.100710551-012-1355-x

Flumerfelt, S., Siriban-Manalang, A. B., & Kahlen, F.-J. (2012). Are agile and lean manufacturing systems employing sustainability, complexity and organizational learning? *The Learning Organization*, *19*(3), 238–247. doi:10.1108/09696471211219976

Fowler, A. (2000). *The Virtuous spiral: A guide to sustainability for NGOs in international development*. Earthscan Publications, Ltd.

Fowler, A. (2003). *The virtuous spiral: A guide to sustainability for NGOs in international development*, Book Review, Earthscan Publications Ltd., London. *Habitat International, 27*(1), 159–161. doi:10.1016/S0197-3975(02)00032-2

Frosch, R. A., & Gallopoulos, N. E. (1989). Strategies for Manufacturing. *Scientific American, 261*(3), 144–152. doi:10.1038cientificamerican0989-144

Giachetti, R. E., Martinez, L. D., Sáenz, O. A., & Chen, C.-S. (2003). Analysis of the structural measures of flexibility and agility using a measurement theoretical framework. *International Journal of Production Economics, 86*(1), 47–62. doi:10.1016/S0925-5273(03)00004-5

Green, S. D. (1999). The dark side of lean construction: exploitation and ideology. *Proceedings IGLC*-7, 21-33.

Gunasekaran, A. (1999). Agile manufacturing: A framework for research and development. *International Journal of Production Economics, 62*(1-2), 87–105. doi:10.1016/S0925-5273(98)00222-9

Hart, S., & Milstein, M. B. (2003). Creating sustainable value. *The Academy of Management Executive, 17*(2), 56–67. doi:10.5465/ame.2003.10025194

Haugh, H. M., & Talwar, A. (2010). How do corporations embed sustainability across the corporation? *Academy of Management Learning & Education, 9*(3), 384–396. doi:10.5465/amle.9.3.zqr384

Huang, C.-Y., Jose A. Ceroni, J. A., Shimon, Y., & Nof, S. Y. (2000). Agility of networked enterprises— Parallelism, error recovery and conflict resolution. *Computers in Industry, 42*(2-3), 275–287. doi:10.1016/S0166-3615(99)00076-7

Jarratt, D., & Fayed, R. F. (2001). The impact of market and organizational challenges on marketing strategy decision-making: A qualitative investigation of the business-to-business sector. *Journal of Business Research, 51*(1), 61–72. doi:10.1016/S0148-2963(99)00040-5

Jayachandran, S., Hewett, K., & Kaufman, P. (2004). Customer response capability in a sense and respond era: The role of customer knowledge process. *Journal of the Academy of Marketing Science, 32*(3), 219–233. doi:10.1177/0092070304263334

Kidd, P. T. (2006). *Agile Manufacturing: A Strategy for the 21st Century*. Retrieved July 25, 2013 from http://www.cheshirehenbury. com/agility/agilitypapers/paper1095.html

Kisperska-Moron, D., & Swierczek, A. (2009). The agile capabilities of Polish companies in the supply chain: An empirical study. *International Journal of Production Economics*, *118*(1), 217–224. doi:10.1016/j.ijpe.2008.08.019

Kodish, J. L., Gibson, D. V., & Amos, J. W. (1995). The development and operation of an agile manufacturing consortium: the case of AAMRC. *Proceedings of the Fourth Annual Conference on Models, Metrics and Pilots*, 2.

Lawler, E. E. III, & Worley, C. G. (2012). Designing organizations for sustainable effectiveness. *Organizational Dynamics, 41*(4), 265–270. doi:.2012.08.001 doi:10.1016/j.orgdyn

Lee, K. H., & Saen, R. F. (2012). Measuring corporate sustainability management: A data envelopment analysis approach. *International Journal of Production Economics*, *140*(1), 219–226. doi:10.1016/j.ijpe.2011.08.024

Li, Q., Nagel, R. N., & Sun, L. (2011). Migrating to Agility 2.0: How social computing creates strategic value. *Organizational Dynamics, 40*(2), 119–126. doi:. orgdyn.2011.01.006 doi:10.1016/j

Lichtenthaler, E. (2007). Managing technology intelligence processes in situations of radical technological change. *Technological Forecasting and Social Change*, *74*(8), 1109–1136. doi:10.1016/j.techfore.2006.10.001

Lin, Y., Desouza, K. C., & Roy, S. (2010). Measuring agility of networked organizational structures via network entropy and mutual information. *Applied Mathematics and Computation*, *216*(10), 2824–2836. doi:10.1016/j.amc.2010.03.132

Livari, J., & Livari, N. (2011). The relationship between organizational culture and the deployment of agile methods. *Information and Software Technology*, *53*(5), 509–520. doi:10.1016/j.infsof.2010.10.008

Longoni, A., Golini, R., & Cagliano, R. (2014). The role of New Forms of Work Organization in developing sustainability strategies in operations. *Int. J. Prod. Econ., 147*(A), 147-160.

Lopes, C. M., Scavarda, A., Hofmeister, L. F., Thomé, A. M. T., & Vaccaro, G. L. R. (2017). An analysis of the interplay between organizational sustainability, knowledge management, and open innovation. *Journal of Cleaner Production*, *142*, 476–488. doi:10.1016/j.jclepro.2016.10.083

Lucas, J., & Vardanyan, A. (2005). *Social enterprises: An Eastern Europe experience. Policy Brief #10*. The William Davidson Institute at the University of Michigan Business School.

Martinez, S. M. (2008). Leadership as an Emergent Phenomenon: A Framework for Complexity and Adaptability. *Proceeding of the 13th International Command and Control Research and Technology Symposia (ICCRTS 2008).*

McNamara, C. (2015). *Basic definition of organization.* Available at: https://managementhelp.org/organizations/definition.htm

Mintzberg, H., Simons, R., & Basu, K. (2002). Beyond Selfishness. *MIT Sloan Management Review*, (Fall), 67–74.

Mohrman, S. A., & Worley, C. G. (2010). The organizational sustainability journey: Introduction to the special issue. *Organizational Dynamics*, *39*(4), 289–294. doi:10.1016/j.orgdyn.2010.07.008

Moore, J. F. (1996). *The Death of Competition: Leadership & Strategy in the Age of Business Ecosystems*. Harper Business.

Ngai, E. W. T., Chau, D. C. K., & Chan, T. L. A. (2011). Information technology, operational, and management competencies for supply chain agility: Findings from case studies. *The Journal of Strategic Information Systems*, *20*(3), 232–249. doi:10.1016/j.jsis.2010.11.002

Noran, O. (2013). Building a support framework for enterprise integration. *Computers in Industry, 64*(1), 29–40. doi:.compind.2012.09.006 doi:10.1016/j

Peltoniemi, M., & Vuori, E. (2004). Business ecosystem as the new approach to complex adaptive business environments. *Frontiers of E-business Research, 2004*, 267–281.

Porter, M., & Kramer, M. (2006). Strategy and society: The link between competitive advantage and corporate social responsibility. *Harvard Business Review*, *84*(12), 78–92. PMID:17183795

ReportB. (1987) Accessed from https://sustainabledevelopment.un.org/content/documents/5987our-common-future.pdf

Ribeiro, I., Kaufmann, J., Schmidt, A., Peças, P., Henriques, E., & Götze, U. (2015). Fostering selection of sustainable manufacturing technologiesea case studyinvolving product design, supply chain and life cycle performance. *Journal of Cleaner Production*, *112*, 3306–3319. doi:10.1016/j.jclepro.2015.10.043

Roberts, N., & Grover, V. (2012). Investigating firm's customer agility and firm performance: The importance of aligning sense and respond capabilities. *Journal of Business Research*, *65*(5), 579–585. doi:10.1016/j.jbusres.2011.02.009

Sarker, S., Munson, C. L., Sarker, S., & Chakraborty, S. (2009). Assessing the relative contribution of the facets of agility to distributed systems development success: An analytic hierarchy process approach. *European Journal of Information Systems*, *18*(4), 285–299. doi:10.1057/ejis.2009.25

Sarker, S., & Sarker, S. (2009). Exploring agility in distributed information systems development teams: An interpretive study in an offshoring context. *Information Systems Research*, *20*(3), 40–461. doi:10.1287/isre.1090.0241

Scheirer, M. A. (2005). Is Sustainability Possible? A Review and Commentary on Empirical Studies of Program Sustainability. *The American Journal of Evaluation*, *26*(3), 320–347. doi:10.1177/1098214005278752

Sharifi, H., & Zhang, Z. (1999). A methodology for achieving agility in manufacturing organisations: An introduction. *International Journal of Production Economics*, *62*(1–2), 7–22. doi:10.1016/S0925-5273(98)00217-5

Sharifi, H., & Zhang, Z. (2001). Agile manufacturing in practice—Application of a methodology. *International Journal of Operations & Production Management*, *21*(5–6), 772–794. doi:10.1108/01443570110390462

Sherehiy, B., Karwowski, W., & Layer, J. K. (2007). A review on enterprise agility: Concepts, frameworks, and attributes. *International Journal of Industrial Ergonomics*, *37*(5), 445–460. doi:.ergon.2007.01.007 doi:10.1016/j

Smart, P. K., Tranfield, D., Deasley, P., Levene, R., Rowe, A., & Corley, J. (2003). Integrating lean and 'high reliability' thinking. *Proceedings of the Institution of Mechanical Engineers. Part B, Journal of Engineering Manufacture*, *217*(5), 733–739. doi:10.1243/095440503322011489

Smith, P. A., Wals, A. E., & Schwarzin, L. (2012). Fostering organizational sustainability through dialogic interaction. *The Learning Organization*.

Thomas, T. E., & Lamm, E. (2012). Legitimacy and organizational sustainability. *Journal of Business Ethics*, *110*(2), 191–203. doi:10.100710551-012-1421-4

Tsourveloudis, N. C., & Valavanis, K. P. (2002). On the measurement of enterprise agility. *Journal of Intelligent & Robotic Systems*, *33*(3), 329–342. doi:10.1023/A:1015096909316 von Rosing, M., Maria Hove, M., & Henrik von Scheel, H. (2013). *Initial thoughts on a Sustainability Framework: Detailing business and IT requirements to a holistic Sustainability Framework*. Retrieved July 04, 2013 from http://www.valueteam.biz/wordpress/wp-content/uploads/2012/12/von-Rosing-M-Hove-M-Scheel-H-Initialthoughts-on-a-Sustainability-Framework_2012.pdf

Wales, T. (2013). Organizational sustainability: What is it, and why does it matter? *Review of Enterprise and Management Studies*, *1*(1), 38–49.

Weerawardena, J., McDonald, R. E., & Mort, G. S. (2010). Sustainability of nonprofit organizations: An empirical investigation. *Journal of World Business*, *45*(4), 346–356. doi:10.1016/j.jwb.2009.08.004

White, A., Daniel, E. M., & Mohdzain, M. (2005). The role of emergent information technologies and systems in enabling supply chain agility. *International Journal of Information Management*, *25*(5), 396–410. doi:10.1016/j.ijinfomgt.2005.06.009

Worley, G. C., & Lawler, E. E. III. (2010). Agility and Organization Design: A Diagnostic Framework. *Organizational Dynamics, 39*(2), 194–204. doi:.orgdyn.2010.01.006 doi:10.1016/j

Zain, M., Rose, R. C., Abdullah, I., & Masrom, M. (2005). The relationship between information technology acceptance and organizational agility in Malaysia. *Information & Management*, *42*(6), 829–839. doi:10.1016/j.im.2004.09.001

Zawawi, N. F. M., & Abd Wahab, S. (2019). Organizational sustainability: A redefinition? *Journal of Strategy and Management*.

Zhang, D. Z. (2011). Towards theory building in agile manufacturing strategies—Case studies of an agility taxonomy. *International Journal of Production Economics*, *131*(1), 303–312. doi:10.1016/j.ijpe.2010.08.010

ADDITIONAL READING

Barth, M., Godemann, J., Rieckman, M., & Stoltenberg, U. (2007a). Developing key competences for sustainable development in higher education. *International Journal of Sustainability in Higher Education*, *8*(4), 416–430. doi:10.1108/14676370710823582

Blaga, S. (2013). Rethinking business sustainability. *Review of Economic Studies and Research*, *6*(1), 5–21.

Cai, H., Sedikides, C., Gaertner, L., Wang, C., Carvallo, M., Xu, Y., O'Mara, E. M., & Jackson, L. E. (2011). Tactical self-enhancement in China: Is modesty at the service of self-enhancement in East Asian culture? *Social Psychological & Personality Science*, *2*(1), 59–64. doi:10.1177/1948550610376599

Capra, F. (2007). Foreword. In A. E. J. Wals (Ed.), *Social Learning towards a Sustainable World* (pp. 13–17). Wageningen Academic Publishers.

Carayannis, E. G., Alexander, J., & Ioannidis, A. (2000). Leveraging knowledge, learning, and innovation in forming strategic government–university–industry (GUI) R&D partnerships in the US, Germany, and France. *Technovation*, *20*(9), 477–488. doi:10.1016/S0166-4972(99)00162-5

Carayannis, E. G., Edgeman, R. L., & Sindakis, S. (2013). Knowledge, information and data analytics for sustainable enterprise excellence (KID4SEE). In World summit on big data and organizational design, Paris.

Carayannis, E. G., Provance, M., & Givens, N. (2011). Knowledge arbitrage, serendipity, and acquisition formality: Their effects on sustainable entrepreneurial activity in regions. *IEEE Transactions on Engineering Management*, *58*(3), 564–577. doi:10.1109/TEM.2011.2109725

Choi, S., & Ng, A. (2011). Environmental and economic dimensions of sustainability and price effects on consumer responses. *Journal of Business Ethics*, *104*(2), 269–282. doi:10.100710551-011-0908-8

Davis, G., O'Callaghan, F., & Knox, K. (2008). Sustainable attitudes and behaviours amongst a sample of non-academic staff. *International Journal of Sustainability in Higher Education*, *10*(2), 136–151. doi:10.1108/14676370910945945

de Haan, G. (2010). The development of ESD-related competencies in supportive institutional frameworks. *International Review of Education*, *56*(1), 315–328. doi:10.100711159-010-9157-9

Dillard, J., Dujon, V., & King, M. C. (2009). *Understanding the social dimension of sustainability*. Routledge.

Doppelt, B. (2003). *Leading change toward sustainability: A change-management guide for business, government and civil society*. Greenleaf.

Dunphy, D. C., Griffiths, A., & Benn, S. (2003). *Organizational change for corporate sustainability: A guide for leaders and change agents of the future*. Routledge.

Eccles, R., Ioannou, I., & Serafeim, G. (2011). *The Impact of a Corporate Culture of Sustainability on Corporate Behaviour and Performance.* Harvard Business School Working Paper 12-035.

Kanter, R. M. (2011). How great companies think differently. *Harvard Business Review, 89*(11), 66–76.

Michelsen, G., & Adomssent, M. (2007). Education for sustainable development strategies in German universities. In A. E. J. Wals (Ed.), *From Çosmetic Reform to Meaningful Integration: Implementing Education for Sustainable Development in Higher Education Institutes – the State of Affairs in Six European Countries* (pp. 21–24). DHO.

Nidumolu, R., Prahalad, C. K., & Rangaswami, M. R. (2009). Why sustainability is now the key driver of innovation. *Harvard Business Review, 87*(9), 56–64.

Pfeffer, J. (2010). Building sustainable organizations: The human factor. *The Academy of Management Perspectives, 24*(1), 34–45.

Schaltegger, S., Ludeke-Freund, F., & Hansen, E. G. (2012). Business cases for sustainability: The role of business model innovation for corporate sustainability. *International Journal of Innovation and Sustainable Development, 6*(2), 95–119. doi:10.1504/IJISD.2012.046944

Segalas, J., Ferrer-Balas, D., Svanstrom, M., Lundqvist, U., & Mulder, K. F. (2009). What has to be learnt for sustainability? A comparison of bachelor engineering education competencies at three European universities. *Sustainability Science, 4*(1), 17–27. doi:10.100711625-009-0068-2

Springett, D., & Kearins, K. (2001). Gaining legitimacy? Sustainable development in business school curricula. *Sustainable Development, 9*(4), 213–221. doi:10.1002d.164

Thomas, T. E. (2007). Educating for sustainability: A double-edged sword? *International Journal of Innovation and Sustainable Development, 2*(3/4), 453–465. doi:10.1504/IJISD.2007.017950

Wals, A. E. J. (Ed.). (2007). *Social Learning Towards a Sustainable World.* Wageningen Academic Publishers. doi:10.3920/978-90-8686-594-9

KEY TERMS AND DEFINITIONS

Organizational Agility: Organizational agility is a company's ability to rapidly transform or adjust in response to changes in the market. In the recent days, there are many examples of how organizational agility can benefit a company.

Organizational Behavior: Organizational behavior can be seen as the study of how people interact within groups and its principles are used to make businesses operate more effectively.

Organizational Compatibility: Inter-organizational compatibility refers to the sharing of common experiences, values, principles, and business strategies among business partners.

Organizational Sustainability: Organizational sustainability means having the leadership, endowment, global insights, and change strategies necessary to rise to the exclusive challenges facing organizations today.

Sustainable Culture: Cultural sustainability relates to sustainable development (and to sustainability) and has to do with the maintaining of cultural beliefs, cultural practices, heritage conservation, culture as its own entity, and attempts to answer the question of whether or not any given cultures will exist in the context of the future. However, from cultural heritage to cultural and creative industries, culture is both an enabler and a driver of the economic, social, and environmental dimensions of sustainable development.

Sustainable Development: Sustainable development is a way of organizing citizens so that it can exist in the long term. This means taking into account both the imperatives present and those of the incoming future, such as the preservation of the environment and natural resources or social and economic equity.

Sustainable Eco-System: If an ecosystem is able to maintain its full functions and properties even though it is harvested, it can be termed as a sustainable ecosystem. It ranged from dealing with domestic, industrial, and agricultural waste is a growing environmental issue with implications for ecosystems and human health.

Chapter 4
Long Tail Leadership:
A Covid Case Study Illustrates the Importance of Understanding Soft Power Affecting Organizations

Diane Spencer-Scarr
https://orcid.org/0000-0002-0970-7040
Curtin University, Australia

ABSTRACT

The increased weighting of digital natives in a fattening long tail has added complexity to organizational leadership, particularly during the global COVID-19 pandemic. Trends affecting the individual come from social, economic, and technological sources and affect leadership behaviors, and this in turn affects society. In order to understand this interconnection, lower-level influences and how they affect the higher-level visible signs are discussed. These lead to influences on behavior. Influences are felt as intensity and embeddedness of engagement, decision-management, feedback ability, and motivators. This chapter begins with a discussion of causes for this phenomenon and concludes with ways to work with the long tail, either from within as a member or externally as a leader. The chapter ends with a brief comment on future research based on findings discussed in this chapter.

INTRODUCTION

The discussion in this chapter is based on original empirical research into 'engagement with digital networked technologies' and involved both qualitative and quantitative research into personality factor correlations related to engagement. This revised

DOI: 10.4018/978-1-7998-4799-1.ch004

chapter summarizes the original chapter and includes discussion on the application of these concepts in a case study, where the soft power of long tail leadership and the agility of an organization led to not simply the survival of the organization during the during the Covid-19 pandemic crisis, but rather to its thriving by accommodating fulfillment of basic human needs such as work, recreation and connection. General relevant literature related to the discussed social phenomenon is still sparse and in order to progress this discussion the literature review is not specifically confined to the background section of this chapter but is dispersed throughout the chapter.

Qualitative research, in the form of interviews and focus groups, revealed significant insights pertinent to this chapter and have been used to substantiate aspects of the discussion. In the initial research it was observed that participants who were deeply engaged with technology also appeared to participate in 'social activism' to a greater degree. This raised the question: what mechanism could translate minor acts of activism on a mass scale into social change and challenges for leaders of organizations

We can see a number of changes rippling through society. One of the most startling is the behavior of the long tail. The previously least influential members of society are becoming more important both as a proportion of the total and in their willingness to exert influence. It appears that the long tail is getting fatter! There are significant behavioral changes at the individual level that can be traced to social trends: the individual believes they have self-worth, they assume their individualism will be acknowledged, and they are increasingly primed for instant gratification as demonstrated in the documentary 'The Social Dilemma'. The long tail is now more assertive! Of great significance are the changed behaviors resulting from engagement with technology: the expectation that in the digital environment things are cheap, fast, connected and that there will be a like-minded peer group to support and assist them. The long tail has expectations! In the long tail it is harder to differentiate leaders from those being led: individuals may simultaneously be both. Most people in society are part of the influential long tail even if they are not aware of it! And it may be that leaders are being led (upward management), and they are not aware of it.

The discussion looks at digital technology as an environment and how the individual operates within the duality of real world and digital environments. It then continues to a discussion on digital technology as a tool and how through engagement with the technology the individual becomes enmeshed and synthesized with the technologies. This leads onto how engagement with technology amplifies individual's behaviors, which affects society and challenges leaders. Each challenge has a suggestion for coping with this social phenomenon. Finally, the chapter concludes with a look at future research directions. It should be noted that the nature of this topic requires a discussion in order to lead the reader to an understanding of the multiple elements and how they interact. To achieve this a narrative style of writing has been used.

BACKGROUND

The origin of the term 'long tail' is from statistical distributions such as the Pareto distribution. The Pareto distribution was named after Vilfredo Pareto a civil engineer and economist who observed a power law probability distribution that is now used in descriptions of social, scientific and many other types of observable phenomena. Generally speaking, the graph of such a distribution will start high and quickly drops off as a concave curved line, approaching zero along the X-axis. Events at the far ends of the axis have an increasingly low probability of occurrence. The Pareto principle applies in many cases, which gave rise to the 80/20 rule: 80% are accounted for by the first 20% of items in the distribution. It should be noted that the distribution is not strictly 80/20, it may vary. Initially Pareto used his distribution to describe wealth-allocation and income distribution. The distribution illustrated how a large portion of wealth of a society is owned by a small percent age of the people within that society. Application of the distribution soon moved to other situations in which a similar distribution of the "small" to the "large." For example: The sizes of human settlements (few cities, many villages), file size distribution of Internet traffic which uses the TCP protocol (few larger files, many small ones), the values of oil reserves in oil fields (few large fields, many small fields), sizes of sand particles, the standardized price returns on individual stocks (Reed & Jorgensen, 2004) and hard disk drive error rates (Schroeder, Damouras, & Gill, 2010). Recently there has been awareness that the influence of technology is making the tail longer and fatter. The formerly least influential 80% of a population are becoming more significant as a proportion of the total. Interest and research into the long tail phenomenon has been growing with the emergence of social media, which has increased the reach and power of the long-tail. This is very evident in the digital network environment where micro-sales to mass customers are now possible (Brynjolfsson, Hu, & Simester, 2011). Research into the long tail is particularly noticeable with regard to marketing where improved and lowered search costs of acquiring customers 'portend an ongoing shift in the distribution of product sales' towards the long tail ("Internet host count history," 2013). This phenomenon is also seen in the social activity of the formerly powerless who mobilize to exert soft power. Examples are the fall of the Berlin Wall, the Arab Spring and the 2013 protests in Turkey. Further examples are seen on a smaller scale such as consumer activism. This is becoming a major trend in society and does not need to be itemized here.

The attributes, qualities and styles of a leader have been discussed and explored from as far back as Aristotle and Plato (Kraut, 2010) to contemporary research into dynamic environments involving chaos theory concepts (D. Snowden, 2003; D. J. Snowden & Boone, 2009). Despite this vast amount of research there still appears to be more questions than answers. This is probably due to the uniqueness of each situation. There are however some common elements that provide a guide to the classification of different leadership styles. The most common styles being: authoritarian (keeps strict, close control), paternalistic (shows concern for followers - receives trust and loyalty), democratic (sharing decision-making), laissez-faire (delegates providing little or no direction), transactional (motivating through rewards and punishments) and transformational (challenge and inspire) (Schultz & Schultz, 1986).

These styles describe the leaders' way of executing leadership: it is their action style. This however is only one aspect of leadership. Leadership also involves a leader's ability to interpret external situational factors as well as the leaders internal 'action logic' (Rooke & Torbert, 2009; D. Snowden & Boone, 2009). This complex feed-back-loop (evaluation of external factors against internal logic) is at the heart of this chapter's argument. Until the advent of digital networked technologies external factors were found in the 'real world', a world which is understood by humans. As will be shown in this discussion, the creation of digital networked technologies is challenging some basic human concepts and creating a duality of environments in which humans now operate as technology is increasingly embedded in society. The consequences of this are being seen in social phenomena such as the long tail breaking the Pareto distribution expectations.

This discussion will contextualize and examine the causes of social phenomenon and behaviors that are presenting challenges to leaders of organizations. By understanding this phenomenon, the leader will be better able to develop strategies suited to their unique situations.

Research Methodology

Empirical research underpinning this discussion explored the general nature of digital network engagement by looking at correlations between personality and engagement. This required mixed method research. Quantitative research was used for personality data and qualitative research for engagement data. Participants were information technology professionals as it was believed this would provide a higher level of engaged participants. A self-reported survey was used for personality and demographic data and personality questions were sourced from the International Personality Item Pool (Goldberg et al., 2006). This involved the Five Factor Model plus four additional NEO PRI sub-scales thought to be important to the research, as well as the REI test giving a total of thirteen personality factors (Pacini & Epstein,

1999). Due to the lack of research into engagement with digital networked technologies a grounded theory approach was used for the qualitative research. This involved a series of three in-depth interviews each building on the previous one. Interviews were transcribed, interpreted, coded and classified. Empirical researched used for this discussion was sourced from the qualitative data. It should be noted that data from the quantitative research has not been used in this discussion.

New research reported in this revised chapter came from focus groups which formed part of a three-year research project related to the transitional requirements of millennials into the workforce. This research is in its final year and is not part of this chapter. However, consent has been given to use information related to the specific arguments of this chapter as a case study to exemplify the concepts discussed.

THE PIVOTAL ROLE OF TECHNOLOGY

Perhaps the most significant influence facing all humans today has been the creation of the digital networked environment: a place that is increasingly ubiquitous and embedded in every aspect of human interaction. The digital networked environment allows for unprecedented self-expression, exploration, exposure to new ideas and cultures and has limited negative consequences. This environment is not simply an extension of the familiar real world environment. It is, as will be discussed, a different environment because the digital environment is adjusting some basic human concepts which are affecting human behavior. There is a common belief that digital networked technologies are 'simply a tool': a means to an end for humans operating in the real world.

It is just the next level of communication. First there was talking face-to-face, then there was writing letters, then telephones now its email, it's just a new way of communicating. (Research participant meSEdl cnote)

This is believed to be an erroneous view. The creation of the digital network was a 'black swan' event that resulted in a new environment in which humans inevitably operate.

In 1697 the Dutch explorer Willem de Vlamingh discovered black swans in Australia. This unexpected event profoundly changed zoology and our understanding of the world as it overturned the previously held Western belief that all swans were white. This required a major reassessment of what was known. As a result of this incident, when a relatively insignificant event in human history occurs that is unprecedented and unexpected but has profound consequences, it is termed a 'Black Swan' event. One such event occurred in 1970 when the USA Department of Defense connected four nodes of computer-to-computer communication known as ARPANET. This simple step ultimately led to personal global digital network connectivity and more importantly, to dramatic social changes. Its effect on human and societal behavior, while commonly acknowledged, is not yet understood. A major reason for this lack of awareness is that digital networked technologies challenge some basic human concepts. Concepts on which humans have operated for millennia. Leaders need to understand this if they wish to lead in this era.

THE DIGITAL WORLD

Humans operate in the real world environment that is comprised of places and spaces, and which is governed by sequential chronological time. Here actions have consequences and memories usually fade. Over the last 30 years humans have created and moved some of their living into the digital environment, which exists within (or as a consequence of) digital networks. In the digital environment places are 0's and 1's and spaces are, as Manuel Castells proposes, spaces of flows (Castells, 2010). The digital environment is governed by instantaneous, eternal, endless or compressed time and actions have limited or no consequences. Here memories are eternal and can survive with absolute clarity. While the collective memory of the real world has been bound to the historical records and remembrances of the privileged few, the digital environment allows the long-tail's voice to be recorded and reflected upon; both within the present, and as the future seeks to look back and reflect on what has been experienced.

History has repeatedly shown that when new or different concepts are introduced to an existing environment an adjustment is necessary. For example: when Columbus introduced Europe to the New World in the fifteenth century. The ubiquitous embedding of digital technologies is forcing the individual to cope with a duality of fundamental concepts. One based on evolutionary experience in the real world, and the other an unknown quantity that the individual, conscious or not, is grappling to cope with. This is uncharted territory that is constantly adapting and changing. The leader needs to understand at least the following core concepts that are altered in the digital environment. While each concept may be discounted for not being substantive, the cumulative effect is undeniable.

Time and Memory

For most humans throughout the ages, time has been regarded as a dimension marked by change, be it change of the seasons, or the state of the altered environment as the individual moves from point A to point B. This traditional concept of time has been the metronome for both individuals and societies. As Lewis Mumford said, "without clocks and the precise timing of activities, ... industrialized societies could not exist" (Giddens, 2006), but what of the digital network environment? According to Castells, in the digital network environment, time has taken on a different form which he terms timeless time. Time, Castells suggests, is compressed and de-sequenced in the digital environment. Consider the example of a tourist withdrawing cash from an ATM on an island resort halfway around the world from their home bank. A transaction like this requires numerous calls on different bank databases and exchange rate calculations: a mammoth task in a non-digital network environment that would have taken hours if not days to process. The tourist standing at the ATM is, however, likely to feel frustrated having to wait more than a few seconds for the transaction to be cleared and the cash dispensed. What has been altered, as a result of the technology, is the human perception of time. While there has only been a clock-time delay of a few seconds, the perception of the frustrated human is that the transaction should be near-instant because it is taking place in the digital network environment: the perception of time has been compressed. Heidegger's discourse on standing-reserve explains how users come to this perception in the digital network environment.

Heidegger suggests resources are expected "... to be immediately at hand, indeed to stand there just so that it may be called for "(Heidegger, 1977, p. 17). The expectation is that service is always available as soon as you require it and in the digital environment there is an even higher expectation: Digital connectivity and services are increasingly expected to be ubiquitous and uninterrupted - it must be 24/7.

The de-sequencing of time, Shiv Visvauathau suggests in his discussion on Castells, creates an instantaneous or eternal time. "Elimination of sequencing creates undifferentiated time which is tantamount to eternity"(Visvauathau, 2001, Sec.11, Par 3). I suggest however that the simultaneous compression and de-sequencing of time in a digital network environment results in both instantaneous and eternal time making the human experience of time in the digital environment very different. An example of instantaneous time would be found in world financial markets where globally dispersed humans interact in real time. Eternal time on the other hand results from the fundamental way in which digital networks operate. At minimal cost, information can be identically copied, shared and stored at great speed in multiple places in the digital network environment without the originators knowledge. Due to the reduced cost and ease with which humans can store information on the digital network, humans are more likely to save retrieved information than spend time evaluating whether it should be deleted or stored. The saved information may well be further copied, stored, shared and archived multiple times making it potentially exist for eternity. Information could therefore be said to potentially exist in eternal time. The enormity of this change has not yet been absorbed by society but there are signs of growing awareness as the digital environment negatively impacts on an individual's real world experiences, for example when misguided Facebook entries undermines job seeking (Mayer-Schonberger,2009).

Time is a key component of traditional memory, which Mayer-Schonberger reminds us, naturally fades as time passes. In the digital environment however, memory is exactly replicated and retained as long as a digital network environment exists: "digital remembering negates [traditional] time" by retaining exact vivid memories. In addition to the potential impact of digital memory on individuals, digital memory has an unprecedented potential to effect social memory.

The custody of humanity's culture as well as collective memories has traditionally been the responsibility of museums and libraries. But as Guy Pessach argues "the transformation from tangible or analogue preservation to digitized cultural retrieval tends to result in partial and gradual privatization of society's memory institutions" (Pessach, 2008, p. 73). This is a potential double-edged sword. On the one hand it offers the utopian view of decentralized and democratized memory institutions and social remembering practices: digital networks and the process of digitization make more information available to more people in more formats. On the other hand, privatization of memory institutions may compromise the democratic vision of social remembering due to biases of the memory institution, be they human, algorithms that filter what information is available, or the agenda of commercial enterprises. In addition to this, digitization of information has the potential to fragment and de-contextualize societal memory.

Regardless of whether one takes a positive or negative view of the overall impact of digitization on memory, there appears to be sufficient evidence that memory within the digital network environment is indeed different to traditional memory, and therefore is an altered or new concept. Whether the individual is aware of it or not, exposure to digital networked technologies makes the individual operate with dual concepts of space and time. This duality is affecting individual and social behavior in apparently erratic ways. Leaders need to be aware of this and adjust strategies accordingly.

Space Becomes Activity

Traditionally we understand 'space' to be geographical and static: a stage on which human activity is played out. To understand the concept of digital network space it is necessary to introduce Gilles Deleuze and his concept of a network being a rhizomic system (Deleuze& Guattari, 1987). To Deleuze a network is a system with no beginning and no end, it is a system of middle containing rhizomic nodes, which prosper and grow proportional to their contribution to the network. A digital network has no central power and therefore a node only gains 'power' according to its ability to perform a useful and reliable function for the network. If a node does not produce results it will become redundant and will ultimately be phased out. Whether a network node 'works' or not is not only determined within the node but emerges from the network itself, of which the node is only one part. Each node must be connected because as Deleuze points out if a node is not connected, from the network perspective, the node does not exist. It is also necessary for nodes to be participatory in order to maintain its nodal status. In other words, the space that an individual occupies in the digital networked environment is the result of both activity and connection. This is very different to real world space where one can passively occupy a location.

This is demonstrated by research participants 'cg' (under 35years) and 'pk' (over 35years) interview answers related to Facebook.

An iPhone, I use it for banking a lot and FB a lot. Checking FB is a standard thing when you are on the phone. Pick it up on the morning and check FB [So that is like your interface to your whole world?] Yeah. [Everything is through FB?] Yeah. [Even though you don't particularly like FB] Yeah. Like I was camping yesterday and/ still had signal in the middle of nowhere and I was on FB it was really ridiculous. (Research participant cgilql)

If someone is like not there, not online you feel they are away... Yeah right now it's always online, I'm never offline. If I'm not on my computer it's on my phone which is always signed in I never sign out of FB on my phone and as soon as somebody writes something to me on my wall or does anything to do with me I get an instant message on my phone screen. [So you never sign out of FB, you are always on FB?] Always [Wow] it's the same with everyone it shows you if you are on your computer and if you go off it will switch to say you are on mobile. So you can still message the person and they will get it. (Research participant cgilq4)

I belong to an investment club and they have got a closed FB group which obviously I am not part of because I am not on FB. So they have to email me when they have bought or sold shares and they just think it is ridiculous ... when we have a function and they take photographs they have to send (email) me the photographs because I don't have access to FB. [Is the expectation that the club have put it on FB therefore you should know about it?] Yes, yes, yes. [Do you have an aversion to that?] I do! There are two of us in the club that are not on FB and so they have to disseminate information to us by email. I don't think that's fair really. If they want to put their whole lives on FB that's their problem. It's not something that I'm comfortable with so I won't do it. (Research participant pkilq6)

When the individual engages with digital networked technologies they become one as Michel Callon and John Law say, "there is no difference between the person and the network of entities on which it acts. Or between the person and the network of entities which acts through the person. Network and person: they are co-extensive" (Callon & Law, 1997, p. 169). As such in order for the individual to be a part of the system they must be both connected and participating - they have to be active.

Castells coined the term a space of flows to describe space in a digital network. In a space of flows he says there is the "possibility of organizing the simultaneity of social practices without geographical contiguity". Felix Stalder expands on this saying "it refers to a specific social condition, rather than nature in general." The space of flows Stalder says "is that stage of human action whose dimensions are created by dynamic movement, rather than by static location"(Stalder, 2002, p. 2). In the digital network environment "the movement takes place through human action and it creates the specific social conditions for our everyday lifes." Traditional space is fixed by geographical boundaries however the digital network environment is not. It is dependent on human action. Space in the digital network environment is fluid and can expand and contract depending on the relational activity resulting from individuals' action on and within the digital network. Examples of this are FaceBook, YouTube and Wikipedia.

If space is defined by the actions occurring between elements in the digital networked environment then it follows that in order to create space in which one can function in the digital environment, one needs to be taking action. This begins to explain why individuals in general appear to have become activists - more likely to express opinions on global or social conditions or events. By taking action the individual not only creates a space in which they can operate, such as creating a FaceBook entry, they also create a way of defining their individuality. From this we begin to see that the concept of space within a digital network environment is indeed different. It is ephemeral and cannot be contained; its size or strength is dependent on the quality and quantity of its connectivity, which may be human or non-human, and on the activity that takes place.

This extended discussion of space is necessary since the dissolving concept of geographical space is impacting on the individuals' self-perception. Not only are geographical boundaries and physical limitations being removed, the concepts replacing them are simultaneously driving people to participate, take action and define themselves by their activism. Individuals and businesses will certainly be advantaged if they are capable of capitalizing on 'digital space' not necessarily through physical ownership but by the quality of their participation.

Locus of Self and Short Term Thinking

The concept locus of self appears to be altered in the digital environment. A good starting point for understanding this concept is Martin Heidegger's concept of dasein or 'being there' ("The Oxford Companion to Philosophy," 1995). For Heidegger all being takes place in time, which is constantly changing, presenting new possibilities for individuals to capitalize on. Time for Heidegger is sequential bringing changes that he feels should be embraced not resisted. Heidegger suggests that an individual is placed in a time and its related environs and that they should extract and experience what is relevant to the individual for the duration of that time because it will inevitably change. If one takes Heidegger's concept of 'being there' but instead of using sequential time applies Castells' concept of 'timeless time' we find that in the digital environment humans conceptually have a new way of 'being' in a de-sequenced, instantaneous and eternal state. Individuals can now be 'present', albeit virtually, in a geographically boundless landscape in 'near instant' time. Similarly, this raises intriguing ideas from Derek Pafit about the individual and their relationship to one's future self (Parfit, 1971). Pafit suggests that the future self is a stranger to the present self and thus attracts less commitment from the present self: Reduced saving for old age is often attributed to this reasoning. If the individual struggles with commitment to future self within the known concepts of time and space in the real world, then it is no wonder that in the digital environment, where time and space are more complex, that individuals invest more in the present: instant gratification. These altered concepts challenge where the individual places their locus of self in the new environment. As businesses increasingly work on, through or in the cloud, taking control of remote desk tops or using remote software to manage their processes, so the employee increasingly finds they are operating according to the constraints and demands of multiple environments. The individual is responding and conforming to the environmental demands, structure and stimuli of the real world environment and one or more digital environments simultaneously. For example: participant 'rg' when discussing remote working behavior.

You actually absorb the corporate culture of the client that you are connecting into. So that while you are still physically in your own environment you are in that that clients building and that must affect the way you look at them and the way you behave even though you are the same person on this end you have changed slightly in some subtle ways. How you think because you are on their site. [So your actual behavior changes?] I think so yes but in subtle ways. Perhaps even the user is not aware of it. (Research participant rgilqi)

Value Exchange Becomes Released Energy

The concept of value exchange, while often associated with Marxism as exchange value, is indeed a basic human concept explored by philosophers as far back as Aristotle to contemporary economists and marketers (Kraut, 2010). It is human instinct to trade some of what one has for things one needs or wants. In the real world 'value exchange' is pre dominantly associated with commodities, which has four attributes; value [relative worth], utility [quality or condition of being useful], exchange value [quantified worth of one's goods or services as expressed in terms of the worth of another] and price [amount expected, required, or given in payment for something].In the real world the concept of value exchange is learned at a very early age. Rarity increases exchange value, which in turn increases price. In the digital environment value exchange is not quite the same and can superficially appear to be irrational, illogical or even chaotic. This can be quite disconcerting to leaders since value exchange by remuneration is often seen as their most effective method of motivation. It is, therefore, necessary to understand some underlying mechanisms of value exchanges in the digital networked environment.

In the digital environment there has been an ever-decreasing entry cost. As a result, there is an ongoing expectation by the user that prices in this environment will continue to be less. This expectation is exacerbated by the fact that early commodities bought or exchanged in the digital environment were in most cases intangible and in digital form, such as music or information. Initially, free entry, participation or access to commodities such as free news on-line, free downloads and 30-day free trial versions of software was not only allowed but was actively encouraged to attract participants to the network. These tactics were necessary because of user naivety and insufficient knowledge of how to capitalize on the digital environment. This created an expectation in users that digitally related activities should incur little to no cost.

This is only a small part of the complex arrangement of value exchange in the digital environment. Take for example the Josh Groban fan club which Clay Shirky describes in his book Cognitive Surplus (Shirky, 2010). Josh Groban, a popular singer, had a website built to provide his fans with information about himself and coming events. The site however led to something far greater than its initial purpose. All four attributes of value exchange manifested in unexpected ways releasing exceptional value to multiple parties at little to no traditional cost. The Josh Groban example illustrates a very different form of value exchange and if understood by leaders it can be a tremendous advantage in identifying motivators of the people they lead.

Once fans were on the Josh Groban website they found they could exchange information with other fans: These self-filtered and like-minded people had a similar passion. New and casual visitors were encouraged to become members and to contribute to the group in the form of comments and photo's. The value exchange provided by fans to the site (building the image of their idol) was in some way different to the real world concept of value exchange. Participants certainly found value (friendship and camaraderie), they also found a sense of utility (providing information about their idol) and possibly exchange value (self-expression) but, on the website, there was no price: no amount was expected, required, or given in payment for the valuable contribution of information provided and received by fans that built the image of Josh Groban. In 2002 the value exchange widened to include social altruism. Josh's fans wanted to buy him a twenty-first birthday gift. Online discussion among fans lead to the decision to raise money for charity in his name (Shirky, 2010, pp. 65-69). The network of fans raised over a thousand dollars (cost to fans), which was handed over to the David Foster Foundation. This pleased their idol (reward for fans), which encouraged the group of personally motivated but technically inexperienced fans, to continue raising funds. The value exchange was so great that it mobilized activist behavior disproportionate to initial expectations of either the site or any individual within the network of fans. At personal cost this small band, now called Grobanites, learned how to build an online auction site to raise even more money for charity in the name of Josh Groban. By 2011 they had raised a million dollars in Josh Groban's name (Grobanites, 2011). This value exchange is certainly different to traditional value exchange. The behaviors in this single example demonstrate a very different range of interactions that were neither traditional real world value exchange nor were they intuitive or obvious. It could be argued that examples such as this are similar to real world examples like fundraising drives by charity organizations but there is a difference. Conceptual changes result in individuals' behavioral changes and behavior changes are a challenge for leaders..

ADAPTING TO CHANGE

The prolific biological diversity known as the Cambrian Explosion occurred over 500 million years ago as a result of a unique combination of high oxygen level and benign environment. It was from this environment, the primordial soup, that a flurry of diverse adapted living organisms emerged (Lewin, 1993, pp.17-19,63-74 and 102-103). Similarly, evidence now abounds of the complex, adaptive diversity of digital networked technologies. Perhaps this will be seen as a modern equivalent: the Digital Explosion. Digital networks are complex in that they are made up of multiple interconnected diverse elements that interact. These elements may be human and non-human. They are adaptive because they have the capacity to change and they increasingly learn from the experience of their elements, for example Google's page ranking (Vaidhyanathan, 2011. Chp 1,2,6).

Today in organizations and businesses almost all functions, communications, access and storing of data, sourcing of materials, selling of products, visualization, relationship and process management, and even staff recruitment, are all subject to the ephemeral and adaptive nature of the digital environment. Despite this it is still argued by some that business is just the same, that it is only the tools that are different. A similar situation occurred with the introduction of electricity where initially it was considered merely a tool to create light. The full impact of electricity on society was only appreciated in hindsight (Carr, 2009). Like electricity, digital networked technology is not simply a tool, it is a lot more and it is changing the course of humanity forever as has clearly been demonstrated during the 2020 Covid-19 pandemic.

For this reason, it is necessary to remove any misconceptions that the digital networked environment can be treated as simply another tool. Examining digital networked technologies enables us to see where it becomes more than a tool, integrating with the user through an iterative process at a core level that shapes their sense of self and how they interact with the world around them.

Primates in the wild can make and use tools as well as solve sophisticated problems (Wolfgang, 2001), but when it comes to "abstract causal variables that govern objects and their relationships in the physical world"(Johnson-Frey, 2003) chimpanzees have difficulty. On the other hand, with humans, understanding of causal relationship emerges in early infancy (Spelke, Breinlinger, Macomber, & Jacobson, 1992). The desire and ability to satisfy abstract perceptual reasoning appears to be a uniquely human attribute.

In his discussion on J J. Gibson's ecological approach to tool-use, Smitsman suggests that humans' use of tools not only shapes and reshapes our environment [e.g. a tractor], but tool-use alters the action potential of the human body [e.g. a shovel becomes a more suitable arm-extension for digging than a hand]. Smitsman points out that the action potential of the human body "evolves in tandem with the evolution of implements for perceiving and acting" [e.g. a flat stone for digging evolves into a shovel with a handle, then a plough pulled by a horse and finally a tractor]. Smitsman also proposes that tool use is a means of conveying insights between generations and humans of different skill levels (Smitsman,1997). In other words, Smitsman suggests that tools not only impact on our physical world but they have the capacity to change how humans perceive their own capability and act as a medium for the transmission of ideas and concepts to other humans and generations. Even simple items that an individual uses as a tool are expected to alter not only their capacity but also their self-perception.

When it comes to considering digital networks as a tool for human use, we find three common properties across a range of disciplines. Tools should be manipulable objects that alter the environment in order to achieve a goal. (Baber, 2003, p. 8;

Frey, 2007, p. 368; St. Amant & Horton, 2008, p. 1203; van Lawick-Goodall,1970, p. 195). Digital networks are certainly manipulable; albeit indirectly via software code, programs and applications, or hardware such as processors and routers. They have also profoundly altered the environment; from the way humans socialize and work to the way humans read books and do financial transactions. Digital networks also satiate human's fundamental need to communicate and share resources and information.

St. Amant and Horton's requirement of the externality of tools poses an interesting problem for digital networks. Consider Deep Brain Stimulation (DBS) where electrodes, a digital network tool [the hardware component], are implanted directly into the human brain [the wetware] creating a symbiotic synthesized network [electrode and accompanying hard and software, neurons, endocrine and muscle system]. In these cases, the electrode, as a digital network tool, cannot easily be considered as external due to the fact that it is deeply imbedded in the human body. This also presents a problem for Gibson who suggested that a tool should be graspable and transportable (Gibson, 1979, p. 41). The DBS electrode is arguably not graspable in the traditional sense, but then neither is an App nor a Blog and yet these digital network tools do conform to the initial three common properties of tool-use: they are manipulable and they alter the environment in order to achieve a goal.

Approaching digital networked technologies from a tool-use perspective highlights how different digital networks are. Digital networked technologies do indeed conform to much of the traditional idea of what a tool is. However as illustrated in the extreme Deep Brain Stimulation example above they have the capacity to embed and synthesize with the human in a way that is different to traditional tools. Even more significant are the less dramatic human/digital-technologies synthesis as explained by participant 'cf' when discussing the smart phone.

I cannot move without my phone. My phone is an extension of my hand. [How come that wasn't your first suggestion of device.] Um, good question. Um I suppose because...l don't know...I don't know... [ls it because it is a part of you?] Yeah it is, it probably is, yeah, it is a part of me. [So it is no longer something separate to you.] No if I haven't got my phone...I am...I am no more. I don't exist without my phone! The worst torture anybody can actually give to somebody else is taking away their phone. When my son and his girlfriend broke up she hid his phone and he was devastated, it was the end of the world. How can you do without your phone? [Do you think everyone is like that?] Yes absolutely! (Participant cfiilql)

From this simple example we see how repeated use, engaging with digital technologies, results in the individual not only embedding and synthesizing with it but also becoming emotionally dependent on it. Clearly there is something more too digital networked technologies than it simply being a tool. Once engaged the user enters an iterative process that not only alters their self-perception but also inevitably alters their action potential, which in turn alters their behaviors and this dynamic process is what the leader must work with.

Superficially digital networks could easily be dismissed as simply being a tool, but closer inspection reveals that digital networks are complex. The more humans engage with the technology the less like a tool it becomes. Human and network becomes a synthesized unit: the complexity depending on the individual's level and intensity of engagement. More significantly multiple changes like this are taking place, rippling through society and resulting in social change such as the long tail.

THE NATURE OF PARETO'S LONG TAIL CHANGES

The shift of influence (power-shift) towards the long tail has been demonstrated in the last three United States presidential campaigns where candidates found they needed digital networked technology if they wanted to reach formerly inactive voters (Clark, 2007; Graff, 2008; Granick, 2006; Grossman, 2008; Kapustka, 2006). Barack Obama led the way with transparency of information to the long tail challenges candidates and makes politicians and governing bodies more accountable (Stelter, 2008; Tynan, 2008). Additionally, lawmakers and the military are experiencing difficulties (Baigorri, 2008; Buxbaum, 2007; Greenemeier, 2008; Gross, 2007) as they try to manage the power-shift to the long tail: While those in authority would like to utilize the easy global dissemination of information to their advantage, they can no longer control the rank and file who have equally easy access and ability (Browne, 2008; Cross, 2007; Leff, 2008). Aggressive use of technology was taken up by Donald Trump in both the 2012 and 2020 election in particular his use of Twitter. Initially his Twittering connected him to his electorate and aided his election by making him appear open and accessible. However, his excessive and unconsidered use of Twittering in the 2020 elections may well have cost him his re-election (Shear. 2019). Leaders need to understand the power of technology and know when to use it and when they should not. This sample of reports in the media shows a significant social trend away from a 'top-down opaque hierarchal system' to a 'bottom-up transparent lateral system'. It demonstrates a global shift towards the long tail that is altering the knowledge-power balance. Sir Francis Bacon said "knowledge is power," and humans' like what they can do with power.

The seeking of, holding onto, concealing, sharing, destroying, preserving, commodifying, manipulating and developing knowledge has driven humans for millennia. There are two parts to knowledge: The information or data and something that processes the data into meaningful and useable knowledge. Traditionally this data or information processing was done by the human but increasingly it is done by digital technologies such as algorithms or software. It is the processed data that becomes knowledge and gives the owner power. Until recently, information or data processing was laborious and limited to a select few. In such a system it was the minority with resources who held power resulting from knowledge (Pareto's 20%). Traditionally a ruler with his information network could manage and control his subjects. Modern leaders however struggle to hold an advantage over well-informed citizens. The Rothschilds, for example, were reputed to have a more efficient messaging service than the governments they dealt with and this gave them an enormous advantage (Ferguson, 2009, pp.86-88). Digital networked technologies change the knowledge-power balance because information flows more freely between connected elements, be they human or non-human, and information is readily available to the majority. Social networking resulted in a dramatic shift of knowledge-power towards the majority, the long tail, who have become active contributors to the knowledge base as well as becoming prolific information seekers. Digital networked technologies have enabled the majority to be supportive or disruptive to authorities in an unprecedented way. This effectiveness is contributing to a change in the individuals' sense of self-worth. Leaders should not dismiss this change in the knowledge power relationship because; in conjunction with other factors, it is changing the expectations of the individuals' they are leading (Spencer-Scarr, 2013). While this change is experienced at an individual level it is having a major social impact because it uses technology for leverage.

Mass customization is the production of goods and services with near mass production efficiency, to meet individual customer's needs (Internet WorldStats) while retaining "monetary price similar to those of mass-produced products" (Fertile, 2013). This strategy creates an increased value perception in the customer because their specified needs or wants are being met "without trade-offs in cost, delivery and quality" (Valz, 2006). When this is combined with global 'me-centric advertising', typified by L'Oreal's "because I'm worth it" slogan which began in the mid-2000s, one can see how the general public develop a heightened sense of increased worth. The 'me-marketing' surge and the online social media explosion started in tandem. The public could not only access information but they could easily share and comment on information. They had a platform and could be heard. The long tail could express themselves and they were being heard by the world who would customize products for their perceived needs. At the same time traditional mass marketing was supporting their increased sense of self-worth with the 'me-centric advertising' creating a heady combination of entitlement, self-worth and self-promotion.

These real world social trends are being re-enforced and enhanced by digital technologies, resulting in major changes within the individual. More importantly the very nature of digital networks plays directly into the individuals' new found sense of self-worth by supplying a feedback loop of micro rewards. This results in heightened desire and the expectation of instant gratification.

The inherent nature of digital networked technologies has exacerbated the individuals' propensity for instant gratification in two ways. Firstly, by lowering the investment threshold to receiving gratification, thereby making it available to more people; and secondly by the way in which the rewards are dispensed. In the digital networked environment micro rewards are dispensed frequently and have been described by a number of subjects as a "treasure hunt" where each result or activity provides incentive for a subsequent action. For example, when probed on the question of why participant 'pk ' spent time engaged with the digital networks, the response was:

Its discovery ... its discovery...You go onto something...I did something the other day where I was looking up something and I ended up reading a film review and then from that film review, reading about the author, now the film review wasn't very good but they referred to the authors previous book on which it was based. They talked about the book and then they said that the book wasn't that great either but that his previous books had been very good and they mentioned one. So I went and looked him up and then I found one of the books that they said was good. Then I Ended up going onto Amazon and buying that book. So it's a process of discovery where you are led on from one thing to another and you think about other things as a result of that. And it just creates this whole area of interest and desire for knowledge. (Research participant pki2q3)

Samuel McClure and associates showed that immediate reward increased activity in areas of the brain that are heavily supplied by the dopamine system (Newlands, Anderson, & Mullin, 2003). Dopamine plays a major role in reinforcing behaviors by creating a sense of pleasure within the individual when released. The continuous micro rewards during online activity releases a steady stream of dopamine that result in an escalating sense of well-being: engagement deepens and intensifies. When contrasting this to the benefits of delayed gratification where motivation demands specific abilities of the individual to continually and accurately imagine the reward in order to delay gratification (McClure, Laibson, Loewenstein, & Cohen, 2004), it becomes easy to see how digital networks feed individuals need for instant gratification. Postponing pleasure for your future self becomes harder, your future self is a stranger to you (Parfit, 1971).

The frequently dispensed micro rewards that an individual receives after minimal cost investment, such as putting in a search query or sharing a photo, makes it difficult for the user to disengage. The process is iterative and thus reinforces the individuals' expectation of micro rewards: the desire and action leading to instant gratification. This is very different to the real world where chronological time and the friction of physical space imposes constraints on our expectations. The instant gratification of the digital environment is a powerful illustration of how a feedback-loop can have an amplifying effect on individuals' behavior. If the feedback-loop is put to good use in organizations, it can alter outcomes.

A CASE STUDY: ADAPTING TO CHANGE IN 2020

The following is a discussion on the adaptive nature of a sandstone college that not only survived but thrived during the 2020 Covid-19 pandemic by applying concepts discussed in this chapter.

The case in this study is a residential college associated with a leading Australian University. The college is a non-profit organization collaboratively run by an elected council, senior executives and the elected student body. The role of council, senior executives and administrative staff is to nurture and guide students in their elected leadership roles as they manage their environment and transition from school-leaver to graduate and beyond. The active role that students take in the management of the case is distinctly different from most other colleges where management tends to be authoritarian, hierarchal and student contribution is marginal. The discussion will now examine the case in context of the previous discussion leading to the significant adaptations made by the case that resulted in organizational growth despite the 2020 global pandemic and the closure of all colleges.

Case Study: Background

On entering St Andrews College, the physical environment imbues one with a feeling of tradition and stability to the point of rigidity and inflexibility. It's beautiful 'Hogwarts' like buildings scream out hierarchy, tradition and ritual, even mystery. It is a place that one is least likely to associate with adaption to change. That however is not the case!

St Andrews College was born out of the Scottish Enlightenment and embodies the principles of inclusion, resolution through discussion, equity and support. Today the college still adheres to the chief values of the Scottish Enlightenment: improvement, virtue, and practical benefit for the individual and society as a whole. In addition to this, the case proactively accommodates the most challenging concept of the Scottish Enlightenment: the rejection of any authority that could not be justified by reason. They have addressed this challenge by creating a 'student led' environment that gives students have an equal voice in running their college. This has attracted high achieving students in all fields of academia, sports and the arts. More importantly the 'student led' environment has attracted a large cohort of students with a desire to be a leader in their selected field. They are to seize the opportunities of this unique supportive environment where they can develop and hone their leadership skills in a meaningful way while studying in preparation for their future.

As with most other similar organizations St Andrew's College has had substantial time to address Maslow's basic survival needs; physiological, shelter and safety needs. The college is proficient in providing a home away from home for their students. In the last decade the college proactively moved towards developing Maslow's more ephemeral needs; relationships and belonging. The aim of this was to aid student leaders as they navigate the minefield of inherited college culture so that they could replace negative cultural behaviors and practices, used to create bonding and relationships, with behaviors and practices better suited to today's cultural climate of respectful inclusion. This was achieved by the leadership program, which develops student leaders' skills and abilities to create inclusive, tolerant, respectful, and safe environments for all college residents. In 2019 nearly half the student cohort participated in the leadership program, and about one third completed it. Completion of the program is a pre-requisite to stand for election.

In 2018 the college initiated the final stage identified in Maslow's needs by supporting research into challenges facing their students' transitions to college and then the workforce. Like many other organizations and institutes senior management was aware of a growing problem with their millennial cohort that was not understood. They took action and dedicated resources to research the problem and development of a solution. The starting point was implementing a three-year focus group study that provided information for the development of the initial program and then ongoing refinement.

Case Study: Methodology

In 2018 a three-year study of millennials began at the college using focus groups (2018, 2019 and 2020). The aim of the study was to identify what millennial students felt they needed in order to successfully transition to the workforce. Each focus group consisted of mixed year level, gender and field of study and was facilitated by a student but overseen by the lead researcher. The focus groups were video recorded, transcribed and all identifies were removed from transcript before analysis began. This research concluded in 2020 and includes the impacts of the Covid-19 pandemic shutdown. Final findings of the three year millennial study will only be available in 2021.

The first of three focus groups was conducted at the end 2018. Based on these outcomes of this focus group a two-part program was developed. Part 1 of the program was designed and implemented in 2019 to address identified extrinsic issues. Being oriented to extrinsic issues, the program was primarily face-to-face mentoring and relationship building events that brought together the millennial digital natives and other cohorts – all activities were real world based. These programs were very successful and provided participants with a sense of belonging, well-being, success and achievement. At the end of 2019, Part 2 of the program was trialed in the form of a small pilot program. Part 2 demonstrated the application of empirical research on which this chapter was based and addressed intrinsic issues identified in the 2018 focus group. Due to the Covid-19 pandemic shutdown, Part 2 was not offered to the wider college community as planned but was offered to student leaders as part of the leadership training program. The pilot program was well received with participants asking if they could participant again the full version in 2021.

Case Study: Discussion

Preliminary results of the focus group clearly indicated that, unlike most other similar research projects undertaken by other institutes, the cause of problems facing this cohort lay in issues previously discussed in the 2014 edition of this chapter and, in part, restated in this chapter. Focus Group participants were aware of problems they were facing and that the problems somehow related specifically to their generation, but they just did not know how to express themselves. Initially, focus group participants felt compelled to dismiss their concerns due to the common view that 'every generation feels that they are different'. It was only with deeper probing into their concerns by the facilitator who was their peer that the participants felt free to express their inner concerns.

To advance this discussion let us return to the three key observations pointed out at the beginning of this chapter that relate to the soft power of long tail leadership in organizations. The key observations being; The long tail is getting fatter, the long tail more assertive, and the long tail has expectations. These observations still hold but now they are being amplified by three Meta factors; Digital natives are now entering the workforce, duality of environment is now the norm, and the Pandemic Crisis has force the adoption of technology globally for all generations. In 2020 technology use became part of meeting basic human needs of security, stability and connectivity.

The Meta Factors

Digital natives have been exposed to digital networked technologies their entire life, they are the first humans to exist in a total duality of environments; the real world and the digital environment. Until now there has been a mix of generations in the long tail that has moderated some long tail behaviors. However now that digital natives are entering the workforce leaders can expect a dramatic amplification of long tail behaviors. Behaviors that stem from very different first principle concepts. Behaviors that result from differences in the way individual experience things. There will be increasing stresses at both ends of the long tail resulting from a lack of understanding. Leaders need to understand and accommodate differences that the dual environment creates on society and its expectations. Understanding will lead to adaptation and adaptation will lead to survival.

Leaders can expect increasing frustration from the long tail because the long tail will grow fatter with digital natives.

As the long tail fattens with digital natives there will be an increased expectation and demand for inclusion, understanding and tolerance. The changing concepts, altered behaviors, and way of experiencing things will be very different to any other cohort or time in history because this generation can only turn to their peer for full understanding and comprehension of their position. This, in is extreme could have led to a case of 'Lord of the files' with digital natives struggling to find their place in a duality of environment without experienced mentors. Leaders need to accept that these are indeed unusual times and that while they may lead, at times it would be wise for them to allow themselves to be led and accept the offerings of this unusual generation who are both children needing guidance and leaders of a new world.

There is however a silver lining. While the Covid 19 pandemic is undeniably a global catastrophe, it has helped avert many of the potential problems discussed in the initial publication of this chapter. The potential problems being those stemming from non-digital natives having to lead in a known, comfortable and tangible environment while adapting to the complexities of an unknown ephemeral environment that is adjusting human behavior.

Pandemic Crisis

Within a matter of a few month cities and countries shut down to prevent spread of the virus and minimize the death rate. It was a situation that challenged the fundamental needs of humans; would they get the virus and die, how could they work to get food and shelter. As leaders in businesses, institutes and governing bodies addressed these basic issues, humans began needing Maslow's third identified need, relationships and a sense of belonging.

Humans were in crisis, the world they knew and understood was collapsing! Solution – take it all online! As reports are showing globally 'going online' is not always an easy or successful process. St Andrew's College presents a different story. The college thrived and has come through 2020 stronger. How was this achieved!

Leadership: Being a student-led community this long tail of digital natives led in an environment in which they were familiar. They took the lead in community building in the online space, not the predominantly non-digitals of the staff and executive council who were adapting to the changed circumstances.

Understanding: The underpinnings of the college's move online was based on research discussed in this chapter and the program developed in 2018. As the 2018 program was designed to operate in a duality of environment its methodology was adopted and adapted by other aspects of the college community . In practical terms this meant that non-digital native staff and council leaders would facilitate an online environment in which the students could lead and develop solutions to overcome the challenges faced during the unfolding pandemic. The long tail of students and in some instances staff were given an opportunity to take the creative lead and rapidly implement solutions that could be rapidly adapted to changing situations.

This resulted in a range of activities from mentoring sessions and educational talks to academic tutorials for both college students and for the wider community where college students tutored struggling high school students for free. The mental well-being of students was maintained by student leaders who conducted weekly catchups online with students, reporting back to admin staff who tracked community connectivity to ensure no-one was left in isolation. Singing, music and creative arts groups moved online which resulted in student's development of new online skills. Sports training continued in isolation but student sport leaders' maintained communication and motivation, reporting back to admin staff to ensure mental well-being. In the real world environment, the non-digital natives led the way with student leaders taking their direction. Senior management set Covid compliance processes and procedures and student leaders implemented them, reporting back if needed.

Awareness: The College took on board research insights regarding adaptation to the duality of environments and focused the energy of student leaders. Guidance from staff resulted in amazing outcomes from the student led programs where different online value exchanges led to rewarding real world outcomes like retention of students through the pandemic and the exceedingly high enrolment for 2021. The agility of senior management was also important. They did not resist appropriating technology to address the situation but retained the good sense to not use it in every instance.

The last point related to awareness is still a work in progress but there are indicators that it is heading in the right direction. This is the identification and igniting of individuals motivators because if the motivation is based on deeply held values and principles of the individual then they and all that they do is more likely to be successful. This is Part 2 of the program which was offered to student leaders at St Andrews College in October of 2020.

HOW THE LONG TAIL CHALLENGES THE LEADER

After considering the fundamental changes taking place, the many ways that the long tail challenges the leader now becomes clearer and can be grouped in the following way; duality of concepts, different human expectations, new value exchanges, agility and motivation.

Duality of concepts: On a daily basis the long tail is confronted with two core concept-bases. This duality, which was extensively discussed in the previous section 'The Pivotal Role Of Technology', affects both individual and societal behavior. The challenge for the leader with regard to this duality of core concept-bases is to be aware that the individual is exposed to and responding to this duality whether the individual is aware of it or not.

Humans are in the process of adaptation to a duality of concepts and leaders can use this understanding to their advantage.

Different human expectations: Individuals in the long tail have a suite of expectations that are different to traditional expectations: They expect to be heard, instantly gratified and receive a continual stream of micro-rewards. This complex suite of expectations is a result of engagement with digital networked technologies. The individual expects to be heard because of mass customization, the 'me-centric' advertising and the capability of the individual to self-publish. The individual also expects to be instantly gratified because engagement with technology results in a series of micro rewards each of which release a small amount of dopamine in the individual. Each dopamine dump creates a micro sense of pleasure that results in a feeling of instant gratification. This iteration of micro-rewards has the potential to change individuals' behavior. This creates a risk. Conditioning humans to expect instant gratification potentially places the individuals' endeavors and goals at the mercy of the manipulators: addictive games are typical of this. The leader must find a way of accommodating these expectations if they wish to release the energy and activism of individuals to their advantage. Digital networked technologies have provided the individual with a low cost means of being heard and being able to mobilize like-minded individuals.

Leaders who wish to focus and direct activist energy to their advantage need to understand this.

New value exchanges: In traditional hierarchal systems rewards are dispensed from the top making it easy to identify leaders from those being led. In the long tail this is more difficult because value exchanges are different and rewards are not obvious. Value exchanges that are not resource rewards make it problematic for traditional leaders to identify motivators. The leader could start by trying to understand individuals' filters (personality, decision-management and engagement) and thus be better placed to orchestrate successful outcomes. In the long tail value-exchanges are often abstract and ephemeral. As such leaders could potentially use them at low cost. On the other hand, a momentum against a leader's objectives could be unleashed by the long tail using value exchanges that the leader may not be able to counter. Dealing with this will be a challenge for leaders because the ubiquitous embedding of digital networked technologies is growing the long tail in new and unprecedented ways.

Understanding the individual and that digital value exchanges do not necessarily conform to traditional reward systems may provide insights in how to lead the long tail.

Agility: A prominent feature of the long tail is agility, which allows the individual to rapidly change not only direction of thought and pursuit but also technology. Participants likened information seeking to a treasure hunt, changing direction in a web like fashion as information piqued their interest. In many ways this has conditioned a short attention span in the long tail who are more easily redirected to the 'new big thing'. For example: If your business is under siege for some 'social justice' issue then it may only last until the next social justice scandal fills the pages of the media and diverts attention. A word of caution though as the digital environments long memory and the inability to "burn the evidence" does mean that leaders need to remain true to their own inner values and respond with consideration. The rapid introduction and easy deployment of new technology, particularly with regard to Apps provides a steady stream of opportunities and problems for the leader.

Awareness of this agility can prepare the leader in resisting and appropriating technology and situations. The leader need not respond to every issue, if they do they should be mindful of the long tail's response.

Motivation: The long tail is driven by personal motivation. Individuals will work tirelessly to achieve a perceived worthwhile end as illustrated in the previously discussed Grobanite example. Another example is the Boston marathon bombing in 2013 where the rapid mass processing of digital imagery led to the quick identification and capture of the perpetrators. This exemplifies some advantages of a bottom-up transparent lateral system that could be useful to leaders. Passion can also be fickle if it is not based on deeply help principles. The ability to link globally enables the long tail to reduce isolation and creates a power shift towards the long tail. On the other hand, this mass effect has inherent weaknesses, one of which is the blockbuster effect where a massive success can be so great that it deprives competing ideas or products of resources. For example, Hollywood blockbusters tend to cause production of similar films or series thereby reducing diversity and restricting smaller players.

Identification and igniting motivators can be advantageous to leaders, particularly if motivation of participants is based on deeply help principles.

From this discussion on how the long tail challenges leaders it is obvious that there is no easy answer. However, it is clear that by understanding the complexities of engaging with digital networked technologies and by being aware of their own engagement leaders can potentially use the soft power of the long tail to their advantage.

FUTURE RESEARCH DIRECTIONS

This discussion is based on ongoing empirical research into understanding engagement with digital networked technologies and its impact on social behaviors such as leadership. Based on research to date, future research directions are: 1) To refine the evaluation instrument to accommodate recent insights related to non-digital natives. 2) To refine the program to be more leader and industry specific. Discussions are underway to incorporate the instrument and associated program to enhance and develop the case study's leadership program so that their organizational memory and culture can be positively sustained.

CONCLUSION

The introduction of this chapter began with a broad view of the long tail phenomenon. It then continued with a contextualization of the long tail and leadership. This led to an in-depth look at elements affecting the long tail: technology as an environment and as a tool as well as the role of the individual and the adaptation process. Finally, the discussion moved to the emergence of a new type of long tail and explored how the long tail is affecting leaders. This chapter has been presented as a discussion to assist the leader in developing an understanding of the origin and nature of both the long tail and digital network technologies that are affecting traditional leadership styles.

Of all the challenges facing leaders of the long tail and the changing nature of the long tail is the greatest risk if using a one-size-fits-all solution. Considering the growing size and nature of the long tail this solution would not only be unsuccessful but could be detrimental to organizations in the future. If a leader is able to understand the long tail, digital networks and the role that they play, and match these to unique opportunities related to their organization, they have the potential to unleash the soft power of the long tail.

REFERENCES

Baber, C. (2003). Cognition and tool use: Forms of engagement in human and animal use of tools. London: Taylor & Francis CRC Press.

Baigorri, M. (2008, July 10). *Pentagon may start using Web 2.0*. Retrieved 11 July, 2008, from http://news.medill.northwestern.edu/washington/news.aspx?id=94823

Bavelier, D., Green, C. S., & Dye, M. W. G. (2010). Children wired for better and for worse. *Neuron*, *67*(September), 682–701. doi:10.1016/j.neuron.2010.08.03520826302 PMID:20826302

BBC Two. (Writer). (2007). Battle of the brains [Television Broadcast]. In Science & Nature: Horizon. United Kingdom: BBC.

Browne, M. (2008). *Gov 2.0 to delete e-gov in 2008*. Retrieved 16 August, 2008, from http://www.zdnet.com.au/news/business/soa/-Gov-2-0-to-delete-e-gov-in-2008/0,139023166,339285045,00.htm?feed=pt_government

Brynjolfsson, E., Hu, Y. J., & Simester, D. (2011). Goodbye Pareto Principle, hello long tail: The effect of search costs on the concentration of product sales. *Management Science*, *57*(8). Advance online publication. doi:10.1287/mnsc.1110.1371

Buxbaum, P. A. (2007). Web of tomorrow. *Military Information Technology Online Archives, 11*(5).

Callon, M., & Law, J. (1997). After the individual in society: Lessons on collectivity from science, technology and society. *Canadian Journal of Sociology*, *22*(2), 165–182. doi:10.2307/3341747

Carducci, B. J. (2009). *The psychology of personality: Viewpoints, research, and applications*. John Wiley and Sons.

Carr, N. (2009). *Big switch: Rewiring the world, from Edison To Google*. W. W. Norton & Company Inc.

Castells, M. (2010). *Rise of the Network society: The information age: Economy, society and culture* (2nd ed., Vol. 1). Blackwell Publishers, Inc.

Clark, D. (2007). *Web 2.0 gives birth to Politics 2.0*. Retrieved 7 July, 2008, from https://gigaom.com/2007/03/19/web-20-gives-birth-to-politics-20/

Cross, M. (2007, June 14). *Open the gates of information.* Retrieved 10 August, 2008, from http://www.guardian.co.uk/society/2007/jun/14/epublic

Deleuze, G., & Guattari, F. (1987). *A thousand plateaus: Capitalism and schizophrenia* (B. Massumi, Trans.). University of Minnesota Press.

Doidge, N. (2007). *The brain that changes itself.* Scribe Publications Pty. Ltd.

Ferguson, N. (2009). *The ascent of money: A financial history of the world.* Penguin Books.

Fertik, M. (2013). *The rich see a different Internet than the poor.* Retrieved from https://www.scientificamerican.com/article.cfm?id=rich-see-different-internet-than-the-poor

Frey, S. H. (2007). What puts the how in where? Tool use and the divided visual streams hypothesis. *Cortex, 43*(3), 368–375. doi:10.1016/S0010-9452(08)70462-317533760 PMID:17533760

Gibson, J. J. (1979). *The ecological approach to visual perception.* Lawrence Erlbaum Associates Inc.

Giddens, A. (2006). *Sociology* (5th ed.). Polity Press.

Goldberg, L. R., Johnson, J. A., Eber, H. W., Hogan, R., Ashton, M. C., & Cloninger, C. R. (2006). The international personality item pool and the future of public-domain personality measures. *Journal of Research in Personality, 40*, 84–96. doi:10.1016/j.jrp.2005.08.007

Graff, G. M. (2008). *McCain and the Internet: Why It matters.* Retrieved 2008, 2008, from https://www.washingtonian.com/blogarticles/people/capitalcomment/8815.html

Granick, J. (2006). *Saving democracy with Web 2.0.* Retrieved 27 July, 2008, from https://www.wired.com/software/webservices/commentary/circuitcourt/2006/10/72001

Greenemeier, L. (2008). *Lawmakers: Terrorists may tap same Web 2.0 Tools as military.* Retrieved from http://www.sciam.com/article.cfm?id=virtual-reality-military

Grobanites. (2011). *Grobanites for charity - Josh Groban 30th birthday donation.* Retrieved 24 June 2011, from http://grobanitesforcharity.org/

Gross, G. (2007). *Expert: U.S. military needs wikis, video-sharing*. Retrieved 26 July, 2008, from https://www.networkworld.com/news/2007/012407-expert-us-military-needs-wikis.html

Grossman, N. (2008, Jul 8). *Obama + Web 2.0 = A (presumptive) presidential nomination*. Retrieved 9 July, 2008, from http://www.bmighty.com/blog/main/archives/2008/07/obama_web_20_a.html

Heidegger, M. (1977). The question concerning technology (W. Lovitt, Trans.). In The Question Concerning Technology and Other Essays. New York: Garland Publishing Inc.

Internet host count history. (2013). Retrieved 08/01, 2013, from http://www.isc.org/solutions/survey/history

Internet World Stats. (2012, October 27). *The digital divide, ICT and the 50x15 initiative*. Retrieved 31 March, 2013, from https://www.internetworldstats.com/links10.htm

Johnson-Frey, S. H. (2003). What's so special about human tool use? *Neuron*, *39*, 201–204. doi:10.1016/S0896-6273(03)00424-012873378 PMID:12873378

Kapustka, P. (2006, December 27). *John Edwards' YouTube candidacy*. Retrieved 27 July, 2008, from http://newteevee.com/2006/12/27/john-edwards-youtube-candidacy/

Kraut, R. (2010). Aristotle's ethic. In E. N. Zalta (Ed.), The Stanford Encyclopaedia of Philosophy. Academic Press.

Leff, M. (2008, July 23). *American-Israel chamber of commerce announces first U.S.-Israel Web 2.0 business exchange: Empowering the connected enterprise*. Retrieved 24 July, 2008, from http://atlanta.dbusinessnews.com/shownews.php?newsid=163248&type_news=latest

Lewin, R. (1993). Complexity - Life on the edge of chaos. London: Phoenix.

Mayer-Schönberger, V. (2009). *Delete: The virtue of forgetting in the digital age*. Princeton University Press.

McClure, S. M., Laibson, D. I., Loewenstein, G., & Cohen, J. D. (2004). Separate neural systems value immediate and delayed monetary rewards. *Science*, *306*(503). Advance online publication. doi:10.1126cience.110090715486304 PMID:15486304

National Telecommunications and Information Administration. (1999). *Falling through the net: Defining the digital divide*. Retrieved from https://www.ntia.doc.gov/report/1999/falling-through-net-defining-digital-divide

Newlands, A., Anderson, A. H., & Mullin, J. (2003). Adapting communicative strategies to computer-mediated communication: An analysis of task performance and dialogue structure. *Applied Cognitive Psychology*, *17*, 325–348. doi:10.1002/acp.868

Pacini, R., & Epstein, S. (1999). The relation of rational and experiential information processing styles to personality, basic beliefs, and the ratio bias phenomenon. *Journal of Personality and Social Psychology*, *76*(6), 972–987. doi:10.1037/0022-3514.76.6.97210402681 PMID:10402681

Parfit, D. (1971). Personal identity. *The Philosophical Review*, *80*(1), 3–27. doi:10.2307/2184309

Pessach, G. (2008). Networked memory institutions: Social remembering, privatization and its discontents. *Cardozo Arts & Ent*, *26*, 71–149.

Reed, W. J., & Jorgensen, M. (2004). The double pareto-lognormal distribution – A new parametric model for size distributions. *Communications in Statistics. Theory and Methods*, *33*(8), 1733–1753. doi:10.1081/STA-120037438

Rooke, D., & Torbert, W. R. (2009). *Seven transformations of leadership. The Essential Guide to Leadership*. Harvard Business School.

Schroeder, B., Damouras, S., & Gill, P. (2010, February 23–26). *Understanding latent sector errors and how to protect against them.* Paper presented at the FAST '10: 8th USENIX Conference on File and Storage Technologies, San Jose, CA, USA.

Schultz, D., & Schultz, S. E. (1986). *Psychology and industry today: An introduction to industrial and organizational* (4th ed.). Macmillan Publishing Co, Inc.

Shear, M. D. (2019). How Trump Reshaped the Presidency in Over 11,000 Tweets. *The New York Times*. https://www.nytimes.com/interactive/2019/11/02/us/politics/trump-twitter-presidency.html

Shirky, C. (2010). *Cognitive surplus: Creativity and generosity in a connected age*. Penguin Books Ltd.

Smitsman, A. W. (1997). The development of tool use: Changing boundaries between organism and environment. In Evolving explanations of development: Ecological approaches to organism–environment systems (pp. 301–329). Washington, DC: American Psychological Association. doi:10.1037/10265-008

Snowden, D. (2003). Complex acts of knowing paradox and descriptive self-awareness. *Bulletin*, *20*(4), 23–28.

Snowden, D. J., & Boone, M. E. (2009). *A leader's framework for decision making. The essential guide to leadership*. Harvard Business School.

Spelke, E. S., Breinlinger, K., Macomber, J., & Jacobson, K. (1992). Origins of knowledge. *Psychological Review*, *99*(October), 605–632. doi:10.1037/0033-295X.99.4.6051454901 PMID:1454901

Spencer-Scarr, D. (2013). *Understanding digital networked technologies: Aiding resistance and appropriation of technology*. Paper presented at the Internet Research 14.0: Resistance and Appropriation, Denver, CO, USA.

Spencer-Scarr, D., & Raward, D. (in press). *Millennials and Transition from Tertiary Study to the Workforce and the Role of Professional Development for Students: A Longitudinal Qualitative Study. Case Study: St Andrew's College, Sydney Australia*. https://www.standrewscollege.edu.au/

Spencer-Scarr, D., & Wilson, H. (n.d.). *Annual Reflective Survey of Student Leadership Program. Case Study: St Andrew's College, Sydney Australia*. https://www.standrewscollege.edu.au/

St. Amant, R., & Horton, T. E. (2008). Revisiting the definition of animal tool use. *Animal Behaviour*, *75*(4), 1199–1208. doi:10.1016/j.anbehav.2007.09.028

Stalder, F. (2002, November 14-16). *The status of objects in the space of flows*. Paper presented at the Doors of Perception Conference, Amsterdam, The Netherlands.

Stelter, B. (2008, July 7). *The Facebooker who friended Obama*. Retrieved 9 July, 2008, from http://www.nytimes.com/2008/07/07/technology/07hughes.html?_r=2&ref=technology&oref=slogin&oref=slogin

The Oxford companion to philosophy. (1995). New York: Oxford University Press Inc.

Tynan, D. (2008, August 20). *Cool political sites for a Web 2.0 election year*. Retrieved 22 August, 2008, from https://www.computerworld.com/action/article.do?command=viewArticleBasic&taxonomyName=networking_and_internet&articleId=9113039&taxonomyId=16&intsrc=kc_feat

Vaidhyanathan, S. (2011). *The Googalization of everything: And why we should worry*. University of California Press.

Valz, D. R. (2006, June 26). *Dynamic pricing models for digital content*. Retrieved from http://appft1.uspto.gov/netacgi/nph-Parser?Sect1=PTO1&Sect2=HITOFF&d=PG01&p=1&u=/netahtml/PTO/srchnum.html&r=1&f=G&l=50&s1=20080154798.PGNR

van Lawick-Goodall, J. (1970). Tool-using in primates and other vertebrates. In Advances in the study of behavior (pp. 195–249). New York, NY: Academic Press.

Visvanathan, S. (2001). *Knowledge and information in the network society*. Paper presented at Globalization - A Symposium on the Challenges of Closer Global Integration, Delhi, India.

Wolfgang, K. (2001). *The mentality of apes* (E. Winter, Trans.). Routledge.

ADDITIONAL READING

Aguiton, C., & Cardon, D. (2007). The Strength of Weak Cooperation: An Attempt to Understand the Meaning of Web 2.0. *Communications & Stratégies*, *65*, 51–65.

Bandura, A. (1986). *Socialfoundationsofthought and action: a social cognitive theory*. Prentice Hall.

Brocas, I., & Carrillo, J. D. (Eds.). (2003). *Psy chology and financial markets: Applications to understanding and remedying irrational decision making* (Vol. 1). Oxford University Press.

Frederick, S., Lowenstein, G., & O'Donoghue, T. (2003). Time Discounting and Time Preference: A Critical Review. In G. Loewenstein, D. Read, & R. F. Baumeister (Eds.), Time and Decision: Economic and Psychological Perspectives on Intertemporal Choice (pp. 13-86). New York: The Russell Sage Foundation.

Giddens, A. (2006). Sociology (5th ed.). Cambridge: Polity Press.

Hongladarom, S. (2002). The Web of Time and the DilemmaofGlobalization. *TheInformationSociety*, *18*(4), 241–249. doi:10.1080/01972240290075093

Lee, W. (1971). *Decision Theory and Human Behaviour*. John Wiley & Sons Inc.

Payne, J. W., Bettman, J. R., & Johnson, E. J. (1993). *The Adaptive Decision Maker*. Cambridge University Press. doi:10.1017/CBO9781139173933

Raban, D. R., & Rafaeli, S. (2007). Investigating ownership and the willingness to share informa tion online. *Computers in Human Behavior*, *23*(5), 2367–2382. doi:10.1016/j.chb.2006.03.013

Reed, E. S. (1996). *Encountering the World: Toward an Ecological Psychology*. Oxford University Press.

Stanovich, K. E. (2010). *Decision Making and Rationality in the Modern World*. Oxford University Press.

Tversky, A., & Kahnema, D. (1981). The Framing of Decisions and the Psychology of Choice. *Science. New Series*, *211*(4481), 453–458.

KEY TERMS AND DEFINITIONS

Activist – in Digital Context: Individuals who participate in the community and society at large taking action with an aim to improving circumstances. In the digital context this is displayed through people being involved with remote causes, forming pressure groups and participating with peers using a reduced real-world commitment of resources.

Black Swan Event: An unexpected event that is itself minor but profoundly changes our understanding of the world. For years it was assumed all swans were white and discovering black swans forced a reassessment of many assumptions.

Digital Networked Technology: It is increasingly difficult to meaningfully distinguish the technology devices, networks, hardware, and software. Therefore, for the purpose of this chapter the phrase *'digital networked technology'* encompasses the complex and dynamic system that makes up the network phenomenon that humans are currently experiencing.

Digital or Online Space: Unlike the real world where space can be passively occupied, in the digital environment an actor must proactively make and maintain activity in order to occupy space in any meaningful way.

Digital or Online Time: In the real-world time is experienced sequentially in a linear way. Time in the digital environment is experienced in a web like fashion and resources are expected to be immediately at hand. It is also seen to be eternal, fragmented, and de-sequenced.

Duality of Concepts: The digital network environment challenges some basic human concepts such as time and space. A *'duality of concepts'* is where the human is exposed to and expected to operate with the contradictory rules of both conceptual frameworks simultaneously.

Long Tail Distribution: The long tail is traditionally associated with a statistical distribution, usually the Pareto principal, where approximately 80% of items in the distribution are accounted for by the first 20%. The tapering of the distribution was named a tail. The Long tail in its contemporary context was first used by Clay Shirky in 2003 and then popularized by Chris Anderson in 2004. It has been noted that the approximately 20% of the tail is behaving in new ways.

Soft Power: There is currently an increasing appreciation of the benefit of leading through influence, by persuasion and example and with the threat of force well hidden. This is seen in political, social and group interactions. The use of soft power requires co-operative techniques such as diplomacy and negotiation.

ENDNOTES

1 The term activist is used not in a purely political sense but rather as indicating someone who is prone to taking action.

2 In this discussion we are only considering the physical location of the tool in relation to the human or environment not the externality of human *cognition* as explored in the fields of philosophy, cognitive science and artificial intelligence.

Chapter 5
Open Innovation Strategies in SMEs:
Development of a Business Model

Hakikur Rahman
Ansted University Sustainability Research Institute, Malaysia

ABSTRACT

Open innovation in enterprises has already obtained its acceptance at all levels of the business industry for adding worth to the business. The value could be in the form of economic expanse or enhancement of knowledge leading to a sustained financial base. Open innovation adopts various strategies to accomplish the task for enhancing the value gain. Varying by size, nature, pattern, or characteristics of the firm, various strategies are being adopted by enterprises. Though largely known to be familiar in corporate business houses, in recent years, open innovation is also becoming increasingly recognizable in small and medium enterprises (SMEs), and the trend is rapidly escalating. However, despite the potency of open innovation strategies, most of the enterprises are yet to find a sustained business model, especially for the SMEs working at the outmost periphery of that value chain. This chapter is trying to formulate a business model incorporating partnership approach from academia, research houses, intermediaries, practitioners, and other stakeholders.

INTRODUCTION

Open innovation has emerged as a new paradigm where firms commercialize external and internal ideas, knowledge, expertise and or technologies and use both external and internal resources. In an open innovation process, models can be launched by taking

DOI: 10.4018/978-1-7998-4799-1.ch005

ideas from internal or external sources and new technology can enter at various stages of the development process. Models can also go to the market in many ways, such as out-licensing of intellectual property or a spin-off venture in addition to traditional sales channels. Usually, open innovation combines internal and external ideas into architectures and systems whose requirements are typically defined by a business model. Eventually, the business model utilizes both external and internal ideas to generate business value, while defining internal mechanisms to claim some portion of that value (Chesbrough, 2003a: xxiv; West, Vanhaverbeke & Chesbrough, 2006). This notion of open innovation, was initially proposed by Chesbrough (2003a; b) and has rapidly gained the interest of both researchers and practitioners, illustrated by a number of special issue publications, dedicated conferences and a fast growing body of literature (Fredberg, Elmquist & Ollila, 2008). This new paradigm inspires enterprises to find the most appropriate business model to commercialize novel products or services, regardless of the existence of any model within the enterprise or must be sought externally (De Jong, Vanhaverbeke, Kalvet & Chesbrough, 2008).

The initiative of open innovation assumes that corporate innovation activities are more like an open system than the conventional (20thcentury) vertically integrated model. It was developed based on the observation of a handful of (large) innovative companies and their deviations from traditional exercise. In some respects, the open innovation model can be seen as a call to a return to the late 19th and early 20th century model of innovation, with a rich, diverse market for technology and small, external oriented R&D labs. Research on obtaining innovations includes searching, enabling, filtering, and attaining each category with its own specific set of mechanisms and conditions. Incorporating innovations has been mostly studied from an absorptive capacity perspective, with less attention given to the impact of competencies, society and culture (including not-invented-here). Commercializing innovations puts the most emphasis on how external innovations create value rather than how firms capture value from those innovations. Therefore, the interaction phase considers both feedback for the linear process and reciprocal innovation processes such as co-creation, network collaboration and community innovation (West and Bogers, 2014).

Depending on the demand and reality, open innovation is based on various principles. Among them, the prime ideology could be the necessity to tap external knowledge to enrich the knowledge of the internal experts; the second could be the essentiality of external R&D for an enterprise to generate significant value; the next could be the trend of research that may not be completely dependent on internal resources and profit would be the main aim of entrepreneurship, irrespective of the ideas; and the important one is the acquisition of strategies that are built on a sustained business model, before reaching to the market. (Chesbrough, 2003b; 2003c; De Jong, Vanhaverbeke, Kalvet & Chesbrough, 2008). Apart from other functions, the business model creates value within the value chain and captures a part of it for the focal firm (Chesbrough, 2006b).

The innovative conception of open innovation identified two modes of knowledge flow: the inbound (or "inside-out") and the outbound (or "outside-in") flow. However, the outbound mode is not directly related to user innovation, and so is not discussed further in this study. The inbound mode of open innovation involves the exploitation of purposive inflows of knowledge to accelerate internal innovation. Such a model combines externally and internally developed technologies to produce an offering that is commercialized by the focal company. Hence, key steps of this process include searching for external innovations, selecting and acquiring suitable innovations, integrating them into the firm's R&D efforts, and bringing them to market (West and Bogers, 2014; Chesbrough, Vanhaverbeke and West, (Eds.). 2014).

In terms of recognizing the effect of culture, or business culture with open innovation, this research has dig into a little. It has found that from the philosophy of open innovation to open innovation culture, there is a call for to conquer the inverted U-shaped curve of open innovation effects, which can also be called the open innovation paradox. Currently, in the 4th Industrial Revolution, the dynamics of open innovation are rapidly escalating with the explosion of the open innovation paradox, which also means open innovation complexity. In these circumstances, the requirement to understand culture, which can control open innovation dynamics, is being augmented. Therefore, some research want to answer the following research question that are noted in this study: How can one define or organize the culture for open innovation dynamics, which can motivate open innovation dynamics, and control the open innovation paradox or open innovation complexity? (Yun, et. al., 2016; Formica and Curley, 2018; Lee, et. al., 2018; Yun, Won and Park, 2016; Yun and Liu, 2019; Yun, Won and Park, 2018; Yun, et. al., 2020).

However, as this study has found, open innovation business model for small and medium scale enterprises (SMEs) is scant. This could be due to the scarce resources of the SMEs community, despite their major contribution in economy and job market, especially in Europe and other developed economies of the world. Furthermore, due to any acceptable and experimentally verified business model most of the developing and transitional economies are also not in a befitting situation in adopting open innovation strategies in their business model.

This chapter intends to establish an open innovation business model synthesizing various other business models that are being developed by contemporary researchers and being adopted and accepted by leading enterprises, though hardly they could be designated as SMEs. But, it is expected that with initial support from the parent entities, the spin-off firms can take significant leaps in strengthening their business engines. Along this perspective, the chapter has developed a business model incorporating crucial supports from all stakeholders in a two tier process. Later on the chapter has focused on a few research and practice challenges and hints on future research aspects before the conclusion.

BACKGROUND

Innovation can be termed as the outcome of a set of activities that utilizes knowledge to create new value to those benefiting from its use (De Sousa, 2006). It is clear that successful innovation under complexity, uncertainty and transformation can only be achieved through collaborative approaches that integrate knowledge inside and outside the enterprise. This model, in turn more popularly known as open innovation business model, is being increasingly used by enterprises throughout the world. It has been observed that this format of open innovation business model is a must for SMEs, which usually lack knowledge of competiveness to fully comply with the innovation process. It has also been observed that larger organizations are increasingly moving away from their traditional R&D approach to a more collaborative approach, varying in nature and context (De Sousa, 2008).

Open innovation reflects the ability of firms to gain access to not only external resources but also utilizing internal resources of innovations using a defined business model to acquire the business value from such innovations (West, 2006). However, for firms seeking to gain additional revenues through open innovation predominantly depends on two factors. Firstly, in strict sense, technology licensing depends on the firm's intellectual property (IP) strategy, which defines the role of the IP for the innovator and for the licensee(s). Secondly, in specific sense, the innovator must develop a business model consistent to the value of the IP and the innovator's positioning in the value network (Chesbrough & Rosenbloom, 2002; West, 2006). Therefore, a firm's business model depends not only on its IP and the value proposition (explicit factors) (Chesbrough & Rosenbloom, 2002; Chesbrough, 2003a), but also on the corresponding business models of the suppliers, customers, competitors and intermediaries (implicit factors) within the value network (West, 2006).

The open innovation business model entails that enterprises can and should use both internal and external ideas and knowledge to advance their innovation processes. It also demands that internal ideas can be taken to the market through external channels (for example, spin-offs, external licensing of intellectual property, or other forms of technology exploitation) to generate additional business value. This new paradigm also inspires enterprises to find the most appropriate business model to commercialize new products or services, regardless whether that model exists within the enterprise or must be taken from external sources (De Jong, Vanhaverbeke, Kalvet & Chesbrough, 2008).

However, this newly evolved business trend is driven by two major factors. Firstly, market democratization is increasing the micro-segmentation and demanding more customized solutions in unexpected, challenging and unpredictable circumstances, which require a higher level of interactions and participations of customers, suppliers and other stakeholders. Secondly, the increasing competitive pressure around the globe and shortened product life-cycles is demanding quicker innovation processes at a reduced cost for the existence and survival of entities of small enterprises.

Examples of innovations developed through open business models proliferate in the livelihood of people at large, ranging from the new mobile phone application, gaming products to new lines of potato chips. This desegregation of the traditional innovation process, requiring internal and external knowledge, has opened space for the emergence of new business models and types of entrepreneurships. Some of these new companies act as 'knowledge brokers' or 'intermediaries', providing the links, knowledge sources and even technical knowledge and expertise, so that firms can accelerate and amplify the effectiveness of their innovation processes (De Sousa, 2008).

The contemporary literature on open innovation (OI) has dealt mainly with large enterprises active in R&D-intensive industries. This has assisted to identify the multi-faceted phenomenon of OI and to reach a richer understanding of how the management and organization of innovation is changing in these companies (OECD, 2008). Furthermore, as suggested by Chesbrough and Crowther (2006), the literature on OI has narrowed in on firms that are active in low-tech industries. With the noteworthy exceptions of Laursen and Salter (2006), Lee et al. (2010) and Vande Vrande et al. (2009), few researchers have paid attention to OI in SMEs and how the utilization of OI practices in SMEs and the benefits derived from them differ from the employment of OI in large enterprises. This study notes the research of Van de Vrande et al. (2009) that focusses on the differences between SMEs and their large counterparts to stress the unique manner in which OI practices contribute to SME performance. Similarly, Lee et al.(2010) also addressed the input of intermediaries as part of the network of a firm. Therefore, this study emphasizes on the fact that by including different dimensions of OI in the analysis can strengthened the research parameters. Moreover, in distinguishing these different dimensions of OI one also extend the review as Dahlander and Gann (2010) who examined a large body of OI literature and contributed significantly to the understanding of what different types of 'openness' entail.

To this end, recent studies in the innovation and technology management domain have proposed several prospective benefits of opening up the innovation process. As found in the literature, this is described as a shift from the traditional or "closed" innovation model, with a main focus on internal research and development (R&D), toward an "open innovation" approach (Chesbrough 2003;Gassmann 2006;

Lichtenthaler 2011). In real meaning, firms engaging in open innovation actively utilize and exploit inward and outward transfer of knowledge and technologies (Chesbrough, Vanhaver-beke, and West 2006). The notion that firms in general and SMEs in particular may benefit from tapping into external resource bases is not novel, but specific knowledge about the effect of different open innovation activities remains limited. Therefore, in this study, it has shed light on which open innovation activities SMEs can engage in to spawn their own innovation efforts (Parida, Westerberg and Frishammar, 2012).

The next section, which is the main trust of the chapter, is focusing on the concept of open innovation business model, discussing about the basis for a business model and developing an open innovation business model using a flexible partnership approach.

BUSINESS MODEL

Basis for a Business Model

A business model can be described as the design of the value creation and capture mechanisms needed to yield profit. One may contend that for a business model to be viable in turbulent and hypercompetitive environments, its dynamics are important and must leverage, out of all key business model modules proposed in different studies, on a combined value and network perspective. However, these different elements present, distinctive challenges for small innovative companies and at the same time larger firms. Moreover, the business model of small firms is sited in the business models of their partners, big companies in actual situations (Gay, 2014).

As a new way of conceptualizing innovation, open innovation business model relaxes many of the assumptions presumed in the Chandlerian model (Chandler, 1990), both in the external supply of innovation to be incorporated into a firm's offerings, as well as the potential demand from outside the firm for its internal innovations. However, this does not mean that any innovation model is feasible, any more than the rise of the Internet and WWW, which meant that any 'e-strategy' was profitable. Moreover, experimentation within the open innovation paradigm has the constraint of establishing a business model for creating or using an innovation strategy, a constraint that may have been obscured by the cross-subsidies often seen with vertical integration (West, Vanhaverbeke & Chesbrough, 2006).

Open innovation as a business management model is currently gaining grounds in many industries. Among them pharmaceutical, consumer products, software, information technology, and a few service sectors are leading the global business. In this aspect, balancing the right size and structure of R&D has become one of main objectives in R&D management today (Chesbrough, 2003a; Gassmann & Reepmeyer, 2005; Gaule, 2006). Based on his own consulting model for open innovation, Gaule (2006) builds heavily on Chesbrough (2003a) to analyze the impact of open innovation on several parts of the organization. He further provides a series of short case studies, for example on Procter & Gamble. Motzek (2007) points to the motivation factors for companies to engage in open innovation. His empirical material is based on two organizations that are based on the ideas of open innovation. This sample is most likely different in character from already established companies that change to embrace open innovation. His motivation factors are rather similar to the general knowledge on motivation factors for entrepreneurs (Fredberg, Elmquist & Ollila, 2008).

Along these contexts, research on open innovation suggests that companies benefit differentially from adopting open innovation strategies; however, it is yet unclear why this is so. One possible explanation is that companies' business models are not attuned to open strategies (Saebi and Foss, 2015). Moreover, because of the acceleration of the second IT revolution and the deepening of the knowledge-based economy, the characteristics of the connected economy that can be linked to markets and technologies in the world are intensified. This means that the necessity of new business models for access to new markets and new business models created by the combination of technologies and markets is being intensified more than ever (Yun, Yang and Park, 2016). Henceforth, the transfer of knowledge plays an important role in innovation and growth. Therefore, emphasis on culture contributes to the innovation, but the balanced way to create culture leads to better transfer and exploitation of knowledge produced by universities in order to stimulate innovation. In (Buckley-Golder et al., 2015) it is defined a business model need to include these five stages: Company Opportunity, Co-Recognition (identifying the business needs), Co-Formulation (focus on meeting the needs and opportunities of the business partner), Co- Creation (partners create opportunity for innovation processes, products or markets), and Commercialization (main purpose of industrial partners is the commercialization) (Ivascu, Cirjaliu and Draghici, 2016).

Chesbrough (2007) argues that a business model has two functions, it creates value and it captures a portion of that value, and that open business models enable enterprises to be more competent in creating and capturing value. He also argues that companies need to adapt their business models to open innovation, as it is a way of generating value from their intellectual property (Chesbrough, 2003c). Chesbrough (2007) further argues that the rising costs of technology development and the shortening product life cycles make it harder for enterprises to justify innovation investments. Using open business models, a firm can beat the cost side through leveraging on external R&D resources to save time and money and at the same time, beat the revenue side by licensing out internal technologies. He also argues that enterprises need to develop their capabilities to experiment with their business models, for instance through alternative brands or spinoffs (to reduce risks) and fundamental changes that require top commitment and support (Chesbrough, 2007; Fredberg, Elmquist & Ollila, 2008).

According to Chesbrough and Schwartz (2007), co-development partnerships are increasingly important in open innovation models. This is in line with Chiaromonte (2006), who argues that the difference of open innovation to traditional outsourcing of innovative capacity is that the outside partners are not seen as suppliers but as peers. Chesbrough and Schwartz (2007) also point out that the use of partners can create business models that reduce R&D expenses, expand innovation output and open up new markets (Fredberg, Elmquist & Ollila, 2008).

For a business model, using partnership approach as mentioned earlier, Fredberg, Elmquist and Ollila (2008) underline the flow chart shown in Figure 1, illustrating the partnership approach in an enterprise.

Figure 1. Illustrating the partnership approach in an entrepreneurship

At first, define the business objectives for partnering

⇩

Then, classify the R&D capabilities of the firm, focusing their core capacity (key source of advantage); critical capacity (vital to success but not key); and contextual capacity (needed to complete the offering, but not differentiator), and

⇩

Finally, align the business models of the two firms.

Based on the above arguments and arguments made by Chesbrough and Rosenbloom (2002), authors like to introduce another flow chart (see Figure 2) illustrating the formulation of innovation strategy in an open innovation business model.

Development of the Business Model

It has been observed that open innovation is increasingly being introduced in international and national organizations for the creation of value. Open innovation is now a practical tool, requiring new strategies and decisions from managers for the exploitation of innovative activities. The basic question that this study seeks to answer is linked to the practice of open innovation in connection with the open business model geared towards the creation of value in marginal companies, as such the small

Figure 2. Shows the formulation of innovation strategies

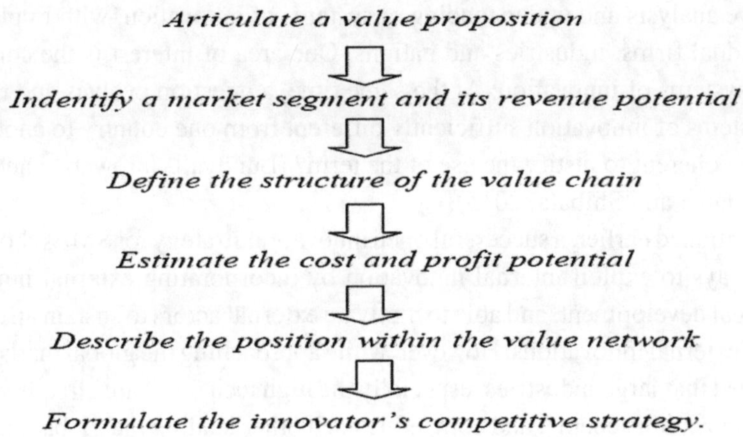

and medium enterprises (SMEs). The study finds that internal sources of knowledge, external sources of knowledge and accentuate working partnerships were adopted by company as strategies to offer resources to change the open business model in order to create value (Alves Aranha, Prado Garcia and Corrêa, 2015). Furthermore, the business model not only creates value within the innovation chain, but also enables the focal actor to capture at least some of that value. Accordingly, the handling of intellectual property rights questions becomes relevant to the ability and willingness of commercial actors to invest resources and undertake risky activities in hopes of developing a successful new process, product, or service (Chesbrough, H. (2015).

Till to date, most of the studies on open innovation business model have examined open innovation at the organizational level, basically for two reasons. Firstly, innovation is traditionally being conceived as the outcome of deliberate actions of a single entrepreneur, and thus R&D competition has also been styled as an innovation race between two or more entrepreneurs. Secondly, the value of a technological invention is realized only through a business model of the enterprise (Chesbrough & Rosenbloom, 2002). While it is very natural that the open innovation business model may easily spill over the boundaries of an enterprise or even an industry (West, Vanhaverbeke, & Chesbrough, 2006).

Along with the appearance of phenomena such as value co-creation, firm networks, and open innovation, open business models have achieved growing attention in contemporary researches. However, most of the scholars from different fields use the open business model, largely without providing a definition. This has led to an overall lack of clarity of the concept itself. Based on a comprehensive review of scholarly literature in the field, commonalities and differences in the perceived nature of the open business model are carved out (Weiblen, 2014). In addition, a number of frameworks have been developed by scholars in recent years in order to improve analysis and understanding of systems of innovation, with implications for individual firms, industries and nations. One area of interest is the concept of national systems of innovation. At the same time, a question evolves and remains, as are systems of innovation sufficiently different from one country to another and internally coherent to justify the use of the term? (Lundvall, Jurowetzki and Lema, 2014; Kodama and Shibata, 2015).

As mentioned earlier, a successful open innovation strategy for SMEs should find creative ways to exploit internal innovation by incorporating external innovation into internal development, and able to motivate external actors to sustain an ongoing stream of external innovations. However, while approaching the global market, it can be observed that large industries, especially the high tech ones, are already involved in open innovation scheme, and competing each other leading the global market. In terms of SMEs with high tech facilities, often generated from universities or research center, they would like to maintain good links to larger organizations, rather than reaching out to the grass roots. On the contrary, SMEs at the local level, equipped with low tech facilities are loosely motivated to promote research, and may not have sufficient resources to identify their needs for innovation through appropriate market analysis, and act accordingly to a defined innovation scheme. The situation becomes more challenging without an appropriate and adaptive business model (West & Gallagher, 2006; Rahman & Ramos, 2010).

An appropriate and adaptive business model may be seen as the totality of how a company selects its clients, defines and differentiates its responses; classifies those tasks it will perform itself and those it will outsource; configures its resources, goes to market, creates utility for clients; and get hold of profits. It is the entire system for delivering utility to clients and gaining a profit from that activity (Pourdehnad, 2007). Figure 3 shows a relationship diagram with the various actors or stakeholders involved in a business model. This evidently envisages the clear bonding among visible groups of stakeholders among the business communities (a partnership approach).

Triple Helix Model (see Figure 4) is another highly discussing model in this arena. According to this model, a spiral of innovation involves government, university, and industry in multiple reciprocal relationships, to create a flexible overlapping innovation system (another partnership approach) (CSR Europe, 2008).

This research would like to point out another business model that may be utilized in SMEs OI process, which has been developed incorporating mixed approach (see Shorthouse, 2008). Figure 5 shows a mixed approach (amalgamated closed and open innovation approaches) business model. Shorthouse (2008) has suggested this as a joint effort to reach the niche market through using both closed and open innovation business model.

Figure 3. Relationship with the stakeholders in a business model
(Adopted from Pourdehnad, 2007)

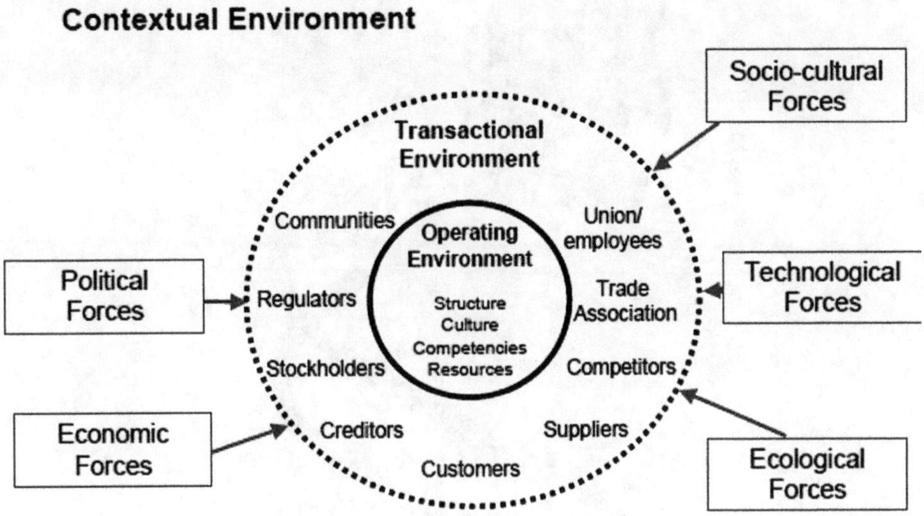

However, this study envisages, attaining a sustainable business model in SMEs exposed to open innovation, one need to follow the following two flow charts (see Figure 6, to find out how to prepare SMEs, and Figure 7, to learn about better positioning them).

Furthermore, a sustainable business model should also follow to the Figure 7.

This study further suggests, the business model should incorporate SMEs being inclusive in the following dimension (See Figure 8).

The proposed business model (to be adopted in a few selected SMEs after a multi-phase survey to be carried out in the next phase of this research) emphasizes on two tiers of relationship; among the core partners in the network (indicated as the core area of the business model) and among the peripheral partners in the network (indicated as the broader area of the business model). In the block, both the segments need not to be isolated from each other. Rather they may remain as active member of the entire community. Therefore, for sustained entrepreneurship the entire group must interact to the grass roots for effective dissemination of open innovation strategies promoting economic and value gain (Rahman & Ramos, 2010). However, while implementing open innovation strategies, despite the introduction of the proposed model, due to the intensity of the competition especially SMEs face tremendous shifting of model architectures adapting the open business environments. Hence, it is recommended that core partners within the network interact faster to provide timely feedback to the peripheral partners for obtaining optimum placement of the business model.

Figure 4. The triple helix model
(Adopted from CSR Europe, 2008b)

Challenges

The market and thus the industry are always changing, depending on the demand and also the supply. Patents may expire in due period or trademarks get updated in due course, exposing huge investment in challenge. Furthermore, open innovation may not be driven by scale or process, but rather by breakthrough science, or a better understanding of human dynamics validating new targets, which may be totally new or unfamiliar to the market. Therefore, the open innovation business model and its research practice must be updated dynamically to fit into the new realities (to suit the behavior of the end-user), which is extremely challenging for SMEs (Jaruzelski & Dehoff, 2008).

Figure 5. A mixed approach business model
(Adopted from Shorthouse, 2008)

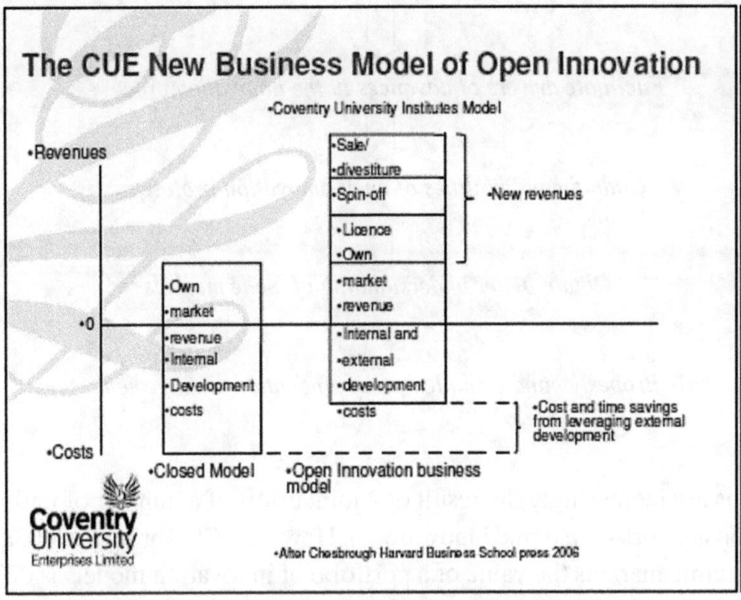

Figure 6. Preparing SMEs towards open innovation business model

Educate and raise SMEs awareness and knowledge

⇩

Identify SME needs

⇩

Facilitate interactions between SMEs & research organizations

⇩

Identify & source partners and opportunities

⇩

Prepare SMEs for successful collaboration

Open innovation systems (Chesbrough, 2003a) are characterized by the flexible way a firm coordinates a large number of innovation models and assess their value. The system is open, because some models come from outside and some internal models go outside. This approach is consistent with former studies that argue that

Figure 7. Positioning SMEs towards open innovation business model

Introduce both the closed and open innovation paradigms as optimized

⇩

Facilitate drivers of advances in the innovation process

⇩

Undo the possibilities of open innovation prototypes

⇩

Obtain better understanding of niche markets

⇩

Properly handle challenges of innovation management

innovations are increasingly the result of a joint effort of a number of multi-parties (innovation networks, systemic innovations). However, Chesbrough (2003a) argues that in dynamic markets the value of a portfolio of innovation models is difficult to estimate and thereby, that the value of patents – as a specific means to 'secure' an innovation's value – is very indeterminate. Moreover, the value of patents (and or

Figure 8. Building block of the proposed business model
(Author)

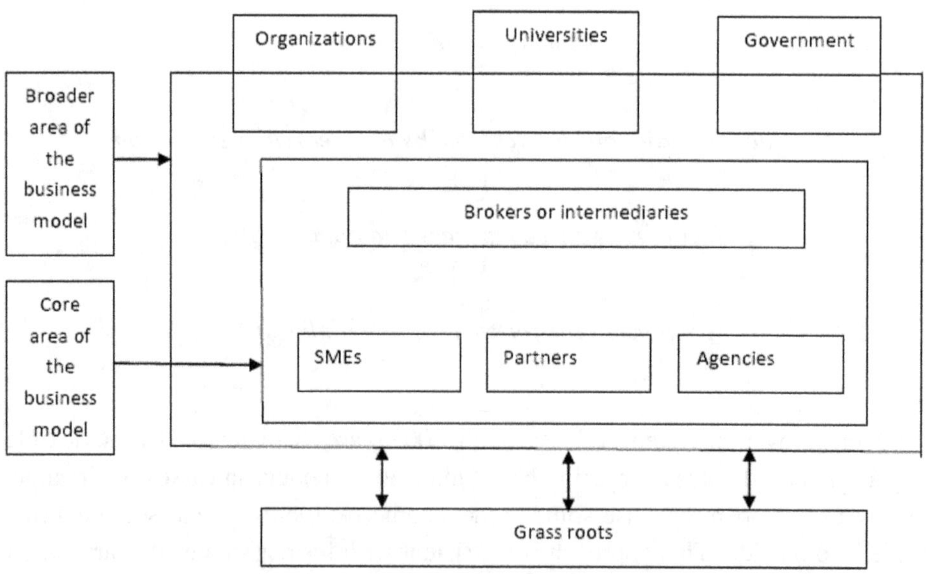

inventions) depends on the specific business model a firm uses to commercialize innovations. Hence, there are different modes of open innovation; they could be spin-offs from research, or out-licensees or technology exploiters. In addition to these, collaboration is not seen as a way out to all innovation problems, but as part of the portfolio in which some if not the majority of models is carried out by the single firm and other models are carried out in partnership with other firms (Dittrich, 2008). This situation exposes SMEs in challenging situations, as they are already exposed to scarce resources and the product life cycles are diminishing.

Among other challenges, the definition of open innovation itself is yet to be made clear-cut. What open innovation is and what it is not, is still being debated. Moreover, open innovation overlaps other concepts such as user generation, crowdsourcing, and distributed innovation. Even though research on open innovation has significantly grown in recent years, there are still many issues that need to be addressed to get insight about open innovation in various contexts. Studies are mostly performed in the context of large firms and in developed countries. Research in the context of developing countries is still almost an untouched spot. Open innovation in the small to medium-sized enterprises (SMEs) context has gained a foothold just very recently. It is crucial to explore some managerial challenges, such as technology transfer, inbound and outbound process, absorptive and disruptive capacity development, particularly in the global open innovation context and it is essential to investigate how open innovation can be implemented for sustainable development (Hossain, 2013).

Therefore, as a newly emerged field of research, open innovation for SME development deserves a prolonged and strategically developed qualitative and quantitative synthesis on available resources, including business models and business practices. Furthermore, while developing an open innovation business model, one should look into the detail of the fundamentals of the innovation process, including the innovation channel, the turn over and also looking into the socio-economic, organizational and cultural differences (Rahman, 2010). Inclusive of above challenges, open innovation for SMEs also deserves further emphasize in resolving issues, like sales, licenses, cash flow, and trust in business relationship; to fulfill the grass roots clientele base by understanding their demand; to develop a transparent business model that add value to it; and to combine appropriate knowledge and technology for building a pipeline of opportunities, enabling a broad-based B2B networking through a sustained organic growth (Rahman & Ramos, 2010).

FUTURE RESEARCH DIRECTIONS

Open innovation is still a moderately new area of research and many of the research questions underline the need to further explore the concept and how enterprises can transform and adapt to this new approach of including external knowledge, resources, and skills in their innovation strategies. The concept is reliant on the organizational and cultural context (Chesbrough, 2007; Fredberg, Elmquist & Ollila, 2008). Similarly, the business model based on the concept is dependent on the strategies and technologies. New technologies will tend to entail new business model. When the technology transforms from one state to another, the value proposition to customers, the value capture by the innovator firm or the relationship of the firm within the value network also transforms (West, 2006; West, Vanhaverbeke & Chesbrough, 2006).

The open innovation model suggests that ideas for innovations can also emerge or go on market from outside the company as well as from inside. The new model assumes that knowledge is spread widely and even the successful innovators with huge R&D resources have to look for the external sources of innovation (Chesbrough, 2006a; Chesbrough, 2006b). The open innovation leverages the role of R&D. Hence, the researchers' job is now, not only to create knowledge, but also to capture it from outside the company. Once a new innovation has taken place, the company can use several business models to bring it to the market. Even if they find that the technology is not suitable for the current business model, it can be licensed or donated to other companies or a new spin-off can be established targeting a new market (Chesbrough 2003a; Chesbrough, 2010). However, the future may reveal that, even if openness in the innovation process is decidedly encouraged there will always be need for some closeness, too (the mixed approach) (Christensen, Olesen & Kjaer, 2005; Viskari, 2006). Open innovation should also consider idea spillovers as a consequence of the company's business model. Spillover ideas are not considered as burden but as opportunities to expand the business model or spin-off a technology outside a firm with a different business concept (Hossain, 2013) .

CONCLUSION

As observed, open Innovation business models explores the capacity of partners to collaborate each other through technological exchanges, letting ideas flow out of the entrepreneurship in order to find better place for the innovation monetization, and flow into the entrepreneurship as new offerings and new business models (Chesbrough, 2003d; Chesbrough, 2006c). The study finds that, the application of open innovation business models implies high levels of competition due to the opportunity to enter into entirely new markets. At first sight it would not be clear to assume an open innovation business model in a multimarket competition environment, because these schemes rely on different objectives and different assumptions.

Hence, it can be mentioned that there is a deep relationship between these three factors (open innovation, complex adaptive systems, and evolutionary change) and they are arranged in a conceptual order based on the name of the model, not in a temporal order. Conceptually, open innovation at a firm goes through a complex adaptive system and then leads to evolutionary transformations. However, in reality, a specific complex adaptive system can trigger open innovation through evolutionary properties at any given firm (Yun, Won and Park, 2016). [c] Under the contemporary economic globalization, traditional closed innovation cannot meet the demand of enterprises for shorter R&D cycle and lower R&D cost. Consequently, enterprises have paid more attentions to open innovation in larger enterprises which is more important (Zhao, Sun and Xu, 2016). Furthermore, in spite of the popularity of open innovation, many firms still struggle to properly manage open innovation. While open innovation poses many new challenges to firms when adopted, it is the internal organizational challenges that are perceived as the most difficult to manage. Therefore, managing the journey from closed to open innovation implies several organizational transformations at various levels of the enterprise and making these transformations is difficult according to various researches (Vanhaverbeke, Chesbrough and West, 2014).

This study also finds and supported by another research (see Alcalde, 2009) that open innovation encourages industry competition through trust, confidence and transparent information interchanges. In this context, in order to avoid the competition, multimarket framework, on one hand, may develop threats and retribution mechanism. On the other hand, open innovation presents predominantly technological exchanges as the major driver of the model. Hence, it could be mentioned that traditional mutual self-control mechanisms would not work in open business models. Moreover, the development of technological exchanges among different market players would imply the penetration in entirely new markets. Thus, diversification would be the logical consequence of technological exchanges in open business models. In conclusion, the study suggests by put forwarding the two phase multi-faceted business model, for further explorations and experimentations.

REFERENCES

Alcalde, M. H. (2009) Multimarket Contact Challenges in Open Innovation Environments. *Proceeding of the ICERI2009 - International Conference of Education, Research and Innovation.*

Alves Aranha, E., Prado Garcia, N. A., & Corrêa, G. (2015). Open innovation and business model: A brazilian company case study. *Journal of Technology Management & Innovation*, *10*(4), 91–98. doi:10.4067/S0718-27242015000400010

Chandler, A. D. Jr. (1990). *Scale and Scope: The Dynamics of Industrial Capitalism*. The Belknap Press of Harvard University.

Chesbrough, H. (2003c). The logic of open innovation: Managing intellectual property. *California Management Review*, *45*(3), 33–58. doi:10.1177/000812560304500301

Chesbrough, H. (2003d). The Governance and Performance of Xerox's Technology Spin-Off Companies. *Research Policy*, *32*(3), 403–421. doi:10.1016/S0048-7333(02)00017-3

Chesbrough, H. (2003e). *Open Innovation: The New Imperative for Creating and Profiting from Technology*. Harvard Business School Publishing Corporation.

Chesbrough, H. (2015). *From open science to open innovation*. Institute for Innovation and Knowledge Management, ESADE.

Chesbrough, H., & Crowther, A. K. (2006). Beyond high tech: Early adopters of open innovation in other industries. *R & D Management*, *36*(3), 229–236. doi:10.1111/j.1467-9310.2006.00428.x

Chesbrough, H., & Schwartz, K. (2007). Innovating business models with co-development partnerships. *Research Technology Management*, *50*(1), 55–59. doi:10.1080/08956308.2007.11657419

Chesbrough, H., Vanhaverbeke, W., & West, J. (Eds.). (2014). *New frontiers in open innovation*. OUP. doi:10.1093/acprof:oso/9780199682461.001.0001

Chesbrough, H. W. (2003a). *Open innovation: the new imperative for creating and profiting from technology*. Harvard Business School Press.

Chesbrough, H. W. (2003b). The era of open innovation. *MIT Sloan Management Review*, *44*(3), 35–41.

Chesbrough, H. W. (2006a) New puzzles and new findings. In H. W. Chesbrough, W. Vanhaverbeke & J. West (Eds.), Open innovation: Researching a new paradigm. Oxford University Press

Chesbrough, H. W. (2006b). Open Innovation: A New Paradigm for Understanding Industrial Innovation. In H. W. Chesbrough, W. Vanhaverbeke & J. West (Eds.), Open innovation: Researching a new paradigm. Oxford University Press.

Chesbrough, H. W. (2006c). *Open Innovation: Researching a New Paradigm*. Oxford University Press.

Chesbrough, H. W. (2007). Why companies should have open business models. *MIT Sloan Management Review*, *48*(2), 22–28.

Chesbrough, H. W. (2010). *Open Innovation: A Key to Achieving Socioeconomic Evolution, How Smaller Companies Can Benefit from Open Innovation*, Retrieved October 30, 2010 from https://www.jef.or.jp/journal/jef_contents_free.asp?c=3707

Chesbrough, H. W., & Rosenbloom, R. S. (2002). The role of the business model in capturing value from innovation: Evidence from Xerox Corporation's technology spin-off companies. *Industrial and Corporate Change*, *11*(3), 529–555. doi:10.1093/icc/11.3.529

Chiaromonte, F. (2006). Open innovation through alliances and partnership: Theory and practice. *International Journal of Technology Management*, *33*(2-3), 111–114.

Christensen, J., Olesen, M., & Kjaer, J. (2005). The Industrial Dynamics of Open Innovation- Evidence from the Transformation of Consumer Electronics. *Research Policy*, *34*(10), 1533–1549. doi:10.1016/j.respol.2005.07.002

Dahlander, L., & Gann, D. M. (2010). How open is innovation? *Research Policy*, *39*(6), 699–709. doi:10.1016/j.respol.2010.01.013

De Jong, J. P. J., Vanhaverbeke, W., Kalvet, T., & Chesbrough, H. (2008). Policies for Open Innovation: Theory, Framework and Cases. Research project funded by VISION Era-Net.

De Sousa, M. (2006). The Sustainable Innovation Engine. *VINE Journal of Information and Knowledge Management Systems*, *36*(4).

De Sousa, M. (2008, Mar.). Open innovation models and the role of knowledge brokers. *Inside Knowledge,* 18-22.

Dittrich, K. (2008). Nokia's strategic change by means of alliance networks. A case of adopting the open innovation paradigm? In P. Sivarajadhanavel & D. Vellingiri (Eds.), *Open Innovation: The Networked R and D.* Icfai's Professional Reference Book Series. Icfai University Press.

CSR Europe. (2008) *R&D Open innovation: Networks with SME.* Open Innovation Network.

Formica, P., & Curley, M. (2018). *Exploring the Culture of Open Innovation.* Emerald. doi:10.1108/9781787437890

Fredberg, T., Elmquist, M., & Ollila, S. (2008). Managing Open Innovation: Present Findings and Future Directions. Report VR 2008:02. VINNOVA - Verket för Innovationssystem/Swedish Governmental Agency for Innovation Systems.

Gassmann, O. (2006). Opening Up the Innovation Process: Towards an Agenda. *R & D Management*, *36*(3), 22–228. doi:10.1111/j.1467-9310.2006.00437.x

Gassmann, O., & Reepmeyer, G. (2005). Organizing Pharmaceutical Innovation: From Science-based Knowledge Creators to Drug-oriented Knowledge Brokers. *Creativity and Innovation Management*, *14*(3), 233–245.

Gaule, A. (2006). *Open Innovation in Action: How to be strategic in the search for new sources of value*. Blackwell.

Gay, B. (2014). Open innovation, networking, and business model dynamics: The two sides. *Journal of Innovation and Entrepreneurship*, *3*(1), 1–20. doi:10.1186/2192-5372-3-2

Golder-Buckley, D., Way, D., & Glover, M. (2015). *Best Practice Strategies for Successful Innovation through University-Business Collaboration*. Research Councils UK.

Hossain, M. (2013). *Open innovation: So far and a way forward. World Journal of Science, Technology and Sustainable Development.*

Ivascu, L., Cirjaliu, B., & Draghici, A. (2016). Business model for the university-industry collaboration in open innovation. *Procedia Economics and Finance*, *39*, 674–678. doi:10.1016/S2212-5671(16)30288-X

Jaruzelski, B. & Dehoff, K. (2008). Beyond Borders: The Global Innovation 1000. *Strategy+Business*, *53*.

Kodama, F., & Shibata, T. (2015). Demand articulation in the open-innovation paradigm. *Journal of Open Innovation*, *1*(1), 2. doi:10.118640852-015-0003-y

Laursen, K., & Salter, A. (2006). Open for innovation: The roleof openness in explaining innovative performance among UK manufacturing firms. *Strategic Management Journal*, *27*(2), 131–150. doi:10.1002mj.507

Lee, M., Yun, J. J., Pyka, A., Won, D., Kodama, F., Schiuma, G., Park, H., Jeon, J., Park, K., Jung, K., Yan, M.-R., Lee, S. Y., & Zhao, X. (2018). How to respond to the fourth industrial revolution, or the second information technology revolution? Dynamic new combinations between technology, market, and society through open innovation. *Journal of Open Innovation*, *2018*(4), 21. doi:10.3390/joitmc4030021

Lee, S., Park, G., Yoon, B., & Park, J. (2010). Open innovationin SMEs—An intermediated network model. *Research Policy*, *39*(2), 290–300. doi:10.1016/j.respol.2009.12.009

Lichtenthaler, U. (2011). Open Innovation: Past Research, Current Debates, and Future Directions. *The Academy of Management Perspectives*, *25*(1), 75–93.

Lundvall, B., Jurowetzki, R., & Lema, R. (2014). *Combining the Global Value Chain and the Innovation System perspectives*. Paper prepared for the 11th Asialics International Conference 2014, Daegu, Korea.

Motzek, R. (2007). *Motivation in Open Innovation: An Exploratory Study on User Innovators*. Saarbrücken: VDM Verlag Dr. Müller.

Organisation for Economic Co-operation and Development (OECD). (2008). *Globalisation and open innovation*. Paris: OECD.

Parida, V., Westerberg, M., & Frishammar, J. (2012). Inbound open innovation activities in high-tech SMEs: The impact on innovation performance. *Journal of Small Business Management*, *50*(2), 283–309. doi:10.1111/j.1540-627X.2012.00354.x

Pourdehnad, J. (2007). Idealized design - An "open innovation" process. In *The Annual W. Edwards Deming Annual Conference*. Purdue University.

Rahman, H. (2010). Open Innovation: Opportunities and Challenges for SMEs. In M. M. Cruz-Cunha & J. Varajão (Eds.), *E-Business Issues, Challenges and Opportunities for SMEs: Driving Competitiveness* (pp. 87–100). IGI Global.

Rahman, H., & Ramos, I. (2010). Open Innovation in SMEs: From Closed Boundaries to Networked Paradigm. *Issues in Informing Science and Information Technology*, *7*, 471–487. doi:10.28945/1221

Saebi, T., & Foss, N. J. (2015). Business models for open innovation: Matching heterogeneous open innovation strategies with business model dimensions. *European Management Journal*, *33*(3), 201–213. doi:10.1016/j.emj.2014.11.002

Shorthouse, S. (2008). Innovation and technology transfer. *The International Conference DISTRICT 2008*.

Spithoven, A., Vanhaverbeke, W., & Roijakkers, N. (2013). Open innovation practices in SMEs and large enterprises. *Small Business Economics*, *41*(3), 537–562. doi:10.100711187-012-9453-9

Van de Vrande, V., de Jong, J., Vanhaverbeke, W., & DeRochemont, M. (2009). Open innovation in SMEs: Trends,motives and management challenges. *Technovation*, *29*(6–7), 423–437. doi:10.1016/j.technovation.2008.10.001

Vanhaverbeke, W., Chesbrough, H., & West, J. (2014). Surfing the new wave of open innovation research. *New Frontiers in Open Innovation, 281*, 287-288.

Viskari, S. (2006). Managing Technologies in Research Organization: Framework for research Surplus Portfolio. Research Report 176. Lappeenranta University of Technology.

Weiblen, T. (2014). The open business model: Understanding an emerging concept. *Journal of Multi Business Model Innovation and Technology*, *2*(1), 35–66. doi:10.13052/jmbmit2245-456X.212

West, J. (2006). Does Appropriability Enable or Retard Open Innovation? In Open Innovation: Researching a New Paradigm. Oxford University Press.

West, J., & Bogers, M. (2014). Leveraging external sources of innovation: A review of research on open innovation. *Journal of Product Innovation Management*, *31*(4), 814–831. doi:10.1111/jpim.12125

West, J. & Gallagher, S. (2006). Challenges of open innovation: the paradox of firm investment in open-source software. *R&D Management*, *36*(3), 319-331.

West, J., Salter, A., Vanhaverbeke, W., & Chesbrough, H. (2014). *Open innovation: The next decade*. Academic Press.

West, J., Vanhaverbeke, W., & Chesbrough, H. (2006). Open Innovation: A Research Agenda. In Open Innovation: Researching a New Paradigm. Oxford University Press.

Yun, J. J., & Liu, Z. (2019). Micro- and macro-dynamics of open innovation with a quadruple-helix model. *Sustainability*, *2019*(11), 3301. doi:10.3390u11123301

Yun, J. J., Park, K., Yang, J., & Jung, W. (2016). The philosophy of "open innovation". *J. Sci. Technol. Policy Manag.*, *2016*(7), 134–153. doi:10.1108/JSTPM-08-2015-0030

Yun, J. J., Won, D., & Park, K. (2016). Dynamics from open innovation to evolutionary change. *Journal of Open Innovation*, *2016*(2), 7–22. doi:10.118640852-016-0033-0

Yun, J. J., Won, D., & Park, K. (2018). Entrepreneurial cyclical dynamics of open innovation. *Journal of Evolutionary Economics*, *2018*(28), 1151–1174. doi:10.100700191-018-0596-y

Yun, J. J., Yang, J., & Park, K. (2016). Open innovation to business model: New perspective to connect between technology and market. *Science, Technology & Society*, *21*(3), 324–348. doi:10.1177/0971721816661784

Yun, Hyo, Zhao, Jung, & Yigitcanlar. (2020). The Culture for Open Innovation Dynamics. *Sustainability*, *12*(12), 1–21.

Zhao, S., Sun, Y., & Xu, X. (2016). Research on open innovation performance: A review. *Information Technology Management*, *17*(3), 279–287. doi:10.100710799-015-0231-7

ADDITIONAL READING

Afuah, A., & Tucci, C. L. (2012). Crowdsourcing as a solution to distant search. *Academy of Management Review*, *37*(3), 355–375. doi:10.5465/amr.2010.0146

Amit, R., & Zott, C. (2012). Creating Value through Business Model Innovation. *MIT Sloan Management Review*, *53*(3), 41–49.

Aquilani, B., Abbate, T., & Codini, A. (2017). Overcoming cultural barriers in open innovation processes through intermediaries: A theoretical framework. *Knowledge Management Research and Practice*, *2017*(15), 447–459. doi:10.105741275-017-0067-5

Belussi, F., Sammarra, A., & Sedita, S. R. (2010). Learning at the boundaries in an "Open Regional Innovation System": A focus on firms' innovation strategies in the Emilia Romagna life science industry. *Research Policy*, *39*(6), 710–721. doi:10.1016/j.respol.2010.01.014

Bock, A. J., Opsahl, T., George, G., & Gann, D. M. (2012). The Effects of Culture and Structure on Strategic Flexibility during Business Model Innovation. *Journal of Management Studies*, *49*(2), 279–305. doi:10.1111/j.1467-6486.2011.01030.x

Bonner, J., & Walker, O. (2004). Selecting influential business-to-business customers in new product development: Relational embeddedness and knowledge heterogeneity considerations. *Journal of Product Innovation Management*, *21*(3), 155–169. doi:10.1111/j.0737-6782.2004.00067.x

Brunswicker, S., & Van de Vrande, V. (2014). Exploring open innovation in small and medium-sized enterprises. *New frontiers in open innovation, 1*, 135-156.

Chesbrough, H. W. (2006). *Open business models: How to thrive in a new innovation landscape*. Harvard Business School Press.

Chesbrough, H. W. (2007). Why companies should have open business models. *MIT Sloan Management Review*, *48*(2), 22.

Curley, M. (2016). Twelve principles for open innovation 2.0. *NATNews*, *533*(7603), 314–316. doi:10.1038/533314a PMID:27193662

Ehrismann, D., & Patel, D. D. (2015). University – Industry collaborations: Models, drivers and cultures. *Swiss Medical Weekly*. Advance online publication. doi:10.4414mw.2015.14086 PMID:25658854

Fortune, A., & Mitchell, W. (2012). Unpacking firm exit at the firm and industry levels: The adaptation and selection of firm capabilities. *Strategic Management Journal*, *22*(7), 794–819. doi:10.1002mj.972

Foss, N. J., Lyngsie, J., & Zahra, S. (2013). The Role of External Knowledge Sources and Organizational Design in Exploiting Strategic Opportunities. *Strategic Management Journal*, *34*(12), 1453–1471. doi:10.1002mj.2135

Gambardella & Panico. (2014). On the Management of Open Innovation. *Research Policy*.

Heredero, C., & Berzosa, D. (2012). *Open Innovation in Firms and Public Administrations: Technologies for Value Creation*. Information Science Reference. doi:10.4018/978-1-61350-341-6

Holm, A. B., Günzel, F., & Ulhøi, J. P. (2013). Openness in innovation and business models: Lessons from the newspaper industry. *International Journal of Technology Management*, *61*(3/4), 324–348. doi:10.1504/IJTM.2013.052674

Jagoda, K., Maheshwari, B., & Gutowski, G. (2012). Deer Creek Land Development (DCLD): Open business model approach to sustaining competitive advantage. *International Journal of Commerce and Management*, *22*(2), 133–144. doi:10.1108/10569211211239430

Laursen, K., & Salter, A. (2014). The Paradox of Openness: Appropriability, External Search and Innovation Collaboration. *Research Policy*, *43*(5), 867–878. doi:10.1016/j.respol.2013.10.004

Lee, S., Park, G., Yoon, B., & Park, J. (2010). Open innovation in SMEs- An intermediated network model. *Research Policy*, *39*(2), 290–300. doi:10.1016/j.respol.2009.12.009

Murphy, P. J., Cooke, R. A., & Lopez, Y. (2013). Firm culture and performance: Intensity's e_ects and limits. *Management Decision*, *2013*(51), 661–679. doi:10.1108/00251741311309715

Poetz, M. K., & Schreier, M. (2012). The value of crowdsourcing: Can users really compete with professionals in generating new product ideas? *Journal of Product Innovation Management*, *29*(2), 245–256. doi:10.1111/j.1540-5885.2011.00893.x

Ritala, P., & Sainio, L. (2014). Coopetition for radical innovation: Technology, market and business-model perspectives. *Technology Analysis and Strategic Management*, *26*(2), 2. doi:10.1080/09537325.2013.850476

Sie, R. L. L. (2010). *Enhancing Open Innovation Through Modelling and Utilizing Knowledge on Coalition Formation (PhD project proposal)*. Dspace Open University of the Netherlands.

Van der Meer, H. (2007). Open Innovation – The Dutch Treat: Challenges in Thinking in Business Models. *Creativity and Innovation Management*, *16*(2), 192–202. doi:10.1111/j.1467-8691.2007.00433.x

Vanhaverbeke, W., & Cloodt, M. (2014). Theories of the firm and open innovation. *New frontiers in open innovation, 256*.

Yun, J. J., Nadhiroh, I. M., & Jung, W. Y. (2013). The relationship between open innovation, entrepreneurship, and introduction of new business models in Korean and Indonesian information technology enterprises. *Korean Social Science Journal*, *40*(2), 81–99. doi:10.100740483-013-0007-9

Yun, J. J., Won, D., & Park, K. (2018). Entrepreneurial cyclical dynamics of open innovation. *Journal of Evolutionary Economics*, *28*(5), 1151–1174. doi:10.100700191-018-0596-y

Zaletelj, V., Sluga, A., & Butala, P. (2008, March). A Conceptual Framework for the Collaborative Modeling of Networked Manufacturing Systems. *Concurrent Engineering, Research and Applications*, *16*(1), 103–114. doi:10.1177/1063293X07084636

KEY TERMS AND DEFINITIONS

Intellectual Property Management (IPM): It is the way of managing intellectual property like; patent renewals, integration, and market assessment either manually or using any automated system by the enterprise itself or by an intermediary. IPM involves IP development (planning and implementation of IP in a conducive environment through proper motivation); Market watch (seeking for opportunities by keeping track of other competitors and infringers); IP exchange (acquiring and selling of spin-offs and or joint R&D); and IPR protection (providing legal protection surviving trade secrets and other disciplinary measures).

Open Innovation Business Model: A form of business model involving inbound and outbound ideas defying boundaries of the companies to gain knowledge, expertise and value intended to be beneficial for the entrepreneurships.

Open Innovation Intermediaries: These are companies or agencies that help other companies implement various facets of open innovation, acting as an enabler or guide to explore the market for ideas without getting in over their heads. There are different kinds of open innovation intermediaries, with some acting as agents, thus representing one side of a transaction, while others take on the role of knowledge brokers or market makers.

Open Innovation Strategy: It could be treated as a mandate or a set of clear vision or a well-defined process incorporating people (employees, clients, suppliers, other stakeholders) in terms of new ways of working, incentives, fading distinction between work and (social) networks; operations ((e-)processes and (e-)infrastructure) in terms of web access, communities, facilitation of knowledge and creativity sharing; policy (written and unwritten rules) regarding intellectual property, privacy, outside communication; and culture (openness, learning, networking) to create the right (and safe) atmosphere.

Spin-Offs: They may refer to Corporate spin-off, a type of corporate transaction forming a new company or entity; Government spin-off, civilian goods which are the result of military or governmental research; Research spin-off, a company founded on the findings of a member or by members of a research group at a university; Spin-off (media), the process of deriving new radio programs, television programs, video games, or novels from already existing ones; or Spin-off product, a new product which uses the brand name of another product which already has a well-developed image. In case of a spin-off, a parent company distributes shares of a subsidiary to the parent company's shareholders. The shares are usually distributed on a pro rata basis and the subsidiary becomes a separate company. State law and the rules of the stock exchanges determine whether a company must seek shareholder approval for a spin-off.

Chapter 6
Assurance for Change Management With COBIT 2019 and CMMC Maturity Frameworks

Jeffrey S. Zanzig
Jacksonville State University, USA

Guillermo A. Francia, III
https://orcid.org/0000-0001-8088-2653
University of West Florida, USA

ABSTRACT

As technology plays an ever-increasing role in carrying out structured tasks in today's society, people are given more time to focus their attention on higher levels of service and personal development. However, technology is in a constant state of change and assurance services are needed to help ensure that technology changes are accomplished properly. The Institute of Internal Auditors has identified 10 steps that can be used to effectively implement changes in technology. This process and its accompanying internal controls can be assessed through an internal audit function that considers issues of both functionality and security. In addition, continuous improvement of the change management process for technology can be evaluated though capability/maturity models to see if organizations are achieving higher levels of accomplishment over time. Such models include the COBIT 2019-supported capability maturity model integration (CMMI) model and the cybersecurity maturity model certification (CMMC) framework used by defense industrial base organizations.

DOI: 10.4018/978-1-7998-4799-1.ch006

INTRODUCTION

The technology of today provides organizations with a tremendous ability to store and process information so that people have more time to focus on higher-level activities that are considered to add more value in meeting customer needs. This does not mean that technology once implemented relieves organizations of the need to understand and revise the functioning of computer systems. Current issues of today including privacy of personal data, theft of trade secrets, and safety of company products and services are all affected by the ability of organizations to properly implement changes to the applications that make up today's technology systems. The following examples illustrate that assurance over technology needs to address both issues of functionality and cybersecurity.

A number of tragic incidents involving computer glitches on the Boeing 737 MAX jet illustrates what can happen when computer software is changed but not adequately tested before being placed into operation. The original issues with the jet resulted from a problem in the plane's flight control system called MCAS that assisted in maintaining a proper balance of the plane while in flight. The system misfired in a manner that "repeatedly and forcefully pushed the planes' noses down, overpowering pilot commands and ending in fatal dives." Since the grounding of the 737 Max, Boeing has been working to revise the software to correct the problem by making such misfires less likely and easier for pilots to counter when they do occur. In their efforts to correct the software, Boeing ran into another glitch that stops the plane's flight control computers from powering up and confirming that the system is ready for flight. The software fix was originally tested mostly on ground-based simulators, which did not show the power-up problems (Pasztor, 2020).

A recent event at Garmin Ltd., who makes navigation systems for cars, boats, and planes, illustrates that organizations must also be careful to ensure that proper cybersecurity measures are built into their technology. The company's Garmin Pilot, which provides weather and flight plan data to pilots was recently interrupted when hackers apparently encrypted a few of its systems, but stopped short of a ransomware attack (Choi, 2020).

The ISACA is well known for its development of international information system auditing and control standards. One of their most significant contributions is a continuing project known as the Control Objectives for Information and related Technology (COBIT) framework. The management process of COBIT 2019 contains four domains:

- Align, Plan and Organize (APO)
- Build, Acquire and Implement (BAI)
- Deliver, Service and Support (DSS)

- Monitor, Evaluate and Assess (MEA)

COBIT 2019 contains explanations of specific management practices than can be tailored to the development of various objectives that a company may wish to accomplish within each domain. Each organization should decide on its own combination of management practices based on the unique environment in which it operates.

In 2020, The Institute of Internal Auditors issued an updated Global Technology Audit Guide (GTAG) entitled *Change and Patch Management Controls Critical for Organizational Success*. It contains information to guide internal auditors when working in conjunction with information technology professionals to manage information technology changes. "Change management can be defined as the systematic set of processes that are executed within an organization's IT function to manage enhancements, updates, installations, implementations, incremental fixes, and patches to production systems. Properly implemented, change management protects the production environment ("live" environment) and provides the organization with a repeatable, measurable, and auditable process that captures all technology-related changes."

The Cybersecurity Maturity Model Certification (CMMC) Framework requires organizations in the Defense Industrial Base sectors to remain in compliance with mandatory practices, procedures, and capabilities to confront evolving cyber threats and intrusions. The chapter will visit this framework and consider its implications to change management as it applies to organizations working with the U.S. Department of Defense.

This chapter considers the COBIT and GTAG guidance along with current change and patch management literature for the purpose of considering how assurance services can be performed to evaluate an organization's process of change management. The remainder of the chapter is conceptually divided into three major topics:

1. The first is a discussion of change management that considers some background on the process of change management, a description of the steps of change management, and internal audit's assessment of a change management process.
2. The second considers a subset of change management known as patch management. This topic covers a description of patch management and considers a comparison of the COBIT 2019 Capability Model (i.e., Capability Maturity Model Integration) and the CMMC Maturity Model and how they can be used to measure the success of an organization's patch management activities from both an operational and security perspective, respectively.
3. The closing sections of the chapter present future research directions and conclusions.

BACKGROUND

Computer systems provide organizations with massive storage capabilities and the ability to process information at a speed that is far beyond human potential. This frees up organizational personnel to spend less time in retrieving and processing information and more time in using information to make better decisions. To illustrate, consider a person who graduated with an accounting degree a few decades ago. An initial task for many new graduates at that time would be to rewrite schedules by hand and make very structured calculations to recompute depreciation. New accountants were often assigned such tasks so more experienced staff members could devote their time to more productive activities. Although trained professionals must still understand the structured processing typically assigned to computers, the technology of today has freed up professionals so that even less experienced persons have additional time to develop their skills and focus more on value-added activities.

Society has come a long way in its use of technology to consistently conduct structured tasks. However, it must also be remembered that the power of technology to provide valuable information is only as good as the system that generates it. The consistency of technology to conduct well-defined tasks comes with some limitations. One is that time allows for system vulnerabilities to be identified and exploited by unscrupulous persons. A second problem is that an incorrectly defined method of processing can result in processing errors that are repeated on a continuous basis. It is therefore imperative that society have respect for the limitations of technology and continually use human reasoning to evaluate and make changes to computer systems as the need arises.

Galligan, Herrygers, and Rau (2019) provide some thoughts regarding how an organization can view their cyber risk profile through the following components of the COSO ERM Framework:

- Governance and Culture – it is important that a company's board of directors either obtain expertise in cybersecurity or make use of advisors with the expertise.
- Strategy and Objective-Setting – when changes happen, an organization should consider additional cyber risks that come with it.
- Performance – cyber risks should be evaluated in terms of how likely they could negatively affect the ability of an organization to achieve its objectives.
- Review and Revision – organizations must put in place governance processes to catch and assess prospective shifts that could change their cyber risk profile.
- Information, Communication, and Reporting – it should be considered how cyber incidents could affect the availability of an organization's information system and data.

Technology exists in a constantly changing environment. Organizational agility in carrying out information system changes is imperative in maintaining the proper functioning and security of technology. Any program of change/patch management must follow a well-defined approach. Assurance services over the programs are needed to help company management to ensure the proper functioning of technology and its accompanying cybersecurity issues. Internal auditors and technology professionals can use the COBIT 2019 and CMMC frameworks to evaluate the capability/maturity of an organization to process technology changes using a skilled approach that allows them to successfully accomplish what is needed in as seamless a manner as possible.

THE STEPS OF CHANGE MANAGEMENT

Emergency situations can arise that may require an expedited process of change to an organization's information system. For example, a security issue could come about due to unanticipated issues from a change in technology. Such situations are addressed by COBIT 2019:

BAI 06.02 Manage Emergency Changes

Carefully manage emergency changes to minimize further incidents. Ensure the emergency change is controlled and takes place securely. Verify that emergency changes are appropriately assessed and authorized after the change.

Metric Example – Number of emergency changes not authorized after the incident. (ISACA, 2018).

Although some emergency changes are inevitable, the need to apply a patch to an organization's information system should attempt to minimize the need for such changes. The GTAG (2020) addresses the application of system patches with the following statement:

The availability of a patch to address a critical security vulnerability can be disruptive and may result in significant resources being redirected from planned work to address the unplanned patch. Organizations with effective patching functions will likely treat a new patch as a predictable and planned change subject to the normal change management process. A new patch is added to the queue to be evaluated, tested, and integrated into an already-scheduled release deployment.

The Institute of Internal Auditors suggest a series of ten steps, that are described in the following paragraphs, that can be used to standardize a system of change management so that it functions in an effective and efficient manner (GTAG, 2020). To more fully describe the steps, specific management practices from COBIT 2019 and other supporting literature are provided as needed. In addition, a comprehensive example illustrates how the steps could be used to improve a company's control over pricing of products for customer quotes and invoicing.

Step 1: Identifying the Need for a Change

System users should be brought in early to a systems development project because of the significant expertise that they have to offer regarding what the system needs to accomplish. This idea also applies to system modifications that are implemented through a process of change management. Persons at all levels that are associated with the system should feel free to make suggestions for improvement (Pollock, 2016). One approach to accomplishing this is to have regular meetings with affected persons to obtain a good understanding of how they currently use the system and any challenges it poses. It is important to include system users who vary in their levels of satisfaction with the current system. More satisfied system users tend to bring up long-term innovations, while dissatisfied persons are more likely to focus on current system problems (Pierce, 2008). Both perspectives are of value in achieving continuous improvement in the ability of an information system to meet the ever-changing needs of its various system users.

In encouraging system users to submit their suggestions, Silverman (2011) states that although financial rewards for suggestions can be a great incentive, some organization employees may value the opportunity to see the implementation of their ideas as being an even greater enticement. This idea captures the basic human desire to give back and be appreciated for contributions in helping others. Another important consideration is that system users should not be the only perspective to be considered. Mathiassen, Ngwenyama, and Aaen (2005) make the observation that more technical persons such as software engineers could be a good source of ideas associated with emerging technologies that persons with less technical skill may not consider.

The importance of establishing an environment to identify areas where changes could make improvements is addressed in COBIT 2019:

APO 04.01 Create an Environment Conducive to Innovation

Create an environment that is conducive to innovation, considering methods such as culture, reward, collaboration, technology forums, and mechanisms to promote and capture employee ideas.

Metric Example – Inclusion of innovation of emerging technology-related objectives in performance goals for relevant staff.

APO 04.03 Monitor and Scan the Technology Environment

Set up a technology watch process to perform systematic monitoring and scanning of the enterprise's external environment to identify emerging technologies that have the potential to create value.

Metric Example – Frequency of environment research and scans performed for identifying innovative ideas and trends.

APO 09.01 Identify I&T Services

Analyze business requirements and the degree to which I&T-enabled services and service levels support business processes. Discuss and agree with the business on potential services and service levels. Compare potential service levels against the current portfolio; identify new or changed services or service level options.

Metric Example – Number of obsolete services identified. (ISACA, 2018).

Step 1 Illustration

A company would like to improve its controls over product pricing in that they have been experiencing inconsistent pricing on customer quotes and sales invoices by their sales staff. The company already makes use of a database and electronic documents for preparing and saving customer quotes and sales invoices. An employee in sales has suggested that the company implement an electronic master price list that would have to be selected from in quoting prices and invoicing customers.

Step 2: Prepare for the Change

A formal structure should be established for the submission of change suggestion. It should include a step-by-step procedure regarding the details of the change, a change test plan, and change rollback to be implemented should a change failure occur (GTAG, 2020). Buckley (2011) refers to the submission as a change inquiry form. In addition to the above components, Buckley recommends that the change inquiry should also include the likely impact of the change and a proposed date of implementation. Because of the considerable effort that goes into a change inquiry, it is helpful to have experienced staff available to assist in ensuring a proper submission.

The necessity of a change manager is an important consideration in this step to evaluate whether the change has adequate potential to be moved forward. In considering the merit of a proposed change, COBIT 2019 suggests understanding current technology capabilities and performing a gap analysis between the current and desired state:

APO 02.02 Assess Current Capabilities, Performance and Digital Maturity of the Enterprise

Assess the performance of current I&T services and develop an understanding of current business and I&T capabilities (both internal and external). Assess current digital maturity of the enterprise and its appetite for change.

Metric Example – Percent of staff satisfied with current capabilities.

APO 02.04 Conduct a Gap Analysis

Identify the gaps between the current and target environments and describe the high-level changes in the enterprise architecture.

Metric Example - Number of significant gaps between current environment and good practices. (ISACA, 2018).

Internal auditors can help to ensure that any change inquiries appearing to have merit are elevated to a change request and assigned a unique number that will allow them to be tracked throughout the change management process (Buckley, 2011).

Step 2 Illustration

A change inquiry form is submitted for the electronic master price list suggestion. For each customer quote, the salesperson would be required to select pricing from a drop-down master price list. The master price list would provide a base price along with predetermined discount percentages that would apply based on the quantity of goods requested. Using the price list information, item descriptions, prices, and quantity discounts would automatically populate the customer quote. The quote would be assigned a unique quote number. If the customer agrees to the terms, this information would automatically be carried to the customer's invoice when the goods are shipped. The change inquiry indicates that the change could be implemented within a four-week period.

Following a careful consideration of the change inquiry, the change manager concludes that the suggestion has merit and should be promoted to the level of a change request with a unique tracking number. The implementation of the change will require setting up the master price list information in the company database and linking it to forms for product quotes prepared by salespersons and sales invoices prepared by billing.

Step 3: Obtain Business Justification

In considering a business justification, an organization needs to make a distinction between a mandatory versus discretionary change. Mandatory change issues often arise due to some legal or regulatory matter that must be addressed. In contrast, a discretionary issue requires a business justification in which the organization must assess the impact, cost, and benefits associated with a change (GTAG, 2020). The significance of continuous evaluation of reporting requirements and the development of a business justification is discussed in COBIT 2019:

APO 01.04 Define and Implement the Organizational Structures

Ensure that required technology and information knowledge is included in the composition of the management structures.

Metric Example – Level of executive satisfaction with management decision making.

BAI 01.02 Initiate a Program

Initiate a program to confirm the expected benefits and obtain authorization to proceed.

Metric Example - Percent of stakeholders approving enterprise need, scope, planned outcome and level of program risk. (ISACA, 2018).

Step 3 Illustration

A manager in Sales believes that the use of an electronic master price list to enforce the company's pricing policies would be of great value in ensuring that appropriate pricing is applied in making customer quotes and invoicing. The current system of allowing persons to manually enter pricing on customer sales quotes and sales invoices can result in inconsistency in the application of pricing to customers.

Step 4: Obtain Approvals

The change request at this point has gone through a process of refinement where it has been fully documented as to the details of the change, a testing program, and its business justification. Before it moves into the next step of being considered for approval, it is important that someone representing the persons requesting the change review it to ensure that it truly reflects what is intended.

Internal auditors can help to ensure that someone with sufficient authority from the affected area supports the change, and that sufficient information is contained within the change request to make an authorization decision.

Step 4 Illustration

A manager in Sales reviews the overall documentation for the change request and concludes that it captures the intent of the proposed change. However, the manager does note that the change request does not adequately describe two special features that should be a part of the new system:

1. The invoicing process would be facilitated through one of two approaches. One would involve an option during invoicing to allow for a lookup of an existing customer quote that would electronically populate the invoice in situations where a customer accepted quote exists. In situations where an accepted quote does not exist, dropdowns on the invoice input form would allow pricing directly from the master price list in the same manner as for making customer quotes.
2. The sales manager suggests that an option be added to allow an override code to enter exclusive pricing for situations involving management-approved special orders.

The chief executive officer and sales department manager agree that the two additional features should be added to the change request.

Step 5: Authorize (via Change Approval Board)

The GTAG (2020) states that it is important to prioritize change requests with respect to other pending changes. Meyer and Lambert (2007) capture the spirit of this in stating that change requests should be prioritized to consider the disruption that could occur if the change is not implemented. Melancon (2006) points out that decisions regarding authorization can be facilitated through the use of a change advisory board. The GTAG (2020) recommends that the authorization process should result in one of three outcomes: authorize, reject, or request additional information. This approach is also supported by Buckley (2011) who feels that change requests should be categorized in the following manner:

- Accepted – the change request provides a practical business benefit and is worth further consideration with the chance for eventual implementation.
- Rejected – the change request should be turned down because it fails to demonstrate a reasonable business benefit.
- On hold/further work is needed – more information is needed before a decision can be made.

In further consideration of this point, Buckley (2011) states that the change can classified by considering how extensively the change affects the overall system:

- Type A – the change affects numerous systems and therefore involves a high level of technical complexity.
- Type B – the change affects only a single system with a medium level of technical complexity.
- Type C – the change affects only a single system with a low level of technical complexity.

Step 5 of the change management process is also addressed as a COBIT 2019 management practice:

BAI 06.01 Evaluate, Prioritize and Authorize Change Requests

Evaluate all requests for change to determine the impact on business processes and I&T services, and to assess whether change will adversely affect the operational environment and introduce unacceptable risks. Ensure that changes are logged, prioritized, categorized, assessed, authorized, planned, and scheduled.

Metric Example – Percent of unsuccessful changes due to inadequate impact assessment. (ISACA, 2018).

Internal auditors can assist in this step of the process by making certain that appropriate persons are evaluating change requests and that the roles and responsibilities of the advisory board are properly documented in its charter. Internal auditors can also help to confirm that each change request undergoes a proper process of risk assessment (Buckley, 2011).

Step 5 Illustration

The change advisory board concludes that the change request for the electronic master price list should be approved for two primary reasons. First, it will improve the accuracy of quoting and invoicing product prices. Second, it will remove the temptation of sales personnel to give too much of a discount to customers so that a sale can be made simply to generate an additional sales commission for the salesperson.

The change advisory board assigns the change as a "Type B" risk because it primarily affects the area of sales. It is felt that the change warrants a medium level of complexity because the electronic master price list must tie into the systems for making customer quotes and performing sales invoicing.

Step 6: Schedule and Coordinate the Change

The GTAG (2020) states that this step of the change process should include the scheduling and assignment of both a change implementer and a change tester. Meyer and Lamber (2007) describe the role of a change implementer being accomplished by an oversight team that includes a variety of skills including persons from the areas of corporate accounting, information technology, internal audit, and others possessing the necessary skills to be addressed by the particular requirements of the change. The oversight team can help to ensure that approved changes are appropriately coordinated and prioritized with other changes that are to be put into operation. COBIT 2019 addresses the importance of the oversight team to implement and track changes:

BAI 05.02 Form an Effective Implementation Team

Establish an effective implementation team by assembling appropriate members, creating trust, and establishing common goals and effectiveness measures.

Metric Example: Stakeholder satisfaction ratings of implementation team.

BAI 06.03 Track and Report Change Status

Maintain a tracking and reporting system to document rejected changes and communicate the status of approved, and in-process changes and complete changes.

Metric Example – Number and age of backlogged change requests. (ISACA, 2018)

Step 6 Illustration

The task of implementing the change is delegated to an oversight team composed of representatives from Sales, Billing, Accounts Receivable, Information Technology, and Internal Audit. Affected persons are informed of the change and why it is being implemented. The oversight team feels that the proposed four-week time frame for implementation is appropriate.

The planned implementation schedule is input into a tracking system and assigned a unique tracking identification number.

Step 7: Test in Appropriate Environment(s)

The GTAG (2020) states that testing of the change should occur in preproduction environments. The reason is that any problems in the operation of the change need to be worked out to the greatest extent possible before the change is implemented. This can help to avoid disruptions in company operations due to issues that could bring down the production environment as a result of unanticipated problems with the change. COBIT 2019 addresses some important testing issues:

BAI 07.04 Establish a test environment

Define and establish a secure test environment representative of the planned business process and IT operations environment in terms of performance, capacity, security, internal controls, operational practices, data quality, privacy requirements and workloads.

Metric Example – Level of comparability between the test environment and future business and operational landscape.

BAI 03.08 Execute solution testing

During development, execute testing continually (including control testing), in accordance with the defined test plan and development practices in the appropriate environment. Engage business process owners and end users in the test team. Identify, log, and prioritize errors and issues identified during testing.

Metric Example – Time and effort to complete tests.

BAI 07.05 Perform Acceptance Tests

Test changes independently in accordance with the defined test plan, prior to migration to the live operational environment.

Metric Example – Number of successful acceptance tests. (ISACA, 2018)

Step 7 Illustration

The implementation team has set up a testing environment that functions like the organization's changed process of entering customer quotes and invoicing. Testing shows that the new system functions appropriately, including the features for carryforward invoicing from customer approved quotations and the option for special order pricing.

Step 8: Implement Change

Internal audit should check security access profiles to "validate that only authorized personnel can migrate a change into the production environment." Once preproduction testing has been completed and the change has been approved, the implementation team should communicate the change to affected stakeholders (GTAG, 2020). Buckley (2011) suggests that the following issues be addressed before implementation:

- Testing is complete with results satisfactory to authorized parties.
- The outage period for implementation has been communicated to those directly impacted by the implementation process.
- Operational teams are available to provide support for the change.

COBIT 2019 emphasizes the importance of communicating the reasons for the change and establishing an appropriate method of implementation:

BAI 05.03 Communicate Desired Vision

Communicate the desired vision for the change in the language of those affected by it. The communication should be made by senior management and include the rationale for, and the benefits of the change; the impacts of not making the change; and the vision, the road map and the involvement required of the various stakeholders.

Metric Example – Stakeholder feedback on level of understanding of the change.

BAI 07.06 Promote to Production and Manage Releases

Promote the accepted solution to the business and operations. Where appropriate, run the solution as a pilot implementation or in parallel with the old solution for a defined period and compare behavior and results. If significant problems occur, revert to the original environment based on the fallback/backup plan.

Metric Example – Percent of stakeholder satisfaction with the implemented solution.

BAI 07.07 Provide Early Production Support

For an agreed period of time, provide early support to the users and information and technology operations to resolve issues and help stabilize the new solution.

Metric Example – Number of additional staff resources provided for support. (ISACA, 2018).

Step 8 Illustration

Testing of the new system for the electronic master price list is complete and the benefits of the system have been communicated to affected system users. To provide for the safest implementation possible, the system changes are implemented using a parallel simulation approach. Support staff have been trained and made available to assist system users.

Step 9: Verify/Validate Change

An evaluation should be made to determine if the implemented change has been successful and that it appropriately meets its design specifications. The GTAG (2020) indicates that the change management process should be evaluated to consider how well proper procedures have been conducted, were internal control and compliance requirements followed during the change, and were any lessons learned to improve the change management process. COBIT 2019 states the importance of reviewing the implemented change:

BAI 07.08 Perform a Post Implementation Review

Conduct a post-implementation review to confirm outcome and results, identify lessons learned, and develop an action plan. Evaluate actual performance and outcomes of the new or changed service against expected performance and outcomes anticipated by the user or customer.

Metric Example – Number and percent of releases that fail to stabilize within an acceptable period.

Step 9 Illustration

Test data provided by Sales works well in evaluating the functioning of the new electronic master price list, including the options to: (1) transfer quotes automatically to invoices when there is a customer accepted quote, and (2) the option to allow for overrides of the master price list for special orders. Results indicate that the change management process was followed and functioned appropriately.

Step 9a: Back Out (If Unsuccessful)

A basic tenet in regard to backing out of unsuccessful changes to software is that programmers should make changes to copies of a program rather than the actual software that is used in operations (Kaitano, 2007). When changes are made directly to operational copies, it is more likely that quick fixes and inappropriate levels of testing will be conducted to minimize the downtime of the system. Serious disruption of company operations can occur if the change later develops issues that could have been detected if more time had been available for implementation and testing. Even if changes are successful and are placed in operation, situations could arise under which the organization would need to return to a prior operating version of the software. An appropriate system of numbering versions of software could be invaluable should such a situation arise.

Step 9a Illustration

The electronic master price list was implemented by making the changes to a copy of the software to allow return to the original processing in case any significant implementation problems arose. This was unnecessary as the implementation was successful.

Step 10: Close Request

The GTAG (2020) states that in closing out the request, any lessons learned that could improve the change management process should be documented and applied to improve the process. COBIT 2019 addresses the final step of closing the change request:

BAI 06.04 Close and Document Changes

Whenever changes are implemented, update the solution, user documentation and procedures affected by the change.

Metric Example – Percent of user documentation and procedures updates performed in a timely manner. (ISACA, 2018)

Step 10 Illustration

The changes for the master price list during customer quotations and invoicing have been appropriately implemented and documented. No new lessons have been observed that require modification of the change management process.

INTERNAL AUDIT'S ASSESSMENT OF CHANGE MANAGEMENT

Internal audit can play a significant role in helping company management to establish and maintain a proper system of change management. "While IT management's responsibility is to protect the production environment and support the organization's pursuit of its business objectives, internal auditors should assess and validate that appropriate risk management processes and controls are in place." Some examples of risks associated with a poor change management program include: "unauthorized or unrecorded changes being applied, system or application failure/downtime, security issues, inefficient business processes, inconsistent results, and even misstated reports and financial statements" (GTAG, 2020). This section considers controls that can be built into the steps of change management and how auditors can best focus their assurance activities by using a risk-based approach. It concludes by illustrating a portion a change management audit program.

Common Controls Over Change Management

The GTAG (2020) points out that the review of an organization's change management process is permitted to be a stand-alone assessment or a part of a larger scale audit. The change management engagement should, as a minimum, "validate authorization, segregation of duties, testing of changes, approval to move changes into production, and validate emergency changes. Specific change management controls can be grouped as follows:

- Preventive controls that will deny changes unless appropriate procedure is followed. Some examples of preventive controls include:
  - Appropriate authorizations by a change advisory board.
  - An implementer does not authorize their own changes.
  - Complete and appropriate change documentation.
  - Minimum required steps are completed.
- Detective controls to consider whether completed changes have resulted in any undesired outcomes. Some examples of detective controls include:
  - Uncovering changes that have not been properly authorized.
  - Monitoring of appropriate change management metrics.
- Corrective controls that take predetermined actions when undesirable results occur as a result of a completed change. Some examples of corrective controls include:
  - Post-implementation reviews.
  - The feeding of change information into early problem diagnosis steps.
- Migration controls to help ensure a smooth transition to the production environment. Some examples of controls over migration include:
  - Migration of a change should be completed by someone independent of the development team in order to reduce the risk of unauthorized changes.
  - Security access profiles of persons migrating a change should be checked to ensure that only authorized persons can migrate a change. (GTAG, 2020)

A Risk-Based Approach to Change Management Assessment

Internal audit functions do not have the resources to review every aspect of the organizations in which the work. For this reason, engagement plans for internal audit should be based on a risk-based approach. A risk assessment process can be defined as the identification and prioritization of risks. A quantitative approach to risk assessment would involve having internal audit compute exposure values for identified risks by taking the potential financial loss of an event occurring times its risk or probability of occurrence. Internal audit can then use the size of the resulting exposure values and other qualitative criteria to assist them in determining the scope and magnitude of a review. In an audit of the change management and control processes of an organization, the GTAG (2020) suggests that internal auditors should consider some of the following general steps in assessing a change management program:

- Understand basic change management components and how the organization implements them.
- Determine whether management has a method to report metrics for process results and effectiveness.
- Determine whether such metrics are actually being used to monitor the processes and promote continuous improvement.
- Confirm whether management has established a secure production environment so that only responsible persons can implement changes.
- Verify that changes to the production environment are documented and maintained in a way that cannot be manipulated or destroyed.

In making concluding audit observations, internal auditors should present both the business value that effective change management processes provide, along with the risks that result when ineffective processes are followed.

Illustration of a Change Management Audit Program

It is a common audit practice to require an audit program to ensure that auditors take appropriate steps to collect and evaluate evidence regarding an assessment of an activity. Table 1 presents an example of one section of a sample audit program for change management.

PATCH MANAGEMENT PROCESS

The process of patch management is an essential part of overall system management that involves the acquisition, testing, and deployment of system or application updates, known as patches, to lessen perceived system vulnerabilities or improve operational efficiency. The concept of patch management can logically be considered as a smaller scale version of the process of change management which is concerned with major system-wide modification activities (Zanzig, Francia & Francia, 2014). All too often organizations are hesitant to develop an appropriate timetable that will enable them to efficiently implement their patching activities. Cavusoglu, Cavusoglu and Zhang (2004) point out that asynchronous patch update is common in practice due to both the managerial costs of patching and concern over the operational risks involved. The unfortunate result is that many systems remain unpatched for months or even years due to a sporadic approach to making needed modifications that provides little, if any, consideration of prioritization and scheduling issues (Shostack, 2003).

An important component in the patch management process is ensuring user compliance with update and vulnerability issues regarding patch management. For

Table 1. Illustration of Change Management Audit Program

Segregation of Duties
Control Objective: To delegate responsibilities such that unintentional errors or intentional, inappropriate actions will be detected.
Risk: Unexpected to adverse results.
Control: At a minimum, separate people/groups perform the responsibilities for change advisory/approval and implementation. Ideally, a separate person or group performs design change and testing of the changes. When this is not feasible or ideal, appropriate detective or monitoring controls are in place.
Work Steps: ▪ Validate that changes are reviewed and approved by an appropriate level of management. ▪ Validate that those who approve changes do not have access to implement them in the production environment. ▪ Determine how changes are tested to ensure they function as intended and do not impair the integrity, availability, or confidentiality of data. ▪ Validate that appropriate detective or monitoring controls are in place to mitigate or enhance segregation of duties controls.

(GTAG, 2020)

instance, during the planning stage, the patching objectives must first be defined by identifying the current vulnerabilities of the system. Also, during the preparation for patching, metrics need to be established and anticipated system changes documented. A comprehensive set of metrics can be delineated into three non-mutually exclusive characterizations: organizational, operational, and technical. Organizational metrics assess the effectiveness of the organization's standards, polices, and procedures used to enhance security. Operational metrics describe how organizational policies and procedures are implemented by technical staff. Finally, the technical set of metrics assesses the adequacy of security imposed on system components (Zanzig, Francia, & Francia, 2019).

COBIT 2019 provides management objectives that can be linked to capability levels for a variety of process activities to assist an organization in assessing the capability level of its patch management process. The Cybersecurity Maturity Model Certification (CMMC) Framework provides a maturity-level model for measuring the capability of an organization to deal with new and evolving cyber threats and intrusions. Together these frameworks weigh the importance of a proper approach to evaluate technology changes while considering accompanying security issues. The next three sections of this chapter present: a description of the COBIT 2019 Capability Levels for Processes model (COBIT model), an explanation of the CMMC and its relationship to levels of the COBIT model, and how these two prominent frameworks can be applied to assess an organization's system of patch management.

COBIT 2019 CAPABILITY LEVELS FOR PROCESSES (COBIT MODEL)

Activities associated with the management objectives of the COBIT 2019 Framework have a capability maturity level assigned to them from the capability levels shown below:

Level 0: Ad-hoc

- Lack of any basic capability.
- Incomplete approach to address governance and management purpose.
- May or may not be meeting the intent of any process practices.

Level 1: Performed

The process more-or-less achieves its purpose through application on an incomplete set of activities that can be characterized as initial or intuitive—not very organized.

Level 2: Managed

The process achieves its purpose through the application of a basic, yet complete, set of activities that can be characterized as performed.

Level 3: Established

The process achieves its purpose in a much more organized way using organizational assets. Processes typically are well defined.

Level 4: Predictable

The process achieves its purpose, is well defined, and its performance is (quantitatively) measured.

Level 5: Optimizing

The process achieves its purpose, is well defined, its performance is measured to improve performance and continuous improvement is pursued. (ISACA, 2018)

CYBERSECURITY MATURITY MODEL CERTIFICATION (CMMC) FRAMEWORK

The CMMC framework builds on the Defense Federal Acquisition Regulations Supplement (DFARS) 252.204-7012, Safeguarding Covered Defense Information and Cyber Incident Reporting. It is developed by the Office of the Undersecretary of Defense for Acquisition and Sustainment (OUSD A&S), University Affiliated Research Centers (UARCs), Federally Funded Research and Development Centers (FFRDC), and Industry stakeholders (Office of the Undersecretary of Defense, 2021).

The framework essentially requires third party assessments of Department of Defense (DoD) organizations' compliance with mandatory practices, procedures and capabilities that are capable to adapt to new and evolving cyber threats and intrusions. In particular, these organizations refer to those entities that belong to the Defense Industrial Base (DIB) sector handling Controlled Unclassified Information (CUI). CMMC is primarily intended to serve as a verification mechanism to ensure that DIB companies implement appropriate cybersecurity practices and processes to protect Federal Contract Information (FCI) and CUI within their unclassified networks. CUI refers to the information created or possessed by the Government or by an entity on behalf of the Government requiring access and dissemination controls. Evidently, a security breach in the protection of CUI could lead to an increased risk in national security. The astute reader is referred to the DoD CUI Program website (U.S. Department of Defense, 2021) for a comprehensive treatment on the subject.

As previously stated, the CMMC framework consists of processes and best practices gleaned from various cybersecurity standards, frameworks, and other references. These processes and practices are organized into a set of 17 domains and mapped into five maturity levels.

The CMMC Framework Domains

The 17 CMMC Framework domains (Carnegie Mellon University and The John Hopkins University Applied Physics Laboratory, LLC, 2020) are as follows:

- Access Control includes access and authorization control mechanisms.
- Asset Management involves identification, documenting and managing assets.
- Audit and Accountability includes audit requirements and processes, protection of audit information and management of audit logs.
- Awareness and Training provides for the security awareness training of personnel.

- Configuration Management establishes configuration baselines and enables configuration and change management.
- Identification and Authentication provides identification and authentication mechanisms including password policies.
- Incident Response enables incident response planning, development, testing and review.
- Maintenance involves maintenance management including controls for conducting system maintenance, off-site maintenance, and media acquisition.
- Media Protection includes the identification, protection, control, and sanitization of media.
- Personnel and Security involves the screening of personnel and the protection of CUI during personnel actions.
- Physical Protection includes the policies and practices for physical protection.
- Recovery includes backups and business continuity planning.
- Risk Management involves risk identification, mitigation and general risk management including those in supply chain.
- Security Assessment includes the development and management system security plans and controls.
- Situational Awareness includes policies, practices, and effectiveness metrics for situational awareness.
- System and Communication Protection entails the development of security requirements and controls for systems and communications.
- System and Information Integrity includes the identification and management of information system flaws, network and system monitoring, and advanced email protections.

The CMMC Framework Maturity Levels

The CMMC framework consists of five certification levels indicating the maturity and resiliency of an organization's cybersecurity infrastructure for safeguarding and securing CUI. The CMMC requires that the organization (contractor) should have a current (i.e., no older than 3 years) CMMC certificate at the CMMC level required by the contract and maintain that certificate at the required level for the duration of the contract (U.S. Department of Defense, 2021). Note that not all five certification levels may be required by the DoD contract. However, each level, except the first, is contingent upon achieving certification of the preceding level. The following describes each level of the CMMC framework, and the practices found within the Configuration Management (CM) domain, if any.

At **CMMC level 1**, the practices are focused on the protection of FCI. It entails the basic safeguarding of federal contract information through rudimentary cyber hygiene.

CMMC level 2 is basically a bridge between levels 1 and 3. This level requires creating documented practices and policies on CMMC implementations for the purpose of repeatability.

- *CM 061. Establish and maintain baseline configurations and inventories of organizational systems.*
- *CM 062. Employ the principle of least functionality by configuring organizational systems to provide only essential capabilities.*
- *CM 063. Control and monitor user-installed software.*
- *CM 064. Establish and enforce security configuration settings for information technology products employed in organizational systems.*
- *CM 065. Track, review, approve, or disapprove, and log changes to organizational systems.*
- *CM 066. Analyze the security impact of changes prior to implementation.* (CMMC, 2020)

CMMC level 3 requires the establishment, maintenance, and resource planning for the implementation of practices for the protection of CUI. Essentially, it covers all the security requirements specified in NIST SP 800-171 and practices from other standards with the ultimate goal of mitigating risks. The CMMC Frequently Asked Questions (FAQs) website describes the connection of the CMMC v1.2 with the NIST SP 800-171 rev 2 (Ross, Pillitteri, Dempsey, Riddle, & Guissanie, 2021) as follows:

CMMC Level 3 includes the 110 security requirements specified in NIST SP 800-171. The CMMC Model also incorporates additional practices and processes from other standards, references, and/or sources such as NIST SP 800-53, Aerospace Industries Association (AIA) National Aerospace Standard (NAS) 9933 "Critical Security Controls for Effective Capability in Cyber Defense", and Computer Emergency Response Team (CERT) Resilience Management Model (RMM). (Office of the Undersecretary of Defense for Acquisition & Sustainment, 2020).

- *CM 067. Define, document, approve, and enforce physical and logical access restrictions associated with changes to organizational systems.*
- *CM 068. Restrict, disable, or prevent the use of nonessential programs, functions, ports, protocols, and services.* (CMMC, 2020)

CMMC level 4 requires the review of practices for effectiveness using established metrics. Further, it calls for corrective actions when necessary and focuses on mitigation of risks on CUI resulting from Advanced Persistent Threats (APTs).

- *CM 073. Employ application whitelisting and an application vetting process for systems identified by the organization.* CMMC, 2020)

CMMC level 5 is involved in the standardization and optimization of processes and practices for the protection of CUI from APTs. At this level, it is expected that the organization has the capability to develop and implement sophisticated cybersecurity mechanisms to address Tactics, Techniques, and Procedures (TTPs) associated with APTs.

- *CM 074. Verify the integrity and correctness of security critical or essential software as defined by the organization.* (CMMC, 2020)

Figure 1 compares capability/maturity levels of the COBIT 2019 and CMMC v1.02 frameworks.

APPLYING THE FRAMEWORKS

The proper functioning of technology requires that organizations possess the agility to quickly and skillfully adapt to meet ever-changing processing requirements. The COBIT 2019 and CMMC frameworks provide a means to evaluate an organization's process of carrying out technology changes to help ensure that such changes are accomplished using best-in-class practices that minimize disruption to company operations. This section presents examples illustrating how organizations can apply the COBIT 2019 and the CMMC frameworks to measure the capability/maturity level of their change management process in an information system environment.

Illustration of Linking COBIT Management Practices to Capability Levels

Table 2 illustrates that specific activities associated with the COBIT BAI 06.02 management practice are assigned a capability level from the previously described COBIT Model.

To help an organization measure its level of capability for a process, the COBIT 2019 framework assigns activities and an accompanying capability level to each of its management practices.

Figure 1. Capability/Maturity levels of the COBIT 2019 and CMMC frameworks

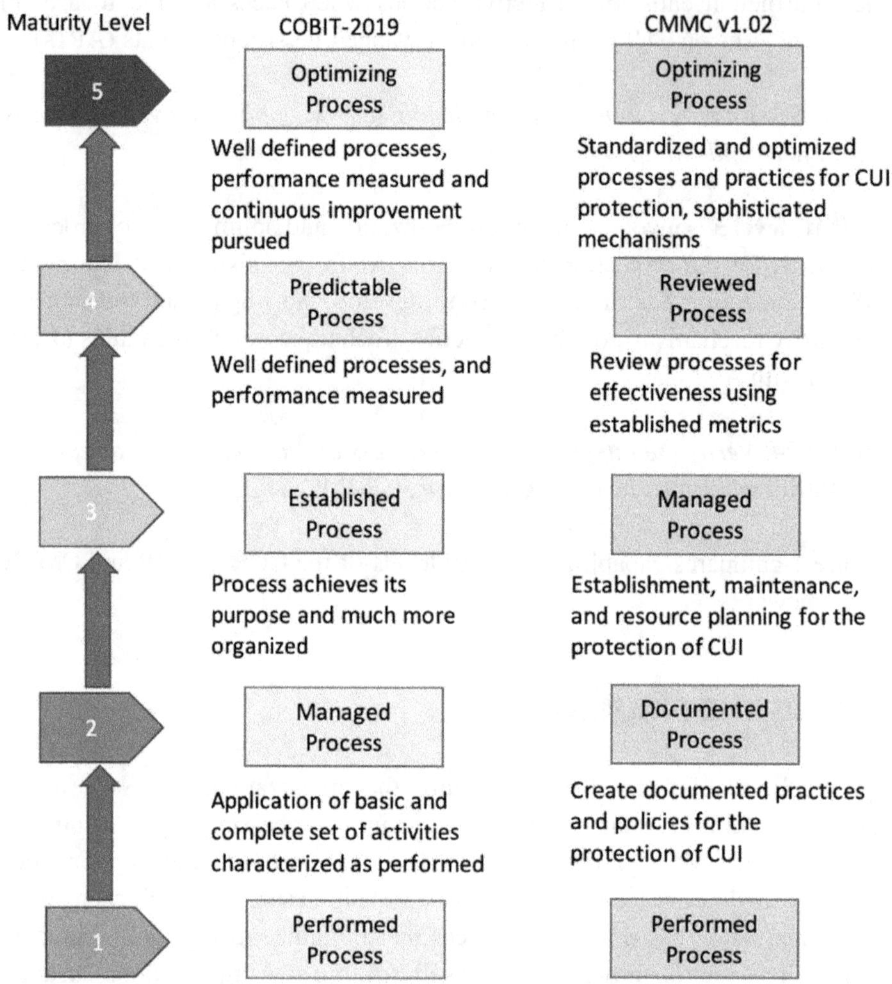

Illustration of the Application of the COBIT 2019 and CMMC Frameworks on an Instance of Patch Management

Table 3 illustrates a side-by-side comparison of the COBIT 2019 framework with the CMMC v1.02 framework at each capability/maturity level.

Table 4 illustrates the same side-by-side comparison as Table 3 but substitutes proposed patch management activities/practices that correspond with the original frameworks.

Table 2. Linking COBIT management practices to capability levels

BAI 06.02 Manage Emergency Changes *Carefully manage emergency changes to minimize further incidents. Ensure the emergency change is controlled and takes place securely. Verify that emergency changes are appropriately assessed and authorized after the change.* *Metric Example – Number of emergency changes not authorized after the incident.*	
Activities:	**Capability Level:**
Activity 1: *Define what constitutes an emergency change.*	**2**
Activity 2: *Ensure that a documented procedure exists to declare, assess, approve preliminary, authorize after the change, and record an emergency change.*	
Activity 3: *Verify that all emergency access arrangements for changes are appropriately authorized, documented and revoked after the change has been applied.*	**3**
Activity 4: *Monitor all emergency changes and conduct post-implementation reviews involving all concerned parties. The review should consider and initiate corrective actions based on root causes such as problems with business process, application system development and maintenance, development and test environments, documentation and manuals, and data integrity.*	**4**

(ISACA, 2018)

FUTURE RESEARCH DIRECTIONS

The updated GTAG by the Institute of Internal Auditors provides a significant enhancement to change management practices. Despite these significant efforts in streamlining the practices, there remain organizational aspects of change and patch management that need to be addressed. These issues suggest the following research directions:

- Development of a system that facilitates an effective communication channel between IT practitioners and internal auditors with regard to change and patch management. This entails the development of an automated system to effectively eliminate gaps and errors and to streamline the process of change and patch management.
- Development of a formal framework for modeling the states of change and patch management processes. The development of a formal framework provides a theoretical foundation for rationalizing each segment of the change and patch management process. A semi-Markov model may be suitable for this proposed formal framework.

- Development of an agile methodology to address the change management issues related to rapid advancements in technology and cybersecurity. This entails the design and development of change management processes that are flexible and adaptable to field advancements using the agile development techniques.

Table 3. Original framework activities/practices

<table>
<tr><td colspan="2">COBIT 2019 (ISACA, 2018)</td><td colspan="2">CMMC v1.02 (CMMC, 2020)</td></tr>
<tr><td colspan="2">Domain</td><td colspan="2">Domain</td></tr>
<tr><td colspan="2">Build, Acquire and Implement (BAI)</td><td colspan="2">Configuration Management</td></tr>
<tr><td colspan="2">Practices</td><td colspan="2">Capabilities</td></tr>
<tr><td colspan="2">BAI 03.10 Maintain solutions.</td><td colspan="2">C013 Establish Configuration Baselines
C014 Perform Configuration and Change Management</td></tr>
<tr><td>Activities</td><td>Capability Level</td><td>Practices</td><td>Maturity Level</td></tr>
<tr><td>Activity 1:
Develop and execute a plan for the maintenance of solution components. Include periodic reviews against business needs and operational requirements such as patch management, upgrade strategies, risk, privacy, vulnerabilities assessment and security requirements.</td><td>2</td><td>Practices
CM 061, CM 062, CM 063, CM 064, CM 065 and CM 066.</td><td>2</td></tr>
<tr><td>Activity 2:
Assess the significance of a proposed maintenance activity on current solution design, functionality and/or business processes.</td><td>3</td><td>Practices
CM 067 and CM 068.</td><td>3</td></tr>
<tr><td>Activity 3:
Ensure that the pattern and volume of maintenance activities are analyzed periodically for abnormal trends.</td><td>4</td><td>Practice
CM 073</td><td>4</td></tr>
<tr><td></td><td></td><td>Practice
CM 074</td><td>5</td></tr>
</table>

CONCLUSION

The purpose of an assurance engagement is to provide an independent assessment of an organization's ability to implement a proper system of governance, risk management, and control processes (Anderson et al., 2017). This chapter considers assurance over changes to an organization's information technology from two

Table 4. Corresponding patch management activities/practices

<table>
<tr><th colspan="2">COBIT 2019 (ISACA, 2018)</th><th colspan="2">CMMC v1.02 (CMMC, 2020)</th></tr>
<tr><th colspan="2">Domain</th><th colspan="2">Domain</th></tr>
<tr><td colspan="2">Build, Acquire and Implement (BAI)</td><td colspan="2">Configuration Management</td></tr>
<tr><th colspan="2">Practices</th><th colspan="2">Capabilities</th></tr>
<tr><td colspan="2">BAI 03.10 Maintain solutions.</td><td colspan="2">C013 Establish Configuration Baselines
C014 Perform Configuration and Change Management</td></tr>
<tr><th>Activities</th><th>Capability Level</th><th>Practices</th><th>Maturity Level</th></tr>
<tr><td>Activity 1:
1. Develop and execute a plan for automated patch management for systems and application software</td><td>2</td><td>Practices
CM 061, CM 062, CM 063, CM 064, CM 065 and CM 066
1. Maintain baseline configurations and inventories of system and application software.
2. Ensure essential capabilities are maintained during the patching process.
3. Control and monitor the patching of user installed software.
4. Ensure that security configuration settings are maintained after patching.
5. Track, review, approve or disapprove and log all patching activities.
6. Test system and application software after patching.</td><td>2</td></tr>
<tr><td>Activity 2:
1. Engage the stakeholders in the patching process.
2. Ensure that the patching process conforms with the change management procedures.</td><td>3</td><td>Practices
CM 067 and CM 068
1. Document and enforce physical and logical access restrictions during the patching process.
2. Ensure that nonessential features, functions, ports, and services remain disabled after the patching process.</td><td>3</td></tr>
<tr><td>Activity 3:
1. Continue to monitor the systems and applications affected by the patching process.</td><td>4</td><td>Practice
CM 073
1. Review and update the application whitelist. Apply the vetting process on new applications.</td><td>4</td></tr>
<tr><td></td><td></td><td>Practice
CM 074
1. Verify the integrity and correctness of patch prior to the actual patching process.
2. Approve or disapprove the patch based on the result of the verification process.</td><td>5</td></tr>
</table>

primary perspectives. First, is a detailed summary of internal audit literature on the proper steps of change management, including various control issues and how an internal auditor can apply a risk-based audit approach using a planned audit program. Secondly, it considers how an assessment of an organization's change/patch management activities could be used to rank an organization's capability/maturity level in its technology environment in terms of established models covering both functionality and cybersecurity issues.

The side-by-side comparison of the COBIT 2019 and the CMMC frameworks illustrates the generic nature of the COBIT 2019 practices and the specificity of the CMMC practices. This is to be expected since the CMMC framework is intended to apply to a specific area, cybersecurity, and to a specific sector of society, the DIB. Indeed, it is apparent that the practices in each framework progress in conformance with the requirements of each level of the capability/maturity models. Measuring change/patch management from the perspective of capability/maturity levels gives an organization assurance of whether they are accomplishing continuous improvement by achieving higher levels of capability/maturity over time.

ACKNOWLEDGMENT

This work is partially supported by the Office of Naval Research (ONR) under grant number N00014-21-1-2025. The United States Government is authorized to reproduce and distribute reprints notwithstanding any copyright notation herein.

REFERENCES

Anderson, U., Head, M., Ramamoorti, S., Riddle, C., Salamasick, M., & Sobel, P. (2017). *Internal Auditing Assurance and Advisory Services*. Internal Audit Foundation.

Buckley, S. (2011). IT Change Management. *Internal Auditor*. Retrieved from https://www.theiia.org/intAuditor/itaudit/2011-articles/it-change-management/

Carnegie Mellon University and The John Hopkins University Applied Physics Laboratory, LLC. (2020). *Cybersecurity Maturity Model Certification (CMMC) v 1.02*. Carnegie Mellon University and The John Hopkins University Applied Physics Laboratory, LLC.

Cavusoglu, H., Cavusoglu, H., & Zhang, J. (2004). Economics of Security Patch Management. *Annual Workshop on the Economics of Information Security*. Retrieved November 14, 2012, from http://ns2.honlab.dc.hu/~mfelegyhazi/courses/BMEVIHIAV15/readings/06_Cavasoglu2006security_patch.pdf

Choi, E. (2020, Jul 28). Business news: Garmin says hack disabled software. *Wall Street Journal*. Retrieved from http://lib-proxy.jsu.edu/login?url=https://www-proquest-com.lib-proxy.jsu.edu/newspapers/business-news-garmin-says-hack-disabled-software/docview/2427462869/se-2?accountid=11662

Galligan, M., Herrygers, S., & Rau, K. (2019). *Managing Cyber Risk in a Digital Age*. Committee of Sponsoring Organizations of the Treadway Commission (COSO).

Global Audit Technology Guide (GTAG) IT Change Management Critical for Organizational Success. (2020). The Institute of Internal Auditors.

ISACA. (2018). *COBIT 2019 Framework: Governance and Management Objectives*. ISACA.

Kaitano, F. (2007). Change Control Audits – A Must for Critical System Functionality. *Internal Auditor*. Retrieved from https://www.theiia.org/intAuditor/itaudit/archives/2007/march/change-control-audits-a-must-for-critical-system-functionality/

Mathiassen, L., Ngwenyama, O., & Aaen, I. (2005). Managing Change in Software Process Improvement. *IEEE Software*, *22*(November/December), 84–91. doi:10.1109/MS.2005.159

Melancon, D. (2006). The Three Cs of IT Change Management. *Internal Auditor*. Retrieved from https://www.theiia.org/intAuditor/itaudit/archives/2006/april/the-three-cs-of-it-change-management/

Meyer, M. J., & Lambert, J. C. (2007). Patch Management: No Longer Just an IT Problem. *The CPA Journal*, (November), 68–72.

Model, C. M. M. C. (2020). *CMMC Model and Assessment Guides*. Retrieved March 2021, from CMMC Model (Appendix A) Excel: https://www.acq.osd.mil/cmmc/docs/CMMCModelExcel_V1.02_20200318.xlsx

Office of the Undersecretary of Defense. (2021). *Cybersecurity Maturity Model Certification*. Retrieved March 2021, from OUSD A&S: https://www.acq.osd.mil/cmmc/index.html

Office of the Undersecretary of Defense for Acquisition & Sustainment. (2020, December 10). *Cybersecurity Maturity Model Certification*. Retrieved March 2021, from CMMC FAQ's: https://www.acq.osd.mil/cmmc/faq.html

Pasztor, A. (2020). Boeing finds another software problem --- glitch adds to string of technical issues delaying return of 737 MAX to service. *Wall Street Journal*. http://lib-proxy.jsu.edu/login?url=https://www-proquest-com.lib-proxy.jsu.edu/newspapers/boeing-finds-another-software-problem-glitch-adds/docview/2340165798/se-2?accountid=11662

Pierce, R. (2008). Using Customer Input to Drive Change in User Assistance. In *Proceedings of the 26th annual ACM international conference on Design of communication (SIGDOC'08)*. ACM. Retrieved from http://doi.acm.org.lib-proxy.jsu.edu/10.1145/1456536.1456541 doi:10.1145/1456536.1456541

Pollock, S. (2016). Change management: It is not a choice. *Talent Management Excellence Essentials*. Retrieved from http://lib-proxy.jsu.edu/login?url=https://search-proquest-com.lib-proxy.jsu.edu/docview/1955087691?accountid=11662

Ross, R., Pillitteri, V., Dempsey, K., Riddle, M., & Guissanie, G. (2021). *NIST SP 800-171 rev 2: Protecting Controlled Unclassified Information in Nonfederal Systems and Organizations. National Institute of Standards and Technology (NIST), Computer Security Division*. U.S. Department of Commerce.

Shostack, A. (2003). Quantifying Patch Management, Secure. *Business Quarterly*, *3*(2), 1–4.

Silverman, R. E. (2011, Oct. 17). Managing & Careers: For Bright Ideas, Ask the Staff --- Companies, Striving to Cut Costs and Encourage Innovation, Seek Suggestions from Rank and File. *Wall Street Journal*. Retrieved from http://search.proquest.com/docview/898496273?accountid=11662

U.S. Department of Defense. (2021). *DoD CUI Program*. Retrieved February 2021, from Controlled Unclassified Information (CUI): https://www.dodcui.mil

U.S. Department of Defense. (2021, January 15). *Part 252-Solicitation Provisions and Contract Clauses*. Retrieved March 2021, from Defense Federal Acquisition Regulation Supplement: https://www.acq.osd.mil/dpap/dars/dfars/html/current/252204.htm#252.204-7021

Zanzig, J., Francia, G. A., & Francia, X. P. (2014). Internal Control Considerations for Information System Changes and Patches. In H. Rahman & R. deSousa (Eds.), Information Systems and Technology for Organizational Agility, Intelligence, and Resilience. Hershey, PA: Business Science Reference. doi:10.4018/978-1-4666-5970-4.ch008

Zanzig, J., Francia, G. A., & Francia, X. P. (2019). Practical Guidance in Achieving Successful Change Management in Information System Environment. In R. da Cruz (Ed.), *New Perspectives on Information Systems Modeling and Design (2019):41* (pp. 41–66). IGI-Global Publishing. www.igi-global.com, doi:10.4018/978-1-5225-7271-8.ch003

ADDITIONAL READING

Agel, A. M. (2019). Governing Digital Transformation Using COBIT 2019: An Ehealth Case Study. *COBIT Focus*, 1-6.

Anderson, M.C., & Martin, J. (2020). CMMC Cybersecurity Maturity Model Certification. *Aerospace & Defense Manufacturing*, 78-82.

Braga, G. (2020). COBIT 2019 and the IIA Guiding Principles of Corporate Governance: Two Frameworks, Many Similarities. *COBIT Focus*, 1-4.

Burnette, R., Cassidy, S., & Clark, S. (2020, February 1). Pentagon Updating Cybersecurity Guidance. *National Defense*, *104*(795), 37.

Drozdov, A. (2019). Impressions From Delivering COBIT 2019 Foundation Training for Auditors. *COBIT Focus*, 1–4.

Ebner, S. W., & Sanchez, R. (2020). CMMC: Tips for Bidding on Government Contracts. *National Defense*, *805*, 18.

Edmead, M. T. (2020). Using COBIT 2019 to Plan and Execute an Organization's Transformation Strategy. *COBIT Focus*, 1–4.

Golden, J. (2020). DOD's cyber certification: Agency imposes a new requirement for contractors in 2020. *New Hampshire Business Review*, *3*, 12.

Graves, B. (2020). Cybersecurity Certification Has Contractors Talking: Pentagon Is Pushing for Audits of All Suppliers. *San Diego Business Journal*, *41*(5), 14.

Horan, J. (2020). DOD's Cybersecurity Maturity Model Certification Program Takes a Step Forward: A breakdown of DOD's recently published interim rule to transition the Pentagon's current cybersecurity regime to the new CMMC program. *Contract Management*, *60*(11), 8–13.

Jones, R. M., & Mikhaeel, M. (2020). Cybersecurity: How to Successfully Navigate CMMC and the DFARS. *Procurement Lawyer*, *55*(3), 1–41.

Lee, C. (2020). CMMC Regulations on the Way Despite Pandemic. *National Defense*, *800*, 22.

Magnuson, S. (2020). Will First CMMC Deadlines Hold Firm? *National Defense*, *798*, 6.

McGrath, M., & Peters, C. (2021, February 1). CMMC Implementation Creates Issues for "Shop Floors.". *National Defense*, *106*(807), 16.

Ojo, O. (2020). Achieving Operational Excellence Using COBIT 2019. *COBIT Focus*, 1–8.

Salman, S. (2020). Digital Transformation Realized Through COBIT 2019. *COBIT Focus*, 1–5.

Sundararajan, V., & Ghodousi, A. (2021). The Most Common Control Deficiencies in CMMC noncompliant DoD contractors. *ISSA Journal*, *19*(2), 31–36.

Williams, L. C. (2020). Pentagon releases CMMC standard for contractors. *Federal Computer Week*, *34*(1), 32–34.

Williams, L. C. (2020). CMMC training underway for auditors. *Federal Computer Week*, *34*(1), 34.

KEY TERMS AND DEFINITIONS

Change Management: A disciplined approach to controlling change and its intended or unintended effects.

Compliance: The state of complying with all rules, laws, regulations, standards, and ethical practices that apply to the organization.

Internal Controls: Systematic measures instituted by an organization to ensure the integrity of its operations.

Maturity Level: The degree of the formality and optimization of a process.

Patch Management: A systematic approach to acquiring, validating, implementing, and deploying a system patch.

Risk Management: A systematic approach to identifying threats and controlling the impact of uncertain events as a consequence of their realization.

Chapter 7
BI and Analytics for Effective Disaster Recovery Management Lessons From the Bayou

Gregory Smith
Xavier University, USA

Thilini Ariyachandra
Xavier University, USA

ABSTRACT

Disaster recovery management requires agile decision making and action that can be supported through business intelligence (BI) and analytics. Yet, fundamental data issues such as challenges in data quality have continued to plague disaster recovery efforts leading to delays and high costs in disaster support. This chapter presents an example of these issues from the 2005 Atlantic hurricane season, where Hurricane Katrina wreaked havoc upon the city of New Orleans forcing the Federal Emergency Management Agency (FEMA) to begin an unprecedented cleanup effort. The chapter brings to light the failings in record keeping during this disaster and highlight how a simple BI application can improve the accuracy and quality of data and save costs. It also highlights the ongoing data driven issues in disaster recovery management that FEMA continues to confront and the need for integrated centralized BI and analytics solutions extending to the supply chain that FEMA needs to become more nimble and effective when dealing with disasters.

DOI: 10.4018/978-1-7998-4799-1.ch007

INTRODUCTION

The devastation of a violent hurricane can etch lasting images into a country's culture and history. Hurricane Katrina, a 2005 Atlantic hurricane, was one such event. Hurricane Katrina remains one of the strongest hurricanes on record to make landfall in the United States, reaching Category 5 at its maximum (Knabb et. al, 2005). The storm affected most of the coastal states along the Gulf of Mexico and ultimately causing at least $80 billion in damage with over 1,800 confirmed deaths (Swenson & Marshall, 2006). The storm's damaging path tracked for over a week starting on August 23, 2005, before dissipating August 30, 2005 (Knabb et. al, 2005). However, it was on August 29, 2005, that the storm will be forever remembered as it was on this date that Hurricane Katrina wreaked havoc upon New Orleans leaving behind almost unbelievable destruction because of the storm's crushing surge.

Hurricane Katrina's storm surge, water pushed towards shore by the force of swirling winds, set in motion a catastrophic failure of New Orlean's aging levee system. This resulted in approximately 80% of the city and many of the nearby parishes being flooded leaving New Orleans the most devastated location in the Gulf region (Fritz et. al, 2008). Remnants of the storm surge persisted for weeks. In addition to the many examples of loss, exploitation, and heroism in New Orleans, cleanup and recovery throughout the region became imperative (Brinkley, 2007; Cutter et. al, 2006; Schneider, 2005). The aftermath left the Federal Government with an unprecedented debris removal effort. It was estimated that the storm generated behind more than 100 million cubic yards of debris which posed a potential threat to the public's health and safety (Luther, 2008). The removal effort was to be tightly controlled and efficient. Unfortunately, neither prospect proved successful as examples of abuse and fleecing were reported (Myers, 2006; U.S. Congress, 2006).

In the Fall of 2006, an independent public accounting firm in Cincinnati, OH, approached the Williams College of Business at Xavier University with an opportunity to assist with a manpower audit they were preparing for the Federal Emergency Management Agency (FEMA). The manpower audit was a review of Hurricane Katrina debris removal for Washington Parish, Louisiana. The firm had completed a formal review of financials, but required outside expertise to help reconcile and mine collected debris data with an ultimate goal of applying business intelligence (BI) to identify unsupported costs for right of way debris removal. They looked to collaborate with Xavier as a way to provide an opportunity for students and faculty to participate on a timely, real-world BI project. The project was to be completed during the Spring of 2007 with final submission to the accounting firm in April of 2007.

This chapter provides an overview of the work performed to identify unsupported costs resulting from ineligible billing for debris removal. It is organized as follows. First, it provides an overview of business intelligence and analytics. Second, it identifies the debris removal problem for Washington Parish. Next, it discusses data collection and database development for the project. Third, it reviews the project and unsupported cost development. Next it describes the value gained by Washington Parish, the ongoing BI and analytics issues that plague FEMA and the impact that holistic BI infrastructure and governance practices can have on similar projects.

BUSINESS INTELLIGENCE

Much like past trends in information systems, BI has a rich background that is several decades old. BI's background can be traced back to decision support systems (DSS) in the mid 1960's (Power, 2003). The purpose of the first decision support systems was to help managers make key decisions. Since then, its functionality has been repackaged with new technology additions. Starting with executive information systems (EIS), DSS has evolved to real time dashboards to specifically address the needs of senior executives (Watson and Frolick, 1993) An EIS provides electronic dashboards, a graphical user interface, that offers an intuitive arrangement of key measures customized for senior executive needs. Furthermore, it grants senior management the ability to drill down to the level of detailed data required.

Gaining access to the data required to support dashboards and drill down functionality can be challenging. Organizational data were mostly in disparate data sources that required coordination to provide a single integrated view of data in the enterprise. Data warehouses offered a solution to the data integration issues of EIS's. A data warehouse is a specially prepared, integrated repository of data for decision making in the organization. Data warehousing along with On-Line Analytical Processing (OLAP) began broadening the realm of EIS and enhanced access to and manipulation of rich data.

Concurrently, the amount of rich data required for decision making vastly increased with the dominance of the digital economy. Severe strains were placed on organizations' information processing abilities to meet changing information demands. Business intelligence (BI) and analytics, another phase in the progression of DSS, provides the needed technology to improve decision-making. It describes the entire infrastructure (e.g., data warehouses) and analytical tools (e.g., OLAP) required to integrate and analyze the growing accumulation of organizational data. It encompasses all the processes and systems needed for gathering, storing, analyzing and accessing data to improve organizational decision making (Liang, Ting-Pend and Liu 2018; Watson, 2006).

Today, with the rise of social media and smart devices, large volumes of data is generated in near real time in different types (i.e., structured, semi structured, unstructured). The resulting big data revolution has evolved BI and impacted every industry (Lee 2017). Data driven decision making has become the norm. BI and analytics functionality is embedded in various devices that individuals, businesses and society interact with to enhance quality of life (Walker and Moran 2019). The BI and analytics market has experienced tremendous growth. It has evolved with the adoption of new technologies such as cloud computing and storage and cognitive analytics (Hwang and Chen 2017). As a result, business agility has become easier for organizations to achieve with cloud storage and analytics enabling faster real-time decision making (Patil and Chavan 2020).

Enhanced with artificial intelligence and machine learning, advanced analytics has enabled data driven decision making to be more pervasive across the organization. Automation of AI based analytics decision making is enabling users to focus on more complex decision making tasks that require more human judgement (Borges, Laurindo, Spinola, Gonçalves, and Mattos 2020). While algorithmic bias and ethical implications of AI based analytics is an important issue in the BI industry, it has led to calls for more regulations globally that has led organizations to step up governance of analytics (Abal Abas et al 2020). With such ongoing efforts, a more conscious approach to advanced analytics that accounts for biases, will eventually enable organizations to adopt responsible, ethical AI analytics solutions for effective decision making. Consequently, BI that empowers frontline users in an organization to use BI and analytic tools for more effective decision making is now becoming a need and a reality within organization (Motamarri, Akter, and Yanamandram 2017). Embedded analytics at the edge is a trend that the Gartner Research sees as a welcome BI and analytics initiative that mature analytics organizations are adopting (Mendoza 2021). Analytics at the edge would enable organizations to sense and react to changes in the market more quickly as data in front line applications will be enhanced with analytics.

In the post pandemic economy, BI and analytics based innovation is expected to be one of the game changing means that organizations plan to use to recover and succeed (Olavsrud 2021). The global market size of big data and analytics was estimated at USD 171.39 billion in 2018 and is projected to reach USD 512.04 billion by 2026, rising at a CAGR of 14.80 percent between 2019 and 2026 (PR Newswire 2020). BI and analytics has become essential infrastructure for firms of all sizes (Bordeleau, Fanny-Eve, Mosconi, and de Santa-Eulalia 2020). BI and analytics solutions ranging from simple 'query and reporting' OLAP applications to complex cognitive analytics systems with automated predictive dynamic dashboards are having a tremendous positive impact on businesses (Henrys 2021).

Despite its growing importance and demand in industry, many companies fail to implement BI and analytics solutions that meet their decision making needs (Liu, Hang and DeBello 2018). According to Gartner Group, more than 87 percent of organizations continue to be classified as having low BI and analytics maturity

(Moore 2018). These organizations have stalled BI efforts characterized by a very basic level of BI capabilities such as spreadsheet based analyses and personal extracts. They struggle to modernize and advance their BI and analytics efforts. Firms continue to struggle to identify the data infrastructure design and analytical tools that would best suit their organization. They often relying on old technology that lacks the capacity to modernize and grow existing decision support infrastructure (Rands 2017). The use of inappropriate, ineffective systems and applications to store and analyze data propagates the creation of disparate data silos. Correspondingly, it hinders efficient organizational information processing, impedes the ability to make agile decision making and may even degrade a company's existing information processing performance.

In addition to the lack of knowledge on what data management solution may fit a given situation, poor data quality is another major issue that impacts BI and analytics success. According to Gartner Research, the average cost of bad data quality on businesses ranges between 9.7 million and 14.2 mission annually (Davie 2019). In the US alone, bad data is estimated to cost more than 3 trillion dollars per year (Redman 2016). Data accuracy and data completeness are among some of the key data quality problems that plague BI and analytics projects. Data accuracy indicates if the data accurately represents reality or is a verifiable source while data completeness describes if all necessary data is present. The BI problem described in this chapter highlights some of the data quality challenges, as well as general data analysis issues stemming from data integration issues commonly witnessed in BI projects today.

METHODOLOGY

In order to understand the BI and analytics issues faced during disaster management, a case study methodology was utilized. This methodology enables an in depth exploration and understanding of a real world situation or phenomenon within a particular context (Tellis 1997). A variety of qualitative data collection approaches can be used in the case study methodology can be used to gain an understanding of the business situation such as interviews, documents and materials from the business situation (Baxter and Jack 2008). Consequently, a descriptive case study approach enabled the investigation and documentation of the BI issues faced by FEMA during the Washington Parish debris cleanup operation.

THE DEBRIS REMOVAL PROBLEM IN WASHINGTON PARISH

Under the guidance of the Department of Homeland Security, the FEMA was responsible for the clean-up efforts for Hurricane Katrina (U.S. Congress, 2006). The goal of the effort was to create a unified workforce among the three stakeholders in the debris removal effort: the debris removal contractors, independent monitoring companies, and the truck drivers hauling debris. The debris removal contractors were responsible for coordinating and completing the loading, hauling, and dumping of debris. The independent monitoring companies were to provide an unbiased, on-site assessment of the removal progress, validate the work performed, and prepare requests for reimbursement from FEMA. The truck drivers assisted in loading, hauling, and dumping the debris under the direction of the debris removal contractors. Truck drivers could be independently employed or employed by the debris removal contractor.

FEMA was responsible for selecting the debris removal contractors for the entire Gulf of Mexico region. Four primary contractors were selected for the debris removal: Ashbritt Inc., CERES Environmental Services Inc., Environmental Chemical Corp. and Phillips and Jordan Inc. Each contractor was provided with a $500 million contract with an additional $500 million option to the Army Corps of Engineers (Myers, 2006). The primary debris removal contractors subsequently subcontracted the work to other debris haulers, with many levels of subcontracting that followed. Ultimately, one debris removal subcontractor (DRS) in a region was responsible for the removal effort and was required to work directly with an independent monitoring company (IMC) hired by the Washington Parish. Both the DRS and IMC maintained records of what was hauled, by whom, when, where from, where to, and the physical amount being carried on a single trip level.

Debris for removal and reimbursement was classified in two ways: right-of-way debris and right-of-entry debris. Right-of-way debris exists on public thoroughfares and impedes traffic, both pedestrian and vehicular. Right-of-entry debris prevents landowners from accessing to their property from a public thoroughfare. For purposes of this study, only right-of-way debris removal data was considered.

Six major forms of debris were to be considered for reimbursement for removal and disposal in the audit. They include: mulch, asbestos, uprooted stumps (stumps), leaning trees and hanging tree limbs (L&H), construction and demolition (C&D) debris, and vegetative debris. For landfill and incineration purposes, only vegetative and C&D debris could be commingled. While each type of waste was able to be safely disposed, some debris might have been contaminated with toxins or hazardous constituents. Therefore, timely removal was imperative for overall recovery efforts to move forward.

Each debris hauling company was required to certify all trucks with the monitoring company that were to be used to collect, haul, and dump debris at landfills. The certification, which included the types of debris that could be hauled and capacity of the truck, was to be completed prior to hauling. This was a qualification for FEMA reimbursement. In each case, a certified truck was assigned a number that was to be displayed on the outside of the vehicle in plain, unobstructed sight. Trucks were dispatched by the DRS to debris sights for removal and disposal.

At the debris site, a carbon paper system was employed to record properties of the load being hauled and dumped. The truck driver was presented with an individually numbered five ticket form, completed by hand, by a FEMA agent in full view of an independent monitor. Items on the ticket included: the longitude and latitude of the site, time and date of loading, the certified truck number, the landfill or incinerator for disposal and type of debris to be hauled. The driver would add his or her name to the form, load the truck with the named debris, and drive the debris to the designated disposal site. At the site, the driver would pull beneath a monitoring tower where the form was lifted to an individual employed by the DRS on the perch via a simply rope and pulley system. The DRS employee verified the truck number, maximum physical capacity, and type of debris in full view of an IMC employee. This individual also estimated the percent of the truck's physical capacity that was filled in five percent increments. The DRS employee recorded this amount on the form. All data discrepancies were to be settled on the tower before separating the tickets. Of the five tickets, two were kept by the DRS, two were kept by the IMC, and one was then returned to the driver via the rope and pulley system. The driver kept the form as a personal receipt for reimbursement for service. The drivers, in many cases, were independent contractors working for fee per haul. Once the form was secured, the driver would then dispose of the debris at the location.

Washington Parish relied exclusively on an IMC to oversee the activities of its right-of- way DRS and handle FEMA reimbursement preparation due to the magnitude of cleanup needed and other pressing needs within the community. The monitoring contractor's responsibility included assuring the Parish that costs billed by the right of way debris removal contractor were accurate and supported. They had an obligation to reconcile costs with the debris removal contractors before the Parish submitted reimbursement requests for FEMA funds.

The risk of generating unsupported costs was high. A simple visual review of data by the accounting firm resulted in questions about the quality of the data being processed and, ultimately, called into question the billing practices of the IMC. The accounting firm's lack of expertise in data handling led them to reach out to Xavier University for assistance. While the project was time consuming, approximately 100 hours, the task was not complex. The project was initially assigned as a group project in an introductory data mining class and later completed by faculty in the management information systems department.

DATA COLLECTION AND DATABASE DEVELOPMENT

The effort required significant data preparation and assaying. The plan was to create and reconcile two separate databases from supplied electronic files, one representing the debris ticket data from the monitoring agency and the other representing the debris ticket data from the hauling company. For both groups, tickets were gathered and the hand written data was manually entered into Excel spreadsheets by employees at both the DRS and IMC. This method of data handling presented many problems for the project team as data quality was low. Misspellings, inaccurate transcriptions, and multiple entries posed serious problems.

The IMC supplied twenty-five separate Excel workbooks to the accounting firm. The workbooks contained over 700 individual spreadsheets in total, each sheet representing a specific debris type and date of entry. In total, 70,166 tickets had information entered. Data entry was not performed daily. Instead, compilations of multiple days of hauling trips were entered together at various times. In addition, the IMC supplied a list of 536 certified trucks. This data was used to generate billing to FEMA for reimbursement.

For the DRS, 683 separate Excel spreadsheets were presented for evaluation. In total, 64,795 tickets had information entered. In a similar manner to the monitoring company's data entry, each sheet represented a specific debris type and data of entry. Again, data entry was not performed daily. In addition, the hauling company supplied an Access database as an attempt to consolidate the spreadsheets. After comparing just one spreadsheet for Vegetative debris to the database and finding numerous errors, the students concluded that completeness should be called into question. So, the prepared database was abandoned as a source for comparison.

For both groups, spreadsheet formatting was similar by debris type. The formatting followed the standard entries from the work tickets. For completeness, 121 spreadsheets for monitoring data and 137 spreadsheets for hauling company data needed reformatting. This effort was necessary as Visual Basic routines were generated to automatically retrieve debris specific data and place them into preformatted Access database tables. Upon completion, two separate databases were constructed with six tables contained within each, five for the debris types and one for the certified trucks. Figure 1 represents final ticket counts by organization in the initial databases.

Figure 1. Count of tickets by organization

Debris Type	IMC	DRS
Asbestos	16	29
L & H	2,652	3,030
Mulch	8,132	8,681
Stumps	5,492	5,324
Vegetation/C&D	53,874	47,731

PROJECT REVIEW AND UNSUPPORTED COST DEVELOPMENT

As this was a governmentally funded manpower audit, there were limitations as to what could be considered for unsupported claims. For purposes of this study, the Xavier team (XU team) was limited to the examination of four specific areas of potential unsupported costs: multiple records for a single ticket, overcapacity hauling, uncertified hauling vehicles, and mis-certified hauling equipment.

Multiple Data Entries

The first comparison was multiple entries for a single ticket. Multiple records were discovered by count querying on individual ticket numbers. The XU team found multiple entries in the DRS's data for asbestos, L&H, and mulch, but none in the IMC's same debris data. This did not present a problem as only the monitoring data was used in FEMA reimbursement billing. For root debris, the XU team discovered 526 tickets had been assigned an additional character to the end of their ticket number. After consulting with the IMC, the team was informed that these tickets had voided and already marked as unsupported claims. For the vegetative and C&D debris data, the team found 6,143 multiple entries in the IMC's data. Of these entries, 297 were entered into the databases from three to five times. The database included a staggering 1,527 entries for the 297 single tickets. After consultation with the monitoring agency, it was determined that while this was a data entry problem, they were going to allow a maximum of two separate entries for the same ticket number in this debris category. So, at most, only 594 entries would be permitted. This would leave 933 questionable entries that had been billed.

Overcapacity Hauling

After removing all questionable entries from the monitoring agency's database, the project focused on overcapacity hauling. The Parish based reimbursement payments to the DRS on estimation of cubic yards hauled to the dump locations. As stated previously, a DRS employee was perched on an elevated tower at the debris disposal site and visually estimated the quantity of debris in the trucks. Guidance from FEMA and the IMC showed that it is unallowable for a truck to be 100 percent full when carrying vegetative or construction and demolition debris. However, the monitor's database included 2,457 truckloads of vegetative and C&D debris estimated at 100 percent per truck. In addition, according to FEMA guidance, estimates of capacities from towers were to be in five percent increments. Because it was not feasible for trucks to be 100 percent full, the maximum capacity claimed should have been at a maximum at 95 percent. Thus, five percent of costs claimed for these loads were questioned.

Uncertified Trucks

The IMC provided a list of 536 trucks with certified capacities for hauling debris. The list included eleven loading vehicles which should not have been certified leaving us with a total of 525 certified trucks. None of the eleven machines billed for service. The XU team matched this list with load tickets included in the generated database for the IMC. The load tickets identified actual trucks which hauled the debris. The comparisons identified 365 trucks in the monitor's database that hauled debris but were not on their list of certified trucks. After questioning the monitoring agency, additional documentation was supplied that supported 308 of the 365 trucks which billed for reimbursement. Documentation was not available for the remaining 57 trucks. Without official certification, the cost of debris hauled in each of truck was not eligible for reimbursement.

Mis-Certified Equipment

The IMC followed the FEMA definition of a certifiable debris hauling vehicle (FEMA, 2003). Therefore, machines used to assist loading were not eligible for certification. Of the 308 trucks that were deemed certified by the IMC in response to the XU team's questioning, 171 were loaders and other non-hauling equipment. In many cases, a certified truck would carry a motorized loader to assist with large debris. While these machines were participants in loading, they were not eligible for reimbursement by FEMA. Ultimately, 662 trucks were deemed certified to haul debris.

Unsupported Cost Development

After full consolidation from project findings, the XU team was left with a total of 63,497 allowable tickets (See Figure 2).

Figure 2. Consolidated database

Debris Type	Ticket Count
Asbestos	16
L & H	2,652
Mulch	8,132
Stumps	4,966
Vegetation/C&D	47,731

This represents the XU team's best attempt to generate a complete database for reimbursement. The Xavier analytics team submitted the findings to the accounting from in April of 2007. After valuing the team's four findings, the accounting firm compiled and returned to us the following unsupported costs:

- The 933 questionable multiple entries had total unsupported billing of $375,000,
- The 2,457 truckloads of vegetative and C&D debris that were estimated at 100% capacity were revalued at 95% capacity. The 5% reduction represents $96,700 in unsupported billing,
- The 57 uncertified trucks had total unsupported billing of $64,000,
- The 171 loaders and other non-hauling equipment that were not reimbursement eligible represented $208,000 in unsupported billing.

Thus, total unsupported claims recognized for purposes of this study summed to $743,700 (OIG, 2007). This amount represents 1.2% of the total approved and paid reimbursements from FEMA for debris and removal in Washington Parish.

DECISION SUPPORT IN DISASTER RESPONSE

Debris removal in Washington Park reveals severe issues with data capture and reporting for decision making in the aftermath of a major disaster. Fleecing was rampant during Katrina according to Myers (2006). In Louisiana and Mississippi alone, the collection, hauling and smashing of debris cost well over 2.5 billion due to the large number of contracts and various tiers of subcontractors that were involved in the cleanup operations. Rapidly deploying infrastructure and feeds to capture data for agile decision making would have exposed irregularities and discouraged mishandling due to data inconsistencies.

According to Roberts (2017) there have been many positive changes to FEMA since Katrina from better leadership to a more local community based approach to post-disaster management. He describes the creation of a social media inspired collaborative bottom up response for disaster management that has emerged since Katrina that enables faster data collection for decision making. However, these new data feeds that are adopted 'on the go' as disasters strike are unstandardized. Coincidently, they create more disparate data feeds that cannot be easily reconciled further propagating integration issues.

After the trials of Katrina, FEMA was given more authority to move resources to impending disaster sites prior to the disaster, to provide a more immediate response once the natural disaster occurs (Roberts 2017). Hurricane Harvey serves as a good example of pre-disaster preparation of resources near the flood zone that was easily deployed after the hurricane struck. This could become a more efficient process supported by forecasting tools and a more data intensive, standardized supply chain process. This would enable greater agility on the ground - post disaster (Gunessee, Subramanian, and Ning 2018). Supply chain agility is crucial to disaster relief and humanitarian efforts (Dubey, Ali, Aital and Venkatesh 2014).

In addition, the importance of transparency in information diffusion is well documented in disaster management (Altay and Pal 2014; Dubey Altay and Blome 2019). Recent research by Dubey, Bryde, Foropon, Graham, Giannakis and Mishra (2020), further suggests that information sharing and transparency can create almost immediate trust among various groups involved in disaster management. This can improve disaster response, cut costs and improve the overall disaster management supply chain. Data driven decision making tools such as BI and analytics are essential features of the disaster management supply chain to create greater sharing, visibility and swift trust. Had such a network been part of FEMA's arsenal during the Washington parish cleanup in the aftermath of Katrina, the time taken for the cleanup, potential fraud and immense costs incurred could have been minimized.

Over the years, FEMA has embraced BI and analytics to its natural disaster prediction process. The sophisticated GIS systems utilized with complex algorithms and AI to forecast the path of a storm, counties affected, etc… are impressive (Altay and Narayanan 2020). However, in the aftermath of major disasters such as hurricane Katrina, FEMA has continued to struggle with data issues and reporting issues. According to a 2019 audit by the Office of the Inspector General, a myriad of IT problems related to data hindered the 2017 response and recovery operations by FEMA (OIG 2019). These challenges included: (1) problems with lack of integration of data feeds when dealing with both internal and external entities within the supply chain, (2) decentralized data practices that do not provide consistent integration and roll up of data in the supply chain to a central data infrastructure, and (3) the lack of centralized governance structures and practices.

Cloud BI and analytics infrastructure has made it more feasible for both large multinational corporations as well as SMEs to gain data integration with lower setup costs (Halper and Stodder 2016). It has improved integration and agility at a lower cost than in the past which has made real time decision making a reality in business (Mihaela 2015). This same infrastructure can be a viable option for FEMA to reduce data quality issues, achieve greater integration and enhance its disaster management supply chain.

FUTURE RESEARCH DIRECTION

Through the adoption of technology, FEMA disaster management has slowly evolved and improved over time. However, compared to the adoption of data driven decision making technologies by private enterprise, FEMA has a long way to go. While BI and analytics practices in organizations are less similar to crises and disaster management, future research in this space can examine how existing BI and analytics efforts by organizations can be translated to FEMA disaster management.

Research is needed on how data practices can be adopted to combat fleecing during disasters. More specifically, researchers need to address how analytics and data transparency be implemented to combat fleecing. There is a need for a framework to examine how agile principles can be applied to the rapid deployment of BI and analytics in high tech and low tech infrastructure environments like disaster management out in the field. More research is needed on how integration and standardization of data collection and reporting be achieved for data driven decision making in disaster aftermath. Existing supply chain research can be extended to discuss how agile supply chain principles, that organizations with mature BI infrastructure use, be adopted to disaster recovery and cleanup practices at organizations such as FEMA. As BI and analytics technology continues to advance, researchers in this space can explore how new BI and analytics technologies such as AI driven analytics automation or advances in cloud computing be adopted to disaster management in a viable manner.

CONCLUSION

The nature and large number of anomalies demonstrate that the IMC did not maintain sufficient records to support the assurances provided to the Parish that the costs billed by the DRS were accurate. With simple integrated database that reduced redundancies, the monitoring contractor would have been able to identify the specific load tickets and other documentation that supported individual invoices from the DRS and thus relieving some concern of unsupported costs. Instead, under the direction of the instructor, a student team in the introductory data mining class was able to create a data extraction routine, carryout data cleansing to improve data accuracy and completeness, build a relational database and finally create straightforward BI reports to identify issues with over billing.

The problems with data accuracy and data completeness described here resulted in 1.2% overbilling. If the amount to the total debris removal budget of FEMA is generalized for the entire Gulf region, the conclusion is a staggering $30 million. The possibility that FEMA may have incurred such a staggering cost due to overbilling is tragic in the wake of a disaster such as Katrina and the financial ruin brought to most of its victims. Yet the financial ramifications resulting from the data quality issues faced by FEMA is a mere example of the costs associated with dirty data.

Data quality remains a global data management issue despite technology advances as the new world of self service has made data quality a more complex issue (Dennis 2019). According to Experian, 90 percent of organizations recognize the impact of lack of data accuracy and data completeness on company financials yet still struggle to establish a data quality strategy (Vescovi 2008). Furthermore, financial hazards are not the only risks that organizations face due to dirty data. Inaccurate data are making organizations more susceptible to government data regulations such as Sarbanes Oxley. There are simple strategies that an organization could follow to enable high data quality within their BI implementations. These include creating validation routines for data entry, exposing shoddy processes, changing human practices, and gaining executive support for data quality strategies. Ultimately, ensuring high data quality is one of the critical success factors that influence the overall success of BI and analytics within organizations.

Collaborative efforts, such as the example described within this piece, are often eye opening events for academicians and practitioners alike. Each gains insight into the other's areas of expertise. With the need for broader applications of business intelligence, organizations are able to utilize skill sets often unavailable to them in-house. In addition, these organizations are able to better evaluate the viability of training their own employees with these skill sets. Likewise, universities gain real-world insight into business problems and are able to bring this experience to their students. This allows students to gain invaluable experience and exposure to business problems in a controlled environment. In this case, both sides, the independent accounting firm and Xavier University, were completely satisfied with the collaboration and look to continue the association into the future. Additionally, the collaborative partnership reveals the importance of a simple integrated BI solution that if expanded to FEMA's disaster management supply chain can vastly enhance the post disaster operations of FEMA and improve its agility during humanitarian crises.

REFERENCES

Abal Abas, Z., Abdul Rahman, A. F. N., Pramudya, G., Wee, S. Y., Kasmin, F., Yusof, N., Md Yunos, N., & Abidin, Z. Z. (2020). Analytics: A review of current trends, future applications and challenges. Compusoft. *International Journal of Advancements in Computing Technology*, *9*(1).

Altay, N., & Narayanan, A. (2020). Forecasting in humanitarian operations: Literature review and research needs. *International Journal of Forecasting*. Advance online publication. doi:10.1016/j.ijforecast.2020.08.001 PMID:32921856

Altay, N., & Pal, R. (2014). Information diffusion among agents: Implications for humanitarian operations. *Production and Operations Management*, *23*(6), 1015–1027. doi:10.1111/poms.12102

Baxter, P., & Jack, S. (2008). Qualitative case study methodology: Study design and implementation for novice researchers. *Qualitative Report*, *13*(4), 544–559.

Bordeleau, Mosconi, & de Santa-Eulalia. (2020). Business intelligence and analytics value creation in Industry 4.0: a multiple case study in manufacturing medium enterprises. *Production Planning & Control, 31*(2-3), 173-185.

Borges, A. F., Laurindo, F. J., Spínola, M. M., Gonçalves, R. F., & Mattos, C. A. (2020). The strategic use of artificial intelligence in the digital era: Systematic literature review and future research directions. *International Journal of Information Management*.

Brinkley, D. (2007). *The great deluge: Hurricane Katrina, New Orleans, and the Mississippi Gulf coast*. Harper Collins.

Cutter, S. L., Emrich, C. T., Mitchell, J. T., Boruff, B. J., Gall, M., Schmidtlein, M. C., Burton, C. G., & Melton, G. (2006). The long road home: Race, class, and recovery from Hurricane Katrina. *Environment*, *48*(2), 8–20. doi:10.3200/ENVT.48.2.8-20

Dennis, A. (2019, July 2). *The Challenges of Data Quality*. Dataversity. https://www.dataversity.net/the-challenges-of-data-quality/

Dubey, R., Ali, S. S., Aital, P., & Venkatesh, V. G. (2014). Mechanics of humanitarian supply chain agility and resilience and its empirical validation. *International Journal of Services and Operations Management*, *17*(4), 367–384. doi:10.1504/IJSOM.2014.059999

Dubey, R., Altay, N., & Blome, C. (2019). Swift trust and commitment: The missing links for humanitarian supply chain coordination? *Annals of Operations Research*, *283*(1), 159–177. doi:10.100710479-017-2676-z

Dubey, R., Bryde, D. J., Foropon, C., Graham, G., Giannakis, M., & Mishra, D. B. (2020). Agility in humanitarian supply chain: An organizational information processing perspective and relational view. *Annals of Operations Research*, 1–21. PMID:33110282

FEMA. (2007). *Debris Management Guide*. Retrieved March 2006, from http://www.fema.gov/government/grant/pa/demagde.shtm#3

Fritz, H. M., Blount, C., Sokoloski, R., Singleton, J., Fuggle, A., McAdoo, B. G., Moore, A., Grass, C., & Banks, T. J. (2008). Hurricane Katrina storm surge reconnaissance. *Journal of Geotechnical and Geoenvironmental Engineering*, *134*(5), 644–656. doi:10.1061/(ASCE)1090-0241(2008)134:5(644)

Gunessee, S., Subramanian, N., & Ning, K. (2018). Natural disasters, PC supply chain and corporate performance. *International Journal of Operations & Production Management*, *38*(9), 1796–1814. doi:10.1108/IJOPM-12-2016-0705

Halper, F., & Stodder, D. (2016). *Transforming Data With Intelligence*. TDWI. https://tdwi.org/webcasts/2016/10/bi-analytics-and-the-cloud-strategies-for-business-agility.aspx

HenrysK. (2021, April 19). *Role of predictive analytics in business*. https://ssrn.com/abstract=3829621

Hwang, K., & Chen, M. (2017). *Big-data analytics for cloud, IoT and cognitive computing*. John Wiley & Sons.

Knabb, R. D., Rhome, J. R., & Brown, D. P. (2005). *Tropical cyclone report, Hurricane Katrina, 23-30, 2005*. National Hurricane Center. https://www.nhc.noaa.gov/pdf/TCR-AL122005_Katrina.pdf

Knights, M. (2008, Apr.). BI Growth to Buck Economic Trends. *IT Pro Fit for Business*.

Lee, I. (2017). Big data: Dimensions, evolution, impacts, and challenges. *Business Horizons*, *60*(3), 293–303. doi:10.1016/j.bushor.2017.01.004

Liang, T., & Liu, L. (2018). Research landscape of business intelligence and big data analytics: A bibliometrics study. *Expert Systems with Applications*, *111*, 2–10. doi:10.1016/j.eswa.2018.05.018

Liu, Y., Han, H., & DeBello, J. (2018). The challenges of business analytics: Successes and failures. *HICSS -51 Conference Proceedings*.

Luther, L. (2008). Disaster debris removal after Hurricane Katrina: status and associated issues: Order Code RL33477. Washington, DC: Congressional Research Service.

Mendoza, N. F. (2021, March 16). *Gartner: Top 10 data and analytics technology trends for 2021*. TechRepublic. https://www.techrepublic.com/article/gartner-top-10-data-and-analytics-technology-trends-for-2021

Meyers, L. (2006, June 6). *Is Katrina cleanup a fleecing of America?* NBC News. https://www.nbcnews.com/id/wbna13153520

Moore, J. (2018). *Gartner Data Shows 87 Percent of Organizations Have Low BI and Analytics Maturity* [Press release]. https://www.gartner.com/en/newsroom/press-releases/2018-12-06-gartner-data-shows-87-percent-of-organizations-have-low-bi-and-analytics-maturity

Motamarri, S., Akter, S., & Yanamandram, V. (2017). Does big data analytics influence frontline employees in services marketing? *Business Process Management Journal*, *23*(3), 623–644. doi:10.1108/BPMJ-12-2015-0182

Muntean, M. (2015). Driving business agility with the use of cloud analytics. *Proceedings of the IE 2015 International Conference*. https://www.conferenceie.ase.ro

Myers, L. (2006). *Is Katrina cleanup a fleecing of America?* Retrieved July 15, 2009 from MSNBC News Web site: http://www.msnbc.msn.com/id/13153520/ns/nightly_news_with_brian_williams-lisa_myers_and_the_nbc_news_investigative_unit/

Newswire, P. R. (2020, February 11). *Big Data and Business Analytics Market Size is Projected to Reach USD 512.04 Billion by 2026* [Press release]. https://www.bloomberg.com/tosv2.html?vid=&uuid=e3122840-a4a1-11eb-94030110c6469ace

Office of Inspector General. (2007). *Review of hurricane Katrina Debris removal activities, Washington Parish, LA* (1603-DR-LA). Denton, TX: Department of Homeland Security.

Office of Inspector General. (2019). *FEMA's Longstanding IT Deficiencies Hindered 2017 Response and Recovery Operations* (OIG-19-58). Denton, TX: Department of Homeland Security.

Olavsrud, T. (2021, March 16). *3 analytics and AI trends that will dominate 2021*. CIO. https://www.cio.com/article/3251720/data-analytics-trends.html

Patil, S. S., & Chavan, R. (2020). Cloud business intelligence: an empirical study. *Stud. Indian Place Names UGC Care J, 27*, 747-754.

Power, D. (2003). *Decision Support Systems: Concepts and Resources for Managers*. Greenwood Publishing.

Rands, K. (2017, September 25). *4 reasons most companies fail at business intelligence*. CIO. https://www.cio.com/article/3221430/4-reasons-most-companies-fail-at-business-intelligence.html

Roberts, P. (2017, September 13). *5 things that have changed about FEMA since Katrina – and 5 that haven't*. The Conversation. https://theconversation.com/5-things-that-have-changed-about-fema-since-katrina-and-5-that-havent-83205

Schneider, K. (2005). Administrative breakdowns in the governmental response to Hurricane Katrina. *Public Administration Review*, *65*(5), 515–516. doi:10.1111/j.1540-6210.2005.00478.x

Strange, K. F. (2003). *Making BI and data warehousing strategic: The key issues*. Gartner Group.

Swenson, D. & Marshall, B. (2006, May 14). Flash flood: Hurricane Katrina Inundation of New Orleans, August 29, 2006. *The Times Picayune*.

Tellis, W. (1997). Application of a case study methodology. *Qualitative Report*, *3*(3), 1–19.

United States Congress. (2006). *A Failure of Initiative: Final Report of the Select Bipartisan Committee to Investigate the Preparation for and Response to Hurricane Katrina*. Washington, DC: Government Printing Office.

Vescovi, P. (2008). *Effective Data Quality Strategies*. Retrieved July 29th, 2009 from Dynamic Business Web site: http://www.dynamicbusiness.com/articles/articles-technology/effective-data-quality-strategies.html/2

Walker, K. L., & Moran, N. (2019). Consumer information for data-driven decision making: Teaching socially responsible use of data. *Journal of Marketing Education*, *41*(2), 109–126. doi:10.1177/0273475318813176

Watson, H. J., & Frolick, M. N. (1993). Determining Information Requirements for an EIS. *Management Information Systems Quarterly*, *17*(3), 255–269. doi:10.2307/249771

Watson, R. T. (2006). *Data management: Databases and organizations* (5th ed.). John Wiley.

ADDITIONAL READING

Ajah, I. A., & Nweke, H. F. (2019). Big data and business analytics: Trends, platforms, success factors and applications. *Big Data and Cognitive Computing*, *3*(2), 32. doi:10.3390/bdcc3020032

Asare, A. O., Addo, P. C., Sarpong, E. O., & Kotei, D. (2020). COVID-19: Optimizing business performance through agile business intelligence and data analytics. *Open Journal of Business and Management*, *8*(5), 2071–2080. doi:10.4236/ojbm.2020.85126

Ashrafi, A., Ravasan, A. Z., Trkman, P., & Afshari, S. (2019). The role of business analytics capabilities in bolstering firms' agility and performance. *International Journal of Information Management*, *47*, 1–15. doi:10.1016/j.ijinfomgt.2018.12.005

Batra, D. (2017). Adapting agile practices for data warehousing, business intelligence, and analytics. *Journal of Database Management*, *28*(4), 1–23. doi:10.4018/JDM.2017100101

George, A., Schmitz, K., & Storey, V. C. (2020). A Framework for Building Mature Business Intelligence and Analytics in Organizations. *Journal of Database Management*, *31*(3), 14–39. doi:10.4018/JDM.2020070102

Larson, D., & Chang, V. (2016). A review and future direction of agile, business intelligence, analytics and data science. *International Journal of Information Management*, *36*(5), 700–710. doi:10.1016/j.ijinfomgt.2016.04.013

Phillips-Wren, G., Daly, M., & Burstein, F. (2021). Reconciling business intelligence, analytics and decision support systems: More data, deeper insight. *Decision Support Systems*, *146*, 113560. doi:10.1016/j.dss.2021.113560

Pool, J. K., Jamkhaneh, H. B., Tabaeeian, R. A., Tavakoli, H., & Shahin, A. (2018). The effect of business intelligence adoption on agile supply chain performance. *International Journal of Productivity and Quality Management*, *23*(3), 289–306. doi:10.1504/IJPQM.2018.089802

Prat, N. (2019). Augmented analytics. *Business & Information Systems Engineering*, *61*(3), 375–380. doi:10.100712599-019-00589-0

Soldić-Aleksić, J., Krasavac, B. C., & Karamata, E. (2020). Business analytics: New concepts and trends. *Management: Journal of Sustainable Business and Management Solutions in Emerging Economies*, *25*(2), 15–29.

Tsoy, M., & Staples, D. S. (2020). What Are the Critical Success Factors for Agile Analytics Projects? *Information Systems Management*, 1–18. doi:10.1080/10580530.2020.1818899

Ukhalkar, P. K., Phursule, D. R. N., Gadekar, D. D. P., & Sable, D. N. P. (2020). Business Intelligence and Analytics: Challenges and Opportunities. *International Journal of Advanced Science and Technology*, *29*, 2669–2676.

Wamba, S. F., & Akter, S. (2019). Understanding supply chain analytics capabilities and agility for data-rich environments. *International Journal of Operations & Production Management*.

Watson, H. J., & Nations, C. (2019). Addressing the growing need for algorithmic transparency. *Communications of the Association for Information Systems*, *45*(1), 26. doi:10.17705/1CAIS.04526

Williams, M., Ariyachandra, T., & Frolick, M. (2017). Business intelligence-success through agile implementation. *Journal of Management & Engineering Integration*, *10*(1), 14–21.

KEY TERMS AND DEFINITIONS

Agile Development: A group of software development methodologies based on iterative development, where requirements and solutions evolve through collaboration between self-organizing cross-functional teams.

Analytics: An umbrella term for data analysis applications. It is the use of "rocket science" algorithms (e.g., machine learning, neural networks) to analyze data.

Artificial Intelligence (AI): Applies advanced analysis and logic-based techniques to interpret events, support and automate decisions, and take actions.

Augmented Analytics: The use of enabling technologies such as machine learning and AI to assist with data preparation, insight generation and insight explanation to augment how people explore and analyze data in analytics and BI platforms.

BI Cloud: An external service provider hosts the technical infrastructure for BI (e.g., servers, BI software) and company data is transmitted, stored, analyzed, and the analyses returned over the internet.

Business Intelligence: A broad category of applications, technologies, and processes for gathering, storing, accessing, and analyzing data to help business users make better decisions.

Data Warehouse: Provides a single version (or source) of the truth for decision support data. The data is extracted from source systems (e.g., operational systems,

ERPs), transformed (e.g., consistent formats), integrated (e.g., around a common key, such as a customer ID), and loaded into the data warehouse.

Machine Learning: Composed of many technologies (such as deep learning, neural networks and natural language processing), used in unsupervised and supervised learning, that operate guided by existing data.

Chapter 8
From Business Intelligence to Data Science: A Decade of Evolution

Virginia M. Miori
Saint Joseph's University, USA

John Yi
Saint Joseph's University, USA

Rashmi Malhotra
Saint Joseph's University, USA

Ronald K. Klimberg
Saint Joseph's University, USA

ABSTRACT

The use of information technology and decision support concepts at the operational business level were slow to take hold in the 20th century. In 2010, the authors documented the evolution and current state of the field of business intelligence and analytics (BIA). In the last decade, however, through the resurgence and mainstream use of artificial intelligence, machine learning algorithms, the development of inexpensive cloud-based mass storage, and the internet-of-things, business intelligence has evolved into data science. In this chapter, the authors trace this evolution across the diverse areas of data science and identify extremely useful advancements and best practices in the field.

DOI: 10.4018/978-1-7998-4799-1.ch008

INTRODUCTION

Prior to 2010, significant growth occurred in the field of business intelligence (BI), a discipline more prevalent in practice than in theory. While there were a number of professional and consulting organizations, few universities had created or adapted their research at that time. BI was thought by some, to be the latest incarnation of management information systems (MIS), but a fundamental change has occurred in the organizational approach to the relevant disciplines. After witnessing the growth of BI, it is important to visit the changes that have taken place in the last decade. With the advent of cloud storage, the internet-of-things, and with the assistance of artificial intelligence and machine learning algorithms, the world has quickly progressed from business intelligence to data science.

Program offerings now span many schools and departments in universities, including business, computer science, statistics, and mathematics. Ten years ago, analytics programs were lumped into rankings with MIS programs. Currently, business analytics and data science programs abound in undergraduate and graduate settings, while online graduate programs have also proliferated, each with their own rankings.

By 2021, 98 colleges and universities were offering undergraduate programs and 627 colleges and universities were offering graduate programs and certificates in the many subfields of data science[1]. Programs focus in areas such as data analytics, data mining, cyber security, and marketing analytics to name a few. Online offerings have abounded.

For purposes of this article, "Data" is considered to encompass all of the traditional functional activities in business such as marketing, manufacturing, accounting, finance, distribution and the support operations provided by the transaction processing systems and other technology. "Science" includes artificial intelligence, machine learning, applied mathematics, data mining and statistical tools developed to solve business problems over this same period.

Assumptions

This article examines the ultimate confluence between efficiency-effectiveness and operational-tactical-strategic. Both dimensions are part of the decision-making process, that has been examined in many arenas from the psychological to the managerial. Some decisions support small issues while others have enormous impact. Theoretical approaches have always advocated for optimize some form of outcome (broadly defined as minimization of cost or maximization of profit) through algorithms or formulae. The practical approaches have usually tried to find "satisfactory" answers through simulation and heuristics. In the end, there are cost-effectiveness tradeoffs that contribute to the selection of the appropriate (or even feasible) decision-making approach. These tradeoffs will be examined on these two dimensions.

Efficiency is the measurement of Output as a function of Input. The formula is simple: Efficiency = Output/Input (e.g., miles/gallon). Operations are fine tuned to ensure the greatest impact of resources in accomplishing a goal. The time-motion expert charts the operation with a stopwatch and clipboard hoping to save precious seconds in highly repetitive operations, seconds which add up to dollars with the operation being repeated thousands or millions of times. On the other hand, effectiveness is not so easy to define. Traditional definitions like "successful in producing a desired or intended result" are less than definitive. What is the desired or intended result? How can it be determined what should be done? Perhaps the simplified "Efficiency is doing things right and Effectiveness is doing the right things" provides guidance. Business practitioners have typically used information and decision technology primarily for efficiency while the academics in the intelligence community were trying to determine what was effective.

Decisions are made at all levels within an organization. At the tactical level, decisions tend to be current in time and use highly detailed data. A clerk at a bank must decide whether to give an automobile loan to a customer based upon the details of an application. Decisions at this level tend to be highly structured, sometimes quite complex, but almost always, well defined by policy and algorithm. At the tactical level, the time horizon grows to weeks, months and maybe a year. Decisions do not require the level of detail but usually involve aggregated data. For example, a branch manager might use summary transaction activity data to make a staff planning decision to assure good service to customers. At the strategic level decisions are made for the long run. There is very little detail or even accuracy in the numbers that may be included in these important and usually very unstructured decisions.

THE "DATA" FLOW

The impact of information management technology on organizations and society increases as new technologies evolve and existing technologies expand. The objective of a computer-based information system is to assist management in solving managerial or organizational problems faster and better than what can be done without computers. To attain this objective, managers may use one or more information technologies. As always, technology and business applications are interrelated and work hand-in-hand. Technologies are developed and are subsequently exploited commercially.

In the 1950s, mainframe computers (IBM and the BUNCH[2]) were the major computation tools (Longbottom, 2017). Through time sharing, multiple simultaneous jobs could be processed at the same time, ensuring high processing utilization levels.

With the appearance of more affordable midrange or minicomputers[3] in the 1970s and 1980s, computing power became accessible to smaller companies, and business areas such as marketing, human resources, design, and manufacturing could have dedicated computers. Systems such as computer-aided design (CAD), computer-aided manufacturing (CAM), and material requirements planning (MRP) improve the productivity of the manufacturing division. Similarly, sales force automation (SFA) and point-of-sale (POS) systems increase the efficiency of the marketing division. During this time, processor utilization was reduced to below 50%. Both mainframe and minicomputers were accessed through dumb or semi-dumb terminals.

While the transaction processing systems (TPS) of this era did much to support the operational decision maker, they provided little support for the tactical or middle-level manager. Management information systems (MIS) were developed as a layer on top of the transaction processing systems. These middle level management information systems provided reporting and analysis capabilities on a monthly or quarterly basis. Managers could monitor their performance against targets through budget analysis, summary reporting and in some cases, graphical output. These systems were aimed at solving the efficiency goal and answered the question of whether a function was operating at some target level. They did not however address the question of whether a company should be taking a very different direction.

In the early 1970s, Scott Morton first articulated the major decision support system (DSS) concepts (Gorry and Scott Morton, 1971). DSS has been linked to the computational approach in electronic data processing (EDP) applications (Alter, 1980), the knowledge-based symbolic approach (Bonezek, et. al., 1980), and the system architecture and development process (Keen, 1980; O'Keefe, 1986).

By the early 1980's microcomputers were introduced, placing computer power and data storage in the hands of individuals with personal computers (PC). Beginning with the Apple II and Visicalc in 1979 followed quickly by the IBM PC and Lotus 1-2-3 in 1981, managers had the potential to address effectiveness decisions. Decision support concepts, could, in theory, provide tactical and possibly strategic decision-makers with a way to ask "effectiveness" questions.

Each PC required the space to store its own operating system and software programs. Processor utilization fell even more, to as low as 5% on average and over time, data became scattered and inaccessible to multiple constituents. Furthermore, the network revolution of the 1990s led to the development of group support systems and hybrid integrated computer systems (Turban, et. al., 1996, 1988).

THE "SCIENCE" FLOW

Organizations typically have had two "parallel cultures": the IT and business cultures (Watson, 2009). However, the evidence that organizations have implemented ever more powerful operational systems demonstrates that at least as far as operational systems are concerned, these cultures have synchronized for operational decision-making. Competitive pressures have driven operational information technology to meet the needs of the efficient organization.

A literature survey on the development of decision support systems by Eom, Lee, Kim, and Somrajan (1998) showed a growing tendency towards group-based decision support systems, executive support systems, and knowledge-based systems. In addition, Mamghani (1997) describes the potential of knowledge-based systems to provide effective computer support for strategic planning. With the increased complexity of problems being solved by knowledge-based systems there was a trend to increase the use of frames and object-oriented implementations (Bogarin and Ebecken, 1996).

Forgionne and Kohli (1995) investigated the benefits of integrating different information technologies.

Significant improvements in making decisions are associated with integrated system usage. The most popular integrated applications are enterprise systems, supply chain management systems, customer relationship management systems, and knowledge management systems. Much of the impetus for the development of these systems came from the need for major system change driven by Y2K (Year 2000) issues and the growth of business process re-engineering. The main focus of enterprise applications is to integrate business and data processes to focus on efficient management of resources. Historically, information systems and information technologies have been used to improve the efficiency of the organization.

Decision support systems have long integrated aspects of statistics (particularly applied to quality initiatives), operations research, and operations management to provide effective business solutions. Since the inception of these operational methods, analysts, scientists and researchers have promoted their use throughout the industrial and service sectors. Rather than being purely theoretical pursuits, developments in these areas have been dedicated toward practical applications. Enterprise level systems have also actively incorporated quantitative complexities in the last decade.

Blockchain, the Internet of Things (IoT), machine learning and artificial intelligences, are all cornerstones of the science. They have transformed cloud computing and therefore enhanced the reach and capabilities of DSS (Gill et al., 2019) and enterprise level systems, enabling applications that range from infrastructure to social media.

DECONSTRUCTING DATA SCIENCE

In order to build an academic program in data science or to establish a data science function within a business organization, it is first critical to define data science in a relevant fashion. The Data Science Framework shown in Figure 1 attempts to create a universal perspective on data science and developments in the last decade. It is important to note that this framework provides a superset, within which programs and organizations may be founded. The field is broad and specializations are varied, it cannot possibly be fully addressed by any single entity.

The Data Science Framework highlights many methodologies and techniques within data science. They are categorized by discipline and discussed in detail in the following sections.

Figure 1. Data science framework

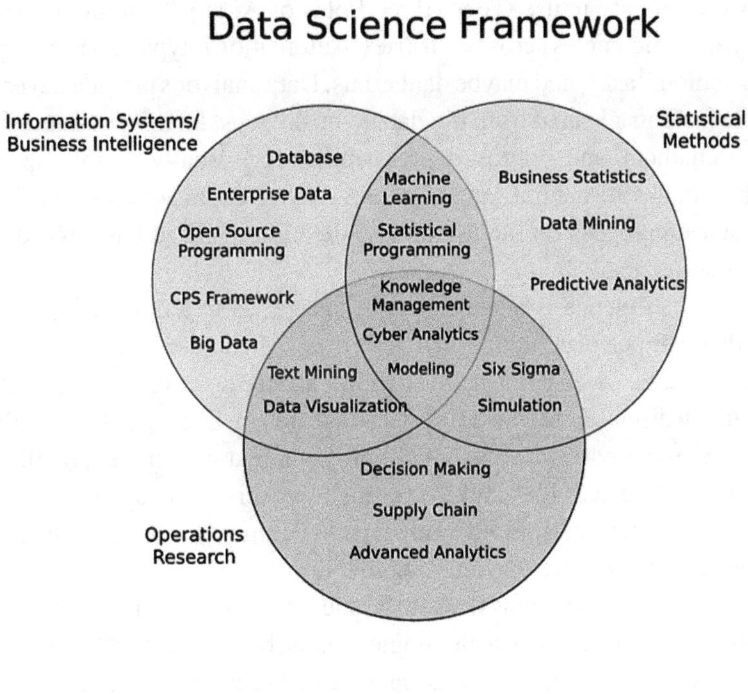

Artificial Intelligence and Machine Learning

With the dawn of the third decade of the new millennium, the power of technology and analytics has proved to be the major driver of economic growth. However, there has been a renewed interest in the use of artificial intelligence (AI) and its subfield – machine intelligence. Irrespective of the nature of business, AI is impacting every facet of business development. AI and the underlying modeling environment is proving to be the next big thing in the application of business intelligence and analytics. The application of AI methodologies is the major enabler for many small, medium, and large service and manufacturing organizations to streamline operations and improve efficiencies. In fact, AI is ushering in the second version of "industrial revolution" – "intelligent machine revolution" (Uzialko, 2019). The "industrial revolution" involved utilizing the physical and mechanical strength of machines to replace manual labor. The "intelligent machine revolution" will harness the mental and cognitive ability of computers to replace or augment mental labor.

AI is now widely used in a variety of business applications such as automation, data analytics, natural language processing to expand and scale operations. Consequently, AI has proven to be a disruptive force in virtually any industry: healthcare, banking, finance, mining, manufacturing, consulting, agriculture, retail, online businesses, construction, gaming, logistics, among others. Automation, data mining, and natural language processing are only a few of the business applications where artificial intelligence is already in use. These three fields of AI are streamlining operations and increasing efficiencies across industries. Automation is typically used to perform repetitive, tedious tasks, and maybe dangerous. Data analytics provide never-before-imaginable insights gleaned from big data to businesses. Intelligent search engines, supportive chatbots, and improved accessibility for visually disabled people are all possible thanks to natural language processing. Organizations worldwide are training their employees on the use and application of AI in business to advance themselves strategically.

Artificial Intelligence is a generic term that refers to a computer hardware or software that can perform human-like activities. AI can perform many tasks such as collecting data, overseeing information, arranging, organization, planning, participating in discussions, and doing deep research on large quantities of data. The objective is to use smart systems that are programmed with human intelligence to perform human-like activities and free human workers to engage in more creative activities that cannot be performed by machines. The most predominant technologies used by businesses are machine learning and deep learning.

Machine learning is now considered to be one of the biggest innovations to augment mental labor. Machine learning technologies enable businesses to effectively analyze and compile data. As structured and unstructured data emerge as a resource, this evolving subfield of AI has now emerged as a full-fledged area that can manually derive rules and build models by analyzing large amounts of data. Machine learning algorithms such as support vector machines, decision trees, random forests, Naive Bayes algorithm, clustering analysis, sentimental analysis, text mining and many more can process vast amounts of data. Further, these algorithms "learn" over time and also work to improve their model and performance. Also, ML algorithms are natural to process the voluminous data captured by connected devices through the Internet of Things.

Machine learning is widely used to optimize search engines, energy management, manage production and supply chains, analyze environmental data, price and product optimization, radical customer personalization, real time operations/logistics optimization, forecasting, predictive maintenance, predictive analytics, and robotics. ML systems can rapidly analyze the constant stream of data from smart devices/systems, identify patterns and anomalies, and make adjustments accordingly. Consequently, machine learning systems are proving to be the major drivers of economic growth and a staple part of the new business intelligence and analytics model of modern businesses. Further, machine learning is giving way to another subfield – deep learning as a full-fledged application.

Deep learning involves the development and use of artificial neural networks (ANN) modeled after the functioning of neurons in the human brain. The main idea is to develop systems that can think and perceive like humans. ANN are composed of "neurons" or nodes – low-power processors organized into multiple layers forming a network that can process and interpret complex data. Typically, ANN consist of multiple layers, with the first layer being the input layer and the last layer being the output layer with multiple in-between layers called hidden layers. Further, the connection between nodes is characterized by a weight value. On receiving an input, a node multiplies the value with weight and checks if the product is higher than a threshold value to qualify for further propagation to other nodes or next layer. The output layer collects all inputs to provide the recommended output or conclusion. The process is emulating the function of human neurons that fire impulse/memories to other neurons to conserve information/knowledge in the human brain. Further, with the passage of time, the ANNs continue to rework the weights based on feedback given by other neurons. As a result, ANN begins to concentrate more on neurons that make right predictions (smart options) as opposed to the neurons that process noise (dumb or irrelevant options).

ANN has evolved as the discipline of deep learning that includes different types of neural networks such as the most popular backpropagation networks, radial basis networks, recurrent networks, convoluted networks, self-organizing maps using different types of learning algorithms such as backpropagation, competitive learning, and simulated annealing (Kohen learning) among others. Deep learning systems power chatbots, natural language processors, robots, self-driving cars, and fraud detection, among others. With high computer processing readily available coupled with smart storage technologies such as Hadoop, deep learning can easily perform more advanced functions that involve analyzing a wide range of factors simultaneously. For instance, deep learning algorithms can easily contextualize information picked from multiple sensors of a self-driving car to make decisions such as changing lanes, reducing speed, to avoid collision, etc. Further, traditional machine learning algorithms typically achieve flat performance once presented with a critical mass of data. On the contrary, deep learning models, powered by a large number of complex webs of neurons, continue to enhance their performance, as more data is presented. As a result, deep learning models are more flexible, scalable, detailed, and continue to provide independent assessment. Also, deep learners also communicate with other intelligent systems to give rise to many subfields of AI as new disciplines such as natural language processing (NLP), speech recognition, and robotics.

Traditionally, computers do not possess the capability to understand spoken or written languages. Machines are programmed using specific programming languages. However, NLP uses machine learning systems including deep learners to enable computers to understand spoken and written English. Consequently, applications such as chatbots can decipher free-form speech and answer adequately. Thus, speech recognizers and NLPs have become an important part of a business's intelligence and analytics toolkit. The applications range from virtual companions, digital lawyers, customer support agents to financial advisors (Gordon, 2020). Another area of AI gaining traction is Computer Vision that empowers smart systems to visualize and analyze images. For instance, Google 's computer vision system can analyze an image and explain the details presented.

Computer vision can be used to visually detect faults and in the transport sector track vehicles that break traffic rules and regulations. Another, popular application of AI is robotics. Robots use different AI technologies such machine learning, computer vision, expert systems, deep learning, and domain-specific knowledge to perform things that human beings can do. One of the most popular applications of robotics is Robotic Process Automation (RPA) that involves using software bots to process, deliver, and execute processes that can be easily automated such as administrative tasks. RPA can improve the resource capacity of an organization, enabling employees to focus on higher-value activities. Thus, robots can perform operational activities, manage supply chain delivery, detect fraud, gather customer data, provide expert customer support, perform predictive maintenance, and automate many other operational activities. It is safe to say that increasingly, artificial intelligence and its emerging subfields such as machine learning, natural language processing, and robotics are an important component of the digital revolution modern businesses are undergoing. These technologies are transforming the business intelligence and analytics model of business.

Statistical Methods, Quality Control and Simulation

The development of statistics dates back to the 17th century therefore methods to analyze and categorize data have existed for centuries. Modern statistical analysis has not substantially changed the original methods, but it has standardized and institutionalized approaches to analysis. Statistical analysis is a critically important part of data science and takes on a special role within the area of quality. Software tools supporting statistical analysis have evolved to include more complex analyses, but more importantly, the open-source programming languages R and Python have made complex statistical analysis readily available at no cost.

Statistical methods form the foundation for data mining techniques and are particularly important in fueling Monte Carlo simulation and associated analysis. Monte Carlo simulation began in the mid 1940's and was used to solve analytically intractable problems. When combined with linear congruential random number generators, simulation techniques rapidly proliferated. The Simulations have expanded decision making by BY 1970, simulation programming languages had been extended, and had found their place in teaching, research and practice. In the last few decades, simulation tool GUIs have evolved into point-and-click approaches, making model creation accessible even to non-programmers.

Data collected in manufacturing and service operations can be fitted to statistical distributions in order to represent the appropriate patterns of an operation. Arrivals and processing times may all be expressed in simulation models, using these distributions. Therefore, the ability to create and validate computer facsimiles of physical models, including alternative scenarios, has clearly been enhanced. These capabilities support evaluation of the impact of changes to any operation resulting in time savings and significant cost reductions. Companies were able to assess changes without needing to alter a physical operation. Further, once scenarios were generated and simulated, hypothesis testing could be applied to determine the statistical significance of operational differences.

The evolving power of statistical analyses and simulation modeling led to significant strides in the quality movement. Though it became prominent in the 1970s, Henry Ford was in fact an early pioneer in quality. Ford established an assembly line and used what are now known as lean principles to create high quality, low-cost automobiles. Walter Andrew Shewhart is known as the father of statistical quality control. While working for Western Electric in 1924, he prepared a short memo containing a schematic of what is now known as a control chart. Shewhart emphasized that bringing a process into a state of statistical control, and keeping it in control, was necessary to predict future output and to manage the process effectively. Joseph Juran's work was the beginning of organized quality control initiatives, and attracted the attention of the Japanese Union of Scientists and Engineers (JUSE).

Over the course of 20 years, Japan embedded this philosophy of disseminating quality management through an entire organization resulting and has been globally recognized as a leader in quality.

While Juran applied Shewhart's methods, he emphasized the human element of quality. At the same time, W. Edwards Deming was actively emphasizing the application of statistical methods to improve designs and enhance product quality. Deming began his work with US manufacturers during World War II. He felt that quality could only be truly achieved if management changed their thinking and presented fourteen points important in the transition, that provided the basis for his advocacy of his own System of Profound Knowledge.

The advancements in Japan and the subsequent influx of higher quality Japanese products into the global marketplace sparked the need for a greater emphasis on quality in the United States. The total quality management (TQM) movement grew out of this need in the early to mid-1970s. TQM embraced the philosophies established by Shewhart, Juran and Deming, and further developed in Japan.

Malcolm Baldrige was inspired by the work of these pioneers in quality and the burgeoning TQM movement during his service as the secretary of commerce under President Ronald Regan from 1981 until his death in 1987. He was instrumental in the passage of the Quality Improvement act of 1987 and the creation of a national quality award which was named for him. Through his advocacy, the TQM philosophies now form that basis for lean manufacturing and service operations.

In 1981, the first Malcolm Baldrige Quality Award (recognized by the president of the United States) was given to Motorola Inc., who was on the leading edge of the quality movement. Motorola demanded total customer satisfaction and strived for this through their trademarked Six Sigma approach.

Six Sigma is an umbrella under which prior quality initiatives fall (quality control, TQM, zero defects, etc.). It is not, however, a simple compilation of techniques, it extends and elaborates upon the previous approaches and remains the leading edge in quality control initiatives. Six Sigma emphasizes a long-term goal of less than 3.4 defects per million opportunities in any manufacturing or service operation. It has been an instrumental tool in more than 125 companies garnering the Malcolm Baldrige Award in the areas of manufacturing, small business, education, service, health care and non-profit.

Multivariate Data Analysis and Data Mining

Statistical theory and developments continued through the 18th, 19th and 20th centuries leading us to a compendium of techniques which in the 21st century fall under the category of multivariate data analysis. These techniques highlighted have become staples within business intelligence and predictive analytics.

Multivariate analysis has been described as "analyses of data that are multivariate in the sense that numerous observations or variables are obtained for each individual or unit studied" (Afifi et. al, 2019). In general, it refers to any statistical analysis allowing the simultaneous investigation of more than two variables. The method of least squares, among the most important statistical methods used in the 19th century, has been widely used in multivariate analysis, and since have moved toward today's predictive multivariate analysis. In the beginning, early eighteenth century, many mathematicians attempted to apply these techniques to astronomical observations. In 1806, Adrien-Marie Legendre published a version of the least squares method that is still used today in his book on paths of comets, where he attempts to identify the orbital equation that best fits the data while considering error. Later, in 1809, Carl Friedrich Gauss claimed to have been using least squares since 1795 with improved results. In the superseding years, this area of study has been significantly extended.

Multivariate techniques are classified into two categories in dependence and interdependence. Dependence techniques are categorized by two primary characteristics: having at least one variable that can be identified as dependent variable, and the type of measurement scale employed by the variables. These techniques are used to predict dependent variables or explain the role of independent variables. There may be a single dependent variable, multiple dependent variables or a series of relationships between dependent and independent variables. The scales on which these variables may be measured include nominal, ordinal, interval, and ratio scales. Nominal and ordinal scales are both nonmetric, and represent simple categories and ordered categories, respectively. Interval and ratio scales, represent quantitative data with representations of magnitude and equidistant difference between neighboring points. The ratio scale, which is the highest level of measurement, is the only scale where the location of the origin is zero.

Dependence techniques began with the method of least squares and are commonly used in many areas of business intelligence because of their predictive nature. For dependent variables with nominal scale, discriminant analysis and logistic regression are prevalently used techniques; for ordinal scale dependent variables, spearman's correlation coefficient is widely used; for both interval or ratio dependent variables, multiple regressions, analysis of variance, and canonical analysis are most well-known techniques. The areas of business applications are wide and they include forecasting, decision analysis, attribution modeling, structural modeling and simulation modeling.

Interdependence techniques are those in which no variables are defined as dependent or independent. Instead, all variables are analyzed simultaneously in an effort to describe the patterns or relationships in the data without explicitly assuming specific distribution for the variables. These techniques are commonly used in areas such as sales and marketing where data collection is continuous, enormous in size, with high dimension, which makes it difficult to accurately understand all the variables.

As with dependence techniques, for variables that are quantitative, factor analysis and principal component analysis are used to condense the size of the dimensions to allow for easier pattern analysis; cluster analysis is used to group or represent structure. For nonmetric variables, correspondence analysis is used to determine the strength of relationships or association between data. In some instances, dummy variable coding can be used to transform the nonmetric variables into metric for factor and cluster analyses. These techniques have also provided the basis for the development of data mining.

Data Mining is the analysis of large observational data sets to find hidden relationships within the data and to summarize it in novel ways that are both transparent in understanding and useful in practice to the data owners and users (Hand et al., 2001). It is especially useful in improving companies' ability to develop learning relationships with their customers including, customer relationship management, consumer segmentation and targeting, resource allocation decisions, and market basket analysis.

Small and large businesses alike are able to build relationships with their customers through continued contact and repetition of their purchasing patterns. This capability has become a standard practice for businesses to search for ways in an effort to improve their competitiveness within the market. Through the use of transaction processing systems to collect the data, store it in data warehouses, and utilize data mining tools to evaluate the data, businesses can improve the quality of their business planning process.

Data mining is also used extensively in marketing in all sectors. Some examples of its usages include financial sector where many companies use data mining tools to detect fraudulent activities (Ngai et al., 2011); in the retail sector, data mining tools are used to match goods to potential customers by preemptively sending out promotional coupons (Corrigan et al., 2014); in the pharmaceutical sector, companies can identify those consumers who are responsive to promotions from those non-responders to improve return on marketing spending (Yi, 2011).

Multivariate analysis and data mining have become more useful tools in business intelligence as more and more evidence of competitive advantage became to be known, along with increase in computing power. Increased education of managers and their increased willingness, and need, to build relationships has established these areas as mainstays in global businesses.

Operations Research

Like statistical analysis, operations research (OR) is a young field when compared to mathematics, OR is a young field when compared with statistics. This new field of OR is defined "as the scientific process of transforming data into insights to making better decisions." (INFORMS, 2020a). The early days of Operations Research was during World War II when George Dantzig discovered the simplex method to solve logistic problems using linear programming. By the end of the war, operations research emerged as a field of study filled with promise. The applications remained primarily military in nature until the early 1950s.

The 1950s, 1960s, and the first half of the 1970s OR research and its applications experienced tremendous growth and success. OR projects expanded to other fields of study, such as manufacturing, health care, transportation, finance, forest management, oil refinery, and water resources. The field of OR was growing internationally and professional societies were being established across Europe. Companies began creating internal operations research groups and universities began developing courses of study centered on the existing and developing areas of operations research. The American Assembly of Collegiate Schools of Business (AACSB) required an OR course as part of the business curriculum. The future of OR looked bright.

Despite this period of tremendous growth, the profession was plagued by serious problems. Even with OR's remarkable past success, Ackoff predicted that OR faces serious problems to avoid its "imminent death," (Ackoff 1987). The elegance of OR methods could only truly be appreciated by researchers and practitioners. Many operations research projects were left unfinished. The managers and business people who had the authority to commission studies and establish projects could not fully trust the methods and therefore felt a lack of confidence when faced with using the results. A main source of their lack of trust was they felt the data was unreliable and not clean. In addition, these decision makers felt threatened. They did not understand the results. The results were presented in a "foreign" language of mathematics that the decision-makers were not fluent in understanding. As early as 1961, Wynne realized the challenge OR specialists will face "consists of stripping the research argument of its mathematical complexities and irrelevancies while retaining the rigorous logic for the executive's understanding," (Wynne 1961). Further as F. Bradshaw noted: "Most managers would rather live with a problem they can't solve than use a solution they don't understand," (Watson and Marett 1979)."

Time, education and the development of more powerful computers began to heal these wounds. New managers, who were more open to optimization methods, simulation and other advanced technologies, were entering the workforce. As universities embraced the methods of operations research and began distilling it into more accessible methods exemplified in operations management, the education of managers improved as well as the acceptance of OR models.

Computers were only used by "tech" people until the mid-1970s with the development of the microprocessor and personal computer (PC). Word processing, spreadsheets and presentation software have become transformational to many organizations. As of today, *"Microsoft Excel is the most familiar, flexible, and widely used business application in the world" (Excel help, 2020).*

In the late 1970s and 1980s, OR groups were able to justify their existence by acting in the capacity of internal consultants. Group members were chartered with visiting business units to market their services. The continued proliferation, adaptation and use of operations research techniques may be easily shown by examining the Franz Edelman Prize awarded first by the combined societies of ORSA and TIMS and now by the Institute for Operations Research and Management Sciences (INFORMS). The Edelman prize recognizes outstanding achievements in the application of operations research by companies and government entities. In addition, the applicants for the prize must demonstrate significant value achieved in applying OR.

Practitioners in operations research have waited patiently for the world to catch up. Astounding advances in computing technology have supported the proliferation of OR techniques, which has in turn contributed to the immense growth of data science.

As shown in Figure 1, data science can be viewed as the confluence of the three disciplines affected by technological advances: Information Systems/Information Technology, Statistics and Operations Research.

THE CONFLUENCE

Gordon Moore, the co-founder of Intel, observed back in 1965 that the amount of processing speed and the amount of memory you can buy for a dollar will double every eighteen months. Moore's prediction has been correct. This exponential growth has been going on for decades and will continue, (Papageorgiou 1983). The speed at which data is being analyzed; the amount of data being analyzed; the variety of data being analyzed are all increasing at an exponential rate. Analytical studies that may have taken weeks or even perhaps months just three decades ago can be easily accomplished in days or hours.

According to Tom Friedman, (Friedman, 2016), change is occurring on the steep rise of an exponential curve. For the coming years, data science and analytics, in particular, will change at an even greater rate. In fact, Friedman believes that for the first time in history, the rate of change will occur at a rate that exceeds the ability to adapt.

As noted in the introduction, the growth in data science in the last decade is owing to the ubiquity of the Internet, the replacement of proprietary network alternatives, and the advent of cloud computing (aided by the emergence of RAID (redundant array of inexpensive/identical disk) disk-storage technologies that facilitate the efficient storage of enterprise historical data). Businesses were created where none had previously existed and existing businesses identified new strategic opportunities.

During the last decade, the decision-making process and the manager's role in that process have dramatically changed. Most organizations today face a significant data explosion and rely on automated data collection tools such as: enterprise resource planning systems, databases, data warehouses, and cloud-based repositories. Historically, managers were disengaged from the decision process, but with the ability to easily analyze and visualize data, managers are more deeply invested in the decision-making process and addressing more complex problems.

In 2021, data is one of the most important organizational assets. "Data is now relevant for leaders across every sector, and consumers of products and services stand to benefit from its application" (Manyika et al., 2011). While "information systems/information technology (IS/IT) spending has been taking a larger and larger proportion of an organization's budget as companies have increasingly embraced analytics as a means for obtaining a competitive advantage." (Klimberg, 2021).

FUTURE RESEARCH

Trends to expect in Cloud Computing include[4] increased cloud-based services and solutions, hybrid and multi-cloud strategies, evolving data protection regulations, containerization and Kubernetes, cloud-native development, serverless computing, cloud-based disaster recovery and the rise of Platform as a Service (PaaS). Future research will address among other these evolving technologies and their impact on the direction of data science.

CONCLUSION

Ten years ago, the rise of Business Intelligence (BI) was documented. In the last decade, there has been a rapid progression from BI to data science. During this time, there has been an acceleration in the usage of the associated tools. This is the evolution of data science, spurred on primarily due to the expansion of the collection of structured and unstructured data, the popularization and mass availability of analytics software, including open-source programming languages such as R and Python, the expansion of cloud storage and computing capabilities, and the Internet of Things. Techniques and tools have been developed widely to support the changing needs in academics and all manner of industry.

The pace of technological progress and technology adoption has accelerated at a pace that has exceeded expectations. Cloud computing has taken many lessons from mainframe computing including virtualization and the establishment roles of client and server. Moving forward, it is anticipated that progress will continue to borrow from the past, while reaching for the future.

ACKNOWLEDGMENT

This paper is dedicated to the memory of our dear colleague Dr. Ira Yermish. Ira led the effort to produce the original BIA paper in 2010. He loved teaching and sharing not only his knowledge but his experiences. He was a true renaissance man and ironman, further enjoyed his cycling, running, triathlons, photography and singing.

REFERENCES

Ackoff, R. L. (1987). O.R., A Post Mortem. *Operations Research*, *35*(3), 471–474. doi:10.1287/opre.35.3.471

Afifi, A., May, S., Donatello, R., & Clark, V. A. (2019). *Practical Multivariate Analysis* (6th ed.). CRC Press. doi:10.1201/9781315203737

Corrigan, H. B., Craciun, G., & Powell, A. M. (2014). How does Target know so much about its customers? Utilizing customer analytics to make marketing decisions. *Marketing Education Review*, *24*(2), 159–166. doi:10.2753/MER1052-8008240206

ExcelHelp. (2020). https://www.excelhelp.com/the-history-of-microsoft-excel/

Friedman, T. L. (2016). *Thank You for Being Late: An Optimist's Guide to Thriving in the Age of Accelerations*. Farrar, Straus and Giroux.

Gill, S. S., Tuli, S., Xu, M., Singh, I., Singh, K. V., Lindsay, D., Tuli, S., Smirnova, D., Singh, M., Jain, U., Pervaiz, H., Sehgal, B., Kaila, S. S., Misra, S., Aslanpour, M. S., Mehta, H., Stankovski, V., & Garraghan, P. (2019). Transformative effects of IoT, Blockchain and Artificial Intelligence on cloud computing: Evolution, vision, trends and open challenges. *Internet of Things*, *8*, 1–26. doi:10.1016/j.iot.2019.100118

Goldsman, D., Nance, R.E., & Wilson, J.R. (2010). A brief history of simulation revisited. *Proceedings of the 2010 Winter Simulation Conference (WSC)*, 567-574.

Gordon, C. (2020, December 31). AI Is Reengineering All Aspects Of Our Human Experience: What Are The Implications? *Forbes*. https://www.forbes.com/sites/cindygordon/2021/12/31/ai-is-reengineering-all-aspects-of-our-human-experience-what-are-the-implications/?sh=7f3325d17a0d

Hand, D., Mannila, H., & Smyth, P. (2001). *Principles of Data Mining*. MIT Press.

Klimberg, R. K. (2015). *Teaching a Data Mining Course in a Business School. In Contemporary Perspectives in Data Mining* (Vol. 2). Information Age Publishing.

Klimberg, R. K. (2021). 2021). The Evolution of Business Analytics and Its Impact on the Service Industry. In M. Davis (Ed.), *Research Handbook on Services Management*. Elgar Publishing.

Longbottom, C. (2017). The Evolution of Cloud Computing : How to Plan for Change. BCS, The Chartered Institute for IT.

Manyika, Chui, Brown, Bughin, Dobbs, Roxburgh, & Hung Byers. (2011). *Big data: The next frontier for innovation competition and productivity*. McKinsey Global Institute Report.

Ngai, E. W. T., Hu, Y., Wong, Y. H., Chen, Y., & Sun, X. (2011). The application of data mining techniques in financial fraud detection: A classification framework and an academic review of literature. *Decision Support Systems*, *50*(3), 559–596. doi:10.1016/j.dss.2010.08.006

Papageorgiou, J. C. (1983). Decision Making in the Year 2000. *Interfaces*, *13*(2), 77–86. Advance online publication. doi:10.1287/inte.13.2.77

Uzialko, A. (2021, April 22). How Artificial Intelligence Will Transform Business. *Business News Daily*. https://www.businessnewsdaily.com/9402-artificial-intelligence-business-trends.html

Watson, H. J., & Marett, P. G. (1979). A Survey of Management Science Implementation Problems. *Interfaces*, *9*(4), 124–128. doi:10.1287/inte.9.4.124

Wynne, B. E. Sr. (1961). A Pattern of Reporting Operations Research to the Business Executive. *Management Technology*, *1*(3), 16–23. doi:10.1287/mantech.1.3.16

Yi, J. (2011). Knowledge-based approach to improving detailing plan in multiple product situations using PDE weights. *Expert Systems with Applications*, *38*(4), 3835–3843. doi:10.1016/j.eswa.2010.09.044

ADDITIONAL READING

Azvine, B., Cui, Z., Majeed, B., & Spott, M. (2007). Operational risk management with real-time business intelligence. *BT Technology Journal*, *25*(1), 154–167. doi:10.100710550-007-0017-5

Bhargava, H. K., Power, D. J., & Sun, D. (2007). Progress in web-based decision support technologies. *Decision Support Systems*, *43*(4), 1083–1095. doi:10.1016/j.dss.2005.07.002

Bonczek, R. H., Holsapple, C. W., & Whinston, A. B. (1980). The Evolving Roles of Models in Decision Support Systems. *Decision Sciences*, *11*(2), 337–356. Advance online publication. doi:10.1111/j.1540-5915.1980.tb01143.x

Castellanos, M., Salazar, N., Casati, F., Dayal, U., & Shan, M.-C. (2006). Predictive business operations management. *International Journal on Computer Science and Engineering*, *2*(5-6), 292–301.

Davenport, T. H. (2006, January). Competing on analytics. *Harvard Business Review*, •••, 98–107. PMID:16447373

Eom, S. B., Lee, B., Kim, E. B., & Somrajan, C. (1998, February). A Survey of Decision Support System Applications (1988-1994). *The Journal of the Operational Research Society*, *49*(2), 109–120. doi:10.1057/palgrave.jors.2600507

Gorry, G. A., & Scott-Morton, M. S. (1971). A Framework for Management Information Systems. *Sloan Management Review*, *11*(2).

Hair, J. F., Black, W. C., Babin, B. J., Anderson, R. E., & Tatham, R. L. (2006). *Multivariate Data Analysis* (6th ed.). Pearson Prentice Hall.

Keen, P. G. W. (1980). Adaptive Design for Decision Support Systems. *Database*, *12*(1).

Lardner, H. (1984). The Origin of Operational Research. *Operations Research*, *32*(2), 465–475. doi:10.1287/opre.32.2.465

Lau, K.-N., Lee, K.-H., Ho, Y., & Lam, P.-Y. (2004). Mining the web for business intelligence: Homepage analysis in the Internet era. *Journal of Database Marketing & Customer Strategy Management*, *12*(1), 32–54. doi:10.1057/palgrave.dbm.3240241

Li, F. L., Cheung, C. F., Lee, W. B., & Kwok, S. K. (2007). Business intelligence for new market development: A web semantic network analysis approach. *International Journal of Enterprise Network Management*, *1*(3), 261–282. doi:10.1504/IJENM.2007.012758

March, S. T., & Hevner, A. R. (2007). Integrated decision support systems: A data warehousing perspective. *Decision Support Systems*, *43*(3), 1031–1043. doi:10.1016/j.dss.2005.05.029

O'Keefe, R. (1986, January). Simulation and Expert Systems: A Taxonomy and some Examples. *Simulation*, *46*(1), 10–16. doi:10.1177/003754978604600102

Power, D. J., & Sharda, R. (2007). Model-driven decision support systems: Concepts and research directions. *Decision Support Systems*, *43*(3), 1044–1061. doi:10.1016/j.dss.2005.05.030

Sahay, B. S., & Ranjan, J. (2008). Real time business intelligence in supply chain analytics. *Information Management & Computer Security*, *16*(1), 28–48. doi:10.1108/09685220810862733

Shim, J. P., Warkentin, M., Courtney, J. F., Power, D. J., Sharda, R., & Carlsson, C. (2002). Past, present, and future of decision support technology. *Decision Support Systems*, *33*(2), 111–126. doi:10.1016/S0167-9236(01)00139-7

Tettamanzi, A. G. B., Carlesi, M., Pannese, L., & Santalmasi, M. (2007). Fuzzy logic and evolutionary algorithms. *Applications of Evolutionary Computing*, *4448*, 230–240.

Turban, E., & Aronson, J. E. (1998). *Decision Support Systems and Intelligent Systems* (5th ed.). Prentice Hall.

ENDNOTES

1 https://www.datascienceprograms.org/

2 IBM and Burroughs, UNIVAC, NCR, Control Data Corporation and Honeywell

3 Digital Equipment Corporation (DEC), Texas Instruments, Hewlett Packard (HP), Data General and others

4 https://consoltech.com/blog/guide-to-2021-cloud-computing-trends/#:~:text=By%202021%2C%20experts%20predict%20that,backend%20operations%20to%20the%20cloud and https://itchronicles.com/cloud/the-evolution-of-cloud-computing-wheres-it-going-next/?spm=a2c65.11461447.0.0.11dd3e01OijvIq

Chapter 9
Towards Making a Sustainable Organization

Hakikur Rahman
Ansted University Sustainability Research Institute, Malaysia

ABSTRACT

Sustainable development refers to an economic, environmental, and social development aspect that meets the demands of the contemporary context and does not prevent future generations from fulfilling their requirements. In this perspective, businesses play an imperative role. However, studies reveal that the progress towards sustainable development has been slow, indicating the need for more concrete guidance that would allow businesses to act strategically and successfully in a sustainable way. There are three distinct, but complementary, dimensions of strategic management as viewed from the perspective of sustainability in order to encourage the integration of sustainability issues into corporate activities and strategies. This chapter looks through various aspects of sustainability towards making a sustainable organization through a vertical literature review. This theoretical discussion contributes to existing research to find relationships between strategic management and sustainable development and tries to provide a schema for further empirical research.

INTRODUCTION

Organization can be defined by an organized group of people or a community with a particular purpose, such as a business or government department (Google definition), while sustainability can be termed as the ability to be maintained at a certain rate or level. It is a form of aspect to avoid the depletion of natural resources in order to maintain an ecological balance (Google definition). Along these perspectives,

DOI: 10.4018/978-1-7998-4799-1.ch009

a sustainable organization can be seen as an organized group of people that aims to advance sustainability and/or include those actions of organizing something sustainably. Unlike many business organizations, sustainable organizations are not limited to implementing sustainability strategies which provide them with economic and cultural benefits attained through environmental responsibility, but also extended towards the overall social development. For sustainable organizations, sustainability can also be an end in itself without supplementary justifications (Wikipedia definition).

In terms of theory, sustainable development refers to an economic, environmental and social development aspect that meets the demands of the contemporary context and does not prevent future generations from fulfilling their necessary requirements. In this perspective, businesses play an imperative function. However, researches reveal that the progress towards sustainable development has been relatively slow, indicating the need for more concrete guidance that would allow businesses to act strategically and successfully in a more sustainable way. There are three distinct, but complementary, dimensions of strategic management as viewed from the perspective of sustainability in order to encourage the integration of sustainability issues into corporate activities and strategies. These three dimensions are: strategy process, strategy content and strategy context. This vertical review tries to contribute to existing research in that it reveals relationships between strategic management and sustainable development and also tries to provide an agenda for supplementary empirical researches (Welford and Jones, 1998; Baumgartner and Rauter, 2017).

As it has been observed in recent research findings, the issue of sustainable development is increasingly present among the concerns of the international academic community in addition to the grass roots communities. However, the depth of the unsustainable practices suggests that insufficient progress has been made to move from an unsustainable lifestyle to sustainable development issues. It has also been observed that by sharing ideas, concepts, tools, experiences learned in different contexts, it is anticipated that one should learn many things that will help the academic communities and companies to develop the skills to make progress towards sustainable development. Particularly, in response to increasing concerns of society about environmental degradation and increasing demands for a transition to a more sustainable society, the business companies are increasingly active in aligning their processes and services with a sustainability agenda. Furthermore, a good management of environmental services has now become the focus of many business strategies tending to the aspiration of 'greening' their infrastructures and product deliveries. Henceforth, the growing demand for "green" products has created major new markets in which visionary entrepreneurs reap the rewards of approaching sustainability. Therefore, by adopting sustainable practices, companies can attain competitive advantage, increase market share and boost shareholder value. In these aspects a sustainable university can be a role model for the organizations that want to embark in the process of transition towards sustainability (Grecu and Ipiña, 2014).

As a response to the transformations that appeared in the economic environment along the contemporary years, novel types of organizations have been developed. As a result, the organizational theories focused on identifying the main characteristics of the sustainable organizations and the knowledge-based ones. Besides, nowadays, they are offered as a key to success in turbulent times. But, a question remains as, why should a company choose between sustainability and knowledge? Could not it be just an added value and at the same time, the relationship with the community and the stock of knowledge that it owns? And if it can, then which will be the particularities of this kind of organization? In order to find an answer to these questions, many studies have been conducted. The results pointed out the fact that, from a theoretical perspective, a sustainable knowledge-based organization represents a formal entity in which economic, environmental and social objectives are achieved by developing the internal knowledge base (Leon, 2013).

This chapter aims to examine how some leading enterprises are integrating sustainability into their planning of future direction and growth. It is expected that the readers will have a strong interest in sustainability and how it should be managed within organizations. Also it is envisaged that by creating and maintaining sustainable organizations is of high priority to companies planning their future in a turbulent and difficult-to-predict operating environment. Hence, the readers will also learn how sustainability may be better integrated into the strategic thinking and management processes. This chapter gives an insight into the past, contemporary and future issues on the importance of integrating sustainability discussion and planning into mainstream strategic management (Perrott, 2015).

BACKGROUND

The expression, sustainable development has evolved through the powerful lobbying of the environmental movement over the past 35 years. Along this route, Bruntland's definition of sustainable development has become widely used. It defined sustainable development as invoking the demands of future generations counterbalanced to the concurrent unmet needs of much of the world's population. As a general concept, sustainable development encompasses three fundamental approaches: economic, environmental, and social developments, which are interrelated and complementary. Hence, the focus of research in sustainability has shifted from local optimization in a single organization to that of the entire supply chain. Moreover, sustainability has become an everlasting movement that has started to impact on how one does business, buys products and even chooses the community leaders. In this aspect, environmental sustainability is a key issue for human societies throughout the 21st century's world. It can be seen as meeting the needs of the contemporary society without compromising the ability of future generations to meet their demands. Furthermore, as environment sustainability is attracting more attention, the literature on current practices focusing on environmental performance has created a stream known as green supply chain management. It is not simply about reducing the quantity of waste of production or using less energy, but is concerned with developing processes that will guide to businesses becoming completely sustainable in the future (Brundtland, 1987; Linton, Klassen and Jayaraman, 2007; Seuring, et. al., 2008; Sarkis, Zhu and Lai, 2011; Tay, et. al., 2015).

Theoretically, the word sustainability refers to the continuation of producing expected outputs without creating any disharmony and imbalance in a system. Contemporary studies show that ICT-based government systems raise barriers and in many instances create digital inequalities between the 'tech-haves' and 'tech-haves not', of which one group reaps the benefits of IT-enabled accessibility by helping each other and one cannot. It is predicted that this phenomenon will not support sustainable e-Participation in which the systems that are expected to provide certain outputs may be disrupted because of some serious factors being ignored during the plan, design and implementation phases. Therefore, a sustainable model for e-Participation may guide the decision makers in state and private levels to implement the systems in certain place and in certain time. Accordingly, adding values and innovations in the various phases of the model will assist the stakeholders to reap the benefits of e-Democracy on continuous basis (EAG, 2005; Horrigan, 2005; Islam, 2008; Upham, et. al., 2012).

Ecopreneurs (entrepreneurs focused to boost economy) from developed countries are not the only ones involved in this existential odyssey of sustainability. In 1993 Professor Anil Gupta of the Indian Institute of Management set up a non-profit non-governmental organisation (NGO) called the Society for Research and Initiatives for Sustainable Technologies and Institutions (SRISTI) to 'strengthen the capacity of grass-roots inventors, innovators and ecopreneurs engaged in conserving biodiversity and developing eco-friendly solutions to local problems'. The key instrument of the NGO is the Honey Bee Network (Gupta 1997: 36- 40), a newsletter in six languages dealing with examples of local ecopreneurship and ways to preserve the intellectual property rights of local inventors in developing countries from being exploited by multinational corporations (MNCs) based in developed countries. Recently, the focus has been on women's indigenous knowledge, given its traditional neglect in India.

The Honey Bee philosophy is aimed at remedying one of the negative free-rider effects of entrepreneurial capitalism: the temptation of bulky corporations from developed economies to take or buy out the innovative technologies of indigenous people in developing counties without giving them sufficient credit for their intellectual discoveries or payment for their ideas and inventions. Such protection and support is critical in order to motivate ecopreneurship in the first place: why bother to innovate and create a green business if the inevitable consequence is to have everything extracted and exploited? The metaphor of the honey bee indicates the cross-fertilization of ideas and initiatives that aim to stimulate, reward and protect the creativity of grass-roots ecopreneurs. Stemming from this affluent Indian tradition, Astad Pastakia (1998: 158) distinguishes between two kinds of ecopreneurs, as such, commercial ecopreneurs and social ecopreneurs (Honey Bee, 2001; Isaak, 2016).

LITERATURE REVIEW

It has been observed that the simultaneous pursuit of economic, environmental, and social sustainability is rapidly becoming part of the established rhetoric for many enterprises across sectors and geographic regions. Along this perspective, the concept of sustainability, and the related notion of sustainable development, has also become part of the common vocabulary in the debates within and across several social sciences such as economics, political science, sociology, and (more in recent times) in management research and practice. In general, scholars refer to the core concept as the specification of a set of actions to be taken by present persons that will not diminish the prospects of future persons to enjoy levels of consumption, wealth, utility, or welfare comparable to those enjoyed by present persons. In management science, the notion of sustainability has been applied to business organizations as social systems that are embedded in larger social and ecological systems with which they share the availability of inputs and the impacts of outputs. In this framing, it has taken on specific meanings related to the capacity of the business organization to serve purposes that include not only economic, but also environmental and social criteria. Furthermore, research in the management sector has generally developed in two main strands addressing two different broad sets of questions, such as: why should companies move beyond serving merely economic purposes, and what makes a company more sustainable. In this regard, answering the question "why (should companies embrace sustainability?)" generated the central and by far the largest empirical effort in the corporate sustainability knowledge domain (Bromley, 2008; Bansal, 2005; Berry and Rondinelli, 1998; Crane and Matten, 2010; Freeman, et. al, 2010; Zollo, 2013).

It reveals that tourism is another form of component in a sustainable society. Over the years it has been observed that heritage and culture are ubiquitous in terms of sustainable development aspect. Wherever there are people (or community), there are culture and heritage. Even in remote polar region and on the top of the highest mountains there is a demand of both natural and cultural heritage, including artifacts left by explorers and awe-inspiring landscapes. Of course, this does not mean that everywhere they are equal in the competition to attract heritage tourists. In fact it has been found that this is far from the case. However, it does mean that culture and heritage require watchful evaluation if they are to be used successfully as attractions in the competitive tourism industry (Wall, 2016).

Within the historical perspectives, for business firms and economy, reasonable consensus is available for the significance of corporate governance (CG) as it attains much attention in the literature. Moreover, recent studies in this field indicate the fact that success factors of business organization is closely associated to CG. The key focus of vast body of literature is depicted through (shown in Table-1):

Table 1. Various factors on business issues

Factors	Literatures
Governance mechanism and its impact on the firm performance	Conyon & He, 2008; La Rocca, Montalto, La Rocca, & StaglianÃ, 2017; Zulkifli, Shukor, & Rahman, 2018; Muma, 2018; Mungwari, 2018; Muniisvaran & Vijayalakshmi, 2018; Muñoz, 2017; Myambo & Munyanyi, 2017; Sbaouelgi, 2018; Obiekwe, 2018
Business firms working with the weak governance structure have more intensity to face the agency issue, where managers place their personal interest ahead of corporate interest	Bosse & Phillips, 2016; Hasanudin et al., 2019; Esenyel & Emeagwali, 2019
Mangers are not very much careful about the funds of stakeholders, comparatively to their own	Letza, Sun, & Kirkbride, 2004; Arora & Sharma, 2016; Azeez, 2015; Francis, Hasan, & Wu, 2015
Diversity in the board through gender specifies its impact on the performance	Bear, Rahman, & Post, 2010; Bernardi, Bean, & Weippert, 2002; Boulouta, 2013; Erhardt, Werbel, & Shrader, 2003
Women empowerment indicates the actions and raising of status for the female through education, literacy and job opportunities in the society	Mosedale, 2005; Malimi, 2017; Mohiuddin, 2018; Mokgari & Pwaka, 2018

The integration of environmental aspects into organizations' strategic and operational decisions is a reality that affects not only the organization which makes decisions, but also its customers

and suppliers (de Camargo Fiorini and Jabbour, 2017). Seeking to incorporate environmental and sustainable practices into the supply chain, organizations have demanded a great deal of information from their partners. Several critical issues that demonstrate the growing concern over sustainability issues are (see Table-2):

Another theory indicates the strong association between the organizational success and satisfaction of shareholders is stewardship theory. Various dimensions are presented in the literature to cover the basic idea of corporate governance. In

Table 2. Various issues on environmental sustainability

Issues	Literatures
Convergence of supply chain and sustainability	Seuring & Müller, 2008; Srivastava, 2007; Zhu & Sarkis, 2004
Information systems (IS) have become important tools for the adoption and management of these new practices	Chen, Tai, & Hung, 2012; Dao, Langella, & Carbo, 2011; Green, Zelbst, Meacham, & Bhadauria, 2012; Green, Zelbst, Bhadauria, & Meacham, 2012; Hu, Li, Chen, & Wang, 2014
IS hold greater promise for addressing environmental issues in organizations; they can support business initiatives in reducing negative environmental impacts	Jenkin, Webster, & McShane, 2011; Khor, Thurasamy, Ahmad, Halim, & May-Chiun, 2015; Sarkis, Koo, & Watson, 2013
It is imperative that organizations understand how to integrate information systems and green initiatives in order to improve business sustainability and identify better practices	Bose and Luo (2011); Wognum, Bremmers, Trienekens, van der Vorst, & Bloemhof, 2011

this regard, total members in the board express the size. It is believed that larger board size can significantly manage the business strategic affairs, comparatively to smaller board size. However, the factor of women empowerment is under observation since last couple years due to its worth in the board through gender diversification. However, the literature contribution for the women empowerment through board diversification and its linkage to capital structure and leverage is very limited (Thabhiranrak and Jermsittiparsert, 2019).

In another aspect of sustainability issue, it has been observed that there is a need for environmental protection and increasing demands for natural resources those are forcing companies to reconsider their business models and restructure their supply chain operations. To improve further, scholars and proactive companies have begun to create more sustainable supply chains. However, what has not been fully addressed is how organizations deal with short-term pressures to remain economically viable while implementing these newly modeled supply chains. In this aspect, Wu and Pagell (2011) use a theory-building through case studies to answer this question: how do organizations balance short-term profitability and long-term environmental sustainability when making supply chain decisions under conditions of uncertainty? They present five sets of propositions that explain how exemplars in green supply chain management make decisions and balance short and long term objectives. They have also identified four environmental postures that help explain the decisions organizations make when dealing with strategic trade-offs among the economic, environmental and social elements of the triple-bottom-line.

This study finds that sustainability in organizations have increasingly gained importance among organizations and their stakeholders around the world. In this context, eco-efficiency has become a consistent tool towards the transition to sustainable development and the efforts of eco- efficiency indicators have been utilized for comparative studies and decision-making tasks, providing better financial, environmental, and social performance. The chapter tried to provide a systematic literature review on the theme of sustainable development from the perspective of eco-efficiency, with the adaptation of the Knowledge Development Process intervention instrument - constructivist (ProKnow-C) (Caiado, et. al., 2017).

In this aspect, Caiado, et. al., (2017) identify and structure the state-of-the-art between Eco-Efficiency and Sustainable Development with a view to:

1. selecting a Bibliographic Portfolio (BP) that is aligned with the perception of the researchers on the theme;
2. performing a bibliometric analysis of the selected BP;
3. performing a thematic synthesis;
4. finding the integration of eco-efficiency and sustainable development with other approaches;
5. proposing an innovative framework to achieve sustainable development through eco-
6. efficiency indicators; and
7. finding paths for further research.

Along this context, this particular study makes multiple new contributions, providing both academics and practitioners a better panorama to achieve sustainable development through eco-efficiency by expanding the literature review, highlighting the synergies and barriers between eco-efficiency and sustainable development and by comparing and analyzing them, showing its relevant features. Furthermore, the study finds that Caiado, et. al., (2017) has tried to synthesize the contributions of the BP according to the BASF indicators, sustainable dimensions and four measurement levels: industry, organization, project and process to better describe the current academic scenario on the subject. Caiado, et. al., (2017) add further that, in 1996, BASF Corporation developed an eco-efficiency methodology to assess both the economic and environmental impacts of chemicals, processes, and products in their lifecycle. The methodology created by BASF has since been further developed and follows the ISO 14040 and ISO 14044 standards for lifecycle assessment (LCA) and also ISO 14045 for Eco-Efficiency assessment. BASF's methodology can be used for sustainable decision making at all levels, from industrial to consumer.

Taking these concepts in consideration, the study progresses further through another area of sustainability: the agriculture. Particularly, organic agriculture offers a unique combination of environmentally-sound practices with low external inputs while contributing to food availability. The objective is to describe the potential of the organic agriculture to provide an alternative way for conventional agricultural practices which leads to a sustainable resource utilization and contributes in mitigating global problems like climate change (Zundel and Kilcher, 2007; Aher, Bhaveshananda and Sengupta, 2012).

Strong, integrated health systems based in primary health care is a function as the first line of defense in emergencies, whether in acute or protracted crises. Hence, a strong health system can be seen as a resilient health system. Conversely, poor-quality primary health care can contribute to the escalation of emergencies through poor standards of infection prevention and control, a lack of appropriate equipment, and untrained staff. Along this context, it has been observed that marginal communities across the developing countries lack strong primary health care.

The success of primary health care is driven by knowledge and capacity-building. Necessary efforts need to be applied to enhance knowledge, including scientific as well as traditional knowledge, to strengthen PHC (Public Health Care), improve health outcomes and ensure access for all people to the right care at the right time and at the most appropriate level of care, respecting their rights, needs, dignity and autonomy. Organizations continue to research and share knowledge and experience, build capacity and improve the delivery of health services and care.

- *Human resources for health*: Fields need to create decent work and appropriate compensation for health professionals and other health personnel working at the primary health care level to respond effectively to people's health needs in a multidisciplinary context. Organizations need to continue to invest in the education, training, recruitment, development, motivation and retention of the PHC workforce, with an appropriate skill mix. Organizations also should strive for the retention and availability of the PHC workforce in rural, remote and less developed areas.
- *Technology*: Organizations should support broadening and extending access to a range of health care services through the use of high- quality, safe, effective and affordable medicines, including, as appropriate, traditional medicines, vaccines, diagnostics and other technologies. They need to promote their accessibility and their rational and safe use and the protection of personal data. Through advances in information systems, it would be better able to collect appropriately disaggregated, high-quality data and to improve information continuity, disease surveillance, transparency, accountability and monitoring of health system performance. Variety of technologies need to be utilized to improve access to health care, enrich health service delivery, improve the quality of service and patient safety, and increase the efficiency and coordination of care. Through digital and other technologies, we will enable individuals and communities to identify their health needs, participate

in the planning and delivery of services and play an active role in maintaining their own health and well-being.

- *Financing*: All countries should to continue to invest in PHC to improve health outcomes. Organizations need to address the inefficiencies and inequities that expose people to financial hardship resulting from their use of health services by ensuring better allocation of resources for health, adequate financing of primary health care and appropriate reimbursement systems in order to improve access and achieve better health outcomes. Henceforth, efforts should be given towards the financial sustainability, efficiency and resilience of national health systems, appropriately allocating resources to PHC based on national context (World Health Organization, 2019).

DISCUSSIONS AND FURTHER ISSUES

In the past decade, research on sustainable innovations has expanded rapidly to increase the understanding of the ways in which new technologies (especially, ICTs) and social practices enable societies to become more sustainable. Many research findings have focused on eco-innovation and the diffusion of clean technologies. Also, in the past decade coherent perspectives have been introduced that look more systemically at the ways in which more sustainable technologies are adopted in society, such as transition management and innovation systems research. This research has contributed to knowledge of factors that induce sustainable innovations, such as regulation and firm characteristics, and also show the interplay of factors in innovation and societal systems that determine the often complex journey of new ideas into products and services (Hall and Clark, 2003; Geels, Hekkert and Jacobsson, 2008; Montalvo, 2008; Boons and Lüdeke-Freund, 2013).

Moreover, sustainable development (SD) is not just obligating society members to fulfill their responsibilities, but can also generate significant competitive advantage. Only recently, organizations increasingly consider SD as a business strategy because it can deliver larger shareholder value and provide access to capital and making stronger performance over time which can improve shared value for both business and society. Considering the present atmosphere where competition is the most important factor in asserting oneself and exerting influence in the developmental process, customer relationship management (CRM) and the significant influence it has brought about in the worldwide scene can be seen as one of the most influential factors contributing to the economic sphere (Gholami, H., et. al., 2015).

In recent decades, and especially in recent days, the attitude of the organizations toward the customer has undergone a change. Looking at the customer turn from consumer to a colleague, a partner, a value creator, or a developer of knowledge and it has given a competitive advantage to organizations. The issues are much more important in higher education due to the structure, nature and manner of communication with students as dominant customers. The importance of these institutions in developing specialized and skilled manpower, as well as are increasingly being viewed as engines of creating human capital needed to support development of local economies (Gholami, H., et. al., 2015).

Along the route of successful entrepreneurship, sustainable supply chain management has developed at an exponential rate into a distinct research field, but its progress towards sustainability is rather modest, and a coherent theoretical foundation for guiding companies towards a stronger integration of sustainability into their operations and supply chains is still absent. This chapter tries to outline how the tradition of critical management studies could foster higher levels of sustainable business and sustainable supply chains. In this aspect, Gold and Schleper (2017) argue that the underlying instrumental logic of contemporary corporate engagement with sustainability, driven by stakeholder pressures, is a vital obstacle when aiming for 'truly' sustainable supply chains. They further mention that by referring to a recognition perspective may dissolve the reified pursuit of profit-seeking and other merely economic performance targets to recall the genuine and in its essence truly radical claim that the concept of sustainable development is inherently a normative one imposed on all of us. Recognition may lead the way for companies to adopt a caring stance for people and the surrounding environment and to respond to the legitimate expectations of all groups in society while conceiving themselves as an integral part of such a society.

While discovering the sustainability factors in health sector, it has been observed that the world has made excellent progress on global health, with changes so great that life expectancy is now around 10 years more than back in 1978, and the risk of dying before the age of 5 years has fallen by around two thirds. Without a doubt, the spectrum of disease is now very different from 40 years ago, due to the demographic and epidemiologic transitions that have occurred. Though the unfinished agenda of preventable child and maternal mortality remains, chronic non-communicable diseases and injuries have replaced acute infections as the major causes of morbidity and mortality, necessitating a change in the profile of health services needed (World Health Organization, 2018). However, the recent havoc in the form of Corona virus (COVID-19) has raised an alarm not only in the health sector, but also in the overall society development thought processes. This form of new virus has at first been detected in China in December 2018, but till this writing in July 2021, the entire population of the globe is suffering from its consequences.

Tourism seems to be one of the world's fastest growing industries, and has been identified as a means of generating national income in less industrialized economies. Many countries have promoted tourism as a major source of national income. Hence, sustainability has become an important topic and concept in relation to tourism planning and development (Kruja and Hasaj, 2010)

Looking into another aspect of sustainable organization and environmental sustainability, it has been perceived that green accounting is another important tool for understanding the influential aspects of natural environment with respect to the economy. The data and information provided by environmental accounts are determined to be in relation to the involvement of natural resources in economic development and costs occurred due to pollution or resource degradation. However, the advantage of corporate environmental accounting initiative is identified as the ability to determine and create awareness regarding costs related to environment, which in turn helps in identifying the techniques for reducing and avoiding costs of such type. It can be mentioned that due to this advantageous feature, the performance of the environment has also been improved. The environmental costs that occur due to the financial outcomes of the firm's operation can be determined by means of a green accounting tool. The operational performance of the organization can be determined with the assistance of certain process like documentation and reporting the emissions of green house gases (GHG). However, the conventional accounting system is determined not to be considered for new or existing demands for natural resources. This demand on natural resources may destabilize sustainability of economic performance and growth, depletion of natural capital, environmental degradation as a social cost of economic activity and also the account of nonmarket goods in gross domestic product (GDP) (Farouk, Cherian and Jacob, 2012).

In contemporary years, there has been growing interest in applying social practice theory to theorizing consumption, specifically in relation to transforming practices that have problematic environmental impacts. Sahakian and Wilhite (2014) tried to address the questions: how do changes in practices occur, and what are the levers for influencing change towards more sustainable consumption practices? They argue that a view of agency distributed across people, things and social contexts is fruitful. They also explore learning through membership in communities of practice, where people are involved in experiments with or exposure to new practices. Carrying on a case study, they relate three case studies in the arena of food consumption practices then discuss the practicalities and pitfalls involved in translating social practice approaches into practicable recommendations for encouraging more sustain- able forms of consumption.

Notwithstanding another important issue, as such social learning is another aspect of sustainability factors and meant to be the collective action and reflection that occurs among different individuals and groups as they work to improve the management of human and environmental interrelations. Social learning for improved human interrelations with the environment must ultimately include us all, because the people are all part of the same system and each of population will inevitably experience the consequences of these change processes.

As another important aspect, environmental management has grown exponentially as a profession over the past half century. Originally a new and largely unwelcome idea, it has now grown to be a major branch in many, if not most, government and non-governmental organizations; and in almost all university programmes. The first 'environment management' jobs appeared in the 1950s as junior posts, typically involved in 'cleaning up the mess', whether as pollution control officers or dog catchers. At that time there were no federal, state or local government departments responsible for environmental management, and no industry would have dreamt of such a thing. Within community sectors, the environmental organizations that existed were mostly concerned with field studies and nature walks.

Environmental legislation has been slowly and somewhat reluctantly introduced into a number of countries and jurisdictions. In the USA it took several tries, in various guises, before the National Environmental Protection Act was passed in 1969. This act, and similar legislation that followed around the globe, required all developments likely to have a 'significant' impact on the environment to undergo an environmental impact assessment. However, unfortunately the legislation did not clearly define 'significant' and assessments were considered to be 'one-off', or 'undertaken and forgotten'. Hence, as environmental problems mounted, environmental protection agencies were created, although they were typically not well funded and functioned primarily as reactive organizations. But, without resources or power, these first agencies could not support a process of social learning or foster the necessary change process for improving environmental management and social wellbeing (Keen, Brown and Dyball, 2005).

Towards making a sustainable transportation system, and driven by the global nature of shipping, maritime governance is characterized by a long history of intergovernmental decision making with the International Maritime Organization (IMO) as central locus of authority. Since the 1980s, maritime governance for the European Union (EU) and its member states is subject to processes of regionalization, especially in the environmental domain. However, dissatisfaction with the ambition level of the IMO as well as lack of effective implementation and enforcement of IMO standards has driven the emergence of four regionally-based initiatives: the use of special areas in IMO Conventions, the adoption of the Paris Memorandum of Understanding (MoU) on Port State Control, the development of the European Union shipping policy domain and the emergence of market based initiatives by ports and cargo-owners. This study observes that each of these regional initiatives are based on cooperation between a regional group of actors and each initiative has become integrated in maritime governance (Van Leeuwen, 2015).

Finally, adding another important aspect of sustainable organization, the provision of sustainability service is discussed here. It is accomplished via three service practices; arranging green shopping trails, answering sustainability questions, and promoting sustainability to green consumers in-store. Analyzed by Fuentes and Fredriksson (2016) it shows that the retailing of sustainable products is not simply a matter of including sustainability products in the range and instructing shop assistants to promote them. Sustainability service – as enacted at W-Store – was dependent on the successful combination and configuration of human competence (service staff) and IT and organizational artifacts. Furthermore, there also needed to be congruence between consumers and their images and between retailers and the version of sustainability they were enacting. Hence, the provision of sustainability service required an investigative and adaptive organization capable of keeping up as well as developing *vis-á-vis* changing sustainability discourses and issues. However, once the necessary conditions had been met, sustainability service worked towards promoting sustainable consumption by making green shopping possible, educating consumers on sustainability issues, and motivating them via positive feedback and dialogue.

CHALLENGES

Among many other seen and unforeseen challenges, the magnitude and urgency of the challenges facing agriculture and food systems demand profound modifications in different aspects of human activity to achieve real transformative change and sustainability. Recognizing that the inherent complexity of achieving sustain-ability is commonly seen as a deterrent to decision-making, the Food and Agriculture Organization of the United Nations (FAO) has approved the 10 Elements of Agroecology as an analytical framework to sustain the design of differentiated paths for agriculture and food systems transformation, hence facilitating improved decision-making by policymakers, practitioners and other stakeholders in differing contexts at a range of levels on a number of scales.

In these aspects, biodiversity, consumers, education and governance are identified as promising entry points to build a structured process using visual narratives that rely on the 10 Elements of Agroecology to graphically dissect prospective social-ecological transition trajectories. We illustrate such applications with examples from agroforestry worldwide, public food procure-ment in Brazil and the United States of America, and agroecology education vis-à-vis secure access to land in Senegal. Nexus approaches are used to highlight and examine salient interactions among different sectors and entry points, and to expand visual narratives describing plausible theories of transformative change towards sustainable agriculture and food systems (Barrios, et. al., 2020).

Furthermore, the global context of sustainability suggests that the discussion of sustainable development has consolidated and increased its impact (e.g. ONU's climate change reports, governmental projects in different levels, academic literature development). Sustainable development has appeared on the agendas of public and private managers, and different kinds of organizations are concerned with making development sustainable, with respect to social, environmental and economic criteria (Cruz and Boehe, 2008).

A growing realization of the un-sustainability of numerous human activities has brought about an increased scrutiny of the sustainability of organizational practices. For example, in the ecological sphere, the core technologies of the industrial age, combined with a profligate use of resources, threaten the viability of life on planet Earth. To illustrate further it can be stated, between 1900 and 2000 the world population increased four-fold; the urban population increased 13-fold, energy use per capita increased six-fold; industrial output increased 40-fold, and the number of marine fish caught increased 35-fold (Peterlin, Pearse and Dimovski, 2015).

Day by day, the world is experiencing the largest wave of urban growth in history. Over half of the world's population is now living in cities and according to the United Nations estimates, by 2050, 66% of the total world's population is expected to be urban. With this rapid urbanization, cities will face various sustainability challenges; including, but not limited to, the poverty expansion, social stress, natural resources shortage, spatial dynamics, and urban pollution with its effect on the climate change phenomenon. Given this unprecedented global urbanization growth and the need for sustainability at all aspects of a city, the concept of "Smart Sustainable Cities" (SSCs) emerged as a desired goal for present and future urban development and attracted the attention of many researchers and practitioners in the field. Their challenge is to ensure that cities are offering improved living conditions for their citizens by solving a set of sustainability challenges at the economic, environmental, and social levels. The Information and Communication Technologies (ICTs) offer high potential for solutions to many of these challenges while ensuring that they are environmentally friendly and viable (Ibrahim, El-Zaart and Adams, 2018).

Tourism has been found as a complex socioeconomic phenomenon based on the growing needs of modem societies for recreation and leisure and has become a major economic activity worldwide and a priority field in policy making at local, regional, national, supranational and international level. It is the result - and a cause - of wide sweeping changes in modem societies with far-reaching consequences for both developed and developing economies. Its spatial extent, in the past involving a few world regions, is becoming increasingly global reaching even far distant places (Coccossis, 2017).

Among others, the great challenges of climate change and the depletion of natural resources are strongly related to the ways in which energy is provided and consumed in contemporary societies. Accordingly, energy governance is concerned with shifting the system of energy provision and consumption towards a more sustainable configuration. Thought process must carry out investigations to which extent such a shift can be managed by intentional policy interventions, and what role local activities can play in fostering change within globally entrenched energy structures are still open questions.

Concepts of 'sustainability transitions' stress the alignment of actors around a shared vision of the future as a means to coordinate change. This is believed to work also at the scale of a city, producing momentum of change in a locally defined infrastructural system. At the same time, empirical accounts and conceptualizations of socio-technical change acknowledge that coordinating such processes is only partially possible, challenged by a multitude of priorities, perceptions and often contradictory views and therefore is necessarily conflict-laden. In reality, and particularly in democratic societies, the search for a shared orientation with regard to such complex systemic endeavors will necessarily remain a distributed and messy process which is in principle prone to mistakes and conflicts. However, questions will remain, as How can such processes of searching, contestation and negotiation be better understood? What does this mean for the organization of decision making processes regarding long-term infrastructural change? (Späth and Rohracher, 2015).

At the end of the day, the current globalization is faced by the challenge to meet the continuously growing worldwide demand for capital and consumer goods by simultaneously ensuring a sustainable evolvement of human existence in its social, environmental and economic dimensions. In order to cope with this challenge, industrial value creation must be geared towards sustainability. Currently, the industrial value creation in the early industrialized countries is shaped by the development towards the fourth stage of industrialization, the so-called Industry 4.0. This development provides immense opportunities for the realization of sustainable manufacturing (Stock and Seliger, 2016).

FUTURE RESEARCH SCOPES

If one talks about the future research scopes of a sustainable organization, one should think about the approaches to 'sustainability transitions' stress the possibility of aligning actors around a shared vision of the future, for example, at the scale of a community, society, or city. Empirical accounts reveal how difficult such coordination often is due to contradictory views involved. How can one better understand related processes of searching and negotiation? What does this mean for the organization of decision making processes regarding long-term infrastructural change? Future research need to reflect on implications of such a perspective on how policies and how governance arrangements should ideally be shaped (Späth and Rohracher, 2015).

In the recent past, the system has been reluctant to see either local or global environmental management as an integral part of the daily affairs. In the era of the industrial revolution, people became so removed from their natural environments that they ceased to see the interconnections between social and natural resources. People consume a banana from across the globe without knowing the social or ecological circumstances under which it was produced; one washes hands, with little awareness of the catchments from which the water comes and where the waste water will go; and turn on the heating, lights and television with little concern about the flows of energy they induce, or how they were generated. People working as environmental managers, in any field, have to contend with these disconnections that exist within communities, as well as those between communities and their natural environment. It is expected that part of an environmental manager's job is to create learning experiences to re-establish the mental connections between our actions and environments, thus creating pathways for social change.

Hence, there is a general recognition throughout the environmental field that it is time to bring social learning and environmental management back together (Keen, Brown and Dyball, 2005).

Furthermore, it must be noted that rapid changes are taking place across the world have had the effect of increasingly actualizing the tasks of corporate strategy and tactic adaptation in order to survive in the competitive struggle. At the same time, the elaboration of strategic plans for sustainable development and competitiveness facilitation based on the assessment of the strengths and weaknesses of activity are points of particular significance, along with the analysis of real possibilities, resources and the existing vulnerabilities of the enterprise towards the external environment. In this aspect, enterprises and organizations of different fields of activity need to search and apply more advanced concepts and tools, focused on quality, continuous improvement and sustainable business success (Salimova, et. al., 2018).

CONCLUSION

The synthesis from the research reveals a lack of a clear definition of sustainability which sets in motion a whole systemic dynamic. The data from the action research exemplify this dynamic. Firstly, there is a pattern of adopting a short-term focus and expediency in decision making. Secondly, problem solving favors the "quick fix" over thoughtful consideration and development of the key components for sustainability. Thirdly, there are gray areas of sustainability issues in developing and transitional economies. This research may also lead to questioning the urgency of implementing the very complex systemic sustainability at this time in view of widespread climate concerns, versus concentrating on the more straightforward carbon footprint reduction (Smith and Sharicz, 2011; Rahman, 2014).

Moreover, the concept of sustainability evokes a multiplicity of meanings, depending on the field. Some researchers have criticized the concept for its vagueness. Notwithstanding this criticism, worldwide efforts to meet the sustainable development goals (SDGs) are in progress and are expected to yield results by 2030. This study aims to addresses two issues and make two primary contributions. Firstly, the concept of sustainability is revisited to develop its integrative understanding. This concept is built on systems thinking –specifically, on the concepts of synergy, emergence, recursion and self-organization. Secondly, an approach is developed to help determine whether the efforts being made towards the SDGs can be expected to be effective (i.e., whether the world can hope to soon be a system that self-organizes towards sustainability) (Donaires, et. al., 2019).

In contrast, the development process for a sustainable corporate brand was examined by reference to the available literature on sustainability in relation to corporate branding. It has been observed that the drivers and factors involved in the development and maintenance of a sustainable corporate brand discussed included the link between corporate identity and corporate brand using Balmer's typology, corporate rebranding, developing a consistent sustainable brand promise, supply chain challenges, signaling and communication issues including the application of discourse theory, the sustainable corporate brand as an innovation credibility, and reputational issues (Stuart, 2011). The discussion of human activities exploiting natural resources and their environmental impact has gained more traction throughout the past decade. Especially, the role corporations play in these developments has caused a shift within corporate strategic considerations. As a result, today, many companies assume increasing responsibility to improve their sustainability performance (Simonarson and Zydorek, 2021).

Finally, the last but not the least, the new world must enclave much innovative approaches to enhance the sustainability at the global and local level, whether for the organizational entity or the state entity to cope the recently apprehended Corona virus (COVID-19) that is hindering the entire thought processes of the humanity crossing all boundaries.

REFERENCES

Aher, S. B., Bhaveshananda, S., & Sengupta, B. (2012). Organic agriculture: Way towards sustainable development. *International Journal of Environmental Sciences*, *3*(1), 209–216.

Arora, A., & Sharma, C. (2016). Corporate governance and firm performance in developing countries: Evidence from India. *Corporate Governance*, *16*(2), 420–436. doi:10.1108/CG-01-2016-0018

Azeez, A. (2015). Corporate governance and firm performance: Evidence from Sri Lanka. *The Journal of Finance*, *3*(1), 180–189.

Bansal, P. (2005). Evolving sustainability: A longitudinal study of corporate sustainable development. *Strategic Management Journal*, *26*(3), 197–218. doi:10.1002mj.441

Barrios, E., Gemmill-Herren, B., Bicksler, A., Siliprandi, E., Brathwaite, R., Moller, S., Batello, C., & Tittonell, P. (2020). The 10 Elements of Agroecology: Enabling transitions towards sustainable agriculture and food systems through visual narratives. *Ecosystems and People*, *16*(1), 230–247. doi:10.1080/26395916.2020.1808705

Baumgartner, R. J., & Rauter, R. (2017). Strategic perspectives of corporate sustainability management to develop a sustainable organization. *Journal of Cleaner Production*, *140*, 81–92. doi:10.1016/j.jclepro.2016.04.146

Bear, S., Rahman, N., & Post, C. (2010). The impact of board diversity and gender composition on corporate social responsibility and firm reputation. *Journal of Business Ethics*, *97*(2), 207–221. doi:10.100710551-010-0505-2

Bee, H. (2001, October–December). Article. *Honey Bee*, *12*(4), 3–5.

Bernardi, R. A., Bean, D. F., & Weippert, K. M. (2002). Signaling gender diversity through annual report pictures: A research note on image management. *Accounting, Auditing & Accountability Journal*, *15*(4), 609–616. doi:10.1108/09513570210441440

Boons, F., & Lüdeke-Freund, F. (2013). Business models for sustainable innovation: State-of-the-art and steps towards a research agenda. *Journal of Cleaner Production*, *45*, 9–19. doi:10.1016/j.jclepro.2012.07.007

Bose, R., & Luo, X. (2011). Integrative framework for assessing firms' potential toundertake Green IT initiatives via virtualization—A theoretical perspective. *TheJournal of Strategic Information Systems*, *20*(1), 38–54. doi:10.1016/j.jsis.2011.01.003

Bosse, D. A., & Phillips, R. A. (2016). Agency theory and bounded self-interest. *Academy of Management Review*, *41*(2), 276–297. doi:10.5465/amr.2013.0420

Boulouta, I. (2013). Hidden connections: The link between board gender diversity and corporate social performance. *Journal of Business Ethics*, *113*(2), 185–197. doi:10.100710551-012-1293-7

Bromley, D. W. (2008). Sustainability. In S. N. Durlauf & L. E. Blume (Eds.), *The new Palgrave dictionary of economics* (2nd ed.). Basingstoke, UK: Palgrave Macmillan. Retrieved July 05, 2021 from http://www.dictionaryofeconomics.com/article?id=pde2008_S000482

Brundtland Commission. (1987). *Our Common Future*. Oxford University Press.

Caiado, R. G. G., de Freitas Dias, R., Mattos, L. V., Quelhas, O. L. G., & Leal Filho, W. (2017). Towards sustainable development through the perspective of eco-efficiency-A systematic literature review. *Journal of Cleaner Production*, *165*, 890–904. doi:10.1016/j.jclepro.2017.07.166

Chen, M. K., Tai, T. W., & Hung, T. Y. (2012). Component selection system for greensupply chain. *Expert Systems with Applications*, *39*(5), 5687–5701. doi:10.1016/j.eswa.2011.11.102

Coccossis, H. (2017). Sustainable tourism and carrying capacity: a new context. In *The Challenge of tourism carrying capacity assessment* (pp. 19–30). Routledge. doi:10.4324/9781315240817-10

Conyon, M., & He, L. (2008). *CEO Turnover and Firm Performance in China's Listed Firms* (CRI 2009-012). Academic Press.

Crane, A., & Matten, D. (2010). *Business ethics* (3rd ed.). Oxford University Press.

Cruz, L. B., & Boehe, D. M. (2008). CSR in the global marketplace: Towards sustainable global value chains. *Management Decision*.

Dao, V., Langella, I., & Carbo, J. (2011). From green to sustainability: InformationTechnology and an integrated sustainability framework. *The Journal of Strategic Information Systems*, *20*(1), 63–79. doi:10.1016/j.jsis.2011.01.002

de Camargo Fiorini, P., & Jabbour, C. J. C. (2017). Information systems and sustainable supply chain management towards a more sustainable society: Where we are and where we are going. *International Journal of Information Management*, *37*(4), 241–249. doi:10.1016/j.ijinfomgt.2016.12.004

Donaires, O. S., Cezarino, L. O., Caldana, A. C. F., & Liboni, L. (2019). Sustainable development goals–an analysis of outcomes. *Kybernetes, 48*(1), 183–207. doi:10.1108/K-10-2017-0401

EAG. (2005). *e-Inclusion: New Challenges and Policy Recommendations*. eEurope Advisory Group, IDABC. Retrieved on July 14, 2021 from http://europa.eu.int/idabc/egovo

Erhardt, N. L., Werbel, J. D., & Shrader, C. B. (2003). Board of director diversity and firm financial performance. *Corporate Governance, 11*(2), 102–111. doi:10.1111/1467-8683.00011

Esenyel, V., & Emeagwali, O. (2019). The relationship between perceived corporate reputation and employee's positive word of mouth behavior: The mediation effect of trust to managers. *Management Science Letters, 9*(5), 673–686. doi:10.5267/j.msl.2019.2.004

Farouk, S., Cherian, J., & Jacob, J. (2012). Green accounting and management for sustainable manufacturing in developing countries. *International Journal of Business and Management, 7*(20), 36. doi:10.5539/ijbm.v7n20p36

Francis, B., Hasan, I., & Wu, Q. (2015). Professors in the boardroom and their impact on corporate governance and firm performance. *Financial Management, 44*(3), 547–581. doi:10.1111/fima.12069

Freeman, R. E., Harrison, J. S., Wicks, A. C., Parmar, B. L., & de Colle, S. (2010). *Stakeholder theory: The state of the art*. Cambridge University Press. doi:10.1017/CBO9780511815768

Fuentes, C., & Fredriksson, C. (2016). Sustainability service in-store: Service work and the promotion of sustainable consumption. *International Journal of Retail & Distribution Management, 44*(5), 492–507. doi:10.1108/IJRDM-06-2015-0092

Geels, F. W., Hekkert, M., & Jacobsson, S. (2008). The micro-dynamics of sustainable innovation journeys [editorial]. *Technology Analysis and Strategic Management, 20*(5), 521–536. doi:10.1080/09537320802292982

Gholami, H., Saman, M. Z. M., Sharif, S., & Zakuan, N. (2015). A CRM strategic leadership towards sustainable development in student relationship management: SD in higher education. *Procedia Manufacturing, 2*, 51–60. doi:10.1016/j.promfg.2015.07.010

Gold, S., & Schleper, M. C. (2017). A pathway towards true sustainability: A recognition foundation of sustainable supply chain management. *European Management Journal, 35*(4), 425–429. doi:10.1016/j.emj.2017.06.008

Grecu, V., & Ipiña, N. (2014). The Sustainable University-A Model for the Sustainable Organization. *Management of Sustainable Development, 6*(2).

Green, K. W. Jr, Zelbst, P. J., Bhadauria, V. S., & Meacham, J. (2012). Doenvironmental collaboration and monitoring enhance organizationalperformance? *Industrial Management & Data Systems, 112*(2), 186–205. doi:10.1108/02635571211204254

Green, K. W. Jr, Zelbst, P. J., Meacham, J., & Bhadauria, V. S. (2012). Green supplychain management practices: Impact on performance. *Supply Chain Management, 17*(3), 290–305. doi:10.1108/13598541211227126

Gupta, A.K. (1997). The Honey Bee Network: Linking Knowledge-Rich Grassroots Innovations. *Development, 40*(4), 36-40.

Hall, J., & Clark, W. (2003). Introduction to the special issue on environmental innovation. *Journal of Cleaner Production, 11*(4), 343–346. doi:10.1016/S0959-6526(02)00070-7

Hasanudin, A. I., Yuliansyah, Y., Said, J., Susilowati, Ch., & Muafi, M. (2019). Management control system, corporate social responsibility, and firm performance. *Entrepreneurship and Sustainability Issues*, *6*(3), 1154–1168. doi:10.9770/jesi.2019.6.3(21)

Horrigan, J. B. (2005). *On Demand Citizens: EGovernment at High Speed.* Pew Internet & American Life Project.

Hu, Z. H., Li, Q., Chen, X. J., & Wang, Y. F. (2014). Sustainable rent-based closed-loopsupply chain for fashion products. *Sustainability*, *6*(10), 7063–7088. doi:10.3390u6107063

Ibrahim, M., El-Zaart, A., & Adams, C. (2018). Smart sustainable cities roadmap: Readiness for transformation towards urban sustainability. *Sustainable Cities and Society*, *37*, 530–540. doi:10.1016/j.scs.2017.10.008

Isaak, R. (2016). The making of the ecopreneur. In *Making Ecopreneurs* (pp. 63–78). Routledge.

Islam, M. S. (2008). Towards a sustainable e-Participation implementation model. *European Journal of ePractice, 5*(10).

Jenkin, T. A., Webster, J., & McShane, L. (2011). An agenda for 'Green' information technology and systems research. *Information and Organization*, *21*(1), 17–40. doi:10.1016/j.infoandorg.2010.09.003

Keen, M., Brown, V. A., & Dyball, R. (Eds.). (2005). *Social learning in environmental management: towards a sustainable future*. Routledge.

Khor, K. S., Thurasamy, R., Ahmad, N. H., Halim, H. A., & May-Chiun, L. (2015). Bridging the gap of green IT/IS and sustainable consumption. *Global Business Review*, *16*(4), 571–593. doi:10.1177/0972150915581101

Kruja, D., & Hasaj, A. (2010). Comparisons of stakeholders' perception towards the sustainable tourism development and its impacts in Shkodra Region, Albania. *Turizam*, *14*(1), 1–12. doi:10.5937/Turizam1001001K

La Rocca, M., Montalto, F., La Rocca, T., & Staglian, Ã, R. (2017). The effect of ownership on firm value: A meta-analysis. *Economic Bulletin*, *37*(4), 2324–2353.

Leon, R. D. (2013). From the sustainable organization to sustainable knowledge-based organization. *Economic Insights - Trends and Challenges*, *65*(2).

Letza, S., Sun, X., & Kirkbride, J. (2004). Shareholding versus stakeholding: A critical review of corporate governance. *Corporate Governance*, *12*(3), 242–262. doi:10.1111/j.1467-8683.2004.00367.x

Linton, J., Klassen, R., & Jayaraman, V. (2007). Sustainable supply chains: An introduction. *Journal of Operations Management*, *25*(6), 1075–1082. doi:10.1016/j.jom.2007.01.012

Malimi, K. (2017). The Influence of Capital Adequacy, Profitability, and Loan Growth on Non-Performing Loans a Case of Tanzanian Banking Sector. International Journal of Economics. *Business and Management Studies*, *4*(1), 38–49.

Mohiuddin, Z. A. (2018). Effect of Lifestyle on Consumer Decision Making: A Study of Women Consumer of Pakistan. Journal of Accounting. *Business and Finance Research*, *2*(1), 12–15.

Mokgari, M. T., & Pwaka, O. (2018). An Evaluation of Effectiveness of Oversight Committees: A Case of City of Johannesburg, Section 79 Committees. *International Journal of Public Policy and Administration Research*, *5*(2), 48–67. doi:10.18488/journal.74.2018.52.48.67

Montalvo, C. (2008). General wisdom concerning the factors affecting the adoption of cleaner technologies: A survey 1990-2007. *Journal of Cleaner Production*, *16*(1), 7–13. doi:10.1016/j.jclepro.2007.10.002

Mosedale, S. (2005). Assessing women's empowerment: Towards a conceptual framework. *Journal of International Development*, *17*(2), 243–257. doi:10.1002/jid.1212

Muma, E. C. (2018). Transformative Constitutionalism in Post-Colonial Africa: A Framework for Democracy and Human Rights Protection. *International Journal of Emerging Trends in Social Sciences*, *3*(1), 29–45. doi:10.20448/2001.31.29.45

Mungwari, T. (2018). Centre for Language and Communication Studies, Chinhoyi University of Technology, Zimbabwe. *International Journal of Social Sciences Perspectives*, *2*(2), 112–125. doi:10.33094/7.2017.2018.22.112.125

Muniisvaran, K., Vijayalakshmi, M. J., & S, F. T. J. (2018). Psychological Support for Mental Health of Mothers to Childhood the Children with Disability. *International Journal of Asian Social Science*, *8*(12), 1186–1191. doi:10.18488/journal.1.2018.812.1186.1191

Muñoz, L. (2017). Is Environmental Externality Management a Correction of Adam Smith's Model to Make it Environmentally Friendly and Shift it Towards Green Markets or is it a Distortion on Top of another Distortion. *International Journal of Economics. Business and Management Studies*, *4*(1), 1–16.

Myambo, A., & Munyanyi, T. (2017). Effectiveness of Labour Court in Labour Dispute Management in Zimbabwe. *International Journal of Social and Administrative Sciences*, *2*(1), 15–30. doi:10.18488/journal.136.2017.21.15.30

Obiekwe, O. (2018). Human Capital Development and Organizational Survival: A Theoretical Review. *International Journal of Management and Sustainability*, *7*(4), 194–203. doi:10.18488/journal.11.2018.74.194.203

Pastakia, A. (1998). Grass-roots Ecopreneurs: Change Agents for a Sustainable Society. *Journal of Organizational Change Management*, *11*(2), 157–170. doi:10.1108/09534819810212142

Perrott, B. E. (2015). Building the sustainable organization: An integrated approach. *The Journal of Business Strategy*, *36*(1), 41–51. doi:10.1108/JBS-06-2013-0047

Peterlin, J., Pearse, N., & Dimovski, V. (2015). Strategic decision making for organizational sustainability: The implications of servant leadership and sustainable leadership approaches. *Economic and Business Review*, *17*(3), 273–290.

Rahman, H. (2014, April-June). Organizational Sustainability: Aspects of Agility. *International Journal of Business Intelligence Research*, *5*(2), 17–38. doi:10.4018/ijbir.2014040102

Sahakian, M., & Wilhite, H. (2014). Making practice theory practicable: Towards more sustainable forms of consumption. *Journal of Consumer Culture*, *14*(1), 25–44. doi:10.1177/1469540513505607

Salimova, T. A., Biryukova, L., Shilkina, A., & Khakhaleva, E. (2018). Towards a methodology of sustainable competitiveness of organization. *International Journal of Civil Engineering and Technology*, *9*(11), 161–172.

Sarkis, J., Koo, C., & Watson, R. T. (2013). Green information systems &technologies-this generation and beyond: Introduction to the special issue. *Information Systems Frontiers*, *15*(5), 695–704. doi:10.100710796-013-9454-5

Sarkis, J., Zhu, Q., & Lai, K. (2011). An organizational theoretic review of green supply chain management literature. *International Journal of Production Economics*, *130*(1), 1–15. doi:10.1016/j.ijpe.2010.11.010

Sbaouelgi, J. (2018). Income Inequality and Economic Growth: Application of Quantile Regression. *Asian Development Policy Review*, *6*(1), 1–14. doi:10.18488/journal.107.2018.61.1.14

Seuring, S., & Müller, M. (2008). From a literature review to a conceptualframework for sustainable supply chain management. *Journal of Cleaner Production*, *16*(15), 1699–1710. doi:10.1016/j.jclepro.2008.04.020

Seuring, S., Sarkis, J., Müller, J., & Rao, P. (2008). Sustainability and supply chain management-an introduction to the special issue. *Journal of Cleaner Production*, *16*(15), 1545–1551. doi:10.1016/j.jclepro.2008.02.002

Simonarson, D., & Zydorek, F. (2021). *Strategic processes towards sustainable development in large, international companies: A cross-case analysis using the Framework for Strategic Sustainable Development*. FSSD.

Smith, P. A., & Sharicz, C. (2011). The shift needed for sustainability. *The Learning Organization*, *18*(1), 73–86. doi:10.1108/09696471111096019

Späth, P., & Rohracher, H. (2015). Conflicting strategies towards sustainable heating at an urban junction of heat infrastructure and building standards. *Energy Policy*, *78*, 273–280. doi:10.1016/j.enpol.2014.12.019

Srivastava, S. K. (2007). Green supply-chain management: A state-of-the-artliterature review. *International Journal of Management Reviews*, *9*(1), 53–80. doi:10.1111/j.1468-2370.2007.00202.x

Stock, T., & Seliger, G. (2016). Opportunities of sustainable manufacturing in industry 4.0. *Procedia CIRP*, *40*, 536–541. doi:10.1016/j.procir.2016.01.129

Stuart, H. J. (2011). An identity based approach to the sustainable corporate brand. *Corporate Communications*.

Tay, M. Y., Abd Rahman, A., Aziz, Y. A., & Sidek, S. (2015). A review on drivers and barriers towards sustainable supply chain practices. *International Journal of Social Science and Humanity*, *5*(10), 892–897. doi:10.7763/IJSSH.2015.V5.575

Thabhiranrak, T., & Jermsittiparsert, K. (2019). Towards sustainable functioning of organization: Women empowerment and corporate management culture. *Journal of Security & Sustainability Issues*, *9*(1), 321–332. doi:10.9770/jssi.2019.9.1(24)

Upham, P., Maughan, J., Raper, D., & Thomas, C. (2012). *Towards sustainable aviation*. Routledge. doi:10.4324/9781849773409

Van Leeuwen, J. (2015). The regionalization of maritime governance: Towards a polycentric governance system for sustainable shipping in the European Union. *Ocean and Coastal Management*, *117*, 23–31. doi:10.1016/j.ocecoaman.2015.05.013

Wall, G. (2016). Tourism and development: Towards sustainable outcomes. In *Cultural tourism and sustainable local development* (pp. 49–64). Routledge.

Welford, R., & Jones, D. (1998). Beyond environmentalism and towards the sustainable organization. *Corporate Environmental Management 1–Systems and Strategies*, 237-257.

Wognum, P. N., Bremmers, H., Trienekens, J. H., van der Vorst, J. G., & Bloemhof, J. M. (2011). Systems for sustainability and transparency of food supplychains—Current status and challenges. *Advanced Engineering Informatics*, *25*(1), 65–76. doi:10.1016/j.aei.2010.06.001

World Health Organization. (2018). A vision for primary health care in the 21st century: towards universal health coverage and the Sustainable Development Goals (No. WHO/HIS/SDS/2018.15). World Health Organization.

World Health Organization. (2019). *Report of the Global conference on primary health care: from Alma-Ata towards universal health coverage and the Sustainable Development Goals* (No. WHO/UHC/IHS/2019.62). World Health Organization.

Wu, Z., & Pagell, M. (2011). Balancing priorities: Decision-making in sustainable supply chain management. *Journal of Operations Management*, *29*(6), 577–590. doi:10.1016/j.jom.2010.10.001

Zhu, Q., & Sarkis, J. (2004). Relationships between operational practices andperformance among early adopters of green supply chain management practices in Chinese manufacturing enterprises. *Journal of Operations Management*, *22*(3), 265–289. doi:10.1016/j.jom.2004.01.005

Zollo, M., Cennamo, C., & Neumann, K. (2013). Beyond what and why: Understanding organizational evolution towards sustainable enterprise models. *Organization & Environment*, *26*(3), 241–259. doi:10.1177/1086026613496433

Zulkifli, N. S., Shukor, Z. A., & Rahman, M. R. C. A. (2018). Intellectual Capital Efficiency and Firm Performance in Malaysia: The Effect of Government Ownership. *Asian Journal of Accounting and Governance*, *8*(Special Issue), 93–105. doi:10.17576/AJAG-2017-08SI-09

Zundel, C., & Kilcher, L. (2007), Organic agriculture and food availability. In *International Conference on Organic Agriculture and Food Security*. Food and Agriculture Organization of the United Nations (FAO).

ADDITIONAL READING

Becker, J. (2004). Making sustainable development evaluations work. *Sustainable Development*, *12*(4), 200–211. doi:10.1002d.236

Berry, M. A., & Rondinelli, D. A. (1998). Proactive corporate environmental management: A new industrial revolution. *The Academy of Management Executive*, *12*(2), 1–13. doi:10.5465/ame.1998.650515

Bhattacharjee, A. (2011). Modern management through ancient Indian wisdom: Towards a more sustainable paradigm. *PURUSHARTHA-A journal of Management. Ethics and Spirituality*, *4*(1), 14–37.

Broman, G., Holmberg, J., & Robört, K. H. (2000). Simplicity without reduction: Thinking upstream towards the sustainable society. *Interfaces*, *30*(3), 13–25. doi:10.1287/inte.30.3.13.11662

Caetano, M., de Araújo, J. B., & Amaral, D. C. (2012). A framework for the application of ecoefficiency to the technology development process. *Journal of Technology Management & Innovation*, *7*(2), 28–38. doi:10.4067/S0718-27242012000200003

Carvalho, H., Govindan, K., Azevedo, S. G., & Cruz-Machado, V. (2017). Modelling green and lean supply chains: An eco-efficiency perspective. *Resources, Conservation and Recycling*, *120*, 75–87. doi:10.1016/j.resconrec.2016.09.025

Charmondusit, K., & Keartpakpraek, K. (2011). Eco-efficiency evaluation of the petroleum and petrochemical group in the map Ta Phut Industrial Estate, Thailand. *Journal of Cleaner Production, 19*(2-3), 241–252. doi:10.1016/j.jclepro.2010.01.013

Charmondusit, K., Phatarachaisakul, S., & Prasertpong, P. (2013). The quantitative ecoefficiency measurement for small and medium enterprise: A case study of wooden toy industry. *Clean Technologies and Environmental Policy, 16*(5), 935–945. doi:10.100710098-013-0693-4

Goldrath, T., Ayalon, O., & Shechter, M. (2015). A combined sustainability index for electricity efficiency measures. *Energy Policy, 86*, 574–584. doi:10.1016/j.enpol.2015.08.013

Hadian, S., & Madani, K. (2015). A system of systems approach to energy sustainability assessment: Are all renewables really green? *Ecological Indicators, 52*, 194–206. doi:10.1016/j.ecolind.2014.11.029

Hart, S. L., & Milstein, M. B. (2003). Creating sustainable value. *The Academy of Management Executive, 17*(2), 56–67. doi:10.5465/ame.2003.10025194

Hellweg, S., Doka, G., Finnveden, G., & Hungerbuhler, K. (2005). Assessing the eco-efficiency of end-of-pipe technologies with the environmental cost efficiency indicator - A case study of solid waste management. *Journal of Industrial Ecology, 9*(4), 189–203. doi:10.1162/108819805775247864

Helminen, R. (2000). Developing tangible measures for eco-efficiency: The case of the Finnish and Swedish pulp and paper industry. *Business Strategy and the Environment, 9*(3), 196–210. doi:10.1002/(SICI)1099-0836(200005/06)9:3<196::AID-BSE240>3.0.CO;2-O

Küpers, W. M. (2011). Integral responsibilities for a responsive and sustainable practice in organization and management. *Corporate Social Responsibility and Environmental Management, 18*(3), 137–150. doi:10.1002/csr.272

Laosirihongthong, T., Samaranayake, P., & Nagalingam, S. (2019). A holistic approach to supplier evaluation and order allocation towards sustainable procurement. *Benchmarking, 26*(8), 2543–2573. doi:10.1108/BIJ-11-2018-0360

Leeuwis, C. (2000). Reconceptualizing participation for sustainable rural development: Towards a negotiation approach. *Development and Change, 31*(5), 931–959. doi:10.1111/1467-7660.00184

Liberatore, A. (1997). *The integration of sustainable development objectives into EU policy-making*. Routledge.

Mårtensson, K., & Westerberg, K. (2016). Corporate environmental strategies towards sustainable development. *Business Strategy and the Environment, 25*(1), 1–9. doi:10.1002/bse.1852

McDonagh, P. (1998). Towards a theory of sustainable communication in risk society: Relating issues of sustainability to marketing communications. *Journal of Marketing Management, 14*(6), 591–622. doi:10.1362/026725798784867699

Nash, D., & Butler, R. (1990). Towards sustainable tourism. *Tourism Management, 11*(3), 263–264. doi:10.1016/0261-5177(90)90051-A

Reddy, K., & Locke, S. (2014). The relationship between ownership structure, capital structure and corporate governance practices: A case study of co-operatives and mutuals in New Zealand. *International Journal of Managerial Finance, 10*(4), 511–536. doi:10.1108/IJMF-12-2012-0130

Romme, A. G. L. (2003). Making a difference: Organization as design. *Organization Science, 14*(5), 558–573. doi:10.1287/orsc.14.5.558.16769

Scialabba, E. N., & Lindenlauf, M. M. (2010). Organic agriculture and climate change. *Renewable Agriculture and Food Systems, 25*(2), 158–169. doi:10.1017/S1742170510000116

Serageidin, I. (1993). Making development sustainable. *Finance & Development, 30*(4).

Shaft, T. M., Sharfman, M. P., & Swahn, M. (2001). Using interorganizational information systems to support environmental management efforts at ASG. *Journal of Industrial Ecology, 5*(4), 95–116. doi:10.1162/10881980160084051

Sharkie, R. (2003). Knowledge creation and its place in the development of sustainable competitive advantage. *Journal of Knowledge Management, 7*(1), 20–31. doi:10.1108/13673270310463590

Shriberg, M. (2002). Toward sustainable management: The University of Michigan Housing Division's approach. *Journal of Cleaner Production, 10*(1), 41–45. doi:10.1016/S0959-6526(01)00021-X

Sikdar, S. K. (2003, August). Sustainable Development and Sustainability Metrics. *AIChE Journal. American Institute of Chemical Engineers, 49*(8), 1928–1932. doi:10.1002/aic.690490802

Suma, V. (2019). Towards sustainable industrialization using big data and internet of things. *Journal of ISMAC, 1*(1), 24–37. doi:10.36548/jismac.2019.1.003

Suto, M. (2003). Capital structure and investment behaviour of Malaysian firms in the 1990s: A study of corporate governance before the crisis. *Corporate Governance*, *11*(1), 25–39. doi:10.1111/1467-8683.00299

Tran, H., Bui, V., Phan, T., Dau, X., Tran, M., & Do, D. (2019). The impact of corporate social responsibility and risk management on financial performance: The case of Vietnamese textile firms. *Management Science Letters*, *9*(7), 1029–1036. doi:10.5267/j.msl.2019.4.003

Wächter, P., Ornetzeder, M., Rohracher, H., Schreuer, A., & Knoflacher, M. (2012). Towards a sustainable spatial organization of the energy system: Backcasting experiences from Austria. *Sustainability*, *4*(2), 193–209. doi:10.3390u4020193

Wen, Y., Rwegasira, K., & Bilderbeek, J. (2002). Corporate governance and capital structure decisions of the Chinese listed firms. *Corporate Governance*, *10*(2), 75–83. doi:10.1111/1467-8683.00271

World Health Organization. (2017). *Promoting health in the SDGs: Report on the 9th Global conference for health promotion, Shanghai, China, 21–24 November 2016: all for health, health for all* (No. WHO/NMH/PND/17.5). World Health Organization.

World Health Organization. (2019). *World health statistics 2019: monitoring health for the SDGs, sustainable development goals*. World Health Organization.

Zandi, G., & Haseeb, M. (2019). The importance of green energy consumption and agriculture in reducing environmental degradation: Evidence from sub-Saharan African countries. *International Journal of Financial Research*, *10*(5), 215–227. doi:10.5430/ijfr.v10n5p215

KEY TERMS AND DEFINITIONS

Economic Development: Economic development can be defined as the creation of wealth from which community benefits are realized. Economic development can also be seen as the process whereby simple, low-income national economies are transformed into modern industrial economies.

Environmental Development: Simply it can be put forward as an economic and social development that respects the environment.

Social Development: Social development is about improving the well-being of every individual in a society so that they can reach their full potential.

Sustainability in Business: In business, sustainability refers to performing business without negatively impacting the environment, community, or society as a whole.

Sustainable Development: Sustainable development can be defined as an organizing principle for meeting various human development goals while simultaneously sustaining the ability of natural systems to provide the natural resources and ecosystem services on which the economy and society depend.

Sustainable Organization: A sustainability organization is primarily an organized group of people that aims to advance sustainability and/or those actions of organizing something sustainably. Unlike many other business organizations, sustainability organizations are not limited to implementing sustainability strategies which provide them with economic and cultural benefits attained through environmental responsibility.

Chapter 10
Critical Success Factors for Organizational Agility:
Q-Study and the Place of IT

Mohamed Amine Marhraoui
ENSIAS Engineering School, Mohammed V University in Rabat, Morocco

Mohammed Abdou Janati Idrissi
ENSIAS Engineering School, Mohammed V University in Rabat, Morocco

Abdellah El Manouar
ENSIAS Engineering School, Mohammed V University in Rabat, Morocco

ABSTRACT

Companies are facing important challenges related to markets' internationalization, regulatory restrictions, and fierce competition especially during the COVID-19 context. Environment is thus characterized by rapid and volatile changes. Organizational agility is the key capability allowing firms to adapt continuously by sensing changes in their environment and responding in an efficient and rapid manner. Previous work has addressed organizational agility enablers, including IT ones, allowing the firm to be more agile. In this chapter, the authors first extend their organizational agility enablers list through an in-depth analysis of consulting firms and governmental agencies reports on agility during the COVID-19 context. The final list contains 28 organizational agility enablers belonging to 10 groups. Then, the authors conduct a Q-study in order to identify what factors are critical for a successful journey towards agility and to analyze the results from an IT perspective.

DOI: 10.4018/978-1-7998-4799-1.ch010

INTRODUCTION

The 1980s has witnessed a downturn in the US economy. There were mainly two recessions in 1980 and 1982 due to the restrictive monetary policy of the Federal Reserve and the effects of the 2nd oil shock (1979). This has caused a slowdown in investment and an increase in the unemployment rate. These two recessions are the strongest after the Second World War (Brunner, 1983).

In this unfavourable economic context, traditional American industry suffered a severe crisis since 1980 due to competition from Europeans, Japanese and emerging Asian industrial countries.

In 1990, the American congress decided to carry out reforms. Thus, the United States Department of Defense has launched an investigation into the American industry to improve its competitiveness.

This is how the story of agility began in the United States as a new model to help revitalize American industry and regain its leadership lost in the 70s and 80s in favour of Japanese and European industries. The notion of agility therefore finds its origins in the military field as the ability to change actions over time (Richards, 1996). Indeed, a group of researchers from Lehigh University in Pennsylvania has been mandated by the United States Department of Defense to define a new strategy for American industry (Nagel & Dove, 1991). Thus, by observing the rate of the environment change, the researchers of the "IACOCCA institute" wrote a report entitled "21st Century Manufacturing Enterprise Strategy. An industry Led view of Agile Manufacturing" which aimed to develop a strategy to strengthen the competitiveness of American industry for the next 15 years (Nagel & Dove, 1991). This report was produced following the organization of a conference to discuss the economic future of the United States with more than 150 researchers. The term "Agile Manufacturing" thus appeared and an annual forum affiliated with Lehigh University was established (Agile Manufacturing Enterprise Forum (AMEF)). The purpose of this forum is to develop a vision of the agile approach, to assess the current state of implementation, to identify and prioritize the necessary changes in practices and related technologies, and to influence the Agile Manufacturing Research Program. In 1995, the results of this research were published in the book "Agile competitors and virtual organizations" (Goldman et al., 1995). The results of the report show that the classic organizational model does not allow companies to provide satisfactory answers to the demands of the post-industrial world characterized by an increasing importance of information and communication.

Indeed, they proposed a new strategy to meet these challenges. This strategy is based on the "Agile Manufacturing" concept driven by four forces: continuous change; quick response; continuous improvement and environmental responsibility. In order to achieve this vision, the company should have key characteristics (competent human resources, continuous learning, technological leadership ...), as well as an agile infrastructure (organizational structures and practices, adoption and transfer of technology, rapid cooperation mechanisms ...). This infrastructure, which enables industrial enterprises to be more agile, may be available through cooperation between enterprises and representatives of industry, government and academia.

Later, during the past decade, rapid technological change has accelerated the production of data. As early as 2012, (Gantz & Reinsel, 2012) predicted an increase in the volume of data to reach 40 zettabytes (40 trillion gigabytes). In addition, according to Stephen Gold, former IBM Marketing Director, 90% of all data in the world has been created in the last 2 years (Brasseur, 2013). This explosion in the amount of information continues exponentially in 2021 and is a source of turbulence in the business environment, and also a development opportunity with the advent of the knowledge society (World bank, 2021).

Indeed, competition has accelerated since the beginning of the third millennium due to economic globalization and the abundance of information leading to rapid and continuous changes in markets and technologies (social networks, artificial intelligence, etc.). The current business environment is characterized by rapid and constant change at several levels: economic, political, technological, regulatory, social and ecological.

The global economy has evolved into a knowledge economy. The intangible capital of a company thus becomes crucial for its development. Indeed, post-industrial society is characterized by a growing importance of knowledge greater than that relating to infrastructure or material capital (Earl, 2001). This revolution is accelerated by the rapid production of knowledge due to scientific and technological progress. In addition, intangible capital has become more important as natural resources are scarce and information is more abundant thanks to investments in R&D, education, collaboration and technological innovation allowing to produce, reconfigure and process a large quantity of data.

Thus, was born the notion of organizational agility which extends the research of agile manufacturing, started in the 90s (Hormozi, 2001), to the entire organization. Organizational agility which is also different from project management methods as it is related to the strategic level for companies allowing them a continuous and a rapid creation of new innovative products. These companies combine agile project management for the development of new software, with a more global vision of agility (Kettunen & Laanti, 2008).

Based on previous work, organizational agility (OA) enablers belonging to six groups namely IT, HR, organizational structure, knowledge management, process and innovation were identified. In this paper, the purpose of the authors is to enrich these OA enablers base by inferring them from field reports especially in the COVD19 context when companies are deploying efforts to be more agile. Then, the main critical success factors are extracted from this base through a Q-study. The authors have chosen to explore representative fields reports from major consulting firms as they reflect the capacities deployed by companies around the world to be more agile and to adapt to COVID19 crisis impacts either on the economic or social levels. Thus, the need for agility has grown among companies in order to survive and achieve a competitive advantage. This agility quest will be more and more increasing in the future as the environment is continuously changing. Consequently, the extracted CSFs list in this chapter may dynamically be updated.

Thus, the chapter is structured as follow. After addressing a literature review in section 2, the authors describe in section 3 the adopted research methodology. Section 4 allows to enrich the OA enablers' base by relying on consulting firms and governmental agencies reports. Then, the authors carry out a Q-sort study allowing to identify the main OA critical success factors. Finally, the authors provide a conclusion of the chapter and highlight their main contributions and research perspectives.

BACKGROUND

Organizational Agility

Organizational agility (OA) is the ability of the enterprise to detect opportunities / risks in its environment and to respond effectively and quickly (Kidd, 1995; Overby et al., 2006). It is a company's ability to adapt to unexpected changes through rapid and innovative responses that exploit change as opportunities for development and growth (Lu, Y. & Ramamurthy, 2011). Detecting these changes in the environment through knowledge management processes enables organizations to prioritize and choose the best solution among possible alternatives, modify business processes, and customize the response in real time (Dove, 2005).

Organizational agility allows the company to maintain competitive leadership by quickly responding to the expectations of its customers, in an era of competition's internationalization, market fragmentation and the growth of external cooperation relationships (Charbonnier, 2006).

According to (Breu et al., 2002), organizational agility is the ability of the company to grow in an environment of continuous and unpredictable change while offering high-performance, high-quality, low-cost products that meet the requirements of consumers.

Furthermore, according to (Holsapple & Li, 2008), organizational agility is the result of combining sensing changes (detecting opportunities / challenges) both internal and environmental, with an ability to use resources to respond proactively / reactively to such changes. This response should be in a fast, flexible and relevant manner. Indeed, two components constitute the organizational agility of the company: 1) The sensing component; 2) The responding component.

Sensing capability is the ability to analyse the requirements of new markets, quickly assess new customer needs and identify development opportunities. It therefore enables the company to predict customer expectations and trends, identify technological advancements and cope with policy and regulatory changes (Overby et al., 2006). Response capacity, on the other hand, is the ability of the company to have different options to act quickly by deploying existing resources or building new resources (Dove, 2001).

On the basis of these two components, (Overby et al., 2006) propose four company profiles. The 1st profile are companies with a highly developed R&D and market intelligence function to detect their environment and having the operational capacities to exploit opportunities.

The 2nd profile of companies is those experiencing changes in their environment but which are unable to respond in a timely manner. The 3rd profile are companies with high production capacities, but may miss opportunities. Moreover, the 4th profile are companies which have neither detection nor response capacities.

Researchers are nowadays talking about "the agile organizations". These are dynamic and adaptable organizations that can be very competitive in the era of "chaos" while being innovative and having weakly coupled structures. These organizations combine harmoniously the characteristics of fluidity and flexibility with a minimum of order, control and predictability (Dyer & Shafer, 2003; Wouter et al., 2015).

Thus, organizational agility helps the company survive in a rapidly changing "chaos" environment characterized by volatility, uncertainty, complexity and ambiguity (VUCA) (Lawrence, 2013).

Volatility means the pace, speed and volume of changes. Therefore, a context is considered volatile when it can evolve in an unpredictable and fast manner (Codreanu, 2016).

Uncertainty is about the difficulties in predicting events (Horney et al., 2010). For example, competition from new entrants into traditional markets through a technological disruption that has created a new business model. Uber in the field of transport allows the user to know how many cars are available while specifying the distance, the waiting time and the price of the race. Also, a political or regulatory decision can create a sudden and unexpected change in the environment (e.g., the obligation for the banks of the countries that have signed an agreement with the United States to comply with the US FATCA by declaring the accounts held by US citizens). The environment is therefore considered uncertain when it is governed by the effect of surprise and the difficulty of predictability.

Complexity is linked to chaos (Kinsinger & Walch, 2012). Change is thus incomprehensible because of the dynamic interactions between the components of a particular sector or market. This interdependence between partners, subcontractors and countries makes the environment more globalized and complex as the current business model of businesses depends on several interacting stakeholders.

Ambiguity is associated with the unknown or with the differences of interpretations (Shaffer & Zalewski, 2011). An example of this last point is the statutory texts which can be interpreted in different ways according to the context or the standards. Another example is the introduction of a new product or the penetration of a new market characterized by a lack of visibility.

Moreover, according to (Winby & Worley, 2014), organizational agility is based on four principles:

1. Define a sustainable strategy appropriate to customer expectations and the constraints of the environment. This strategy is in line with the objectives and values of the company.
2. Early identification of opportunities / weak signals, and communication to decision-makers to anticipate changes and act accordingly.
3. Test possible solutions for an adequate response, better learning and permanent innovation.
4. Ability to implement possible solutions in order to implement the desired changes.

The organizational agility topic has interested researchers from different disciplines: human resources (Dyer & Shafer, 2003; Breu et al., 2002; Charbonnier, 2006), operations management (Sharifi & Zhang, 2001), Information technology (Tallon et al., 2019; Overby et al., 2006; Karimi-Alaghehband & Rivard, 2019), supply chain management (Lin et al., 2006) and strategic management (Teece et al., 2016).

Moreover, organizational agility can help companies to ensure a sustainable performance. Indeed, agile companies can respond effectively to unexpected changes and thereby increase the speed of execution to optimize supply chain performance (Baskerville, 2005). An agile company thus identifies the needs of the market, the possibilities for improving its products and implements the necessary actions to seize these opportunities. Therefore, agility is a necessary ability for the company to adapt to changes in stakeholder requirements for sustainability, and therefore to be more efficient economically, socially and environmentally (Marhraoui & El Manouar, 2017).

Finally, organizational agility is different from the "Lean" paradigm. Indeed, "Lean" mainly concerns JIT (Just-in-time) production (Womack et al., 1990), "Kanban" production (Monden, 1983; Ohno, 1988) and optimization of the use of resources (Womack & Jones, 2003; Ohno, 1988). However, lean is inappropriate for an uncertain environment (Wendler, 2013). Lean is effective in producing a large quantity of standard products in a predictable environment. On the contrary, agility is adequate when it comes to a VUCA environment allowing to meet variable and limited quantity demand.

Characteristics of Agile Firms

Agile companies have in common one or more detection / response characteristics, mainly: awareness, responsiveness, speed, flexibility, competence and integration.

While awareness is the ability to accurately detect and anticipate a change in the environment (Dove, 2005), reactivity is associated with making adequate decisions and taking effective action to respond to changes (Dyer & Shafer, 2003).

Flexibility, on the other hand, is the ability to adapt to change by reconfiguring the same existing resources (Bernardes & Hanna, 2009) and changing the state of a system at the operational level using the same available resource base. In addition, competence is linked to productivity, efficiency and quality. Speed means a short production cycle, optimized time to market for new products and rapid process execution (Sharifi & Zhang, 1999). Finally, integration refers to intra-company coordination (Yahaya et al., 1999) and also inter-company integration through alliances, virtual companies and collaborative platforms (Sharifi & Zhang, 2001).

There are three types of organizational agility: customer agility, partners agility and operational / internal agility (Weill et al., 2002).

Customer agility is the ability to engage customers in the development of innovative products by sharing new ideas, co-creating products or testing by giving feedback on new features. Customer agility is therefore the ability to detect and respond to opportunities for innovation and competitive action linked to customer needs (Roberts & Grover, 2012).

Agility towards partners is the ability to take advantage of knowledge, skills and strengths of business partners in order to identify and implement new business opportunities. For example, it allows suppliers to participate in the design of products and services with higher added value (Izza et al., 2008).

The exploitation of these innovative opportunities with precision and speed is achieved thanks to the operational agility of the company (Sambamurthy, 2003). In order to improve the good ability to

information processing, operational agility is based, according to (Huang et al., 2014), on a two-step process: the construction of information flow network and the implementation of organizational control.

MAIN FOCUS OF THE CHAPTER

Issues, Controversies, Problems

Based on the literature review presented earlier, companies should deploy the necessary means in order to adapt to their environment and thus ensure their survival. Previous research has focused on the impact of some enablers on firm's agility. However, there is a lack in the literature of studies encompassing the main enablers which can help companies in their efforts towards a successful agile transformation. These are critical success factors of organizational agility.

Furthermore, as specified earlier, the organizational agility topic has interested different disciplines namely HR, IT and strategic management. However, there are very few studies encompassing the main agility enablers and comparing their respective impact. Moreover, most articles tackling the impact of IT on organizational agility have found positive causal relationship. In fact, information technologies are a major lever for supporting communication, information processing and decision-making processes. These are management applications for internal and external activities, covering human resources management and business processes as well as managing the relationship with partners (customers, suppliers, etc.). IT also includes software that enables production management to reduce operating costs and improve the reliability and quality of delivered products. In addition, the access to IT resources is becoming increasingly democratized with the advent of on-demand cloud solutions available in SAAS (Software As A Service) mode. Thus, the company can easily and quickly take advantage of IT opportunities that are most relevant to its development perspectives.

Indeed, the major differentiation between companies today is the access and exploitation of reliable, up-to-date, available and relevant information.

Information technologies, when adopted and controlled by the internal and external users of the company, ensure therefore a better flow of information enabling communication, the day-to-day business management and effective decision-making in a turbulent environment.

However, there are some controversies on the dark side of IT use (Seo & La Paz, 2008). Indeed, IT can present some problems in data collection, data integration difficulties, information accuracy and the effective adoption of new systems. Also, IT applications when badly managed and deployed may hinder organizational agility (Overby et al., 2006). In fact, monolithic applications are very costly to adapt to changing customers' requirements, and some old systems may be difficult to connect with the ecosystem of suppliers and customers. Moreover, the implementation of ERP systems for instance may hinder organizational agility. Indeed, firms may have difficulties in developing new agile capabilities when they stick to the processes emanating from the implementation of ERP (Galliers, 2007; Kharabe, & Lyytinen, 2012). This can create more complexity inside the company due to tight integration between business processes (Gupta et al., 2006).

Thereby, the main research question in this study is the following:

What are the main critical success factors (CSF) allowing the firms to be more agile? What is the place of information technology enablers among these CSFs?

Methodology

In order to answer the research question stated earlier, the authors present the adopted methodology in this study as described in figure 1 below. Based on previous research (Marhraoui & El Manouar, 2017), six agility enablers categories were identified namely IT, HR, organizational structure, knowledge management, innovation, process. Then, authors have extracted agility enablers from consulting firms/ governmental agencies reports. Consequently, by merging the two pre-cited lists, they have established an exhaustive list of organizational agility enablers classified by categories.

Then, authors have carried out a Q-study, as described by (Brown, 1993) in order to identify the main critical success factors of organizational agility and to deduce the place of IT among the other enablers. Indeed, the quantitative analysis was based on a survey. Each participant classifies the statements corresponding to organizational agility enablers on according to a normally distributed 7-point Q-scale ranging from -3 to +3. Then, a factor analysis allows to calculate the Q-sort value per factor for each statement. The consensus about a statement was thus calculated, as described thereafter, in order to classify the most important enablers which constitutes the critical success factors of organizational agility.

SOLUTIONS AND RECOMMENDATIONS

Organizational Agility Enablers

A previous work of (Marhraoui & El Manouar, 2017) has focused on a systematic literature review in order to extract the enablers of organizational agility. These are grouped into six categories (IT, HR, organizational structure, knowledge management, innovation, process) as described in figure 2 below.

IT enablers include data governance, the company's IT resources, the use of mobile applications, service-oriented architecture and artificial intelligence. Indeed, service-oriented architecture (SOA) improves alignment between service-based

Figure 1. The adopted methodology

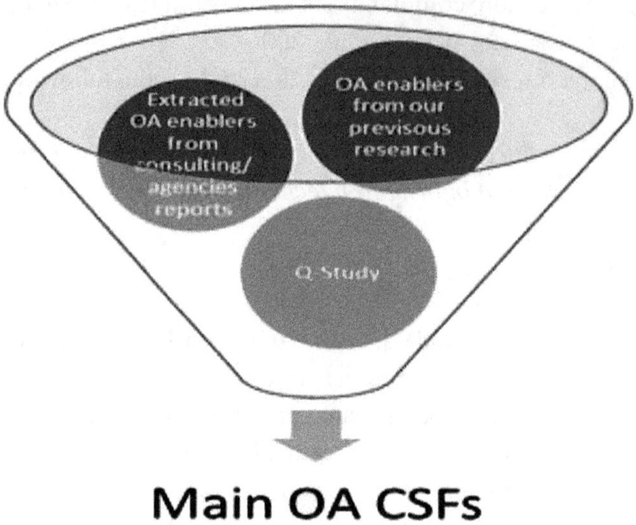

Figure 2. Organizational agility enablers groups

systems and business requirements. Thus, the use of the services offered by APIs (Application Programming Interface) allows better modularity and optimized/unique access to data, whatever the nature of the Human Machine Interface (Web, Mobile, Desktop).

In addition, (Marhraoui & El Manouar) have found that either collaboration or decision-oriented knowledge management systems have a positive impact on organizational agility. The first type is related to the capture and sharing of knowledge. It includes content management systems (CMS), document management systems (DMS), intranet / extranet portals, groupware as well as workflows (Bali et al., 2009). On one hand, groupware tools refer to the set of utilities that facilitate work across different groups (Gross & Koch, 2007). They include messaging, group calendars, information sharing in discussion forums, and electronic conferencing (Prax, 2012). Workflows tools, on the other hand, do not just put people in touch with each other but structures the information flows in order to offer the right information at the right time to the right stakeholder in the process (Prax, 2012). The second type is related to systems allowing decision-making based on discovery and the relevance of knowledge. It is linked to decision support systems based on data warehouses and data exploration techniques. In addition, artificial intelligence and machine learning allow companies to learn how to recognize complex patterns and how to make intelligent decisions (Santo, 2010). This second type is also related to advanced analyses based on large data sets (Russom, 2011).

Also, companies can enhance their agility by facilitating knowledge sharing while maintaining a balance between managing knowledge and change. The challenge for companies is therefore to provide the knowledge at the right time so that it is available before the time of use in order to anticipate emerging needs, meet current needs and eliminate obsolete needs (Dove, 2003).

Moreover, HR practises are another enablers' group which includes the open behaviour/mindset of employees, their skills development and effective teamwork. Indeed, the company must foster a culture and mentality oriented towards agility as well as associated behaviours (Dyer and Shafer, 2003). These include encouraging initiative, employee versatility, rapid reconfiguration of human resources, collective collaboration as well as continuous learning.

In addition, the organizational structure, when flat and composed of independent/multi-disciplinary business units, enables organizational agility as each operational entity within a system of reduced complexity is closer to customers (Barrand, 2006). This allows the company to react effectively to the changing environment, as each unit focuses on a market, a product line or a specific customer segment (Gallagher & Worrell, 2008). In addition, the flat structure improves coordination and collaboration among employees for better agility in rapidly changing environments (Lunenburg, 2011). The flat organizational structure allows for a stronger connection with the outside world, a simplification of working procedures and taking advantage of the collaborative potential of the employee.

Added to this are flexible processes which can be modelled and adjusted to changing business needs. They allow the company to detect effectively change in its environment and respond in a personalized way (Dove, 2005; Benner & Tushman, 2003). Also, (Schonenberg et al., 2008) developed the concept of PAIS (Process Aware Information Systems) allowing the company to adjust its business processes to changes in the environment.

The 6th enabler's category is related to the design of innovative products which helps the company to adapt to the turbulent environment. This makes it possible to introduce new products to meet customer needs and to transform the business by entering new emerging markets (Brown & Eisenhardt, 1995). The innovative company starts with a minimalist and doable product (MVP: Minimum Viable Product) and refines it based on the attitudes of early customers. This allows the company to increase the time to penetrate a new market (Time to Market), to validate the product and adapt it to user needs. The Design Thinking approach allows the company to strengthen this co-creation of products and services with its customers / communities, and thus build a company focusing its resources on high added value actions.

In order to complete the list of organizational agility enablers gathered through the study of the literature, authors conducted an analysis of consulting firms and government agencies reports.

Indeed, as mentioned in table 1, 11 reports from major consulting firms (Mckinsey, BCG, Bain, Capgemini, Mazars, Deloitte, Pwc, Ey, Accenture, OliverWyman) on organizational agility as well as 4 reports from government agencies and international organizations (Oecd, Eupan, WE Forum) were analysed in order to extract the agility enablers of organizational agility. The majority of these reports is published during the COVID19 pandemic. This is due to the necessity of being agile in order to meet challenging times and to anticipate by learning lessons for the "new normal".

By using the TagCrowd web tool (Steinbock & Pea, 2007), authors were able to highlight the frequency of the most cited words. Then, they qualified these words to bring out those corresponding to organizational agility enablers. The results of the extracted enablers by occurrence frequency are described in figure 3.

The extracted results were grouped into ten categories. In addition to confirming the 6 categories tackled by (Marhraoui & El Manouar, 2017), 4 new categories were added related to leadership & vision, execution capabilities, customer experience and partnership. Thus, the obtained list of 28 organizational agility enablers is grouped into 10 groups as described in figure 4 below.

The added enablers following the frequency analysis are highlighted in green. Indeed, leadership and vision category encompass the engagement of executive

Table 1. List of consulting firms/international organizations reports

Source	Title	Firm/ Agency	Year	Reference
Consulting firm reports	Agile resilience in the UK: Lessons from COVID-19 for the 'next normal'	Mckinsey	2020	(Chong et al., 2020)
	When the Ground Shifts, It Pays to Be Agile	BCG	2020	(Danoesastro et al., 2020)
	Doing agile right	Bain	2020	(Rigby et al., 2020)
	Leading with Agility and Responsible Innovation in Response to Covid-19: MedTech Industry Anchor Response	Accenture	2020	(O'Halloran et al., 2020)
	Soar in the Face of Disruption.	Accenture	2020	(Roark et al., 2020)
	Five Predictions for COVID-19 Driven Agility across the Life Science Value Chain	Capgemini	2020	(Iyengar et al., 2020)
	COVID-19: Which Critical Choices Should Businesses Make Next?	EY	2020	(Weidemeyer, 2020)
	Using Agility and Tech to Help Clients Meet Regulatory Commitments amid COVID-19	Pwc	2020	(Lines, 2020)
	COVID-19: Board Agility in a Time of Crisis	Deloitte	2020	(Foutty, 2020)
	Agile Working in Uncertain Times	Mazars	2020	(Beaupere, 2020)
	Organizational agility. Why large corporations often struggle to adopt the inventions created by their innovation units and how to improve success rates in rapidly changing environment	Oliver Wyman	2018	(Prats et al., 2018)
Government and international organization agencies' reports	4 Digital Technologies That Can Help Supply Chains Take Flight.	WEF	2020	(Al Essa, 2020)
	Winning the race for survival: How advanced manufacturing technologies are driving business-model innovation.	WEF	2020	(Joglekar et al., 2020)
	Common Assessment Framework. The European model for improving public organisations through self-assessment	EUPAN	2020	(Eupan, 2020)
	Achieving Public Sector Agility at Times of Fiscal Consolidation.	OECD	2015	(OECD, 2015)

board of directors, the strategic thinking of leaders, their transformation focus and the investments which they allocate to succeed transformation projects. In addition, execution is another added enabler's category which is related to effective project/ program management, team's management, planning and scaling capabilities. Moreover, another category related to customer experience was added. It relates to adapted products and services to customers' needs and to designing an optimal customer journey. Finally, partnerships are important in order to enhance firm's agility. This added category group relates to having a large network of partners and a strong collaboration across the supply chain.

Figure 3. The results of the extracted enablers by occurrence frequency

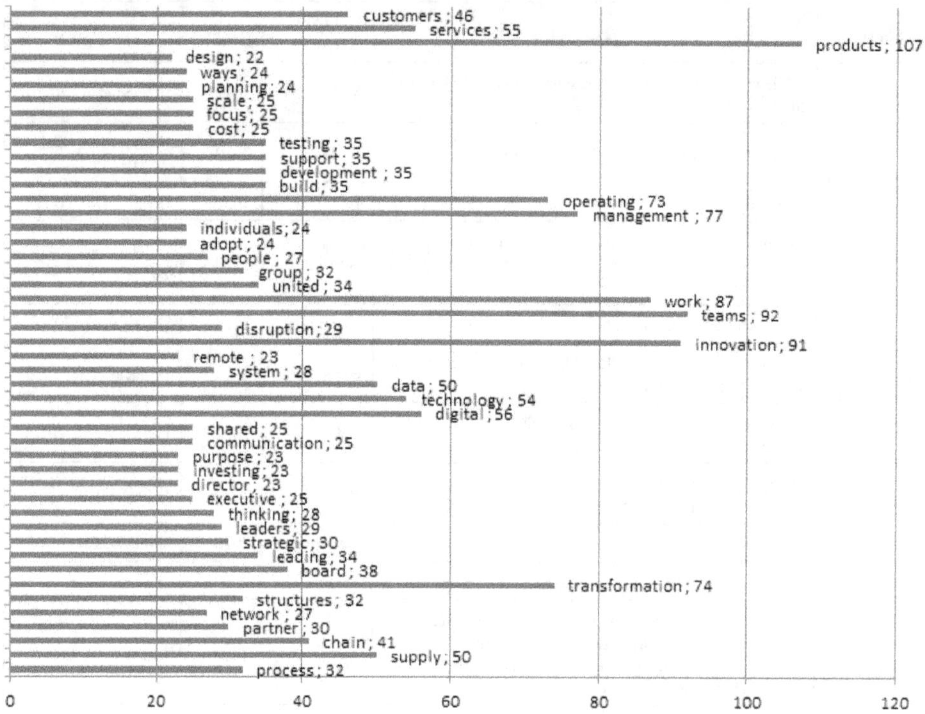

Q-Study: Main Critical Success Factors (CSA) of Organizational Agility

1. Data Collection

Authors conducted a Q-study in order to extract the main critical success factors among the list of 28 organizational agility enablers obtained in section 3. Based on open-source "Easy-HtmlQ" with Firebase in combination with Ken-Q-Analysis (Banasick, 2019), authors developed an online anonymous survey for their Q-study. The HtmlQ files were downloaded (https://github.com/shawnbanasick/easy-htmlq/archive/master.zip) and the setting files were adapted for this study. The survey, whose URL is https://agility-enablers.netlify.app/#/, consists of a series of guided steps for classifying the proposed statements stemming from the list of the OA enablers as described in table 2 below. Participants first see the individual statements selected randomly and split them up into three piles: a pile for statements they tend to disagree with, a pile for cards they tend to agree with, and a pile for the rest.

Figure 4. Obtained list of 28 organizational agility enablers grouped into 10 groups

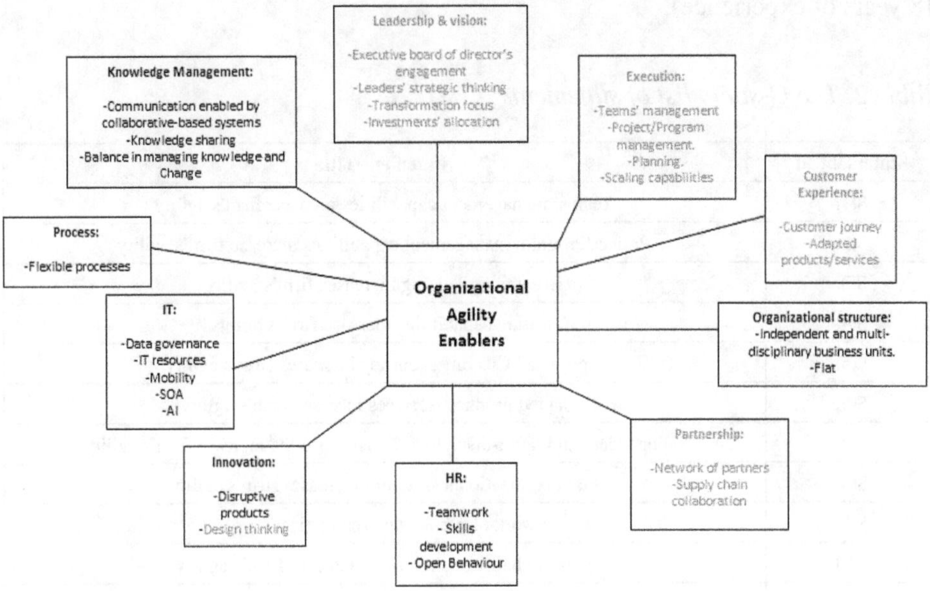

Then, participants rank statements according to a normally distributed 7-point scale (Annex 1). This scale represents significance (Brown, 1980), in this case most disagree (-3 column) to most agree (+3 column). The middle of the distribution represents a neutral opinion. Participants take the cards from the "AGREE" pile and read them again. Next, they select the statement they most agree with and place it on right side of the score sheet the "+3". In the same way, they read the cards in the "DISAGREE" pile again and select the statement they most disagree with and place it on the left side of the score sheet the "-3". Next, they select the statements they second most agree/disagree with and place them under "+2"/"-2". Participants follow this procedure for all cards in the "AGREE" and "DISAGREE" piles. Finally, they read the "NEUTRAL" cards again and arrange them in the remaining open boxes of the score sheet.

Authors sent the survey to a list of 500 reliable contacts. In order to obtain reliable answers, the databases of contacts were provided by a training establishment which collaborates with executives, managers and non-managers, namely the PMI (Project Management Institute) which is the organization of reference offering best practices and certifications recognized worldwide in project and portfolio management.

The number of Q-sorts responses for the study's sample is 48 which constitute a response rate of nearly 10%. 56% of participants are from Morocco, 36% from Europe, 4% from America and 4% from other African countries. Most of the participants are managers (15% of project managers, 50% of senior/board managers and 35%

of CEOs) who have between 10 and 30 years of experience (the average is nearly 18 years of experience).

Table 2. The Q-study list of statements

Statement Id	Statement Title
St1.	Teams' management capabilities increase firm's agility
St2.	Project/Program management capabilities increase firm's agility
St3.	Execution planning increases firm's agility
St4.	Scaling capabilities increase firm's agility
St5.	Optimized Customer journey increases firm's agility
St6.	Adapted products/services increase firm's agility
St7.	Independent and multi-disciplinary business units increase firm's agility
St8.	Flat organizational structure increases firm's agility
St9.	Network of partners increases firm's agility
St10.	Supply chain collaboration increases firm's agility
St11.	Teamwork increases firm's agility
St12.	Employees' skills development increases firm's agility
St13.	Open behavior increases firm's agility
St14.	Disruptive products increase firm's agility
St15.	Design thinking adoption increases firm's agility
St16.	Data governance increases firm's agility
St17.	Information technology resources/infrastructure increase firm's agility
St18.	Digital mobility increases firm's agility
St19.	Service Oriented Architecture increases firm's agility
St20.	Artificial intelligence enabled products/applications increase firm's agility
St21.	Flexible processes increase firm's agility
St22.	Communication enabled by collaborative-based systems increases firm's agility
St23.	Knowledge sharing increases firm's agility
St24.	Balance in managing knowledge and Change increases firm's agility
St25.	Executive board of director's engagement increases firm's agility
St26.	Leaders' strategic thinking increases firm's agility
St27.	Transformation's focus increases firm's agility
St28.	Investments' allocation increases firm's agility

2. Results

Following a factor analysis, 3 factors were extracted from the collected data using centroid factor method such that each factor represents a unique viewpoint (Brown, 1980). Then, authors applied a varimax rotation. Each statement has obtained a Q-sort value per factor as described in figure 5.

Figure 5. Q-sort value of the 28 statements per factor

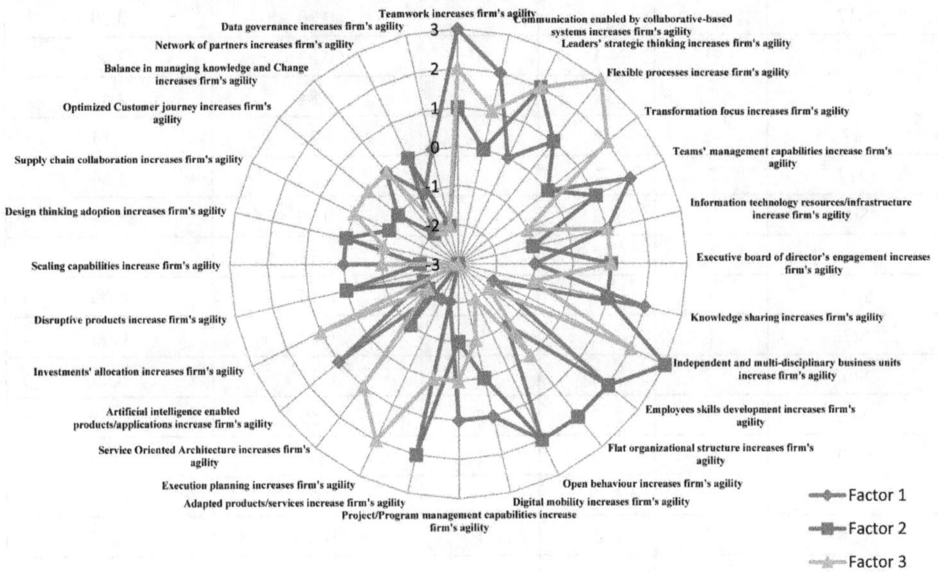

Each statement has a z-score variance allowing to have an insight about the consensus degree on this statement among the 3 factors (table 3 below). In order to classify the most critical factors, authors have chosen to calculate a score for each statement (formula (1) below) by summing the Q-sort values for the 3 factors and weighted by z-score variance so as to keep the statements with the highest Q-sort values and the highest consensus (corresponding to the white part of table 3).

$$\text{Score(St)} = \sum(\text{Q-sort value F})/(\text{z-score variance}) \qquad (1)$$

Table 3. Classification of statements

Statement Id	Factor 1	Factor 2	Factor 3	Z-Score Variance	Statement Score
St11.	3	1	2	0,19	32,26
St22.	2	0	1	0,13	22,39
St26.	0	2	2	0,19	20,94
St21.	1	1	3	0,35	14,41
St27.	0	0	2	0,42	4,81
St1.	2	1	-1	0,55	3,61
St17.	1	-1	1	0,30	3,29
St25.	-1	1	1	0,33	3,06
St23.	2	1	-1	0,81	2,47
St7.	-2	3	2	1,38	2,17
St12.	2	2	-2	1,22	1,64
St8.	-1	2	0	0,70	1,43
St13.	2	2	-2	1,53	1,31
St18.	1	0	-1	0,14	0,00
St2.	1	-1	0	0,42	0,00
St6.	-2	2	0	0,71	0,00
St3.	-2	-3	2	1,59	-1,89
St19.	-2	-1	1	0,50	-4,04
St20.	1	-2	-2	0,69	-4,35
St28.	-2	-2	1	0,63	-4,77
St14.	-3	0	-3	1,00	-5,99
St4.	0	-2	-1	0,45	-6,61
St15.	0	0	-1	0,14	-7,14
St10.	-1	-1	0	0,17	-11,56
St5.	-1	-1	0	0,15	-13,70
St24.	0	-2	0	0,07	-29,85
St9.	-1	0	-2	0,07	-41,10
St16.	0	-2	-2	0,06	-65,57

3. Discussion: Analysis From an IT Perspective

Authors conclude that the main critical success factors are related to teamwork, communication enabled by collaborative-based systems, leaders' strategic thinking, flexible processes, transformation focus, teams' management capabilities and information technology resources/infrastructure. The complete list of ranked critical success factors is presented in table 4 below and grouped into the corresponding category.

Table 4. OA critical success factors

OA Critical Success Factors	Category	Rank
Teamwork	HR	1
Communication enabled by collaborative knowledge management systems	Knowledge Management	2
Leaders' strategic thinking	Leadership & Vision	3
Flexible processes	Process	4
Transformation focus	Leadership & Vision	5
Teams' management capabilities	Execution	6
Information technology resources/infrastructure	IT	7
Executive board of director's engagement	Leadership & Vision	8
Knowledge sharing	Knowledge Management	9
Independent and multi-disciplinary business units	Organizational structure	10
Employees' skills development	HR	11
Flat organizational structure	Organizational structure	12
Open behavior	HR	13

In percentage, 23% of the found critical success factors are related to human resources category. The same percentage is related to leadership & vision enablers category. Otherwise, knowledge management and organizational structure account for 15% of the critical success factors each. Then, the rest of CSFs is equally shared (7%) by the execution, the process and the IT enablers categories.

From an IT perspective, authors can notice that there is only one critical success factor, which is ranked 7th, related to the IT category. In fact, 6 of the most ranked OA critical success factors are related to HR and leadership categories. It means that putting in place information technology infrastructure and applications is important but not sufficient in order to ensure an effective agile transformation of the firm.

Indeed, an enterprise cannot be agile without a clear vision, a transformation focus, an involvement of strategic leaders and an upskilling of its employees in order to acquire the adequate competencies and behaviour. This latter facilitates the acceptance and effective use of information systems. Consequently, putting in place IT applications like ERP, CRM, and Decision Support Systems is essential but can help the company to be more agile only if effective change management is carried oud and systems are adopted by employees across the organization.

Also, knowledge management is an important agility's enabler category encompassing knowledge sharing and communication which can be enhanced by the effective use of knowledge management systems (KMS). This latter which has two components namely collaborative KMS and decision-oriented KMS have a positive impact on organizational agility as found in previous study (Marhraoui & El Manouar, 2017).

In addition, organizations should enable their structures to be flatter and to share knowledge across independent and multi-disciplinary business units. Processes should also be optimized and modelled in order to be more flexible and to avoid bottlenecks across stakeholders.

FUTURE RESEARCH DIRECTIONS

Future studies will extend the Q-study for extracting critical success factors to a larger sample of respondents. In addition, authors plan to conduct qualitative case studies on firms in order to perform in-depth analysis across different contexts as the importance of organizational agility critical success factors may vary depending on the enterprise sector. Indeed, authors plan to study a very specific sector of activity through a field study by comparing the resulted CSFs of a set of companies belonging to the same sector (telecommunications, energy, banking, etc.).

Also, other quantitative studies will allow to confirm the positive impact of the major highlighted enablers on organizational agility through structural equation modelling and to verify thus the cause-and-effect relationship between the CSF and organizational agility constructs.

Finally, another perspective could be to propose predictive scenarios for the evolution of organizational agility depending on the impact of one or a set of critical success factors. The purpose is to provide companies, through the use of machine learning models, with a tool allowing them to prepare the adequate set of enablers in order to enhance their future organizational agility level.

CONCLUSION

In this chapter, authors have addressed an important topic in the context of COVID19. Firms should be agile and focus on the most important enablers.

Authors believe that each company, depending on its context and the evolution of its activity's sector, may be faced with different challenges which would require the implementation of different projects resulting from the highest organizational agility's priority levers in order to enhance its survival and / or its sustainable performance.

On one hand, the presented work is an original contribution as it proposes a whole vision about organizational agility enablers. On the other hand, authors have identified through their Q-study, 13 critical success factors belonging mainly to HR and leadership categories.

Moreover, authors conclude that IT enablers are important for allowing firms to adapt to their environment but are not sufficient. Firms should focus, as part of their digital transformation programs, not only on implementing new digital capabilities but also on enhancing employees' skills, communication and leadership capabilities. Investments in digital transformation programs should then not only be dedicated to technical applications and putting in place IT infrastructures but also to effective change management across the company.

REFERENCES

Bali. (2009). *Knowledge Management" Primer*. Routledge. doi:10.4324/9780203894712

Banasick, S. (2019). Ken-Q Analysis (Version 1.0.6) [Software]. Available from https://shawnbanasick.github.io/ken-q-analysis/ doi:10.5281/zenodo.1300201

Barrand, J. (2006). *Le Manager agile: Vers un nouveau management pour affronter la turbulence*. Dunod.

Baskerville, R., Mathiassen, L., Pries-Heje, J., & DeGross, J. (Eds.). (2005). *Business Agility and Information Technology Diffusion: IFIP TC8 WG 8.6 International Working Conference, May 8-11, 2005, Atlanta, Georgia, USA* (Vol. 180). Springer Science & Business Media.

Benner, M. J., & Tushman, M. L. (2003). Exploitation, exploration, and process management: The productivity dilemma revisited. *Academy of Management Review*, *28*(2), 238–256. doi:10.5465/amr.2003.9416096

Brasseur, C. (2013). *Enjeux et usages du Big Data. Technologies, méthodes et mises en œuvre*. Lavoisier.

Breu, K., Christopher, J. H., Strathern, M., & Bridger, D. (2002). Workforce Agility: The New Employee Strategy for the Knowledge Economy. *Journal of Information Technology*, *17*(1), 21–31. doi:10.1080/02683960110132070

Brown, S. L., & Eisenhardt, K. M. (1995). Product development: Past research, present findings, and future directions. *Academy of Management Review*, *20*(2), 343–378. doi:10.5465/amr.1995.9507312922

Brown, S. R. (1980). *Political Subjectivity: Application of Q Methodology in Political Science*. Yale University Press.

Brown, S. R. (1993). A primer on Q methodology. *Operant Subjectivity*, *16*(3/4), 91–138.

Brunner, K. (1983). *The Recession of 1981/1982 in the Context of Postwar Recessions*. Academic Press.

Charbonnier, A. (2006). *L'agilité organisationnelle: un nouveau défi pour la GRH*. Congrès de l'AGRH.

Chong, Handscomb, & Williams. (n.d.). *Agile Resilience in the UK: Lessons from COVID-19 for the 'next normal'*. https://www.mckinsey.com/business-functions/organization/our-insights/agile-resilience-in-the-uk-lessons-from-covid-19-for-the-next-normal

Codreanu, A. (2016). A VUCA action framework for a VUCA environment. Leadership challenges and solutions. *Journal of Defense Resources Management*, *7*(2), 31–38.

Danoesastro, M., Rehberg, B., Ritter, D., Krishna, A., Hildebrandt, P., & Islam, M. (2020). *When the Ground Shifts, It Pays to Be Agile*. BCG Global. https://www.bcg.com/publications/2020/understanding-why-agile-will-help-move-the-needle-post-covid-19

Dove, R. (2005). Agile Enterprise Cornerstones: Knowledge, Values, and Response Ability. In *Business Agility and Information Technology Diffusion* (pp. 313–330). Springer. doi:10.1007/0-387-25590-7_20

Dyer, L., & Shafer, R. (2003). *Dynamic Organizations: Achieving Marketplace and Organizational Agility with People* (CAHRS Working Paper 03-04). Ithaca, NY: Cornell University, School of Industrial and Labor Relations, Center for Advanced Human Resource Studies.

Earl, M. (2001). Knowledge Management Strategies: Toward a Taxonomy. *Journal of Management Information Systems*, *18*(1), 215–233. doi:10.1080/07421222.2001.11045670

Eupan. (2020). *Common Assessment Framework. The European model for improving public organisations through self-assessment*. European CAF Resource Centre – European Institute of Public Administration.

Foutty, J., & Sinclair, D. (2020). *COVID-19: Board Agility in a Time of Crisis*. Deloitte Global. https://www2.deloitte.com/global/en/pages/about-deloitte/articles/covid-19/covid-19-and-the-board-a-chairs-point-of-view.html

Gallagher, K. P., & Worrell, J. L. (2008). Organizing IT to promote agility. *Information Technology Management*, *9*(1), 71–88. doi:10.100710799-007-0027-5

Galliers, R. D. (2006). Strategizing for Agility: Confronting Information. *Agile Information Systems, 1*.

Gantz & Reinsel. (2012). The digital universe in 2020: Big data, bigger digital shadows, and biggest growth in the far east. *IDC iView: IDC Analyze the Future, 2007*(2012), 1-16.

Goldman, S. L., Nagel, R. N., & Preiss, K. (1995). *Agile competitors and virtual organizations: strategies for enriching the customer* (Vol. 8). Van Nostrand Reinhold.

Gross, T., & Koch, M. (2007). *Computer-supported cooperative work*. Oldenbourg. doi:10.1524/9783486593419

Gupta, A. K., Smith, K. G., & Shalley, C. E. (2006). The interplay between exploration and exploitation. *Academy of Management Journal*, *49*(4), 693–706. doi:10.5465/amj.2006.22083026

Holsapple, C. W., & Li, X. (2008). *Understanding organizational agility: a workdesign perspective*. Kentucky Univ Lexington School Of Management.

Hormozi, A. M. (2001). Agile manufacturing: The next logical step. *Benchmarking*, *8*(2), 132–143. doi:10.1108/14635770110389843

Horney, N., Pasmore, B., & O'Shea, T. (2010). Leadership agility: A business imperative for a VUCA world. *Human Resource Planning*, *33*(4), 34.

Huang, P. Y., Pan, S. L., & Ouyang, T. H. (2014). Developing information processing capability for operational agility: Implications from a Chinese manufacturer. *European Journal of Information Systems*, *23*(4), 462–480. doi:10.1057/ejis.2014.4

Iyengar, N., Radcliffe, A., & Silvester, E. (2020). Five Predictions for COVID-19 Driven Agility across the Life Science Value Chain. *Capgemini Worldwide*. https://www.capgemini.com/2020/06/covid-19-predictions-for-life-sciences/

Izza, S., Imache, R., Vincent, L., & Lounis, Y. (2008). An approach for the evaluation of the agility in the context of enterprise interoperability. In *Enterprise Interoperability III* (pp. 3–14). Springer. doi:10.1007/978-1-84800-221-0_1

JoglekarN.ParkerG.SraiJ. S. (2020) *Winning the race for survival: How advanced manufacturing technologies are driving business-model innovation*. World Economic Forum. https://papers.ssrn. com/sol3/papers.cfm?abstract_id=3604242

Karimi-Alaghehband, F., & Rivard, S. (2019). Information technology outsourcing and architecture dynamic capabilities as enablers of organizational agility. *Journal of Information Technology*, *34*(2), 129–159. doi:10.1177/0268396218816271

Kettunen, P., & Laanti, M. (2008). Combining agile software projects and large-scale organizational agility. *Software Process Improvement and Practice*, *13*(2), 183–193. doi:10.1002pip.354

Kharabe, A., & Lyytinen, K. J. (2012). *Is implementing ERP like pouring concrete into a company? Impact of enterprise systems on organizational agility*. Academic Press.

Kidd, P. T. (1995). *Agile manufacturing: A strategy for the 21st century*. Academic Press.

Kinsinger, P., & Walch, K. (2012). Living and leading in a VUCA world. Thunderbird University.

Lawrence, K. (2013). Developing leaders in a VUCA environment. *UNC Executive Development*, *2013*, 1–15.

Lin, C. T., Chiu, H., & Chu, P. Y. (2006). Agility index in the supply chain. *International Journal of Production Economics*, *100*(2), 285–299. doi:10.1016/j.ijpe.2004.11.013

Lines, M. (2020). *Using Agility and Tech to Help Clients Meet Regulatory Commitments amid COVID-19*. PwC. https://www.pwc.co.uk/services/operate/insights/using-agility-and-tech-to-help-clients-meet-regulatory-commitmen.html

Lu, Y. (2011). Understanding the link between information technology capability and organizational agility: An empirical examination. *Management Information Systems Quarterly*, *35*(4), 931–954. doi:10.2307/41409967

Lunenburg, F. C. (2011). Self-efficacy in the workplace: Implications for motivation and performance. *International Journal of Management, Business, and Administration, 14*(1), 1-6.

Marhraoui, M. A., & El Manouar, A. (2017, October). IT innovation and firm's sustainable performance: The mediating role of organizational agility. In *Proceedings of the 9th International Conference on Information Management and Engineering* (pp. 150-156). Academic Press.

Marhraoui, M. A., & Manouar, A. E. (2017). *Towards a new framework linking knowledge management systems and organizational agility: An empirical study*. arXiv preprint arXiv:1707.08182.

Marhraoui, M. A., & Manouar, El, A. (2017). IT-Enabled organizational agility-proposition of a new Framework. *Journal of Theoretical & Applied Information Technology*, *95*(20).

Monden, Y. (1983). *Toyota Production System: Practical Approach to Production Management.* Industrial Engineering and Management Press, Institute of Industrial Engineers.

Nagel, R. N., & Dove, R. (1991). *21st century manufacturing enterprise strategy: An industry-led view*. Diane Publishing.

O'Halloran, A. M., Waelchli, Z., Schulz, F., Lauber, J., Provoost, F., Schattenberg, D., Bavery, S., & Schulte, G. (2020). *Leading with Agility and Responsible Innovation in Response to Covid-19: MedTech Industry Anchor Response*. Accenture.

OCDE. (2015). *Achieving Public Sector Agility at Times of Fiscal Consolidation*. OECD Public Governance Reviews, Éditions OCDE. doi:10.1787/9789264206267-

Ohno, T. (1988). *Toyota Production System: Beyond Large-Scale Production*. CRC Press.

Overby, E., Bharadwaj, A., & Sambamurthy, V. (2006). Enterprise agility and the enabling role of information technology. *European Journal of Information Systems*, *15*(2), 120–131. doi:10.1057/palgrave.ejis.3000600

Prats, J., Siota, J., Gillespie, D., & Singleton, N. (2018). *Organizational agility. Why large corporations often struggle to adopt the inventions created by their innovation units and how to improve success rates in rapidly changing environment*. Oliver Wyman.

Richards, C. W. (1996). *Agile Manufacturing: Beyond Lean?* Production and Inventory Management Journal, Second Quarter.

Rigby, Elk, & Perez. (2020). *Doing agile right*. Bain.

Roark, C., Herreria, B., & Ilomechina, N. (2020). *Soar in the Face of Disruption*. Accenture.

Roberts, N., & Grover, V. (2012). Leveraging information technology infrastructure to facilitate a firm's customer agility and competitive activity: An empirical investigation. *Journal of Management Information Systems*, *28*(4), 231–270.

Sambamurthy, V., Bharadwaj, A., & Grover, V. (2003). Shaping agility through digital options: Reconceptualizing the role of information technology in contemporary firms. *Management Information Systems Quarterly*, 237–263.

Schonenberg, H., Mans, R., Russell, N., Mulyar, N., & van der Aalst, W. (2008). Process flexibility: A survey of contemporary approaches. In *Advances in enterprise engineering I* (pp. 16–30). Springer.

Seo, D., & La Paz, A. I. (2008). Exploring the dark side of IS in achieving organizational agility. *Communications of the ACM*, *51*(11), 136–139.

Shaffer, L. S., & Zalewski, J. M. (2011). Career advising in a VUCA environment. *NACADA Journal*, *31*(1), 64–74.

Sharifi, H., & Zhang, Z. (1999). A Methodology for Achieving Agility in Manufacturing Organisations: An Introduction. *International Journal of Production Economics*, *62*(1), 7–22.

Sharifi, H., & Zhang, Z. (2001). Agile manufacturing in practice-Application of a methodology. *International Journal of Operations & Production Management*, *21*(5/6), 772–794.

Steinbock, D., & Pea, R. (2007). *Wearable tag clouds: Visualizations to facilitate new collaborations*. Academic Press.

Tallon, P. P., Queiroz, M., Coltman, T., & Sharma, R. (2019). Information technology and the search for organizational agility: A systematic review with future research possibilities. *The Journal of Strategic Information Systems*, *28*(2), 218–237.

Teece, D., Peteraf, M., & Leih, S. (2016). Dynamic capabilities and organizational agility: Risk, uncertainty, and strategy in the innovation economy. *California Management Review*, *58*(4), 13–35.

Weidemeyer, F. (2020). *COVID-19: Which Critical Choices Should Businesses Make Next?* https://www.ey.com/en_gl/long-term-value/covid-19-critical-choices-businesses-should-make

Weill, P., Subramani, M., & Broadbent, M. (2002). *IT infrastructure for strategic agility*. Academic Press.

Wendler, R. (2013, September). The structure of agility from different perspectives. In *2013 Federated Conference on Computer Science and Information Systems* (pp. 1177-1184). IEEE.

Winby, S., & Worley, C. G. (2014). Management processes for agility, speed, and innovation. *Organizational Dynamics*, *43*(3), 225–234.

Womack, J. P., & Jones, D. T. (2003). *Banish waste and create wealth in your corporation*. Recuperado de http://www. kvimis. co.in/sites/kvimis. co. in/files/ ebook_attachments/James

Womack, J. P., Jones, D. T., & Roos, D. (2007). *The machine that changed the world: The story of lean production—Toyota's secret weapon in the global car wars that is now revolutionizing world industry*. Simon and Schuster.

World Bank. (2021). *World Development Report 2021: Data for Better Lives*. The World Bank.

Wouter, A., De Smet, A., & Weerda, K. (2015). Agility: It Rhymes with Stability. *The McKinsey Quarterly*.

Yahaya, Y., Sarhadi, Y. M., & Gunasekaran, A. (1999). Agile Manufacturing: The Drivers, Concepts and Attributes. *International Journal of Production Economics*, *62*(1), 33–43.

ADDITIONAL READING

Al-Omoush, K. S., Simón-Moya, V., & Sendra-García, J. (2020). The impact of social capital and collaborative knowledge creation on e-business proactiveness and organizational agility in responding to the COVID-19 crisis. *Journal of Innovation & Knowledge*, *5*(4), 279–288. doi:10.1016/j.jik.2020.10.002

Eisenhardt, K. M., & Martin, J. A. (2000). Dynamic capabilities: What are they? *Strategic Management Journal*, *21*(10-11), 1105–1121. doi:10.1002/1097-0266(200010/11)21:10/11<1105::AID-SMJ133>3.0.CO;2-E

Harreld, J. B., O'Reilly, C. A. III, & Tushman, M. L. (2007). Dynamic capabilities at IBM: Driving strategy into action. *California Management Review*, *49*(4), 21–43. doi:10.2307/41166404

Nejatian, M., & Zarei, M. H. (2013). Moving towards organizational agility: Are we improving in the right direction? *Global Journal of Flexible Systems Managment, 14*(4), 241–253. doi:10.100740171-013-0048-3

Sherehiy, B., Karwowski, W., & Layer, J. K. (2007). A review of enterprise agility: Concepts, frameworks, and attributes. *International Journal of Industrial Ergonomics, 37*(5), 445–460. doi:10.1016/j.ergon.2007.01.007

Tallon, P. P., & Pinsonneault, A. (2011). Competing perspectives on the link between strategic information technology alignment and organizational agility: Insights from a mediation model. *Management Information Systems Quarterly, 35*(2), 463–486. doi:10.2307/23044052

Teece, D. J. (2007). Explicating dynamic capabilities: The nature and microfoundations of (sustainable) enterprise performance. *Strategic Management Journal, 28*(13), 1319–1350. doi:10.1002mj.640

Teece, D. J., Pisano, G., & Shuen, A. (1997). Dynamic capabilities and strategic management. *Strategic Management Journal, 18*(7), 509–533. doi:10.1002/(SICI)1097-0266(199708)18:7<509::AID-SMJ882>3.0.CO;2-Z

Wanasida, A. S., Bernarto, I., Sudibjo, N., & Purwanto, A. (2021). The Role of Business Capabilities in Supporting Organization Agility and Performance During the COVID-19 Pandemic: An Empirical Study in Indonesia. The Journal of Asian Finance. *Economics and Business, 8*(5), 897–911.

Wendler, R. (2013, September). The structure of agility from different perspectives. In *2013 Federated Conference on Computer Science and Information Systems* (pp. 1177-1184). IEEE.

Worley, C. G., & Lawler, E. E. III. (2010). Agility and organization design: A diagnostic framework. *Organizational Dynamics, 39*(2), 194–204. doi:10.1016/j.orgdyn.2010.01.006

Yang, C., & Liu, H. M. (2012). Boosting firm performance via enterprise agility and network structure. *Management Decision, 50*(6), 1022–1044. doi:10.1108/00251741211238319

Yusuf, Y. Y., Sarhadi, M., & Gunasekaran, A. (1999). Agile manufacturing: The drivers, concepts and attributes. *International Journal of Production Economics, 62*(1-2), 33–43. doi:10.1016/S0925-5273(98)00219-9

Zabala, A., Sandbrook, C., & Mukherjee, N. (2018). When and how to use Q methodology to understand perspectives in conservation research. *Conservation Biology*, *32*(5), 1185–1194. doi:10.1111/cobi.13123 PMID:29707822

Zain, M., Rose, R. C., Abdullah, I., & Masrom, M. (2005). The relationship between information technology acceptance and organizational agility in Malaysia. *Information & Management*, *42*(6), 829–839. doi:10.1016/j.im.2004.09.001

KEY TERMS AND DEFINITIONS

Critical Success Factor: The limited number of areas/elements which are necessary for the success of a business program. These are the areas a company or a department must focus on and successfully implement to reach its objectives.

Enablers: Are all practises that can be leveraged in order to support and facilitate reaching company's strategic goals.

Factor Analysis: A statistical technique used to uncover the latent structure of a set of variables. It reduces attribute space from a larger number of variables to a smaller number of factors.

Knowledge Management System: Refers to IT applications that store and retrieve knowledge, improve collaboration, locate knowledge sources, look for hidden knowledge, captures and uses knowledge in order to improve decision-making.

Organizational Agility: Is the ability of detecting opportunities and challenges in the environment and using the adequate resources to respond to such changes in a fast and relevant manner.

APPENDIX

Figure 6. The adopted Q-study scale for the survey

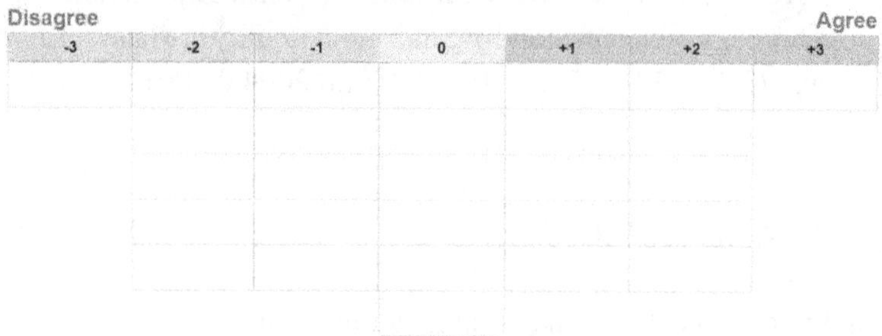

Compilation of References

Abal Abas, Z., Abdul Rahman, A. F. N., Pramudya, G., Wee, S. Y., Kasmin, F., Yusof, N., Md Yunos, N., & Abidin, Z. Z. (2020). Analytics: A review of current trends, future applications and challenges. Compusoft. *International Journal of Advancements in Computing Technology*, *9*(1).

Abrahamsson, P., Salo, O., Ronkainen, J., & Warsta, J. (2002). *Agile software development methods.* VTT Publishing.

Ackoff, R. L. (1987). O.R., A Post Mortem. *Operations Research*, *35*(3), 471–474. doi:10.1287/opre.35.3.471

Afifi, A., May, S., Donatello, R., & Clark, V. A. (2019). *Practical Multivariate Analysis* (6th ed.). CRC Press. doi:10.1201/9781315203737

Aguilera, R., Rupp, D., Williams, C., & Ganapathi, J. (2007). Putting the S back in corporate social responsibility: A multilevel theory of social change in organizations. *Academy of Management Review*, *32*(3), 836–863. doi:10.5465/amr.2007.25275678

Aher, S. B., Bhaveshananda, S., & Sengupta, B. (2012). Organic agriculture: Way towards sustainable development. *International Journal of Environmental Sciences*, *3*(1), 209–216.

Alberts, D. S., & Hayes, R. E. (2003). *Power to the Edge: Command, Control in the Information Age*. US Department of Defense, Command and Control Research Program.

Alcalde, M. H. (2009) Multimarket Contact Challenges in Open Innovation Environments. *Proceeding of the ICERI2009 - International Conference of Education, Research and Innovation.*

Altay, N., & Narayanan, A. (2020). Forecasting in humanitarian operations: Literature review and research needs. *International Journal of Forecasting*. Advance online publication. doi:10.1016/j.ijforecast.2020.08.001 PMID:32921856

Altay, N., & Pal, R. (2014). Information diffusion among agents: Implications for humanitarian operations. *Production and Operations Management*, *23*(6), 1015–1027. doi:10.1111/poms.12102

Alves Aranha, E., Prado Garcia, N. A., & Corrêa, G. (2015). Open innovation and business model: A brazilian company case study. *Journal of Technology Management & Innovation*, *10*(4), 91–98. doi:10.4067/S0718-27242015000400010

Anderson, U., Head, M., Ramamoorti, S., Riddle, C., Salamasick, M., & Sobel, P. (2017). *Internal Auditing Assurance and Advisory Services*. Internal Audit Foundation.

Antunes, P., Simões, D., Carriço, L., & Pino, J. A. (2013). An end-user approach to business process modeling. *Journal of Network and Computer Applications, 36*(6), 1466–1479. doi:. jnca.2013.03.014 doi:10.1016/j

Armbrust, M., Fox, A., Griffith, R., Joseph, A. D., Katz, R. H., Konwinski, A., . . . Zaharia, M. (2009). *Above the clouds: a Berkeley view of cloud computing* (Report No. UCB/EECS-2009-28). University of Berkeley, UC Berkeley reliable adaptive distributed systems laboratory.

Arora, A., & Sharma, C. (2016). Corporate governance and firm performance in developing countries: Evidence from India. *Corporate Governance, 16*(2), 420–436. doi:10.1108/CG-01-2016-0018

Aydin, M. N., Harmsen, F., & Van Slooten, K., & Stegwee, R. (2009). An agile information systems development method in use. *Turkish Journal of Electrical Engineering and Computer Sciences*, *12*(2), 127–138.

Azeez, A. (2015). Corporate governance and firm performance: Evidence from Sri Lanka. *The Journal of Finance*, *3*(1), 180–189.

Babcock, C. (2010). *Management Strategies for the Cloud Revolution*. McGraw Hill Professional.

Baber, C. (2003). Cognition and tool use: Forms of engagement in human and animal use of tools. London: Taylor & Francis CRC Press.

Baigorri, M. (2008, July 10). *Pentagon may start using Web 2.0*. Retrieved 11 July, 2008, from http://news.medill.northwestern.edu/washington/news.aspx?id=94823

Bali. (2009). *Knowledge Management" Primer*. Routledge. doi:10.4324/9780203894712

Banasick, S. (2019). Ken-Q Analysis (Version 1.0.6) [Software]. Available from https://shawnbanasick.github.io/ken-q-analysis/ doi:10.5281/zenodo.1300201

Bansal, P. (2005). Evolving sustainability: A longitudinal study of corporate sustainable development. *Strategic Management Journal*, *26*(3), 197–218. doi:10.1002mj.441

Barczyk, C. C., & Duncan, D. G. (2012). Social Networking Media: An Approach for the Teaching of International Business. *Journal of Teaching in International Business*, *23*(2), 98–122. doi:10.1080/08975930.2012.718703

Barrand, J. (2006). *Le Manager agile: Vers un nouveau management pour affronter la turbulence*. Dunod.

Barrios, E., Gemmill-Herren, B., Bicksler, A., Siliprandi, E., Brathwaite, R., Moller, S., Batello, C., & Tittonell, P. (2020). The 10 Elements of Agroecology: Enabling transitions towards sustainable agriculture and food systems through visual narratives. *Ecosystems and People*, *16*(1), 230–247. doi:10.1080/26395916.2020.1808705

Barwise, P., & Meehan, S. (2010). The One Thing You Must Get Right When Building a Brand. *Harvard Business Review*, 80–84.

Baskerville, R., Mathiassen, L., Pries-Heje, J., & DeGross, J. (Eds.). (2005). *Business Agility and Information Technology Diffusion: IFIP TC8 WG 8.6 International Working Conference, May 8-11, 2005, Atlanta, Georgia, USA* (Vol. 180). Springer Science & Business Media.

Baumgartner, R. J., & Rauter, R. (2017). Strategic perspectives of corporate sustainability management to develop a sustainable organization. *Journal of Cleaner Production*, *140*, 81–92. doi:10.1016/j.jclepro.2016.04.146

Bavelier, D., Green, C. S., & Dye, M. W. G. (2010). Children wired for better and for worse. *Neuron*, *67*(September), 682–701. doi:10.1016/j.neuron.2010.08.03520826302 PMID:20826302

Baxter, P., & Jack, S. (2008). Qualitative case study methodology: Study design and implementation for novice researchers. *Qualitative Report*, *13*(4), 544–559.

BBC Two. (Writer). (2007). Battle of the brains [Television Broadcast]. In Science & Nature: Horizon. United Kingdom: BBC.

Bear, S., Rahman, N., & Post, C. (2010). The impact of board diversity and gender composition on corporate social responsibility and firm reputation. *Journal of Business Ethics*, *97*(2), 207–221. doi:10.100710551-010-0505-2

Bee, H. (2001, October–December). Article. *Honey Bee*, *12*(4), 3–5.

Bemrose Bob. (2014). *Implementing and Integrating SaaS Solutions at Small Businesses.* Presented to the Interdisciplinary Studies Program of University of Oregon Applied Information Management. Approved by Dr. Kara McFall. Small Business SAAS Integration.

Benner, M. J., & Tushman, M. L. (2003). Exploitation, exploration, and process management: The productivity dilemma revisited. *Academy of Management Review*, *28*(2), 238–256. doi:10.5465/amr.2003.9416096

Berlanga, R., Lanza-Cruz, I., & Aramburu, M. J. (2019). Quality Indicators for Social Business Intelligence. *Sixth International Conference on Social Networks Analysis, Management and Security (SNAMS)*, 229-236. 10.1109/SNAMS.2019.8931862

Bernardi, R. A., Bean, D. F., & Weippert, K. M. (2002). Signaling gender diversity through annual report pictures: A research note on image management. *Accounting, Auditing & Accountability Journal*, *15*(4), 609–616. doi:10.1108/09513570210441440

Boons, F., & Lüdeke-Freund, F. (2013). Business models for sustainable innovation: State-of-the-art and steps towards a research agenda. *Journal of Cleaner Production*, *45*, 9–19. doi:10.1016/j.jclepro.2012.07.007

Bordeleau, Mosconi, & de Santa-Eulalia. (2020). Business intelligence and analytics value creation in Industry 4.0: a multiple case study in manufacturing medium enterprises. *Production Planning & Control, 31*(2-3), 173-185.

Borges, A. F., Laurindo, F. J., Spínola, M. M., Gonçalves, R. F., & Mattos, C. A. (2020). The strategic use of artificial intelligence in the digital era: Systematic literature review and future research directions. *International Journal of Information Management.*

Bose, R., & Luo, X. (2011). Integrative framework for assessing firms' potential toundertake Green IT initiatives via virtualization—A theoretical perspective. *TheJournal of Strategic Information Systems*, *20*(1), 38–54. doi:10.1016/j.jsis.2011.01.003

Bosse, D. A., & Phillips, R. A. (2016). Agency theory and bounded self-interest. *Academy of Management Review*, *41*(2), 276–297. doi:10.5465/amr.2013.0420

Bottani, E. (2009). On the assessment of enterprise agility: Issues from two case studies. *International Journal ofLogistics: ResearchandApplications*, *12*(3), 213–230. doi:10.1080/13675560802395160

Boulouta, I. (2013). Hidden connections: The link between board gender diversity and corporate social performance. *Journal ofBusiness Ethics*, *113*(2), 185–197. doi:10.100710551-012-1293-7

Boyd, D. (2008). *Taken out of context: American teen sociality in networked publics*. School of Information, University of California-Berkeley.

Boyd, D. M., & Ellison, N. B. (2008). Social network sites: Definition, history, and scholarship. *Journal of Computer-Mediated Communication*, *13*(1), 210–230. doi:10.1111/j.1083-6101.2007.00393.x

Brasseur, C. (2013). *Enjeux et usages du Big Data. Technologies, méthodes et mises en œuvre*. Lavoisier.

Breu, K., Christopher, J. H., Strathern, M., & Bridger, D. (2002). Workforce Agility: The New Employee Strategy for the Knowledge Economy. *Journal of Information Technology*, *17*(1), 21–31. doi:10.1080/02683960110132070

Brinkley, D. (2007). *The great deluge: Hurricane Katrina, New Orleans, and the Mississippi Gulf coast*. Harper Collins.

Bromley, D. W. (2008). Sustainability. In S. N. Durlauf & L. E. Blume (Eds.), *The new Palgrave dictionary of economics* (2nd ed.). Basingstoke, UK: Palgrave Macmillan. Retrieved July 05, 2021 from http://www.dictionaryofeconomics.com/article?id=pde2008_S000482

Browaeys, M.-J., & Fisser, S. (2012). Lean and agile: An epistemological Reflection. *The Learning Organization*, *19*(3), 207–218. doi:10.1108/09696471211219903

Brower, H. H. (2011). Sustainable development through service learning: A pedagogical framework and case example in a third world context. *Academy of Management Learning & Education*, *10*(1), 58–76. doi:10.5465/AMLE.2011.59513273

Browne, M. (2008). *Gov 2.0 to delete e-gov in 2008*. Retrieved 16 August, 2008, from http://www.zdnet.com.au/news/business/soa/-Gov-2-0-to-delete-e-gov-in-2008/0,139023166,339285045,00.htm?feed=pt_government

Brown, J. S. (2012). *Learning in and for the 21st Century. Singapure*. National Institute of Education.

Brown, S. L., & Eisenhardt, K. M. (1995). Product development: Past research, present findings, and future directions. *Academy of Management Review*, *20*(2), 343–378. doi:10.5465/amr.1995.9507312922

Brown, S. L., & Eisenhardt, K. M. (1998). *Competing on the edge, strategy as structured Chaos*. Harvard Business School Press.

Brown, S. R. (1980). *Political Subjectivity: Application of Q Methodology in Political Science*. Yale University Press.

Brown, S. R. (1993). A primer on Q methodology. *Operant Subjectivity*, *16*(3/4), 91–138.

Brundtland Commission. (1987). *Our Common Future*. Oxford University Press.

Brunner, K. (1983). *The Recession of 1981/1982 in the Context of Postwar Recessions*. Academic Press.

Brynjolfsson, E., Hu, Y. J., & Simester, D. (2011). Goodbye Pareto Principle, hello long tail: The effect of search costs on the concentration of product sales. *Management Science*, *57*(8). Advance online publication. doi:10.1287/mnsc.1110.1371

Buckley, S. (2011). IT Change Management. *Internal Auditor*. Retrieved from https://www.theiia.org/intAuditor/itaudit/2011-articles/it-change-management/

Buxbaum, P. A. (2007). Web of tomorrow. *Military Information Technology Online Archives, 11*(5).

Buys, L., Mengersen, K., Johnson, S., Buuren, N. V., & Chauvin, A. (2014). Creating asustainability scorecard as a predictive tool for measuring the complex social, economic and environmental impacts of industries, a case study: Assessing the viability and sustainability of the dairy company A. *Journal of Environmental Management*, *133*, 184–192. doi:10.1016/j.jenvman.2013.12.013 PMID:24374467

Buyya, R., Yeo, C. S., & Venugopal, S. (2008). *Market-oriented cloud computing: Vision, hype, and reality for delivering it services as computing utilities*. Academic Press.

Cadambi P., Easwaran S. (2016). *Transforming Your SaaS Business a strategic guide for optimizing business performance.* KPMG LLP International Whitepaper.

Caiado, R. G. G., de Freitas Dias, R., Mattos, L. V., Quelhas, O. L. G., & Leal Filho, W. (2017). Towards sustainable development through the perspective of eco-efficiency-A systematic literature review. *Journal of Cleaner Production*, *165*, 890–904. doi:10.1016/j.jclepro.2017.07.166

Callon, M., & Law, J. (1997). After the individual in society: Lessons on collectivity from science, technology and society. *Canadian Journal of Sociology*, *22*(2), 165–182. doi:10.2307/3341747

Carayannis, E. G., & Provance, M. (2008). Managing firm innovativeness: Towards a composite index builton firm innovative posture, propensity and performance attributes. *International Journal of Innovationand Regional Development*, *1*(1), 90–107. doi:10.1504/IJIRD.2008.016861

Carayannis, E. G., Sindakis, S., & Walter, C. (2015). Business model innovation as lever of organizational sustainability. *The Journal of Technology Transfer*, *40*(1), 85–104. doi:10.100710961-013-9330-y

Carducci, B. J. (2009). *The psychology of personality: Viewpoints, research, and applications.* John Wiley and Sons.

Carnegie Mellon University and The John Hopkins University Applied Physics Laboratory, LLC. (2020). *Cybersecurity Maturity Model Certification (CMMC) v 1.02.* Carnegie Mellon University and The John Hopkins University Applied Physics Laboratory, LLC.

Carraro, G., & Chong, F. (2006). *Software as a service (SaaS): An enterprise perspective, A Microsoft Whitepaper.* Retrieved March 24th, 2012 from http://msdn.microsoft.com/en-us/library/aa905332.aspx

Carr, N. (2009). *Big switch: Rewiring the world, from Edison To Google.* W. W. Norton & Company Inc.

Carr, N. G. (2003). IT doesn't matter. *EDUCAUSE Review, 38*, 24–38. PMID:12747161

Carson P., Botter L., Krujelskis S. (2013, July). Going to The Cloud vs Doing It In-House. *Information Today,* 4-10.

Castells, M. (2010). *Rise of the Network society: The information age: Economy, society and culture* (2nd ed., Vol. 1). Blackwell Publishers, Inc.

Cavusoglu, H., Cavusoglu, H., & Zhang, J. (2004). Economics of Security Patch Management. *Annual Workshop on the Economics of Information Security.* Retrieved November 14, 2012, from http://ns2.honlab.dc.hu/~mfelegyhazi/courses/BMEVIHIAV15/readings/06_Cavasoglu2006security_patch.pdf

Chandler, A. D. Jr. (1990). *Scale and Scope: The Dynamics of Industrial Capitalism.* The Belknap Press of Harvard University.

Charbonnier, A. (2006). *L'agilité organisationnelle: un nouveau défi pour la GRH.* Congrès de l'AGRH.

Charbonnier-Voirin, A. (2011). The development and partial testing of the psychometric properties of a measurement scale of organizational agility. *M@n@gement, 14*(2), 119-156.

Charlton, T., Devlin, M., & Drummond, S. (2009). Using Facebook to improve communication in undergraduate software development teams. *Computer Science Education, 19*(4), 273–292. doi:10.1080/08993400903384935

Cheng, C., Zhong, H., & Cao, L. (2020). Facilitating speed of internationalization: The roles of business intelligence and organizational agility. *Journal of Business Research, 110*, 95–103. doi:10.1016/j.jbusres.2020.01.003

Chen, M. K., Tai, T. W., & Hung, T. Y. (2012). Component selection system for greensupply chain. *Expert Systems with Applications, 39*(5), 5687–5701. doi:10.1016/j.eswa.2011.11.102

Chesbrough, H. (2015). *From open science to open innovation.* Institute for Innovation and Knowledge Management, ESADE.

Chesbrough, H. W. (2006a) New puzzles and new findings. In H. W. Chesbrough, W. Vanhaverbeke & J. West (Eds.), Open innovation: Researching a new paradigm. Oxford University Press

Chesbrough, H. W. (2006b). Open Innovation: A New Paradigm for Understanding Industrial Innovation. In H. W. Chesbrough, W. Vanhaverbeke & J. West (Eds.), Open innovation: Researching a new paradigm. Oxford University Press.

Chesbrough, H. W. (2010). *Open Innovation: A Key to Achieving Socioeconomic Evolution, How Smaller Companies Can Benefit from Open Innovation*, Retrieved October 30, 2010 from https://www.jef.or.jp/journal/jef_contents_free.asp?c=3707

Chesbrough, H. (2003c). The logic of open innovation: Managing intellectual property. *California Management Review, 45*(3), 33–58. doi:10.1177/000812560304500301

Chesbrough, H. (2003d). The Governance and Performance of Xerox's Technology Spin-Off Companies. *Research Policy, 32*(3), 403–421. doi:10.1016/S0048-7333(02)00017-3

Chesbrough, H. (2003e). *Open Innovation: The New Imperative for Creating and Profiting from Technology.* Harvard Business School Publishing Corporation.

Chesbrough, H. W. (2003a). *Open innovation: the new imperative for creating and profiting from technology.* Harvard Business School Press.

Chesbrough, H. W. (2003b). The era of open innovation. *MIT Sloan Management Review, 44*(3), 35–41.

Chesbrough, H. W. (2006c). *Open Innovation: Researching a New Paradigm.* Oxford University Press.

Chesbrough, H. W. (2007). Why companies should have open business models. *MIT Sloan Management Review, 48*(2), 22–28.

Chesbrough, H. W., & Rosenbloom, R. S. (2002). The role of the business model in capturing value from innovation: Evidence from Xerox Corporation's technology spin-off companies. *Industrial and Corporate Change, 11*(3), 529–555. doi:10.1093/icc/11.3.529

Chesbrough, H., & Crowther, A. K. (2006). Beyond high tech: Early adopters of open innovation in other industries. *R & D Management, 36*(3), 229–236. doi:10.1111/j.1467-9310.2006.00428.x

Chesbrough, H., & Schwartz, K. (2007). Innovating business models with co-development partnerships. *Research Technology Management, 50*(1), 55–59. doi:10.1080/08956308.2007.11657419

Chesbrough, H., Vanhaverbeke, W., & West, J. (Eds.). (2014). *New frontiers in open innovation*. OUP. doi:10.1093/acprof:oso/9780199682461.001.0001

Chiaromonte, F. (2006). Open innovation through alliances and partnership: Theory and practice. *International Journal of Technology Management*, *33*(2-3), 111–114.

Choi, E. (2020, Jul 28). Business news: Garmin says hack disabled software. *Wall Street Journal*. Retrieved from http://lib-proxy.jsu.edu/login?url=https://www-proquest-com.lib-proxy.jsu.edu/newspapers/business-news-garmin-says-hack-disabled-software/docview/2427462869/se-2?accountid=11662

Chong, Handscomb, & Williams. (n.d.). *Agile Resilience in the UK: Lessons from COVID-19 for the 'next normal'*. https://www.mckinsey.com/business-functions/organization/our-insights/agile-resilience-in-the-uk-lessons-from-covid-19-for-the-next-normal

Chou, A., & Chou, D. (2011). *Cloud Computing from the perspective of system analysis*. Paper presented at the 2011 Southwest Decision Science Institute Conference.

Chou, D. C., & Chou, A. Y. (2008). *Software as a Service (SaaS) as an outsourcing model: an economic analysis*. Paper presented at the 2011 Southwest Decision Science Institute Conference.

Christensen, J., Olesen, M., & Kjaer, J. (2005). The Industrial Dynamics of Open Innovation-Evidence from the Transformation of Consumer Electronics. *Research Policy*, *34*(10), 1533–1549. doi:10.1016/j.respol.2005.07.002

Churakova, I., & Mikhramova, R. (2009-2010). *Software as a service: Study and analysis of saas business model and innovation ecosystems* [Unpublished Master's thesis]. Universiteit Gent.

CIPD. (2012). *Responsible and Sustainable Business: HR leading the way – A collection of "thought pieces"*. CIPD.

CISCO. (2020). *Cisco Annual Internet Report (2018–2023) White Paper*. Retrieved July, 2020, from https://www.cisco.com/c/en/us/solutions/collateral/executive-perspectives/annual-internet-report/white-paper-c11-741490.html

Clark, D. (2007). *Web 2.0 gives birth to Politics 2.0*. Retrieved 7 July, 2008, from https://gigaom.com/2007/03/19/web-20-gives-birth-to-politics-20/

Coccossis, H. (2017). Sustainable tourism and carrying capacity: a new context. In *The Challenge of tourism carrying capacity assessment* (pp. 19–30). Routledge. doi:10.4324/9781315240817-10

Codreanu, A. (2016). A VUCA action framework for a VUCA environment. Leadership challenges and solutions. *Journal of Defense Resources Management*, *7*(2), 31–38.

Consulting, I. (2011a). *"Social media around the world" study*. Retrieved July 05, 2013, from www.slideshare.net/InSitesConsulting/social-media-around-the-world-2011-9537752

Conyon, M., & He, L. (2008). *CEO Turnover and Firm Performance in China's Listed Firms* (CRI 2009-012). Academic Press.

Corrigan, H. B., Craciun, G., & Powell, A. M. (2014). How does Target know so much about its customers? Utilizing customer analytics to make marketing decisions. *Marketing Education Review*, *24*(2), 159–166. doi:10.2753/MER1052-8008240206

Cortada, J. (2012). *The Business of Social Business: What works and how its done*. IBM Institute for Business Value. Retrieved August 02, 2013, from https://www.ibm.com/midmarket/common/att/pdf/IBV_2012_The_business_of_social_business.pdf

Crane, A., & Matten, D. (2010). *Business ethics* (3rd ed.). Oxford University Press.

Cross, M. (2007, June 14). *Open the gates of information*. Retrieved 10 August, 2008, from http://www.guardian.co.uk/society/2007/jun/14/epublic

Cruz, L. B., & Boehe, D. M. (2008). CSR in the global marketplace: Towards sustainable global value chains. *Management Decision*.

CSR Europe. (2008) *R&D Open innovation: Networks with SME*. Open Innovation Network.

Cutter, S. L., Emrich, C. T., Mitchell, J. T., Boruff, B. J., Gall, M., Schmidtlein, M. C., Burton, C. G., & Melton, G. (2006). The long road home: Race, class, and recovery from Hurricane Katrina. *Environment*, *48*(2), 8–20. doi:10.3200/ENVT.48.2.8-20

D'Aveni, R. A., Dagnino, G. B., & Smith, K. G. (2010). *The age of temporary advantage*. Academic Press.

D'Aveni, R. A., Dagnino, G. B., & Smith, K. G. (2010, December). The age of temporary advantage. *Strategic Management Journal*, *31*(13), 1371–1547. doi:10.1002mj.897

Dahlander, L., & Gann, D. M. (2010). How open is innovation? *Research Policy*, *39*(6), 699–709. doi:10.1016/j.respol.2010.01.013

Danoesastro, M., Rehberg, B., Ritter, D., Krishna, A., Hildebrandt, P., & Islam, M. (2020). *When the Ground Shifts, It Pays to Be Agile*. BCG Global. https://www.bcg.com/publications/2020/understanding-why-agile-will-help-move-the-needle-post-covid-19

Dao, V., Langella, I., & Carbo, J. (2011). From green to sustainability: Information Technology and an integrated sustainability framework. *The Journal of Strategic Information Systems*, *20*(1), 63–79. doi:10.1016/j.jsis.2011.01.002

De Brún, A., & McAuliffe, E. (2020). Identifying the context, mechanisms and outcomes underlying collective leadership in teams: Building a realist programme theory. *BMC Health Services Research*, *20*(1), 1–13. doi:10.118612913-020-05129-1 PMID:32228574

de Camargo Fiorini, P., & Jabbour, C. J. C. (2017). Information systems and sustainable supply chain management towards a more sustainable society: Where we are and where we are going. *International Journal of Information Management*, *37*(4), 241–249. doi:10.1016/j.ijinfomgt.2016.12.004

De Jong, J. P. J., Vanhaverbeke, W., Kalvet, T., & Chesbrough, H. (2008). Policies for Open Innovation: Theory, Framework and Cases. Research project funded by VISION Era-Net.

De Sousa, M. (2008, Mar.). Open innovation models and the role of knowledge brokers. *Inside Knowledge,* 18-22.

De Sousa, M. (2006). The Sustainable Innovation Engine. *VINE Journal of Information and Knowledge Management Systems, 36*(4).

Dede, C. (2005). Planning for Neomillenial learning styles: Implications for investments in technology and faculty, In D. G. Oblinger & J. L. Oblinger (Eds.), *Educating the Net Generation*, (pp. 228–249). Retrieved August 02, 2013, from https://www.educause.edu/educatingthenetgen

Deleuze, G., & Guattari, F. (1987). *A thousand plateaus: Capitalism and schizophrenia* (B. Massumi, Trans.). University of Minnesota Press.

Demyen, S. (2020). Employees' Perspective on the Usefulness of Social Media for an Organisation. Analele Universitatii "Eftimie Murgu" Resita. Fascicola II. *Studii Economice*, *27*, 17–31.

Dennis, A. (2019, July 2). *The Challenges of Data Quality*. Dataversity. https://www.dataversity.net/the-challenges-of-data-quality/

Dittrich, K. (2008). Nokia's strategic change by means of alliance networks. A case of adopting the open innovation paradigm? In P. Sivarajadhanavel & D. Vellingiri (Eds.), *Open Innovation: The Networked R and D*. Icfai's Professional Reference Book Series. Icfai University Press.

Dodge, R., Daly, A., Huyton, J., & Sanders, L. (2012). The challenge of defining wellbeing. *International Journal of Wellbeing*, *2*(3), 222–235. doi:10.5502/ijw.v2i3.4

Doidge, N. (2007). *The brain that changes itself.* Scribe Publications Pty. Ltd.

Donaires, O. S., Cezarino, L. O., Caldana, A. C. F., & Liboni, L. (2019). Sustainable development goals–an analysis of outcomes. *Kybernetes*, *48*(1), 183–207. doi:10.1108/K-10-2017-0401

Dorn, J., Grün, C., Werthner, H., & Zapletal, M. (2007). A Survey of B2B Methodologies and Technologies: From Business Models towards Deployment Artifacts. *Proceedings of 40th Hawaii International Conference on Systems Science (HICSS-40-2007).*

Douma, S., & Schreuder, H. (2012). *Economic Approaches to Organizations*. Pearson Education.

Dove, R. (2005). Agile Enterprise Cornerstones: Knowledge, Values, and Response Ability. In *Business Agility and Information Technology Diffusion* (pp. 313–330). Springer. doi:10.1007/0-387-25590-7_20

Downes, S. (2008). *Places to go: YouTube*. Innovate. Retrieved July 02, 2013, from https://innovateonline.info/

Dubey, R., Ali, S. S., Aital, P., & Venkatesh, V. G. (2014). Mechanics of humanitarian supply chain agility and resilience and its empirical validation. *International Journal of Services and Operations Management*, *17*(4), 367–384. doi:10.1504/IJSOM.2014.059999

Dubey, R., Altay, N., & Blome, C. (2019). Swift trust and commitment: The missing links for humanitarian supply chain coordination? *Annals of Operations Research*, *283*(1), 159–177. doi:10.100710479-017-2676-z

Dubey, R., Bryde, D. J., Foropon, C., Graham, G., Giannakis, M., & Mishra, D. B. (2020). Agility in humanitarian supply chain: An organizational information processing perspective and relational view. *Annals of Operations Research*, 1–21. PMID:33110282

Dunlap, J. C., & Lowenthal, P. R. (2011). Learning, unlearning, and relearning: Using Web 2.0 technologies to support the development of lifelong learning skills. In G. D. Magoulas (Ed.), *E-infrastructures and technologies for lifelong learning: Next generation environments* (pp. 292–315). University of London. doi:10.4018/978-1-61520-983-5.ch012

Dybå, T., & Dingsøyr, T. (2008). Empirical studies of agile software development: A systematic review. *Information and Software Technology*, *50*(9-10), 833–859. doi:10.1016/j.infsof.2008.01.006

Dyer, L., & Shafer, R. (2003). *Dynamic Organizations: Achieving Marketplace and Organizational Agility with People* (CAHRS Working Paper 03-04). Ithaca, NY: Cornell University, School of Industrial and Labor Relations, Center for Advanced Human Resource Studies.

EAG. (2005). *e-Inclusion: New Challenges and Policy Recommendations*. eEurope Advisory Group, IDABC. Retrieved on July 14, 2021 from http://europa.eu.int/idabc/egovo

Earl, M. (2001). Knowledge Management Strategies: Toward a Taxonomy. *Journal of Management Information Systems*, *18*(1), 215–233. doi:10.1080/07421222.2001.11045670

Eccles, R., Ioannou, I., & Serafeim, G. (2011). *The Impact of a Corporate Culture of Sustainability on Corporate Behaviour and Performance*. Harvard Business School Working Paper 12-035.

Edwards, J. (2016). *6 benefits of being a social business*. Retrieved July, 2020, from https://www.theidm.com/blog/6-benefits-of-being-a-social-business

Eersing, R. L., Loeffler, D. N., Tracy, M. B., & Onu, L. (2007). Pentru Voi Fundatia. *Journal of Community Practice*, *15*(1), 193–215. doi:10.1300/J125v15n01_09

Elkington, J. (1994). Towards the sustainable corporation. *California Management Review*, *36*(2), 90–100. doi:10.2307/41165746

Elkington, J. (1998). *Cannibals with forks: The triple bottom line of the 21st Century*. New Society Publishers.

Elkington, J. (2004). Enter the triple bottom line. In A. Henriques & J. Richardson (Eds.), *The Triple Bottom Line: Does It All Add up?* (pp. 1–16). Earthscan.

Erhardt, N. L., Werbel, J. D., & Shrader, C. B. (2003). Board of director diversity and firm financial performance. *Corporate Governance*, *11*(2), 102–111. doi:10.1111/1467-8683.00011

Esenyel, V., & Emeagwali, O. (2019). The relationship between perceived corporate reputation and employee's positive word of mouth behavior: The mediation effect of trust to managers. *Management Science Letters*, *9*(5), 673–686. doi:10.5267/j.msl.2019.2.004

Eupan. (2020). *Common Assessment Framework. The European model for improving public organisations through self-assessment*. European CAF Resource Centre – European Institute of Public Administration.

Eva, N., Cox, J. W., Tse, H. M., & Lowe, K. B. (2019). From competency to conversation: A multi-perspective approach to collective leadership development. *The Leadership Quarterly*, *101346*. Advance online publication. doi:10.1016/j.leaqua.2019.101346

ExcelHelp. (2020). https://www.excelhelp.com/the-history-of-microsoft-excel/

Farouk, S., Cherian, J., & Jacob, J. (2012). Green accounting and management for sustainable manufacturing in developing countries. *International Journal of Business and Management*, *7*(20), 36. doi:10.5539/ijbm.v7n20p36

FEMA. (2007). *Debris Management Guide*. Retrieved March 2006, from http://www.fema.gov/government/grant/pa/demagde.shtm#3

Ferguson, N. (2009). *The ascent of money: A financial history of the world*. Penguin Books.

Ferreira, M. J., Moreira, F., & Seruca, I. (2019). Digital Transformation Towards a New Context of Labour: Enterprise 4.0. In Technological Developments in Industry 4.0 for Business Applications (vol. 1, pp 26-49). Information Science Reference (IGI). Doi:10.4018/978-1-5225-4936-9.ch002

Ferreira, M. J., Moreira, F., & Seruca, I. (2014). *A traditional organization towards a new dimension of labour – social business. In Information systems and Technology for Organizational Agility, Intelligence, and Resilience*. Information Science Reference. doi:10.4018/978-1-4666-5970-4.ch009

Ferreira, M. J., Moreira, F., & Seruca, I. (2017). Organizational training within Digital Transformation: The ToOW model. *Proceedings of the 19th International Conference on Enterprise Information Systems (ICEIS 2017)*, *2*, 526-532. 10.5220/0006366105260532

Ferriter, W. H. (2010). Digitally speaking. *Educational Leadership*, *68*, 87–88.

Fertik, M. (2013). *The rich see a different Internet than the poor*. Retrieved from https://www.scientificamerican.com/article.cfm?id=rich-see-different-internet-than-the-poor

Florea, L., Cheung, Y. H., & Herndon, N. C. (2013). For all good reasons: Role of values in organizational sustainability. *Journal of Business Ethics*, *114*(3), 393–408. doi:10.100710551-012-1355-x

Flumerfelt, S., Siriban-Manalang, A. B., & Kahlen, F.-J. (2012). Are agile and lean manufacturing systems employing sustainability, complexity and organizational learning? *The Learning Organization*, *19*(3), 238–247. doi:10.1108/09696471211219976

Forbes. (2011). *How to Build a Social Business*. Retrieved July 02, 2013, from https://www.forbes.com/sites/danschawbel/2011/10/13/how-to-build-a-social-business/

Formica, P., & Curley, M. (2018). *Exploring the Culture of Open Innovation*. Emerald. doi:10.1108/9781787437890

Foulger, T., Ewbank, A., Kay, A., Popp, S., & Cater, H. (2009). Moral spaces in MySpace: Preservice teachers' perspectives about ethical issues in social networking. *Journal of Research on Technology in Education*, *42*(1), 1–28. doi:10.1080/15391523.2009.10782539

Foutty, J., & Sinclair, D. (2020). *COVID-19: Board Agility in a Time of Crisis*. Deloitte Global. https://www2.deloitte.com/global/en/pages/about-deloitte/articles/covid-19/covid-19-and-the-board-a-chairs-point-of-view.html

Fowler, A. (2000). *The Virtuous spiral: A guide to sustainability for NGOs in international development*. Earthscan Publications, Ltd.

Fowler, A. (2003). *The virtuous spiral: A guide to sustainability for NGOs in international development*, Book Review, Earthscan Publications Ltd., London. *Habitat International*, *27*(1), 159–161. doi:10.1016/S0197-3975(02)00032-2

Francis, B., Hasan, I., & Wu, Q. (2015). Professors in the boardroom and their impact on corporate governance and firm performance. *Financial Management*, *44*(3), 547–581. doi:10.1111/fima.12069

Fredberg, T., Elmquist, M., & Ollila, S. (2008). Managing Open Innovation: Present Findings and Future Directions. Report VR 2008:02. VINNOVA - Verket för Innovationssystem/Swedish Governmental Agency for Innovation Systems.

Freeman, R. E., Harrison, J. S., Wicks, A. C., Parmar, B. L., & de Colle, S. (2010). *Stakeholder theory: The state of the art*. Cambridge University Press. doi:10.1017/CBO9780511815768

Frey, S. H. (2007). What puts the how in where? Tool use and the divided visual streams hypothesis. *Cortex*, *43*(3), 368–375. doi:10.1016/S0010-9452(08)70462-317533760 PMID:17533760

Friedman, T. L. (2016). *Thank You for Being Late: An Optimist's Guide to Thriving in the Age of Accelerations*. Farrar, Straus and Giroux.

Friedrich, T. L., Vessey, W. B., Schuelke, M. J., Ruark, G. A., & Mumford, M. D. (2009). A framework for understanding collective leadership: The selective utilization of leader and team expertise within networks. *The Leadership Quarterly*, *20*(6), 933–958. doi:10.1016/j.leaqua.2009.09.008

Fritz, H. M., Blount, C., Sokoloski, R., Singleton, J., Fuggle, A., McAdoo, B. G., Moore, A., Grass, C., & Banks, T. J. (2008). Hurricane Katrina storm surge reconnaissance. *Journal of Geotechnical and Geoenvironmental Engineering*, *134*(5), 644–656. doi:10.1061/(ASCE)1090-0241(2008)134:5(644)

Frosch, R. A., & Gallopoulos, N. E. (1989). Strategies for Manufacturing. *Scientific American, 261*(3), 144–152. doi:10.1038cientificamerican0989-144

Fuentes, C., & Fredriksson, C. (2016). Sustainability service in-store: Service work and the promotion of sustainable consumption. *International Journal of Retail & Distribution Management, 44*(5), 492–507. doi:10.1108/IJRDM-06-2015-0092

Gallagher, K. P., & Worrell, J. L. (2008). Organizing IT to promote agility. *Information Technology Management, 9*(1), 71–88. doi:10.100710799-007-0027-5

Gallaugher, J., & Ransbotham, S. (2010). Social Media and Customer Dialog Management at Starbucks. *MIS Quarterly Executive, 9*(4), 197–212.

Galliers, R. D. (2006). Strategizing for agility: confronting information systems inflexibility in dynamic environments. *The Transfer and Diffusion of Information Technology for Organizational Resilience*, 361-362.

Galliers, R. D. (2006). Strategizing for Agility: Confronting Information. *Agile Information Systems, 1.*

Galligan, M., Herrygers, S., & Rau, K. (2019). *Managing Cyber Risk in a Digital Age.* Committee of Sponsoring Organizations of the Treadway Commission (COSO).

Gantz & Reinsel. (2012). The digital universe in 2020: Big data, bigger digital shadows, and biggest growth in the far east. *IDC iView: IDC Analyze the Future, 2007*(2012), 1-16.

Garcia, L., & Ferreira, M. J. (2012). *Facebook as a supporting tool for collaborative/cooperative teaching. Global Journal of Educational Research.*

Gartner. (2009). *Gartner fact checks the five most-common SaaS assumption.* Gartner Report.

Gassmann, O. (2006). Opening Up the Innovation Process: Towards an Agenda. *R & D Management, 36*(3), 22–228. doi:10.1111/j.1467-9310.2006.00437.x

Gassmann, O., & Reepmeyer, G. (2005). Organizing Pharmaceutical Innovation: From Science-based Knowledge Creators to Drug-oriented Knowledge Brokers. *Creativity and Innovation Management, 14*(3), 233–245.

Gaule, A. (2006). *Open Innovation in Action: How to be strategic in the search for new sources of value.* Blackwell.

Gay, B. (2014). Open innovation, networking, and business model dynamics: The two sides. *Journal of Innovation and Entrepreneurship, 3*(1), 1–20. doi:10.1186/2192-5372-3-2

Geels, F. W., Hekkert, M., & Jacobsson, S. (2008). The micro-dynamics of sustainable innovation journeys [editorial]. *Technology Analysis and Strategic Management, 20*(5), 521–536. doi:10.1080/09537320802292982

Gholami, H., Saman, M. Z. M., Sharif, S., & Zakuan, N. (2015). A CRM strategic leadership towards sustainable development in student relationship management: SD in higher education. *Procedia Manufacturing*, *2*, 51–60. doi:10.1016/j.promfg.2015.07.010

Ghorbel, A., Ghorbel, M., & Jmaiel, M. (2017). Privacy in Cloud Computing Environment: A Survey and Research Challenges. *Journal of Supercomputing*. . doi:10.1007/s11227-016-1953-y

Giachetti, R. E., Martinez, L. D., Sáenz, O. A., & Chen, C.-S. (2003). Analysis of the structural measures of flexibility and agility using a measurement theoretical framework. *International Journal of Production Economics*, *86*(1), 47–62. doi:10.1016/S0925-5273(03)00004-5

Gibson, J. J. (1979). *The ecological approach to visual perception*. Lawrence Erlbaum Associates Inc.

Giddens, A. (2006). *Sociology* (5th ed.). Polity Press.

Gill, S. S., Tuli, S., Xu, M., Singh, I., Singh, K. V., Lindsay, D., Tuli, S., Smirnova, D., Singh, M., Jain, U., Pervaiz, H., Sehgal, B., Kaila, S. S., Misra, S., Aslanpour, M. S., Mehta, H., Stankovski, V., & Garraghan, P. (2019). Transformative effects of IoT, Blockchain and Artificial Intelligence on cloud computing: Evolution, vision, trends and open challenges. *Internet of Things*, *8*, 1–26. doi:10.1016/j.iot.2019.100118

Gioti, H., Ponis, S. T., & Panayiotou, N. (2018). Social business intelligence: Review and research directions. *Journal of Intelligence Studies in Business*, *8*(2), 23–42. doi:10.37380/jisib.v8i2.320

Global Audit Technology Guide (GTAG) IT Change Management Critical for Organizational Success. (2020). The Institute of Internal Auditors.

Goldberg, L. R., Johnson, J. A., Eber, H. W., Hogan, R., Ashton, M. C., & Cloninger, C. R. (2006). The international personality item pool and the future of public-domain personality measures. *Journal of Research in Personality*, *40*, 84–96. doi:10.1016/j.jrp.2005.08.007

Golder-Buckley, D., Way, D., & Glover, M. (2015). *Best Practice Strategies for Successful Innovation through University-Business Collaboration*. Research Councils UK.

Goldman, S. L., Nagel, R. N., & Preiss, K. (1995). *Agile competitors and virtual organizations: strategies for enriching the customer* (Vol. 8). Van Nostrand Reinhold.

Gold, S., & Schleper, M. C. (2017). A pathway towards true sustainability: A recognition foundation of sustainable supply chain management. *European Management Journal*, *35*(4), 425–429. doi:10.1016/j.emj.2017.06.008

Goldsman, D., Nance, R.E., & Wilson, J.R. (2010). A brief history of simulation revisited. *Proceedings of the 2010 Winter Simulation Conference (WSC)*, 567-574.

Gonçalves, N. P., & Sapateiro, C. M. (2008). Aspects for Information Systems Implementation: Challenges and impacts. A higher education institution experience. *Tékhne-Revista de Estudos Politécnicos*, (9), 225–241.

Gordon, C. (2020, December 31). AI Is Reengineering All Aspects Of Our Human Experience: What Are The Implications? *Forbes*. https://www.forbes.com/sites/cindygordon/2021/12/31/ai-is-reengineering-all-aspects-of-our-human-experience-what-are-the-implications/?sh=7f3325d17a0d

Govindaraju, R., Akbar, R., & Suryadi, K. (2018). IT Infrastructure Transformation and Its impact on IT Capabilities in the Cloud Computing Context. International Journal on Electrical Engineering and Informatics, 10(2).

Graff, G. M. (2008). *McCain and the Internet: Why It matters*. Retrieved 2008, 2008, from https://www.washingtonian.com/blogarticles/people/capitalcomment/8815.html

Granick, J. (2006). *Saving democracy with Web 2.0*. Retrieved 27 July, 2008, from https://www.wired.com/software/webservices/commentary/circuitcourt/2006/10/72001

Gray, K., Annabell, L., & Kennedy, G. (2010). Medical students' use of Facebook to support learning: Insights from four case studies. *Medical Teacher*, *32*(12), 971–976. doi:10.3109/0142159X.2010.497826 PMID:21090950

Grecu, V., & Ipiña, N. (2014). The Sustainable University-A Model for the Sustainable Organization. *Management of Sustainable Development, 6*(2).

Greenemeier, L. (2008). *Lawmakers: Terrorists may tap same Web 2.0 Tools as military*. Retrieved from http://www.sciam.com/article.cfm?id=virtual-reality-military

Greenhow, C. (2011). Online social networking and learning: What are the interesting research questions? *International Journal of Cyber Behavior, Psychology and Learning*, *1*(1), 36–50. doi:10.4018/ijcbpl.2011010104

Greenhow, C., Robelia, B., & Hughes, J. E. (2009). Web 2.0 and classroom research: What path should we take now? *Educational Researcher*, *38*, 246–259. doi:10.3102/0013189X09336671

Green, K. W. Jr, Zelbst, P. J., Bhadauria, V. S., & Meacham, J. (2012). Doenvironmental collaboration and monitoring enhance organizationalperformance? *Industrial Management & Data Systems*, *112*(2), 186–205. doi:10.1108/02635571211204254

Green, K. W. Jr, Zelbst, P. J., Meacham, J., & Bhadauria, V. S. (2012). Green supplychain management practices: Impact on performance. *Supply Chain Management*, *17*(3), 290–305. doi:10.1108/13598541211227126

Green, S. D. (1999). The dark side of lean construction: exploitation and ideology. *Proceedings IGLC*-7, 21-33.

Green, T., & Bailey, B. (2010). Academic uses of Facebook: Endless possibilities or endless peril? *TechTrends*, *54*(3), 20–22. doi:10.100711528-010-0398-z

Grobanites. (2011). *Grobanites for charity - Josh Groban 30th birthday donation*. Retrieved 24 June 2011, from http://grobanitesforcharity.org/

Gross, G. (2007). *Expert: U.S. military needs wikis, video-sharing*. Retrieved 26 July, 2008, from https://www.networkworld.com/news/2007/012407-expert-us-military-needs-wikis.html

Grossman, N. (2008, Jul 8). *Obama + Web 2.0 = A (presumptive) presidential nomination*. Retrieved 9 July, 2008, from http://www.bmighty.com/blog/main/archives/2008/07/obama_web_20_a.html

Gross, T., & Koch, M. (2007). *Computer-supported cooperative work*. Oldenbourg. doi:10.1524/9783486593419

Guamushig, T.-M., Lopez, C.-P., Santorum, M., & Aguilar, J. (2019). Characterization of a Fourth Generation Virtual Organization Based on Industry 4.0. *2019 International Conference on Information Systems and Software Technologies (ICI2ST), Information Systems and Software Technologies (ICI2ST), 2019 International Conference On*, 182–186. 10.1109/ICI2ST.2019.00033

Gunasekaran, A. (1999). Agile manufacturing: A framework for research and development. *International Journal of Production Economics*, *62*(1-2), 87–105. doi:10.1016/S0925-5273(98)00222-9

Gunessee, S., Subramanian, N., & Ning, K. (2018). Natural disasters, PC supply chain and corporate performance. *International Journal of Operations & Production Management*, *38*(9), 1796–1814. doi:10.1108/IJOPM-12-2016-0705

Gupta, A.K. (1997). The Honey Bee Network: Linking Knowledge-Rich Grassroots Innovations. *Development*, *40*(4), 36-40.

Gupta, A. K., Smith, K. G., & Shalley, C. E. (2006). The interplay between exploration and exploitation. *Academy of Management Journal*, *49*(4), 693–706. doi:10.5465/amj.2006.22083026

Hagel, J., Brown, J. S., & Davison, L. (2010). *The Power of Pull: How Small Moves, Smartly Made, Can Set Big Things in Motion*. Basic Books.

Hall, J., & Clark, W. (2003). Introduction to the special issue on environmental innovation. *Journal of Cleaner Production*, *11*(4), 343–346. doi:10.1016/S0959-6526(02)00070-7

Halper, F., & Stodder, D. (2016). *Transforming Data With Intelligence*. TDWI. https://tdwi.org/webcasts/2016/10/bi-analytics-and-the-cloud-strategies-for-business-agility.aspx

Ham, C.-D., Lee, J., Hayes, J. L., & Bae, Y. H. (2019). Exploring sharing behaviors across social media platforms. *International Journal of Market Research*, *61*(2), 157–177. doi:10.1177/1470785318782790

Hand, D., Mannila, H., & Smyth, P. (2001). *Principles of Data Mining*. MIT Press.

Harris, A. L., & Rea, A. (2009). Web 2.0 and virtual world technologies: A growing impact on IS education. *Journal of Information Systems Education*, *20*(2), 137–144.

Hart, S., & Milstein, M. B. (2003). Creating sustainable value. *The Academy of Management Executive*, *17*(2), 56–67. doi:10.5465/ame.2003.10025194

Hasanudin, A. I., Yuliansyah, Y., Said, J., Susilowati, Ch., & Muafi, M. (2019). Management control system, corporate social responsibility, and firm performance. *Entrepreneurship and Sustainability Issues*, *6*(3), 1154–1168. doi:10.9770/jesi.2019.6.3(21)

Haugh, H. M., & Talwar, A. (2010). How do corporations embed sustainability across the corporation? *Academy of Management Learning & Education*, *9*(3), 384–396. doi:10.5465/amle.9.3.zqr384

Heidegger, M. (1977). The question concerning technology (W. Lovitt, Trans.). In The Question Concerning Technology and Other Essays. New York: Garland Publishing Inc.

HenrysK. (2021, April 19). *Role of predictive analytics in business*. https://ssrn.com/abstract=3829621

Herbert, L., Ross, C. F., & Rose, E. (2010). *Real-world insights into SaaS implementation success*. Report to Forrester Group.

Hew, K. F. (2011). Students' and teachers' use of Facebook. *Computers in Human Behavior*, *27*(2), 662–676. doi:10.1016/j.chb.2010.11.020

Hibbard, C. (2010). How Twitter helped Discovery Channel during a hostage crisis. *Social Media Examiner*. Retrieved July 04, 2013, from www.socialmediaexaminer.com/discovery-channel-case-study/

Highsmith, J., & Cockburn, A. (2001). Agile software development: the business of innovation. *International Journal of Computer, 34*(9), 120-122.

Hinchcliffe, D. (2020). *Revisiting How to Cultivate Connected Organizations in an Age of Coronavirus*. Retrieved August, 2020, from https://dionhinchcliffe.com/category/social-business/social-collaboration/

Hiriyappa, B. (2008). *Strategic Management for Chartered Accountants*. New Age International Pvt Ltd Publishers.

Hogan, M. (2008). *Cloud computing & databases, how databases can meet the demands of cloud computing*. Whitepaper report to ScaleDB.

Holsapple, C. W., & Li, X. (2008). *Understanding organizational agility: a workdesign perspective*. Kentucky Univ Lexington School Of Management.

Hormozi, A. M. (2001). Agile manufacturing: The next logical step. *Benchmarking*, *8*(2), 132–143. doi:10.1108/14635770110389843

Horney, N., Pasmore, B., & O'Shea, T. (2010). Leadership agility: A business imperative for a VUCA world. *Human Resource Planning*, *33*(4), 34.

Horrigan, J. B. (2005). *On Demand Citizens: EGovernment at High Speed*. Pew Internet & American Life Project.

Hossain, M. (2013). *Open innovation: So far and a way forward. World Journal of Science, Technology and Sustainable Development.*

Huang, C.-Y., Jose A. Ceroni, J. A., Shimon, Y., & Nof, S. Y. (2000). Agility of networked enterprises— Parallelism, error recovery and conflict resolution. *Computers in Industry, 42*(2-3), 275–287. doi:10.1016/S0166-3615(99)00076-7

Huang, P. Y., Pan, S. L., & Ouyang, T. H. (2014). Developing information processing capability for operational agility: Implications from a Chinese manufacturer. *European Journal of Information Systems, 23*(4), 462–480. doi:10.1057/ejis.2014.4

Hu, Z. H., Li, Q., Chen, X. J., & Wang, Y. F. (2014). Sustainable rent-based closed-loopsupply chain for fashion products. *Sustainability, 6*(10), 7063–7088. doi:10.3390u6107063

Hwang, K., & Chen, M. (2017). *Big-data analytics for cloud, IoT and cognitive computing*. John Wiley & Sons.

IBM. (2012). *The business of social business: What works and how it's done*. Retrieved July 04, 2013, from https://www.ibm.com/midmarket/common/att/pdf/IBV_2012_The_business_of_social_business.pdf

IBM. (2013). *Social Business: Patterns in achieving social business success by leading and pioneering organizations*. IBM Institute for Business Value. Retrieved July 05, 2013, from IBM website: http://social.bz/download/IBM-social-patterns.pdf

Ibrahim, M., El-Zaart, A., & Adams, C. (2018). Smart sustainable cities roadmap: Readiness for transformation towards urban sustainability. *Sustainable Cities and Society, 37*, 530–540. doi:10.1016/j.scs.2017.10.008

Internet host count history. (2013). Retrieved 08/01, 2013, from http://www.isc.org/solutions/survey/history

Internet World Stats. (2012, October 27). *The digital divide, ICT and the 50x15 initiative*. Retrieved 31 March, 2013, from https://www.internetworldstats.com/links10.htm

Isaak, R. (2016). The making of the ecopreneur. In *Making Ecopreneurs* (pp. 63–78). Routledge.

ISACA. (2018). *COBIT 2019 Framework: Governance and Management Objectives*. ISACA.

i-SCOOP. (n.d.). *Social business guide: Context and business dimensions*. https://www.i-scoop.eu/social-business/

Islam, M. S. (2008). Towards a sustainable e-Participation implementation model. *European Journal of ePractice, 5*(10).

Ivascu, L., Cirjaliu, B., & Draghici, A. (2016). Business model for the university-industry collaboration in open innovation. *Procedia Economics and Finance, 39*, 674–678. doi:10.1016/S2212-5671(16)30288-X

Iyengar, N., Radcliffe, A., & Silvester, E. (2020). Five Predictions for COVID-19 Driven Agility across the Life Science Value Chain. *Capgemini Worldwide*. https://www.capgemini.com/2020/06/covid-19-predictions-for-life-sciences/

Izza, S., Imache, R., Vincent, L., & Lounis, Y. (2008). An approach for the evaluation of the agility in the context of enterprise interoperability. In *Enterprise Interoperability III* (pp. 3–14). Springer. doi:10.1007/978-1-84800-221-0_1

Jafari, S. M., & Asgarnajafi, F. (2017). Social Business Intelligence Utilization in Organization: The Importance of Unstructured Knowledge. *Proceedings of the International Conference on Intellectual Capital, Knowledge Management & Organizational Learning*, 109–115.

Jandrić, P. (2020). Creativity and Collective Intelligence. In M. Peters & R. Heraud (Eds.), *Encyclopedia of Educational Innovation*. Springer. doi:10.1007/978-981-13-2262-4_65-1

Jarche, H. (2011). *Social learning for business*. Retrieved July 9, 2013, from http://www.jarche.com/2011/01/social-learning-for-business/

Jarrahi, M. H., & Sawyer, S. (2013). Social Technologies, Informal Knowledge Practices, and the Enterprise. *Journal of Organizational Computing and Electronic Commerce*, *23*(1-2), 110–137. doi:10.1080/10919392.2013.748613

Jarratt, D., & Fayed, R. F. (2001). The impact of market and organizational challenges on marketing strategy decision-making: A qualitative investigation of the business-to-business sector. *Journal of Business Research*, *51*(1), 61–72. doi:10.1016/S0148-2963(99)00040-5

Jaruzelski, B. & Dehoff, K. (2008). Beyond Borders: The Global Innovation 1000. *Strategy+Business*, *53*.

Jayachandran, S., Hewett, K., & Kaufman, P. (2004). Customer response capability in a sense and respond era: The role of customer knowledge process. *Journal of the Academy of Marketing Science*, *32*(3), 219–233. doi:10.1177/0092070304263334

Jenkin, T. A., Webster, J., & McShane, L. (2011). An agenda for 'Green' information technology and systems research. *Information and Organization*, *21*(1), 17–40. doi:10.1016/j.infoandorg.2010.09.003

JoglekarN.ParkerG.SraiJ. S. (2020) *Winning the race for survival: How advanced manufacturing technologies are driving business-model innovation*. World Economic Forum. https://papers.ssrn.com/sol3/papers.cfm?abstract_id=3604242

Johnson-Frey, S. H. (2003). What's so special about human tool use? *Neuron*, *39*, 201–204. doi:10.1016/S0896-6273(03)00424-012873378 PMID:12873378

Joiner, B. (2019). Leadership Agility for Organizational Agility. *Journal of Creating Value*, *5*(2), 139–149. doi:10.1177/2394964319868321

Junco, R., & Cole-Avent, G. A. (2008). An introduction to technologies commonly used by college students. *New Directions for Student Services*, *124*(124), 3–17. doi:10.1002s.292

Kaitano, F. (2007). Change Control Audits – A Must for Critical System Functionality. *Internal Auditor*. Retrieved from https://www.theiia.org/intAuditor/itaudit/archives/2007/march/change-control-audits-a-must-for-critical-system-functionality/

Kang, S., Myung, J., Yeon, J., Ha, S.-w., Cho, T., Chung, J.-m., & Lee, S.-g. (2009). *A Standardized Maturity Model for Designing SaaS Service Guideline*. Academic Press.

Kang, S., Myung, J., Yeon, J., Ha, S.-w., Cho, T., Chung, J.-m., & Lee, S.-g. (2010). *A Standardized Maturity Model for Designing SaaS Service Guideline*. Academic Press.

Kaplan, A. M., & Haenlein, M. (2010). Users of the world, unite! The challenges and opportunities of social media. *Business Horizons*, *53*(1), 59–68. doi:10.1016/j.bushor.2009.09.003

Kapustka, P. (2006, December 27). *John Edwards' YouTube candidacy*. Retrieved 27 July, 2008, from http://newteevee.com/2006/12/27/john-edwards-youtube-candidacy/

Karimi-Alaghehband, F., & Rivard, S. (2019). Information technology outsourcing and architecture dynamic capabilities as enablers of organizational agility. *Journal of Information Technology*, *34*(2), 129–159. doi:10.1177/0268396218816271

Keen, M., Brown, V. A., & Dyball, R. (Eds.). (2005). *Social learning in environmental management: towards a sustainable future*. Routledge.

Kemp, S. (2020). *Digital 2020 Global Overview Report, DataReportal*. https://datareportal.com/reports/digital-2020-global-digital-overview

Kettunen, P., & Laanti, M. (2008). Combining agile software projects and large-scale organizational agility. *Software Process Improvement and Practice*, *13*(2), 183–193. doi:10.1002pip.354

Kharabe, A., & Lyytinen, K. J. (2012). *Is implementing ERP like pouring concrete into a company? Impact of enterprise systems on organizational agility*. Academic Press.

Khor, K. S., Thurasamy, R., Ahmad, N. H., Halim, H. A., & May-Chiun, L. (2015). Bridging the gap of green IT/IS and sustainable consumption. *Global Business Review*, *16*(4), 571–593. doi:10.1177/0972150915581101

Kidd, P. T. (1995). *Agile manufacturing: A strategy for the 21st century*. Academic Press.

Kidd, P. T. (2006). *Agile Manufacturing: A Strategy for the 21st Century*. Retrieved July 25, 2013 from http://www.cheshirehenbury. com/agility/agilitypapers/paper1095.html

Kim, P. (2012). *The definition of social business*. Retrieved from http://dachisgroup.com/2012/06/the-definition-of-social-business/

Kim, W. (2009). Cloud Computing: Today and Tomorrow. *Journal of Object Technology*, *8*(1), 65–72. doi:10.5381/jot.2009.8.1.c4

Kinsinger, P., & Walch, K. (2012). Living and leading in a VUCA world. Thunderbird University.

Kisperska-Moron, D., & Swierczek, A. (2009). The agile capabilities of Polish companies in the supply chain: An empirical study. *International Journal of Production Economics*, *118*(1), 217–224. doi:10.1016/j.ijpe.2008.08.019

Klimberg, R. K. (2015). *Teaching a Data Mining Course in a Business School. In Contemporary Perspectives in Data Mining* (Vol. 2). Information Age Publishing.

Klimberg, R. K. (2021). 2021). The Evolution of Business Analytics and Its Impact on the Service Industry. In M. Davis (Ed.), *Research Handbook on Services Management*. Elgar Publishing.

Knabb, R. D., Rhome, J. R., & Brown, D. P. (2005). *Tropical cyclone report, Hurricane Katrina, 23-30, 2005*. National Hurricane Center. https://www.nhc.noaa.gov/pdf/TCR-AL122005_Katrina.pdf

Knights, M. (2008, Apr.). BI Growth to Buck Economic Trends. *IT Pro Fit for Business*.

Kodama, F., & Shibata, T. (2015). Demand articulation in the open-innovation paradigm. *Journal of Open Innovation*, *1*(1), 2. doi:10.118640852-015-0003-y

Kodish, J. L., Gibson, D. V., & Amos, J. W. (1995). The development and operation of an agile manufacturing consortium: the case of AAMRC. *Proceedings of the Fourth Annual Conference on Models, Metrics and Pilots*, 2.

Koelliker. (2016). Maximize Business Agility with Cloud-Based Knowledge Management. *KMWorld, S17*.

Kotter, J. P. (1995). Leading Change: Why Transformation Efforts Fail. *Harvard Business Review OnPoint*, 60-67.

Kovács, A. I., & Ueno, H. (2004). Towards complex adaptive information systems. *Proceedings of the 2nd International Conference on Information Technology and Application*.

Kraut, R. (2010). Aristotle's ethic. In E. N. Zalta (Ed.), The Stanford Encyclopaedia of Philosophy. Academic Press.

Kruja, D., & Hasaj, A. (2010). Comparisons of stakeholders' perception towards the sustainable tourism development and its impacts in Shkodra Region, Albania. *Turizam*, *14*(1), 1–12. doi:10.5937/Turizam1001001K

La Rocca, M., Montalto, F., La Rocca, T., & Staglian, Ã, R. (2017). The effect of ownership on firm value: A meta-analysis. *Economic Bulletin*, *37*(4), 2324–2353.

Lampe, C., Ellison, N., & Steinfield, C. (2006). A Face (book) in the crowd: Social searching vs. social browsing. CSCW '06, Banff, Alberta.

Laursen, K., & Salter, A. (2006). Open for innovation: The role of openness in explaining innovative performance among UK manufacturing firms. *Strategic Management Journal*, *27*(2), 131–150. doi:10.1002mj.507

Lawler, E. E. III, & Worley, C. G. (2012). Designing organizations for sustainable effectiveness. *Organizational Dynamics, 41*(4), 265–270. doi:.2012.08.001 doi:10.1016/j.orgdyn

Lawrence, K. (2013). Developing leaders in a VUCA environment. *UNC Executive Development, 2013*, 1–15.

Lee, I. (2017). Big data: Dimensions, evolution, impacts, and challenges. *Business Horizons, 60*(3), 293–303. doi:10.1016/j.bushor.2017.01.004

Lee, K. H., & Saen, R. F. (2012). Measuring corporate sustainability management: A data envelopment analysis approach. *International Journal of Production Economics, 140*(1), 219–226. doi:10.1016/j.ijpe.2011.08.024

Lee, M., Yun, J. J., Pyka, A., Won, D., Kodama, F., Schiuma, G., Park, H., Jeon, J., Park, K., Jung, K., Yan, M.-R., Lee, S. Y., & Zhao, X. (2018). How to respond to the fourth industrial revolution, or the second information technology revolution? Dynamic new combinations between technology, market, and society through open innovation. *Journal of Open Innovation, 2018*(4), 21. doi:10.3390/joitmc4030021

Lee, S., Park, G., Yoon, B., & Park, J. (2010). Open innovationin SMEs—An intermediated network model. *Research Policy, 39*(2), 290–300. doi:10.1016/j.respol.2009.12.009

Leff, M. (2008, July 23). *American-Israel chamber of commerce announces first U.S.-Israel Web 2.0 business exchange: Empowering the connected enterprise*. Retrieved 24 July, 2008, from http://atlanta.dbusinessnews.com/shownews.php?newsid=163248&type_news=latest

Lehman, C. M., DuFrene, D. D., & Lehman, M. W. (2010). YouTube video project: A "Cool" way to learn communication ethics. *Business Communication Quarterly, 73*(4), 444–449. doi:10.1177/1080569910385382

Leon, R. D. (2013). From the sustainable organization to sustainable knowledge-based organization. *Economic Insights - Trends and Challenges, 65*(2).

Letza, S., Sun, X., & Kirkbride, J. (2004). Shareholding versus stakeholding: A critical review of corporate governance. *Corporate Governance, 12*(3), 242–262. doi:10.1111/j.1467-8683.2004.00367.x

Levy, P. (1999). *Collective Intelligence: Mankind's Emerging World in Cyberspace*. Perseus Books.

Lewin, R. (1993). Complexity - Life on the edge of chaos. London: Phoenix.

Liang, T., & Liu, L. (2018). Research landscape of business intelligence and big data analytics: A bibliometrics study. *Expert Systems with Applications, 111*, 2–10. doi:10.1016/j.eswa.2018.05.018

Lichtenthaler, E. (2007). Managing technology intelligence processes in situations of radical technological change. *Technological Forecasting and Social Change, 74*(8), 1109–1136. doi:10.1016/j.techfore.2006.10.001

Lichtenthaler, U. (2011). Open Innovation: Past Research, Current Debates, and Future Directions. *The Academy of Management Perspectives, 25*(1), 75–93.

Lin, C. T., Chiu, H., & Chu, P. Y. (2006). Agility index in the supply chain. *International Journal of Production Economics*, *100*(2), 285–299. doi:10.1016/j.ijpe.2004.11.013

Lines, M. (2020). *Using Agility and Tech to Help Clients Meet Regulatory Commitments amid COVID-19.* PwC. https://www.pwc.co.uk/services/operate/insights/using-agility-and-tech-to-help-clients-meet-regulatory-commitmen.html

Linton, J., Klassen, R., & Jayaraman, V. (2007). Sustainable supply chains: An introduction. *Journal of Operations Management*, *25*(6), 1075–1082. doi:10.1016/j.jom.2007.01.012

Lin, Y., Desouza, K. C., & Roy, S. (2010). Measuring agility of networked organizational structures via network entropy and mutual information. *Applied Mathematics and Computation*, *216*(10), 2824–2836. doi:10.1016/j.amc.2010.03.132

Liu, Y., Han, H., & DeBello, J. (2018). The challenges of business analytics: Successes and failures. *HICSS -51 Conference Proceedings*.

Liu, Y. (2010). Social media tools as a learning resource. *Journal of Educational Technology Development and Exchange*, *3*(1), 101–114. doi:10.18785/jetde.0301.08

Livari, J., & Livari, N. (2011). The relationship between organizational culture and the deployment of agile methods. *Information and Software Technology*, *53*(5), 509–520. doi:10.1016/j.infsof.2010.10.008

Longbottom, C. (2017). The Evolution of Cloud Computing : How to Plan for Change. BCS, The Chartered Institute for IT.

Longoni, A., Golini, R., & Cagliano, R. (2014). The role of New Forms of Work Organization in developing sustainability strategies in operations. *Int. J. Prod. Econ.*, *147*(A), 147-160.

Lopes, C. M., Scavarda, A., Hofmeister, L. F., Thomé, A. M. T., & Vaccaro, G. L. R. (2017). An analysis of the interplay between organizational sustainability, knowledge management, and open innovation. *Journal of Cleaner Production*, *142*, 476–488. doi:10.1016/j.jclepro.2016.10.083

Lu, Y., & Ramamurthy, K. (2011). Understanding The Link Between Information Technology Capability and Organizational Aglity: An Empirical Examination. MIS Quarterly, 35(4), 931-954.

Lucas, J., & Vardanyan, A. (2005). *Social enterprises: An Eastern Europe experience. Policy Brief #10.* The William Davidson Institute at the University of Michigan Business School.

Lundvall, B., Jurowetzki, R., & Lema, R. (2014). *Combining the Global Value Chain and the Innovation System perspectives*. Paper prepared for the 11th Asialics International Conference 2014, Daegu, Korea.

Lunenburg, F. C. (2011). Self-efficacy in the workplace: Implications for motivation and performance. *International Journal of Management, Business, and Administration, 14*(1), 1-6.

Luther, L. (2008). Disaster debris removal after Hurricane Katrina: status and associated issues: Order Code RL33477. Washington, DC: Congressional Research Service.

Lu, Y. (2011). Understanding the link between information technology capability and organizational agility: An empirical examination. *Management Information Systems Quarterly*, *35*(4), 931–954. doi:10.2307/41409967

Lynn. (2016). Agility, Flexibility & Insight. Is That Your Cloud? *KMWorld, S21.*

Mackay, F. (2010). Business schools respond to demand for use of social media. *The New York Times*. Retrieved July 10, 2013, from http://www.nytimes.com/2010/03/31/education/31iht-riedmba.html?p

Majchrzack, A., Cherbakov, L., & Ives, B. (2009). Harnessing the Power of the Crowds with Corporate Social Networking "How IBM does it". *MIS Quarterly Executive*, *8*(2), 103–198.

Malimi, K. (2017). The Influence of Capital Adequacy, Profitability, and Loan Growth on Non-Performing Loans a Case of Tanzanian Banking Sector. International Journal of Economics. *Business and Management Studies*, *4*(1), 38–49.

Malone, T. W., Laubacher, R., & Dellarocas, C. N. (2009). *Harnessing Crowds: Mapping the Genome of Collective Intelligence.* MIT Sloan Research Paper No. 4732-09. Retrieved July 12, 2013, from http://ssrn.com/abstract=1381502 doi:10.2139/ssrn.1381502

Manyika, Chui, Brown, Bughin, Dobbs, Roxburgh, & Hung Byers. (2011). *Big data: The next frontier for innovation competition and productivity*. McKinsey Global Institute Report.

Marhraoui, M. A., & El Manouar, A. (2017, October). IT innovation and firm's sustainable performance: The mediating role of organizational agility. In *Proceedings of the 9th International Conference on Information Management and Engineering* (pp. 150-156). Academic Press.

Marhraoui, M. A., & Manouar, A. E. (2017). *Towards a new framework linking knowledge management systems and organizational agility: An empirical study*. arXiv preprint arXiv:1707.08182.

Marhraoui, M. A., & Manouar, El, A. (2017). IT-Enabled organizational agility-proposition of a new Framework. *Journal of Theoretical & Applied Information Technology*, *95*(20).

Martin, A., & van Bavel, R. (2013). *Assessing the Benefits of Social Networks for Organizations.* Retrieved November 18, from http://ftp.jrc.es/EURdoc/JRC78641.pdf

Martinez, S. M. (2008). Leadership as an Emergent Phenomenon: A Framework for Complexity and Adaptability. *Proceeding of the 13th International Command and Control Research and Technology Symposia (ICCRTS 2008).*

Mathiassen, L., Ngwenyama, O., & Aaen, I. (2005). Managing Change in Software Process Improvement. *IEEE Software*, *22*(November/December), 84–91. doi:10.1109/MS.2005.159

Mayer-Schönberger, V. (2009). *Delete: The virtue of forgetting in the digital age*. Princeton University Press.

McAfee, A. (2009). *Enterprise 2.0: New Collaborative Tools for Your Organization's Toughest Challenges*. Harvard Business Review Press.

McClure, S. M., Laibson, D. I., Loewenstein, G., & Cohen, J. D. (2004). Separate neural systems value immediate and delayed monetary rewards. *Science*, *306*(503). Advance online publication. doi:10.1126cience.110090715486304 PMID:15486304

McKinsey & Company. (2012). *The social economy: Unlocking value and productivity through social technologies*. Retrieved November 19 from https://www.mckinsey.com/insights/high_tech_telecoms_internet/the_social_economy

McNamara, C. (2015). *Basic definition of organization*. Available at: https://managementhelp.org/organizations/definition.htm

Melancon, D. (2006). The Three Cs of IT Change Management. *Internal Auditor*. Retrieved from https://www.theiia.org/intAuditor/itaudit/archives/2006/april/the-three-cs-of-it-change-management/

Mell, P., & Grance, T. (2011). *The NIST Definition of Cloud Computing-Recommendations of the National Institute of Standards and Technology*. NIST Special Publication, 800-145.

Mendoza, N. F. (2021, March 16). *Gartner: Top 10 data and analytics technology trends for 2021*. TechRepublic. https://www.techrepublic.com/article/gartner-top-10-data-and-analytics-technology-trends-for-2021

Meyer, M. J., & Lambert, J. C. (2007). Patch Management: No Longer Just an IT Problem. *The CPA Journal*, (November), 68–72.

Meyers, L. (2006, June 6). *Is Katrina cleanup a fleecing of America?* NBC News. https://www.nbcnews.com/id/wbna13153520

Mintzberg, H., Simons, R., & Basu, K. (2002). Beyond Selfishness. *MIT Sloan Management Review*, (Fall), 67–74.

Model, C. M. M. C. (2020). *CMMC Model and Assessment Guides*. Retrieved March 2021, from CMMC Model (Appendix A) Excel: https://www.acq.osd.mil/cmmc/docs/CMMCModelExcel_V1.02_20200318.xlsx

Mohiuddin, Z. A. (2018). Effect of Lifestyle on Consumer Decision Making: A Study of Women Consumer of Pakistan. Journal of Accounting. *Business and Finance Research*, *2*(1), 12–15.

Mohrman, S. A., & Worley, C. G. (2010). The organizational sustainability journey: Introduction to the special issue. *Organizational Dynamics*, *39*(4), 289–294. doi:10.1016/j.orgdyn.2010.07.008

Mokgari, M. T., & Pwaka, O. (2018). An Evaluation of Effectiveness of Oversight Committees: A Case of City of Johannesburg, Section 79 Committees. *International Journal of Public Policy and Administration Research*, *5*(2), 48–67. doi:10.18488/journal.74.2018.52.48.67

Monden, Y. (1983). *Toyota Production System: Practical Approach to Production Management.* Industrial Engineering and Management Press, Institute of Industrial Engineers.

Montalvo, C. (2008). General wisdom concerning the factors affecting the adoption of cleaner technologies: A survey 1990-2007. *Journal of Cleaner Production*, *16*(1), 7–13. doi:10.1016/j.jclepro.2007.10.002

Moore, J. (2018). *Gartner Data Shows 87 Percent of Organizations Have Low BI and Analytics Maturity* [Press release]. https://www.gartner.com/en/newsroom/press-releases/2018-12-06-gartner-data-shows-87-percent-of-organizations-have-low-bi-and-analytics-maturity

Moore, J. F. (1996). *The Death of Competition: Leadership & Strategy in the Age of Business Ecosystems*. Harper Business.

Moran, M., Seaman, J., & Tinti-Kane, H. (2011). *Teaching, learning, and sharing: How today's higher education faculty use social media.* Pearson Learning Solutions and Babson Survey Research Group. Retrieved July 15, 2013, from http://www.pearsonlearningsolutions.com/educators/pearson-social-media-survey-2011-bw.pdf

Morton, R., Lindsay, C., & Ching, C. (2006). *Why your business needs agile software development.* Report to Vision Consulting Group.

Mosedale, S. (2005). Assessing women's empowerment: Towards a conceptual framework. *Journal of International Development*, *17*(2), 243–257. doi:10.1002/jid.1212

Motahari-Nezhad, H. R., Stephenson, B., & Singhal, S. (2009). Outsourcing business to cloud computing services: Opportunities and challenges. *IEEE Internet Computing*, 10.

Motamarri, S., Akter, S., & Yanamandram, V. (2017). Does big data analytics influence frontline employees in services marketing? *Business Process Management Journal*, *23*(3), 623–644. doi:10.1108/BPMJ-12-2015-0182

Motzek, R. (2007). *Motivation in Open Innovation: An Exploratory Study on User Innovators.* Saarbrücken: VDM Verlag Dr. Müller.

Mullen, R., & Wedwick, L. (2008). Avoiding the digital abyss: Getting started in the classroom with YouTube, digital stories, and blogs. *The Clearing House: A Journal of Educational Strategies, Issues and Ideas*, *82*(2), 66–69. doi:10.3200/TCHS.82.2.66-69

Muma, E. C. (2018). Transformative Constitutionalism in Post-Colonial Africa: A Framework for Democracy and Human Rights Protection. *International Journal of Emerging Trends in Social Sciences*, *3*(1), 29–45. doi:10.20448/2001.31.29.45

Mungwari, T. (2018). Centre for Language and Communication Studies, Chinhoyi University of Technology, Zimbabwe. *International Journal of Social Sciences Perspectives*, *2*(2), 112–125. doi:10.33094/7.2017.2018.22.112.125

Muniisvaran, K., Vijayalakshmi, M. J., & S, F. T. J. (2018). Psychological Support for Mental Health of Mothers to Childhood the Children with Disability. *International Journal of Asian Social Science*, *8*(12), 1186–1191. doi:10.18488/journal.1.2018.812.1186.1191

Muñoz, L. (2017). Is Environmental Externality Management a Correction of Adam Smith's Model to Make it Environmentally Friendly and Shift it Towards Green Markets or is it a Distortion on Top of another Distortion. *International Journal of Economics. Business and Management Studies*, *4*(1), 1–16.

Muntean, M. (2015). Driving business agility with the use of cloud analytics. *Proceedings of the IE 2015 International Conference*. https://www.conferenceie.ase.ro

Murthy, A. (2010). Tapping into SaaS and pre-packaged products to drive optimization. *Infosys, FINsights Issue on IT Optimization.*

Myambo, A., & Munyanyi, T. (2017). Effectiveness of Labour Court in Labour Dispute Management in Zimbabwe. *International Journal of Social and Administrative Sciences*, *2*(1), 15–30. doi:10.18488/journal.136.2017.21.15.30

Myers, A. (2013). *McKensey Global Survey Finds Social Tools Tacking Hold in the Networked Enterprise*. Retrieved August 02, 2013, from https://www.cmswire.com/cms/social-business/mackinse

Myers, L. (2006). *Is Katrina cleanup a fleecing of America?* Retrieved July 15, 2009 from MSNBC News Web site: http://www.msnbc.msn.com/id/13153520/ns/nightly_news_with_brian_williams-lisa_myers_and_the_nbc_news_investigative_unit/

Nagel, R. N., & Dove, R. (1991). *21st century manufacturing enterprise strategy: An industry-led view*. Diane Publishing.

National Telecommunications and Information Administration. (1999). *Falling through the net: Defining the digital divide*. Retrieved from https://www.ntia.doc.gov/report/1999/falling-through-net-defining-digital-divide

Nema, P. (2010). *Best practices for adopting SaaS: a holistic evaluation approach: A Silicon Valley*. Bank report and white paper.

Newlands, A., Anderson, A. H., & Mullin, J. (2003). Adapting communicative strategies to computer-mediated communication: An analysis of task performance and dialogue structure. *Applied Cognitive Psychology*, *17*, 325–348. doi:10.1002/acp.868

Newswire, P. R. (2020, February 11). *Big Data and Business Analytics Market Size is Projected to Reach USD 512.04 Billion by 2026* [Press release]. https://www.bloomberg.com/tosv2.html?vid=&uuid=e3122840-a4a1-11eb-94030110c6469ace

Ngai, E. W. T., Chau, D. C. K., & Chan, T. L. A. (2011). Information technology, operational, and management competencies for supply chain agility: Findings from case studies. *The Journal of Strategic Information Systems*, *20*(3), 232–249. doi:10.1016/j.jsis.2010.11.002

Ngai, E. W. T., Hu, Y., Wong, Y. H., Chen, Y., & Sun, X. (2011). The application of data mining techniques in financial fraud detection: A classification framework and an academic review of literature. *Decision Support Systems*, *50*(3), 559–596. doi:10.1016/j.dss.2010.08.006

O'Halloran, A. M., Waelchli, Z., Schulz, F., Lauber, J., Provoost, F., Schattenberg, D., Bavery, S., & Schulte, G. (2020). *Leading with Agility and Responsible Innovation in Response to Covid-19: MedTech Industry Anchor Response*. Accenture.

Obiekwe, O. (2018). Human Capital Development and Organizational Survival: A Theoretical Review. *International Journal of Management and Sustainability*, *7*(4), 194–203. doi:10.18488/journal.11.2018.74.194.203

OCDE. (2015). *Achieving Public Sector Agility at Times of Fiscal Consolidation*. OECD Public Governance Reviews, Éditions OCDE. doi:10.1787/9789264206267-

Office of Inspector General. (2007). *Review of hurricane Katrina Debris removal activities, Washington Parish, LA* (1603-DR-LA). Denton, TX: Department of Homeland Security.

Office of Inspector General. (2019). *FEMA's Longstanding IT Deficiencies Hindered 2017 Response and Recovery Operations* (OIG-19-58). Denton, TX: Department of Homeland Security.

Office of the Undersecretary of Defense for Acquisition & Sustainment. (2020, December 10). *Cybersecurity Maturity Model Certification*. Retrieved March 2021, from CMMC FAQ's: https://www.acq.osd.mil/cmmc/faq.html

Office of the Undersecretary of Defense. (2021). *Cybersecurity Maturity Model Certification*. Retrieved March 2021, from OUSD A&S: https://www.acq.osd.mil/cmmc/index.html

Ohno, T. (1988). *Toyota Production System: Beyond Large-Scale Production*. CRC Press.

Olavsrud, T. (2021, March 16). *3 analytics and AI trends that will dominate 2021*. CIO. https://www.cio.com/article/3251720/data-analytics-trends.html

Organisation for Economic Co-operation and Development (OECD). (2008). *Globalisation and open innovation*. Paris: OECD.

Orr, E., Mita, S., Ross, C., Simmering, M., Arseneault, J., & Orr, R. (2009). The influence of shyness on the use of Facebook in an undergraduate sample. *Cyberpsychology & Behavior*, *12*(3), 337–340. doi:10.1089/cpb.2008.0214 PMID:19250019

Osterwalder, A., Pigneur, Y., & Tucci, C. L. (2005). Clarifying business models: Origins, present, and future of the concept. *Communications of the Association for Information Systems*, *16*, 16. doi:10.17705/1CAIS.01601

Overby, E., Bharadwaj, A., & Sambamurthy, V. (2006). Enterprise agility and the enabling role of information technology. *European Journal of Information Systems*, *15*(2), 120–131. doi:10.1057/palgrave.ejis.3000600

Pacini, R., & Epstein, S. (1999). The relation of rational and experiential information processing styles to personality, basic beliefs, and the ratio bias phenomenon. *Journal of Personality and Social Psychology*, *76*(6), 972–987. doi:10.1037/0022-3514.76.6.97210402681 PMID:10402681

Papageorgiou, J. C. (1983). Decision Making in the Year 2000. *Interfaces*, *13*(2), 77–86. Advance online publication. doi:10.1287/inte.13.2.77

Parfit, D. (1971). Personal identity. *The Philosophical Review*, *80*(1), 3–27. doi:10.2307/2184309

Parida, V., Westerberg, M., & Frishammar, J. (2012). Inbound open innovation activities in high-tech SMEs: The impact on innovation performance. *Journal of Small Business Management*, *50*(2), 283–309. doi:10.1111/j.1540-627X.2012.00354.x

Pastakia, A. (1998). Grass-roots Ecopreneurs: Change Agents for a Sustainable Society. *Journal of Organizational Change Management*, *11*(2), 157–170. doi:10.1108/09534819810212142

Pasztor, A. (2020). Boeing finds another software problem --- glitch adds to string of technical issues delaying return of 737 MAX to service. *Wall Street Journal*. http://lib-proxy.jsu.edu/login?url=https://www-proquest-com.lib-proxy.jsu.edu/newspapers/boeing-finds-another-software-problem-glitch-adds/docview/2340165798/se-2?accountid=11662

Patil, S. S., & Chavan, R. (2020). Cloud business intelligence: an empirical study. *Stud. Indian Place Names UGC Care J, 27*, 747-754.

Paul, J. (2009). *The Doritos Guru chips in*. Retrieved November 29, 2013, from https://strategyonline.ca/2009/04/01/decondoritos-20090401/

Peltoniemi, M., & Vuori, E. (2004). Business ecosystem as the new approach to complex adaptive business environments. *Frontiers of E-business Research*, *2004*, 267–281.

Peng, B., Cui, B., & Li, X. (2009). Implementation Issues of A Cloud Computing Platform. *Bulletin of the IEEE Computer Society Technical Committee on Data Engineering*.

Perrott, B. E. (2015). Building the sustainable organization: An integrated approach. *The Journal of Business Strategy*, *36*(1), 41–51. doi:10.1108/JBS-06-2013-0047

Pessach, G. (2008). Networked memory institutions: Social remembering, privatization and its discontents. *Cardozo Arts & Ent*, *26*, 71–149.

Peterlin, J., Pearse, N., & Dimovski, V. (2015). Strategic decision making for organizational sustainability: The implications of servant leadership and sustainable leadership approaches. *Economic and Business Review*, *17*(3), 273–290.

Pierce, R. (2008). Using Customer Input to Drive Change in User Assistance. In *Proceedings of the 26th annual ACM international conference on Design of communication (SIGDOC'08)*. ACM. Retrieved from http://doi.acm.org.lib-proxy.jsu.edu/10.1145/1456536.1456541 doi:10.1145/1456536.1456541

Pinto, B. (2009). *Using Twitter to teach.* ABC News. Retrieved July 15, 2013, from https://abcnews.go.com/GMA/Weekend/story?id=7140272&page=1

Pollock, S. (2016). Change management: It is not a choice. *Talent Management Excellence Essentials*. Retrieved from http://lib-proxy.jsu.edu/login?url=https://search-proquest-com.lib-proxy.jsu.edu/docview/1955087691?accountid=11662

Porter, M., & Kramer, M. (2006). Strategy and society: The link between competitive advantage and corporate social responsibility. *Harvard Business Review*, *84*(12), 78–92. PMID:17183795

Positivo Tecnologia. (2018). *Social business: entenda o que é e quais são as melhores práticas.* Author.

Pourdehnad, J. (2007). Idealized design - An "open innovation" process. In *The Annual W. Edwards Deming Annual Conference*. Purdue University.

Power, D. (2003). *Decision Support Systems: Concepts and Resources for Managers*. Greenwood Publishing.

Prats, J., Siota, J., Gillespie, D., & Singleton, N. (2018). *Organizational agility. Why large corporations often struggle to adopt the inventions created by their innovation units and how to improve success rates in rapidly changing environment.* Oliver Wyman.

Prensky, M. (2001). Digital natives, digital immigrants. *On the Horizon, 9*(5), 1–6. Retrieves July, 2020, from https://www.meupositivo.com.br/panoramapositivo/social-business-entenda-o-que-e-e-quais-sao-as-melhores-praticas/

PulsePoint Group and The Economist Intelligence Unit. (2012). *The Economics of the Socially Engaged Enterprise*. Retrieved November 18, from http://www.pulsepointgroup.com/sites/default/files/AP-Presentation-4_27_12.pdf

Rahman, H. (2010). Open Innovation: Opportunities and Challenges for SMEs. In M. M. Cruz-Cunha & J. Varajão (Eds.), *E-Business Issues, Challenges and Opportunities for SMEs: Driving Competitiveness* (pp. 87–100). IGI Global.

Rahman, H. (2014, April-June). Organizational Sustainability: Aspects of Agility. *International Journal of Business Intelligence Research*, *5*(2), 17–38. doi:10.4018/ijbir.2014040102

Rahman, H., & Ramos, I. (2010). Open Innovation in SMEs: From Closed Boundaries to Networked Paradigm. *Issues in Informing Science and Information Technology*, *7*, 471–487. doi:10.28945/1221

Rands, K. (2017, September 25). *4 reasons most companies fail at business intelligence*. CIO. https://www.cio.com/article/3221430/4-reasons-most-companies-fail-at-business-intelligence.html

Rappa, M. (2010). *Business models on the Web*. Retrieved Feb 11th, 2012 from http://digitalenterprise.org/models/models.html

Reed, W. J., & Jorgensen, M. (2004). The double pareto-lognormal distribution – A new parametric model for size distributions. *Communications in Statistics. Theory and Methods*, *33*(8), 1733–1753. doi:10.1081/STA-120037438

ReportB. (1987) Accessed from https://sustainabledevelopment.un.org/content/documents/5987our-common-future.pdf

Ribeiro, I., Kaufmann, J., Schmidt, A., Peças, P., Henriques, E., & Götze, U. (2015). Fostering selection of sustainable manufacturing technologiesea case studyinvolving product design, supply chain and life cycle performance. *Journal of Cleaner Production*, *112*, 3306–3319. doi:10.1016/j.jclepro.2015.10.043

Richards, C. W. (1996). *Agile Manufacturing: Beyond Lean?* Production and Inventory Management Journal, Second Quarter.

Ried, S., Rymer, J. R., & Iqbal, R. (2008). *SaaS Maturity Model by Forrester*. Report to Forrester Group. Retrieved Feb 23rd, 2012 from https://www.forrester.com/Forresters+SaaS+Maturity+Model/fulltext/-/E-RES46817?docid=46817

Rigby, Elk, & Perez. (2020). *Doing agile right*. Bain.

Roark, C., Herreria, B., & Ilomechina, N. (2020). *Soar in the Face of Disruption*. Accenture.

Roberts, P. (2017, September 13). *5 things that have changed about FEMA since Katrina – and 5 that haven't*. The Conversation. https://theconversation.com/5-things-that-have-changed-about-fema-since-katrina-and-5-that-havent-83205

Roberts, N., & Grover, V. (2012). Investigating firm's customer agility and firm performance: The importance of aligning sense and respond capabilities. *Journal of Business Research*, *65*(5), 579–585. doi:10.1016/j.jbusres.2011.02.009

Roberts, N., & Grover, V. (2012). Leveraging information technology infrastructure to facilitate a firm's customer agility and competitive activity: An empirical investigation. *Journal of Management Information Systems*, *28*(4), 231–270.

Rooke, D., & Torbert, W. R. (2009). *Seven transformations of leadership. The Essential Guide to Leadership*. Harvard Business School.

Rosenberg, D. (2009). *How to evaluate SaaS for your business*. Retrieved March 20th, 2012 from http://news.cnet.com/8301-13846_3-10172508-62.html

Ross, R., Pillitteri, V., Dempsey, K., Riddle, M., & Guissanie, G. (2021). *NIST SP 800-171 rev 2: Protecting Controlled Unclassified Information in Nonfederal Systems and Organizations. National Institute of Standards and Technology (NIST), Computer Security Division*. U.S. Department of Commerce.

Rostami, T., Akbari, M. K., & Javan, M. S. (2014). Benefits, Weaknesses, Opportunities and Risks of SaaS Adoption from Iranian Organizaitons Perspective. Advances in Computer Science: an International Journal, 3(1).

Sääksjärvi, M., Lassila, A., & Nordström, H. (2005). *Evaluating the software as a service business model: From CPU time-sharing to online innovation sharing.* Paper presented at the IADIS International Conference e-Society.

Saebi, T., & Foss, N. J. (2015). Business models for open innovation: Matching heterogeneous open innovation strategies with business model dimensions. *European Management Journal*, *33*(3), 201–213. doi:10.1016/j.emj.2014.11.002

Sahakian, M., & Wilhite, H. (2014). Making practice theory practicable: Towards more sustainable forms of consumption. *Journal of Consumer Culture*, *14*(1), 25–44. doi:10.1177/1469540513505607

Salesforce.com. (2008). *The 7 secrets of SaaS startup success.* Whitepaper report of Salesforce.com over SaaS implementation issues.

Salimova, T. A., Biryukova, L., Shilkina, A., & Khakhaleva, E. (2018). Towards a methodology of sustainable competitiveness of organization. *International Journal of Civil Engineering and Technology*, *9*(11), 161–172.

Sambamurthy, V., Bharadwaj, A., & Grover, V. (2003). Shaping agility through digital options: Reconceptualizing the role of information technology in contemporary firms. *Management Information Systems Quarterly*, 237–263.

Sarker, S., Munson, C. L., Sarker, S., & Chakraborty, S. (2009). Assessing the relative contribution of the facets of agility to distributed systems development success: An analytic hierarchy process approach. *European Journal of Information Systems*, *18*(4), 285–299. doi:10.1057/ejis.2009.25

Sarker, S., & Sarker, S. (2009). Exploring agility in distributed information systems development teams: An interpretive study in an offshoring context. *Information Systems Research*, *20*(3), 40–461. doi:10.1287/isre.1090.0241

Sarkis, J., Koo, C., & Watson, R. T. (2013). Green information systems &technologies-this generation and beyond: Introduction to the special issue. *Information Systems Frontiers*, *15*(5), 695–704. doi:10.100710796-013-9454-5

Sarkis, J., Zhu, Q., & Lai, K. (2011). An organizational theoretic review of green supply chain management literature. *International Journal of Production Economics*, *130*(1), 1–15. doi:10.1016/j.ijpe.2010.11.010

Sbaouelgi, J. (2018). Income Inequality and Economic Growth: Application of Quantile Regression. *Asian Development Policy Review*, *6*(1), 1–14. doi:10.18488/journal.107.2018.61.1.14

Scheirer, M. A. (2005). Is Sustainability Possible? A Review and Commentary on Empirical Studies of Program Sustainability. *The American Journal of Evaluation*, *26*(3), 320–347. doi:10.1177/1098214005278752

Schneider, K. (2005). Administrative breakdowns in the governmental response to Hurricane Katrina. *Public Administration Review*, *65*(5), 515–516. doi:10.1111/j.1540-6210.2005.00478.x

Schonenberg, H., Mans, R., Russell, N., Mulyar, N., & van der Aalst, W. (2008). Process flexibility: A survey of contemporary approaches. In *Advances in enterprise engineering I* (pp. 16–30). Springer.

Schroeder, B., Damouras, S., & Gill, P. (2010, February 23–26). *Understanding latent sector errors and how to protect against them.* Paper presented at the FAST '10: 8th USENIX Conference on File and Storage Technologies, San Jose, CA, USA.

Schultz, D., & Schultz, S. E. (1986). *Psychology and industry today: An introduction to industrial and organizational* (4th ed.). Macmillan Publishing Co, Inc.

Seo, D., & La Paz, A. I. (2008). Exploring the dark side of IS in achieving organizational agility. *Communications of the ACM*, *51*(11), 136–139.

Seuring, S., & Müller, M. (2008). From a literature review to a conceptualframework for sustainable supply chain management. *Journal of Cleaner Production*, *16*(15), 1699–1710. doi:10.1016/j.jclepro.2008.04.020

Seuring, S., Sarkis, J., Müller, J., & Rao, P. (2008). Sustainability and supply chain management-an introduction to the special issue. *Journal of Cleaner Production*, *16*(15), 1545–1551. doi:10.1016/j.jclepro.2008.02.002

Shaffer, L. S., & Zalewski, J. M. (2011). Career advising in a VUCA environment. *NACADA Journal*, *31*(1), 64–74.

Sharifi, H., & Zhang, Z. (1999). A Methodology for Achieving Agility in Manufacturing Organisations: An Introduction. *International Journal of Production Economics*, *62*(1), 7–22.

Sharifi, H., & Zhang, Z. (1999). A methodology for achieving agility in manufacturing organisations: An introduction. *International Journal of Production Economics*, *62*(1–2), 7–22. doi:10.1016/S0925-5273(98)00217-5

Sharifi, H., & Zhang, Z. (2001). Agile manufacturing in practice-Application of a methodology. *International Journal of Operations & Production Management*, *21*(5/6), 772–794.

Sharifi, H., & Zhang, Z. (2001). Agile manufacturing in practice—Application of a methodology. *International Journal of Operations & Production Management*, *21*(5–6), 772–794. doi:10.1108/01443570110390462

Shear, M. D. (2019). How Trump Reshaped the Presidency in Over 11,000 Tweets. *The New York Times*. https://www.nytimes.com/interactive/2019/11/02/us/politics/trump-twitter-presidency.html

Sherehiy, B., Karwowski, W., & Layer, J. K. (2007). A review of enterprise agility: Concepts, frameworks, and attributes. *International Journal of Industrial Ergonomics*, *37*(5), 445–460. doi:10.1016/j.ergon.2007.01.007

Shirky, C. (2010). *Cognitive surplus: Creativity and generosity in a connected age*. Penguin Books Ltd.

Shorthouse, S. (2008). Innovation and technology transfer. *The International Conference DISTRICT 2008.*

Shostack, A. (2003). Quantifying Patch Management, Secure. *Business Quarterly, 3*(2), 1–4.

Sideraworks. (2013). *What Is Social Business?* Retrieved July 17, 2013, from https://www.sideraworks.com/wp-content/uploads/2012/03/WhatIsSocialBusiness_SideraWorks.pdf

SIIA. (2001). *Software as a Service strategic background, Software and Information Industry Association report on SaaS*. SIIA.

Silius, K., Kailanto, M. & Tervakari, A-M. (2011). Evaluating the Quality of Social Media in an Educational Context. *iJET, 6*(3), 21-26.

Silverman, R. E. (2011, Oct. 17). Managing & Careers: For Bright Ideas, Ask the Staff --- Companies, Striving to Cut Costs and Encourage Innovation, Seek Suggestions from Rank and File. *Wall Street Journal.* Retrieved from http://search.proquest.com/docview/898496273?accountid=11662

Simonarson, D., & Zydorek, F. (2021). *Strategic processes towards sustainable development in large, international companies: A cross-case analysis using the Framework for Strategic Sustainable Development*. FSSD.

Smart, P. K., Tranfield, D., Deasley, P., Levene, R., Rowe, A., & Corley, J. (2003). Integrating lean and 'high reliability' thinking. *Proceedings of the Institution of Mechanical Engineers. Part B, Journal of Engineering Manufacture, 217*(5), 733–739. doi:10.1243/095440503322011489

Smith, P. A., & Sharicz, C. (2011). The shift needed for sustainability. *The Learning Organization, 18*(1), 73–86. doi:10.1108/09696471111096019

Smith, P. A., Wals, A. E., & Schwarzin, L. (2012). Fostering organizational sustainability through dialogic interaction. *The Learning Organization.*

Smitsman, A. W. (1997). The development of tool use: Changing boundaries between organism and environment. In Evolving explanations of development: Ecological approaches to organism–environment systems (pp. 301–329). Washington, DC: American Psychological Association. doi:10.1037/10265-008

Snowden, D. (2003). Complex acts of knowing paradox and descriptive self-awareness. *Bulletin, 20*(4), 23–28.

Snowden, D. J., & Boone, M. E. (2009). *A leader's framework for decision making. The essential guide to leadership*. Harvard Business School.

Späth, P., & Rohracher, H. (2015). Conflicting strategies towards sustainable heating at an urban junction of heat infrastructure and building standards. *Energy Policy, 78*, 273–280. doi:10.1016/j.enpol.2014.12.019

Spelke, E. S., Breinlinger, K., Macomber, J., & Jacobson, K. (1992). Origins of knowledge. *Psychological Review, 99*(October), 605–632. doi:10.1037/0033-295X.99.4.6051454901 PMID:1454901

Spencer-Scarr, D. (2013). *Understanding digital networked technologies: Aiding resistance and appropriation of technology*. Paper presented at the Internet Research 14.0: Resistance and Appropriation, Denver, CO, USA.

Spencer-Scarr, D., & Raward, D. (in press). *Millennials and Transition from Tertiary Study to the Workforce and the Role of Professional Development for Students: A Longitudinal Qualitative Study. Case Study: St Andrew's College, Sydney Australia*. https://www.standrewscollege.edu.au/

Spencer-Scarr, D., & Wilson, H. (n.d.). *Annual Reflective Survey of Student Leadership Program. Case Study: St Andrew's College, Sydney Australia*. https://www.standrewscollege.edu.au/

Spieth, P., Schneider, S., Clauß, T., & Eichenberg, D. (2019). Value drivers of social businesses: A business model perspective. *Long Range Planning Journal, 52*(3), 427–444. doi:10.1016/j.lrp.2018.04.004

Spithoven, A., Vanhaverbeke, W., & Roijakkers, N. (2013). Open innovation practices in SMEs and large enterprises. *Small Business Economics, 41*(3), 537–562. doi:10.100711187-012-9453-9

Srivastava, S. K. (2007). Green supply-chain management: A state-of-the-artliterature review. *International Journal of Management Reviews, 9*(1), 53–80. doi:10.1111/j.1468-2370.2007.00202.x

St. Amant, R., & Horton, T. E. (2008). Revisiting the definition of animal tool use. *Animal Behaviour, 75*(4), 1199–1208. doi:10.1016/j.anbehav.2007.09.028

Stalder, F. (2002, November 14-16). *The status of objects in the space of flows*. Paper presented at the Doors of Perception Conference, Amsterdam, The Netherlands.

Steinbock, D., & Pea, R. (2007). *Wearable tag clouds: Visualizations to facilitate new collaborations*. Academic Press.

Stelter, B. (2008, July 7). *The Facebooker who friended Obama*. Retrieved 9 July, 2008, from http://www.nytimes.com/2008/07/07/technology/07hughes.html?_r=2&ref=technology&oref=slogin&oref=slogin

Stock, T., & Seliger, G. (2016). Opportunities of sustainable manufacturing in industry 4.0. *Procedia CIRP, 40*, 536–541. doi:10.1016/j.procir.2016.01.129

Strange, K. F. (2003). *Making BI and data warehousing strategic: The key issues*. Gartner Group.

Streitz, N., Prante, T., Röcker, C., Alphen, D. V., Magerkurth, C., Stenzel, R. & Plewe, D. A. (2003). Ambient Displays and Mobile Devices for the Creation of Social Architectural Spaces. *The Kluwer International series on Computer Supported Cooperative Work, 2*, 387-409.

Stuart, H. J. (2011). An identity based approach to the sustainable corporate brand. *Corporate Communications*.

Stuckenberg, S., Fielt, E., & Loser, T. (2011). The impact of software-as-a-service on business models of leading software vendors: experiences from three exploratory case studies. *Proceedings of the 15th Pacific Asia Conference on Information Systems (PACIS 2011).*

StuzoGroup. (2013). *Doritos-Become The Doritos Guru.* Retrieved November 29, 2013, from http://www.stuzo.com/case-studies/Stuzo_CaseStudy_Doritos_BecometheDoritosGuru.pdf

Swenson, D. & Marshall, B. (2006, May 14). Flash flood: Hurricane Katrina Inundation of New Orleans, August 29, 2006. *The Times Picayune.*

Syncapse. (2013). *The Value of a Facebook Fan 2013: Revisiting Consumer Brand Currency In Social Media.* Retrieved November 25, 2013, from www2.syncapse.com/e/15032/Value-of-a-Fan-Report-2013-pdf/4mqfc/328355212

Tagtmeier, C. (2010). Facebook vs. Twitter: Battle of the social network stars. *Computers in Libraries, 30*, 6–10.

Tallon, P. P., Queiroz, M., Coltman, T., & Sharma, R. (2019). Information technology and the search for organizational agility: A systematic review with future research possibilities. *The Journal of Strategic Information Systems, 28*(2), 218–237.

Tay, M. Y., Abd Rahman, A., Aziz, Y. A., & Sidek, S. (2015). A review on drivers and barriers towards sustainable supply chain practices. *International Journal of Social Science and Humanity, 5*(10), 892–897. doi:10.7763/IJSSH.2015.V5.575

Teece, D., Peteraf, M., & Leih, S. (2016). Dynamic capabilities and organizational agility: Risk, uncertainty, and strategy in the innovation economy. *California Management Review, 58*(4), 13–35.

Tellis, W. (1997). Application of a case study methodology. *Qualitative Report, 3*(3), 1–19.

Thabhiranrak, T., & Jermsittiparsert, K. (2019). Towards sustainable functioning of organization: Women empowerment and corporate management culture. *Journal of Security & Sustainability Issues, 9*(1), 321–332. doi:10.9770/jssi.2019.9.1(24)

The Oxford companion to philosophy. (1995). New York: Oxford University Press Inc.

Thomas, T. E., & Lamm, E. (2012). Legitimacy and organizational sustainability. *Journal of Business Ethics, 110*(2), 191–203. doi:10.100710551-012-1421-4

Timmermans, F., & Katainen, J. (2019). *Towards a sustainable Europe by 2030.* European Commission. Retrieved August, 2020, https://ec.europa.eu/commission/sites/beta-political/files/rp_sustainable_europe_30-01_en_web.pdf

Timmers, P. (1998). Business models for electronic markets. *Electronic Markets, 8*(2), 3–8. doi:10.1080/10196789800000016

Tsourveloudis, N. C., & Valavanis, K. P. (2002). On the measurement of enterprise agility. *Journal of Intelligent & Robotic Systems, 33*(3), 329–342. doi:10.1023/A:1015096909316

Tynan, D. (2008, August 20). *Cool political sites for a Web 2.0 election year*. Retrieved 22 August, 2008, from https://www.computerworld.com/action/article.do?command=viewArticleBasic&taxonomyName=networking_and_internet&articleId=9113039&taxonomyId=16&intsrc=kc_feat

U.S. Department of Defense. (2021). *DoD CUI Program*. Retrieved February 2021, from Controlled Unclassified Information (CUI): https://www.dodcui.mil

U.S. Department of Defense. (2021, January 15). *Part 252-Solicitation Provisions and Contract Clauses*. Retrieved March 2021, from Defense Federal Acquisition Regulation Supplement: https://www.acq.osd.mil/dpap/dars/dfars/html/current/252204.htm#252.204-7021

United States Congress. (2006). *A Failure of Initiative: Final Report of the Select Bipartisan Committee to Investigate the Preparation for and Response to Hurricane Katrina*. Washington, DC: Government Printing Office.

Upham, P., Maughan, J., Raper, D., & Thomas, C. (2012). *Towards sustainable aviation*. Routledge. doi:10.4324/9781849773409

Uzialko, A. (2021, April 22). How Artificial Intelligence Will Transform Business. *Business News Daily*. https://www.businessnewsdaily.com/9402-artificial-intelligence-business-trends.html

Vaidhyanathan, S. (2011). *The Googalization of everything: And why we should worry*. University of California Press.

Valz, D. R. (2006, June 26). *Dynamic pricing models for digital content*. Retrieved from http://appft1.uspto.gov/netacgi/nph-Parser?Sect1=PTO1&Sect2=HITOFF&d=PG01&p=1&u=/netahtml/PTO/srchnum.html&r=1&f=G&l=50&s1=20080154798.PGNR

Van Belleghem, S. (2012). *The Conversation Company, Boost your Business Through Culture. People & Social Media*. Kogan Page.

Van de Vrande, V., de Jong, J., Vanhaverbeke, W., & DeRochemont, M. (2009). Open innovation in SMEs: Trends,motives and management challenges. *Technovation*, *29*(6–7), 423–437. doi:10.1016/j.technovation.2008.10.001

van Lawick-Goodall, J. (1970). Tool-using in primates and other vertebrates. In Advances in the study of behavior (pp. 195–249). New York, NY: Academic Press.

Van Leeuwen, J. (2015). The regionalization of maritime governance: Towards a polycentric governance system for sustainable shipping in the European Union. *Ocean and Coastal Management*, *117*, 23–31. doi:10.1016/j.ocecoaman.2015.05.013

Vanhaverbeke, W., Chesbrough, H., & West, J. (2014). Surfing the new wave of open innovation research. *New Frontiers in Open Innovation, 281*, 287-288.

Vannoy, S. A., & Palvia, P. (2010). The Social Influence Model of Technology Adoption. *Communications of the ACM*, *53*(8), 149–153. doi:10.1145/1743546.1743585

Vescovi, P. (2008). *Effective Data Quality Strategies*. Retrieved July 29th, 2009 from Dynamic Business Web site: http://www.dynamicbusiness.com/articles/articles-technology/effective-data-quality-strategies.html/2

Viskari, S. (2006). Managing Technologies in Research Organization: Framework for research Surplus Portfolio. Research Report 176. Lappeenranta University of Technology.

Visvanathan, S. (2001). *Knowledge and information in the network society*. Paper presented at Globalization - A Symposium on the Challenges of Closer Global Integration, Delhi, India.

von Rosing, M., Maria Hove, M., & Henrik von Scheel, H. (2013). *Initial thoughts on a Sustainability Framework: Detailing business and IT requirements to a holistic Sustainability Framework*. Retrieved July 04, 2013 from http://www.valueteam.biz/wordpress/wp-content/uploads/2012/12/von-Rosing-M-Hove-M-Scheel-H-Initialthoughts-on-a-Sustainability-Framework_2012.pdf

Wales, T. (2013). Organizational sustainability: What is it, and why does it matter? *Review of Enterprise and Management Studies*, *1*(1), 38–49.

Walker, K. L., & Moran, N. (2019). Consumer information for data-driven decision making: Teaching socially responsible use of data. *Journal of Marketing Education*, *41*(2), 109–126. doi:10.1177/0273475318813176

Wall, G. (2016). Tourism and development: Towards sustainable outcomes. In *Cultural tourism and sustainable local development* (pp. 49–64). Routledge.

Wankel, L., & Wankel, C. (2011). Connecting on campus with new media: Introduction to higher education administration with social media. *Cutting Edge Technologies in Higher Education*, *2*, xi–xviii.

Watson, H. J., & Frolick, M. N. (1993). Determining Information Requirements for an EIS. *Management Information Systems Quarterly*, *17*(3), 255–269. doi:10.2307/249771

Watson, H. J., & Marett, P. G. (1979). A Survey of Management Science Implementation Problems. *Interfaces*, *9*(4), 124–128. doi:10.1287/inte.9.4.124

Watson, R. T. (2006). *Data management: Databases and organizations* (5th ed.). John Wiley.

Weerawardena, J., McDonald, R. E., & Mort, G. S. (2010). Sustainability of nonprofit organizations: An empirical investigation. *Journal of World Business*, *45*(4), 346–356. doi:10.1016/j.jwb.2009.08.004

Weiblen, T. (2014). The open business model: Understanding an emerging concept. *Journal of Multi Business Model Innovation and Technology*, *2*(1), 35–66. doi:10.13052/jmbmit2245-456X.212

Weidemeyer, F. (2020). *COVID-19: Which Critical Choices Should Businesses Make Next?* https://www.ey.com/en_gl/long-term-value/covid-19-critical-choices-businesses-should-make

Weill, P., Subramani, M., & Broadbent, M. (2002). *IT infrastructure for strategic agility*. Academic Press.

Weill, P., Subramani, M., Broadbent, M., & Building, I. (2002). Infrastructure for Strategic Agility. *Sloan Management Review*, *44*(1), 57–65.

Welford, R., & Jones, D. (1998). Beyond environmentalism and towards the sustainable organization. *Corporate Environmental Management 1–Systems and Strategies*, 237-257.

Wendler, R. (2013, September). The structure of agility from different perspectives. In *2013 Federated Conference on Computer Science and Information Systems* (pp. 1177-1184). IEEE.

West, J. & Gallagher, S. (2006). Challenges of open innovation: the paradox of firm investment in open-source software. *R&D Management*, *36*(3), 319-331.

West, J. (2006). Does Appropriability Enable or Retard Open Innovation? In Open Innovation: Researching a New Paradigm. Oxford University Press.

West, J., Salter, A., Vanhaverbeke, W., & Chesbrough, H. (2014). *Open innovation: The next decade*. Academic Press.

West, J., Vanhaverbeke, W., & Chesbrough, H. (2006). Open Innovation: A Research Agenda. In Open Innovation: Researching a New Paradigm. Oxford University Press.

West, J., & Bogers, M. (2014). Leveraging external sources of innovation: A review of research on open innovation. *Journal of Product Innovation Management*, *31*(4), 814–831. doi:10.1111/jpim.12125

White, A., Daniel, E. M., & Mohdzain, M. (2005). The role of emergent information technologies and systems in enabling supply chain agility. *International Journal of Information Management*, *25*(5), 396–410. doi:10.1016/j.ijinfomgt.2005.06.009

Wikipedia. (2013). *United Breaks Guitars*. Retrieved March 03, 2013, from https://en.wikipedia.org/wiki/United_Breaks_Guitars

Winby, S., & Worley, C. G. (2014). Management processes for agility, speed, and innovation. *Organizational Dynamics*, *43*(3), 225–234.

Wognum, P. N., Bremmers, H., Trienekens, J. H., van der Vorst, J. G., & Bloemhof, J. M. (2011). Systems for sustainability and transparency of food supplychains—Current status and challenges. *Advanced Engineering Informatics*, *25*(1), 65–76. doi:10.1016/j.aei.2010.06.001

Wolfgang, K. (2001). *The mentality of apes* (E. Winter, Trans.). Routledge.

Womack, J. P., & Jones, D. T. (2003). *Banish waste and create wealth in your corporation.* Recuperado de http://www. kvimis. co.in/sites/kvimis. co. in/files/ebook_attachments/James

Womack, J. P., Jones, D. T., & Roos, D. (2007). *The machine that changed the world: The story of lean production—Toyota's secret weapon in the global car wars that is now revolutionizing world industry*. Simon and Schuster.

Wong, D. M. L. (2020). *Individual use of Enterprise 2.0 and its impact on social capital within large organisations* [PhD Thesis]. Computing and Information Systems - Theses [380]. Retrieved September, 2030, from https://minerva-access.unimelb.edu.au/handle/11343/241865

Woolley, B., & Hobbs, G. (2008). Agility in Information System. *ACIS 2008 Proceedings*.

World Bank. (2021). *World Development Report 2021: Data for Better Lives*. The World Bank.

World Health Organization. (2018). A vision for primary health care in the 21st century: towards universal health coverage and the Sustainable Development Goals (No. WHO/HIS/SDS/2018.15). World Health Organization.

World Health Organization. (2019). *Report of the Global conference on primary health care: from Alma-Ata towards universal health coverage and the Sustainable Development Goals* (No. WHO/UHC/IHS/2019.62). World Health Organization.

Wouter, A., De Smet, A., & Weerda, K. (2015). Agility: It Rhymes with Stability. *The McKinsey Quarterly*.

Wu, Z., & Pagell, M. (2011). Balancing priorities: Decision-making in sustainable supply chain management. *Journal of Operations Management*, *29*(6), 577–590. doi:10.1016/j.jom.2010.10.001

Wynne, B. E. Sr. (1961). A Pattern of Reporting Operations Research to the Business Executive. *Management Technology*, *1*(3), 16–23. doi:10.1287/mantech.1.3.16

Xin, M., & Levina, N. (2008). Software-as-a-service model: Elaborating client-side adoption factors. *Proceedings of the 29th International Conference on Information Systems*.

Yahaya, Y., Sarhadi, Y. M., & Gunasekaran, A. (1999). Agile Manufacturing: The Drivers, Concepts and Attributes. *International Journal of Production Economics*, *62*(1), 33–43.

Yi, J. (2011). Knowledge-based approach to improving detailing plan in multiple product situations using PDE weights. *Expert Systems with Applications*, *38*(4), 3835–3843. doi:10.1016/j.eswa.2010.09.044

Yin, R. (2009). *Case Study Research: Design and Methods*. SAGE Publication, Inc.

Young, J. (2010). How social networking helps teaching (and worries some professors). *The Chronicle of Higher Education*. Retrieved July 18, 2013, from http://chronicle.com/article/How-Social-Networking-Helps/123654/

Yun, Hyo, Zhao, Jung, & Yigitcanlar. (2020). The Culture for Open Innovation Dynamics. *Sustainability*, *12*(12), 1–21.

Yun, J. J., & Liu, Z. (2019). Micro- and macro-dynamics of open innovation with a quadruple-helix model. *Sustainability*, *2019*(11), 3301. doi:10.3390u11123301

Yun, J. J., Park, K., Yang, J., & Jung, W. (2016). The philosophy of "open innovation". *J. Sci. Technol. Policy Manag.*, *2016*(7), 134–153. doi:10.1108/JSTPM-08-2015-0030

Yun, J. J., Won, D., & Park, K. (2016). Dynamics from open innovation to evolutionary change. *Journal of Open Innovation, 2016*(2), 7–22. doi:10.118640852-016-0033-0

Yun, J. J., Won, D., & Park, K. (2018). Entrepreneurial cyclical dynamics of open innovation. *Journal of Evolutionary Economics, 2018*(28), 1151–1174. doi:10.100700191-018-0596-y

Yun, J. J., Yang, J., & Park, K. (2016). Open innovation to business model: New perspective to connect between technology and market. *Science, Technology & Society, 21*(3), 324–348. doi:10.1177/0971721816661784

Yunus, M. (2007). *Creating a World Without Poverty: Social Business and the Future of Capitalism.* Public Affairs.

Zain, M., Rose, R. C., Abdullah, I., & Masrom, M. (2005). The relationship between information technology acceptance and organizational agility in Malaysia. *Information & Management, 42*(6), 829–839. doi:10.1016/j.im.2004.09.001

Zakić, N., Jovanović, A., & Stamatović, M. (2008). External and Internal Factors Affecting the Product and Business Process Innovation. *Facta Universitatis Series: Economics and Organization, 5*(1), 17–29.

Zanzig, J., Francia, G. A., & Francia, X. P. (2014). Internal Control Considerations for Information System Changes and Patches. In H. Rahman & R. deSousa (Eds.), Information Systems and Technology for Organizational Agility, Intelligence, and Resilience. Hershey, PA: Business Science Reference. doi:10.4018/978-1-4666-5970-4.ch008

Zanzig, J., Francia, G. A., & Francia, X. P. (2019). Practical Guidance in Achieving Successful Change Management in Information System Environment. In R. da Cruz (Ed.), *New Perspectives on Information Systems Modeling and Design (2019):41* (pp. 41–66). IGI-Global Publishing. www.igi-global.com, doi:10.4018/978-1-5225-7271-8.ch003

Zawawi, N. F. M., & Abd Wahab, S. (2019). Organizational sustainability: A redefinition? *Journal of Strategy and Management.*

Zhang, D. Z. (2011). Towards theory building in agile manufacturing strategies—Case studies of an agility taxonomy. *International Journal of Production Economics, 131*(1), 303–312. doi:10.1016/j.ijpe.2010.08.010

Zhao, F., & Kemp, L. (2012). Integrating Web 2.0-based informal learning with workplace training. *Educational Media International, 49*(3), 231–245. doi:10.1080/09523987.2012.738015

Zhao, S., Sun, Y., & Xu, X. (2016). Research on open innovation performance: A review. *Information Technology Management, 17*(3), 279–287. doi:10.100710799-015-0231-7

Zhu, Q., & Sarkis, J. (2004). Relationships between operational practices andperformance among early adopters of green supply chain management practices in Chinese manufacturing enterprises. *Journal of Operations Management, 22*(3), 265–289. doi:10.1016/j.jom.2004.01.005

Zollo, M., Cennamo, C., & Neumann, K. (2013). Beyond what and why: Understanding organizational evolution towards sustainable enterprise models. *Organization & Environment*, *26*(3), 241–259. doi:10.1177/1086026613496433

Zulkifli, N. S., Shukor, Z. A., & Rahman, M. R. C. A. (2018). Intellectual Capital Efficiency and Firm Performance in Malaysia: The Effect of Government Ownership. *Asian Journal of Accounting and Governance*, *8*(Special Issue), 93–105. doi:10.17576/AJAG-2017-08SI-09

Zundel, C., & Kilcher, L. (2007), Organic agriculture and food availability. In *International Conference on Organic Agriculture and Food Security*. Food and Agriculture Organization of the United Nations (FAO).

About the Contributors

Hakikur Rahman is an academic over 27 years has served leading education institutes and established various ICT4D projects funded by ADB, UNDP and World Bank in Bangladesh. He is currently serving as a Post Doctoral Researcher at the University of Minho, Portugal under the Centro Algoritmi. He has written and edited over 25 books, more than 50 book chapters and contributed over 100 articles on computer education, ICTs, knowledge management, open innovation, data mining and e-government research in newspapers, journals, and conference proceedings. Graduating from the Bangladesh University of Engineering and Technology in 1981, he has done his Master's of Engineering from the American University of Beirut in 1986 and completed his PhD in Computer Engineering from the Ansted University, BVI, UK in 2001.

* * *

Maria João Ferreira is Associate Professor at the Science and Technology Department at Universidade Portucalense, Porto, Portugal. Graduated in Applied Mathematics and Computation at Portucalense University, she was awarded with a M.Sc. (1993) and a Ph.D. (2003) degrees in Computation by the University of Manchester. Currently, she teaches subjects in the areas of IT in Organizations and Information Systems at undergraduate and master level while supervising M.Sc. and Ph.D. students. She is both a researcher at REMIT - Research on Economics, Management and Information Technologies- at Universidade Portucalense - and at ISTTOS - Centro Algoritmi, at University of Minho. Her research focuses on Information Systems, Digital Transformation in Organizations. She was coordinator during 10 years of the MSc in Information Technologies in Education. She is a co-author of several scientific publications on national and international conferences, book chapters and journals and has been involved in several conferences as a program committee member, organizer committee member and local-chair member. She is also an Editorial Board Member of the IJADS and the IJAS.

Guillermo A. Francia, III received his Ph.D. in Computer Science from New Mexico Tech. Before joining Jacksonville State University (JSU), he was the chairman of the Computer Science department at Kansas Wesleyan University. In 1996, Dr. Francia received one of the five national awards for Innovators in Higher Education from Microsoft Corporatión. His research and teaching interests include embedded and industrial control systems security, vehicular network security, machine learning, and unmanned aerial vehicle security. He is a two-time recipient of a Fulbright award (UK, 2017 and Malta, 2007) related to cyber security projects and is the 2018 winner of the National CyberWatch Center Innovations in Cyber Security Education award. He has successfully managed research projects funded by the National Science Foundation, Department of Defense, Department of Energy, National Security Agency, Department of Homeland Security, and the Eisenhower Foundation. Professor Francia has widely published in books, journals, and conference articles in several branches of cybersecurity. He held Distinguished Professor and Director of the Center for Information Security and Assurance positions at JSU prior to joining the University of West Florida. In July 2019, he received an appointment as Commissioner of the Computing Accreditation Commission of ABET. Currently, Dr. Francia is serving as Faculty Scholar and Professor at the UWF Center for Cybersecurity.

Kamran Janamian was born 1985 in Esfahan, Iran. As he is a Baha'i in an Islamic country, education in official schools and universities of Iran was forbidden for him by the government due to racist policy and religious discrimination of the government. After college, he joined BIHE (Baha'i Institute for Higher Education) university, an online university formed and supported by hundreds of Baha'i and non-Baha'i scholars around the world. He graduated autumn 2007 in BA of accounting and then graduated MBA in spring of 2009. He managed to work on Information Systems starting from his graduate thesis on MBA. As a personal habit he likes programming and this helps him a lot in his work as Auditor and Information System consulter in more than 8 private companies in Iran. He coded and wrote many accounting software and patches in VB.NET and Ruby languages, helping accountants on automating their tasks. He was a contributor of ITQM 2013 and is an instructor in BIHE University right now.

Ronald (Ron) K. Klimberg, Ph.D., is a Professor in the Decision and System Sciences Department of the Haub School of Business at Saint Joseph's University, USA. Professor Klimberg received his B.S. in Information Systems from the University of Maryland, his M.S. in Operations Research from George Washington University, and his Ph.D. in Systems Analysis and Economics for Public Decision-Making from the Johns Hopkins University. Before joining the faculty of Saint

Joseph's University in 1997, he was a professor at Boston University (10 years), an operations research analyst for the Food and Drug Administration (FDA) (10 years) and a consultant (7 years). Ron was the 2007 recipient of the Tengelmann Award for his excellence in scholarship, teaching, and research. His research has been directed toward the development and application of quantitative methods, e.g., statistics, forecasting, data mining, and management science techniques, such that the results add value to the organization and the results are effectively communicated. Dr.Klimberg published 4 books, including Fundamentals of Predictive Analytics using JMP, edited 15 books and over 70 articles and has made over 100 presentations at national and international conferences in the areas of management science, business intelligence, business analytics, information systems, statistics, data mining and operations management. In addition, Ron has over 20 years of consulting providing statistical and analytical support to private and public organizations. Dr. Klimberg expertise is directed toward the development and application of quantitative methods, e.g., statistics, forecasting, optimization, efficiency analysis, data mining, and management science techniques, such that the results add value to the organization and the results are effectively communicated. He is currently a member of INFORMS, DSI, and MCDM.

Rashmi Malhotra is a professor of decision and system sciences at Saint Joseph's University. Dr. Malhotra specializes in the area of artificial intelligence, object-oriented systems, knowledge management, and business intelligence. She has published over 50 research articles in various journals that include European Journal of Operational Research, Omega—The International Journal of Management Science, Journal of Intelligent Systems, Knowledge-based Systems, and International Journal of Electronic Business and more than 87 proceedings publications. In addition, she has presented around 104 papers in different academic conferences. In addition, she is the Editor-in-Chief of the International Journal of Business Intelligence and Systems Engineering (IJBISE) (Inderscience Publishers). She also serves on the editorial boards of International Journal of Applied Management Science, International Journal of Data Analysis Techniques and Strategies, International Journal of Management Research, International Journal of Strategic Decision Sciences (IJSDS), Journal of Management Systems, Collaborative Filtering Using Data Mining and Analysis, and Journal of Distributed Sensor Networks.

Virginia Miori, Ph.D., is a Full Professor and Chair of the Decision and System Sciences Department in the Haub School of Business at Saint Joseph's University in Philadelphia, Pennsylvania. She is a graduate of the LeBow College of Business at Drexel University, holding a doctoral degree in Operations Research. She also holds an MS in Operations Research from Case Western Reserve University and an MS in Systems Engineering and Transportation from the University of Pennsylvania. In addition to being chair, Dr. Miori was the Academic Coordinator of the Master of Science in Business Intelligence and Analytics at Saint Joseph's University for 8 years, an internationally ranked program. She has 20 years of teaching experience and over 14 years of industry experience in developing and implementing statistical and operations research models in the area of supply chain/logistics. She has been recognized as a high-quality instructor, presenting at a number of teaching symposiums. She is active in research in the areas of learning health systems, unconscious bias in healthcare data, health care informatics, healthcare operations, rehab center effectiveness, supply chain management modeling, scheduling, simulation, and predictive analytics. She has received several research and service awards. Dr. Miori has published over 35 scholarly articles and coauthored one text book. She actively engages in interdisciplinary research, applying data science to institutional and industry problems.

Fernando Moreira is Head of Science and Technology Department. He is graduated in Computer Science (1992), M.Sc. in Electronic Engineering (1997) and PhD in Electronic Engineering (2003), both at Faculty of Engineering of the University of Porto, and Habilitation (2018). He is a member of the Science and Technology Department at Portucalense University since 1992, currently as Full Professor and a visiting professor at the University of Porto Business School. He teaches subjects related to undergraduate and post-graduate studies. He supervises several PhD and M.Sc. students. He is a (co-)author more than 200 scientific publications with peer-review on national and international journals and conferences. He serves as a member of the Editorial Advisory Board for several journals and books. He organized several special issues from JCR journals. He has already regularly served as a member of Programme and Scientific committees of national and international conferences. He was the MSc in Computation coordinator during the last ten years. He holds editorial experience, and he is co-editor of several books. He is associated with NSTICC, ACM and IEEE. His principal research areas are mobile computing, ICT in Higher Education, Mobile learning, Social business and Digital transformation. Awarded with Atlas Elsevier Award, April 2019.

Isabel Seruca is an Associate Professor and a Researcher at the Science and Technology Department of Portucalense University, Porto, Portugal, where she teaches subjects in the area of Information Systems and she is the Department Coordinator of the Erasmus+ Programme. She graduated in Applied Mathematics and Computation at Portucalense University and she has an MSc and a PhD degree both in Computation from the University of Manchester Institute of Science and Technology (UMIST). She is the coordinator of the Data Analysis and Decision

Support Systems Group of REMIT (Research on Economics, Management and Information Technologies), Portucalense University and member of ISTTOS (Centro Algoritmi), a research unit in Information Systems and Technologies institutionally hosted by University of Minho. Her research interests are in the Information Systems area, namely in topics such as Business Intelligence, Data and Web Mining, Social Business, Reuse and Patterns. She has participated in several Erasmus Intensive Programmes in the topics of Business Intelligence (Erasmus IP Miss LOGO 2008, 2009 and 2010), Web Mining (Erasmus IP WISDOM 2011, 2012 and 2013) and Data Science (Erasmus IP DasBuG 2014). She is a member of several program committees of international conferences and workshops, a co-editor of books and conference proceedings in Enterprise Information Systems and she has published several papers in refereed conferences and journals in the areas of Data Mining, Semantic Web, Social Business and Patterns.

Diane Spencer-Scarr uses a second order cybernetic approach to develop an understanding of the complex relationship between human and digital networked technology, which she refers to as digital-engagement. Digital-engagement explores the relationship between the individual (particularly personality and decision-making) and digital networked technologies in order to understand why some individuals successfully manage their digital-engagement and others are disadvantaged. Diane is currently exploring the challenges and opportunities facing digital natives as they transition into the workforce and take up their role as leaders in the Digital Networked Age. Starting her career from an artistic and educational background Diane moved into IT becoming a partner in a consulting business involved in various aspects of information technology including scoping and implementing information technology projects and liaising between stakeholders to deliver IT solutions. Diane's entrepreneurial activities led to the launch of a number of online businesses. Diane has served as an editor for academic journals, authored academic papers, contributed book chapters, and is an accomplished speaker and workshop facilitator. Mensa NSW supported Diane's research into improving organization participation and was reported at the Mensa International conferences in the USA and Europe (2013). Diane is currently researching issues related to transitioning Alpha generation graduates into the workforce as they take on their role as industry leaders.

John C. Yi is an Associate Professor in the Decision and System Sciences Department of the Haub School of Business at Saint Joseph's University. He teaches the core analytics classes in both undergraduate and graduate programs. His research focuses on sales and marketing resource optimization, sales forecasting, and improving college-level teaching. He has over 20 publications in peer-reviewed journals, and has won several awards for research. Prior to entering academia in 2006, Professor

Yi forecasted both new and inline products, optimized sales and marketing resources, and improved business processes for Johnson&Johnson, Sanofi-Aventis, and GEC.

Jeffrey S. Zanzig is a Professor of Accounting in the School of Business and Industry at Jacksonville State University in Jacksonville, Alabama. He received both his Bachelor's and Master's of Business Administration degrees from Jacksonville State University. He also holds a Master's of Accounting from the University of Alabama at Birmingham, a Master's of Science in Computer Systems and Software Design from Jacksonville State University, and a Ph.D. in Accounting from the University of Mississippi. His professional designations include: Certified Public Accountant, Certified Internal Auditor, Certified Management Accountant, and Certified in Financial Management. He has authored a variety of articles in the areas of accounting, auditing, and information systems. He received the 2006 Max Block Distinguished Article Award for Informed Comment from the New York State Society of Certified Public Accountants. Dr. Zanzig is also affiliated with the Center for Information Security and Assurance at Jacksonville State University.

Index

A

Activist – in Digital Context 135
Agile Development 190, 216
agile systems 83, 89
agility 1, 3, 7, 12-13, 22, 27-29, 31, 33, 37, 39, 41-43, 57-61, 63-67, 69-70, 72, 75-99, 102, 104, 125-127, 167, 187, 194, 200, 208-213, 215-216, 261, 269-283, 288-297
analytics 5, 100, 197-201, 207-213, 215-216, 218-219, 223-226, 228, 232-237
artificial intelligence (AI) 216, 223
ASP, Application Service Provider 70
assurance 163-165, 167, 179, 190, 192
Augmented Analytics 215-216

B

BI Cloud 216
Black Swan Event 103, 135
business 1-16, 19, 21-23, 25-70, 72-79, 81, 83-86, 88-102, 116, 127, 129, 131-133, 137-162, 169-173, 175, 177, 179, 181, 185, 193-195, 197-201, 209-216, 218-226, 228-233, 235-240, 242-244, 247-248, 254, 256-258, 260-261, 265-266, 268, 271-277, 279-280, 288-292, 296-297
Business Agility 57, 63, 67, 70, 200, 213, 289-290
business intelligence 3, 15, 21-23, 27-28, 30-31, 46, 72-73, 84, 197-199, 210-216, 218-219, 224-226, 228-230, 233, 236-237, 261
business model 34, 37, 45-46, 50-57, 60-61, 63-66, 68, 72, 74, 88, 90-91, 93, 101, 137-140, 142-153, 155-160, 162, 273-274

C

change management 57, 59-60, 64, 163, 165, 167-168, 170, 173, 177-182, 185, 187, 189-190, 192-196, 261, 288-289
CIS, Cloud Information System 70
Cloud Information Systems 39-40, 57-59
COBIT 2019 163-165, 167-168, 170-171, 173-177, 179, 182-183, 187-188, 192-193, 195-196
Codvid 103
collective intelligence 1, 3, 12-13, 22, 27, 31-32, 36-37
compliance 45, 49, 125, 165, 177, 181, 184, 196
COVID19 269, 272, 280, 288
Critical Success Factor 287, 297
critical success factors 36, 49, 210, 216, 269, 272, 276-277, 282, 286-289
cybersecurity 2, 163-167, 182, 184-185, 187, 190, 192-193, 195

D

data collection 199, 201, 204, 208-209, 229, 233, 276, 282
data integration 199, 201, 209, 276
data mining 204, 210, 218-219, 224, 227-228, 230, 235
data preparation 197, 204, 216

data quality 175, 197, 201, 204, 209-211, 214
data science 215, 218-219, 223, 227, 232-233
data warehouse 199, 216-217
decision support 199, 201, 207, 214-216, 218, 221-222, 235-237, 279, 287
decision-making 3, 74, 80, 86, 91, 95, 106, 199, 219-220, 222, 233, 245, 251, 263, 276, 279, 297
digital networked technology 116, 118, 135
Digital or Online Space 135
Digital or Online Time 135
digitalization 1-2
duality of concepts 126, 135

E

Economic development 249, 267
enablers 88, 269, 271-272, 276-280, 282-283, 287-289, 292, 297
Environmental Development 267

F

factor analysis 230, 277, 285, 297

I

Institute of Internal Auditors 163, 165, 168, 189, 193
intellectual property 46, 138, 140, 143, 145, 154, 161-162, 241
Intellectual Property Management (IPM) 161
internal audit 163, 165, 174-176, 179-180, 192
Internal Control 177, 194
internal controls 163, 175, 196
ISACA 164, 167, 169-171, 173, 175-177, 179, 183, 189, 193
it 1-5, 7, 10-19, 21-27, 31-32, 39-68, 70, 73-86, 88-92, 94, 99, 102, 104-128, 130, 135, 138-140, 142-147, 151-153, 161-162, 165-166, 168-179, 181, 184, 186-187, 189, 192-194, 197-201, 205-206, 208-209, 212-213, 216, 219-220, 222-223, 226-231, 233-235, 238-244, 246-252, 254-256, 260-261, 267, 269, 271-273, 275-277, 279-281, 283, 286-287, 289-291, 293, 295, 297
IT capabilities 40, 43-44, 61, 67

K

Knowledge Management System 297

L

Long Tail Distribution 135

M

machine learning 200, 216-219, 222-226, 279, 288
maturity level 55, 183, 187-188, 192, 196
Maturity Model 51, 55, 64-65, 67-68, 89, 163, 165, 182, 184, 192-193, 195
Mobile Learning 36, 38

N

nomadic workers 3, 38

O

open innovation 96, 137-162
open innovation business model 139-140, 142, 144-146, 148-152, 162
open innovation intermediaries 162
open innovation strategies 137, 139, 143, 147, 157
Open Innovation Strategy 146, 162
organization 2-19, 21-27, 29-32, 35, 37, 41-46, 52, 55-57, 63-64, 69, 72-78, 80-86, 88-94, 96-99, 104, 121, 129, 141, 143, 158, 165-168, 171, 176, 178-182, 185, 187, 190, 192, 195-196, 199-201, 204-205, 210, 220, 222-224, 226, 228, 233, 238-240, 242-243, 245, 247-251, 253, 256, 259-268, 270-271, 283, 288, 290, 296
organizational agility 12, 27-29, 31, 37, 39, 43, 83-87, 89-90, 94, 99, 102, 167,

194, 269, 271-280, 282-283, 288-297
Organizational behavior 78, 102
Organizational Compatibility 102
organizational sustainability 72, 74-75, 77, 79-80, 86, 90-91, 93-94, 96-99, 102, 261

P

pandemic 103-104, 116, 121-125, 196, 200, 280, 296
patch management 165, 167, 181-182, 188-189, 191-194, 196

Q

Q-study 269, 272, 277, 282, 284, 288-289, 298

R

responding 60, 76, 113, 126, 269, 272-273, 295
risk management 5, 46, 179, 185, 190, 196, 236, 267

S

SaaS implementation 39-41, 44, 48-51, 53, 55, 58-63, 65, 67-68, 70
SaaS, Software as a Service 70
sensing 9, 269, 272-273
SLA, Service-Level Agreement 70
SMEs 46, 137, 139-142, 145-151, 156-157, 209
Social Business 1-15, 21-23, 25-38
social business intelligent 1, 23
social development 238-239, 267
social media 1-3, 5, 7, 9-10, 13-16, 19, 21-26, 28, 30-34, 36-37, 105, 119, 199, 208, 222
Social Software 4, 38
social tools 1-2, 7, 33, 38
soft power 103-105, 123, 128-129, 136
space 36, 41, 110-113, 121, 125, 133, 135, 141, 209, 221, 297
spin-offs 140, 151, 161-162
St Andrews College 121, 125
strategic movement 39, 41, 44, 57-60, 64-65
sustainability 4, 72-81, 85-86, 88-91, 93-102, 137, 158, 238-245, 247-249, 251-259, 261-263, 265-268, 274
Sustainability in Business 268
Sustainable Culture 102
sustainable development 2, 78, 93, 99, 101-102, 151, 156, 238-240, 242, 245, 247-248, 252, 254-259, 262-268
Sustainable Eco-System 102
sustainable organization 72, 75, 77, 92, 238-239, 249, 251, 253, 256, 259-261, 263, 268
SWOT ANALYSIS ON SAAS 59

T

time 4-5, 7, 12, 14-15, 40-46, 48-49, 52, 60, 62-63, 65, 73, 78-84, 88, 92, 108-110, 113, 119-120, 122, 124, 134-135, 142-143, 146, 163-164, 166, 175, 177-178, 192, 199, 203, 208-209, 219-221, 224-225, 227-228, 231-233, 237, 240-241, 246-247, 250, 253-255, 270, 272-273, 275, 279-280, 291
Training and Education Professionals 38

V

value proposition 51, 140, 152
VUCA 273, 275, 290-292, 294

W

well-being 1, 3, 12-13, 22, 27, 38, 120, 123, 125, 247, 267

www.ingramcontent.com/pod-product-compliance
Lightning Source LLC
LaVergne TN
LVHW080559300926
849162LV00005B/1002
* 9 7 8 1 7 9 9 8 4 7 9 9 1 *